BIAFRA

BIAFRA

A Military History

ROY DORON

INDIANA UNIVERSITY PRESS

This book is a publication of

Indiana University Press
Office of Scholarly Publishing
Herman B Wells Library 350
1320 East 10th Street
Bloomington, Indiana 47405 USA

iupress.org

First Printing 2025

Library of Congress Cataloging-in-Publication Data

Names: Doron, Roy author
Title: Biafra : a military history / Roy Doron.
Description: Bloomington : Indiana University Press, 2025. | Includes bibliographical references and index.
Identifiers: LCCN 2025007410 (print) | LCCN 2025007411 (ebook) | ISBN 9780253073860 hardback | ISBN 9780253073877 paperback | ISBN 9780253073891 ebook | ISBN 9780253073884 adobe pdf
Subjects: LCSH: Nigeria—History—Civil War, 1967–1970
Classification: LCC DT515.836 .D67 2025 (print) | LCC DT515.836 (ebook) | DDC 966.905/2—dc23/eng/20250430
LC record available at https://lccn.loc.gov/2025007410
LC ebook record available at https://lccn.loc.gov/2025007411

For Ethan and Olanna

Dedicated to the memory of all who fought, suffered, died, and survived the war from 1967 to 1970.

CONTENTS

PREFACE

ONE SUNNY DAY IN LAGOS in 2007, while researching the Nigerian Civil War at the Nigerian Institute of International Affairs (NIIA), I boarded a boat on Victoria Island heading toward the then still secluded beach at Tarkwa Bay, near the mouth where Lagos Lagoon meets the Atlantic Ocean. After some time watching the freighters enter and leave the nearby port of Apapa, I decided to tour the area. My guide took me to the regular points of interest on the island, such as the lighthouse and Lord Lugard's old mansion, of which only the brick chimney partially remains. On the way back to the beach to reboard the boat and return to the bustle of Nigeria's major metropolis, I noticed several homes that seemed to differ from those around them; they were similar in appearance to one another and felt more impersonal than the others I had encountered. My guide told me that these homes were once the barracks where soldiers of the Nigerian 3rd Marine Commando Division lived while learning amphibious tactics and taking swimming lessons before their deployment.

I was approached by an older man who seemed curious as to why I'd be so interested in these homes. When I told him I was researching the civil war for a project that would become my dissertation, he told me he had come from Northern Nigeria as a swimming instructor during the war and simply never left. We spoke for about half an hour, wherein he explained in detail how he would train soldiers during their three-week stay at Tarkwa Bay, what their regimen was like, and how important the skills they learned were, especially at the war's beginning when the soldiers landed at Bonny, Calabar, and finally Port Harcourt. I could sense two things about this man. First, I felt his intense pride at being not only a soldier but an instructor. Second, I sensed a profound sadness in him because no one had ever bothered to listen to his war stories, despite the fact that he had lived there most of his adult life, on a site that in any other country would most likely have become a war memorial. As the boat driver would most likely not have waited for me to return to Lagos, I had to rush back to the beach, and as we stood to part ways, the man stiffened and gave me a crisp military salute, and his chest swelled with pride. I turned around to see dozens of his neighbors listening intently to our conversation, learning about this man (whose name I have forgotten, I am ashamed to say) who had lived there since the 1960s but whose story they had never bothered to listen to before.

A few weeks later, I traveled to Enugu, the former Biafran capital, to visit the National Archives there. One afternoon, I stopped at the Presidential Hotel, the site where Biafra's leader, Chukwuemeka Ojukwu, declared Biafra's independence on May 30, 1967. I had just spent the day scavenging the city's bookstores and markets for literature on the war and decided to spend the afternoon at the location where Biafra began. I was sitting on the balcony of the hotel bar reading my newly purchased books, drinking Gulder, Nigeria's best beer, and watching the middle-aged businessmen play tennis in the courts below when a young man approached me. He worked at the hotel as a custodian and looked like he was in his early twenties. He asked me what I was reading, and I showed him the stack of books. He suddenly got a thoughtful look on his face and glanced around to make sure we were alone. He leaned in and whispered, "We still believe"—meaning the Igbo people's enduring belief in Biafra.

These two random encounters illustrate the dichotomy of the civil war in Nigeria. On the one hand there was a veteran who fought in the war and lived his entire life in the place where he had served, yet his story was neglected and his experiences ignored. On the other hand there was a young man who obviously had no lived experience of the war yet had a clear connection to a particular aspect of the war's memory and the country that was lost.

The Nigerian Civil War, also known as the Biafran War, remains one of the most politically charged and divisive issues in contemporary Nigerian politics. Overshadowing all other aspects of the war, the genocide of the Igbo remains the conflict's most painful unresolved legacy. For many, especially but not exclusively the Igbo, the idea that the war was genocidal is irrefutable. For many others in the country, the Igbos' fate was a painful, avoidable tragedy but not an orchestrated act of extermination. A small minority of Nigerians believe that the Igbo orchestrated the entire crisis, which began with a bloody failed coup on January 15, 1966, and that whatever they suffered after that was ultimately their own doing.

The story of the Nigerian Civil War, like most other wars, is infinitely more complex than the laser focus on genocide that has erased many other legacies of the war. For example, the war was the first time a modern African military conducted large-scale amphibious operations. The war's legacies are more than the question of genocide, as the conflict shaped the lived experiences of all Nigerians, from the victims of the senseless violence in places like the picturesque town of Asaba to the man I met decades later, still living in his former military post. The Nigerian Civil War profoundly altered life for all Nigerians, regardless of where they stood ethnically or politically. With this book, I attempt to tell the story for all those who fought, suffered, or died, military and civilian.

Roy Doron
Winston-Salem, 2024

ACKNOWLEDGMENTS

THIS BOOK HAS BEEN A long time in the making and would not have been possible without the support of countless individuals who helped, encouraged, and cajoled me into finishing this task. First and foremost, I need to thank my doctoral advisor, Toyin Falola. Without his guidance, encouragement, and belief in my abilities, I would not be an academic, and this book would never have been done. Thank you for all you have done for me as both an advisor and a friend.

Along with Dr. Falola, there are many others who have mentored me along the way and without whom I might have not been able to set my sights on this path. Drs. James Felak and Carol Thomas and the late Dauril Alden from the University of Washington saw in me something that I may not have and kept me on track to become a historian. During my graduate studies, I had the privilege of being mentored by some of the greats in the field, such as Antony Hopkins, HW Brands, Juliet Walker, Catherine Boone, Neville Hoad, the late Barbara Harlow, and many others.

My friends and colleagues in the history department at the University of Texas have been good to me, and I thank them for all they have done and continue to do as we grow together in the field: Tyler Fleming, Matt Heaton, Ann Genova, Charlie Thomas, Steve Salm, Kwame Essien, Sylvester Gundona, Emily Brownell, Danielle Porter-Sanchez, Chris Albi, Andrew Paxman, Creighton Chandler, and many, many others who, if I list them here, will take up more space than I am allocated.

My travels around the world researching for this work would not have been possible without some of the most generous hosts, especially in Nigeria, where travel can be challenging for an Oyibo, Onye Ocha, Bature, and so on. I must thank all who hosted and helped me navigate the nuances of Nigeria: Saheed

Aderinto, who gave me a place to stay and chop suya in Ibadan; the late Ademola Babalola—I will always remember your encouraging words while carrying your bag of snails; Chief Eze of the National Archives in Enugu for opening his home to me; and Sydney Emezue for the jokes and help with all things Igbo—if I am an Onye Ocha, you are the Onye Oji. Axel Hartniet-Sievers and everyone at the Heinrich Boll Foundation when it was still in Lagos, you provided me more than just a workspace but a place where I felt at home during my first days in Nigeria. The entire staff at the Nigerian Institute of International Affairs, your thankless work archiving the documents of and maintaining the memory of the war has been instrumental in my work here. To Danilo Sturla, Tom Rodermond, Maarten Boudewijn, and Alexey Kokhanchik, the expats who opened their homes to me in Nigeria, sometimes without knowing me beforehand, I owe for their hospitality and friendship. Last, I need to thank my uncle Uzi Frankel, who was working in Lagos at the time of my first visit. Without him, my early days in Nigeria would have been much more trepidatious, and it would have taken me much longer to find my place there.

Very few academics succeed without friends, mentors, and intellectual guides. I have been very fortunate to have several whom I have been able to call all of the above. Doug Anthony was probably the first to help, when I was a young graduate student. Timothy Stapleton helped push me in the direction of military history, a place few Africanists feel comfortable, and he has supported me all along the way, especially in helping to create the *Journal of African Military History*, which has given a voice to all of us with an interest in military matters in African history. The entire board of the journal has been instrumental in all things military, but none more so than Michelle Moyd and Alicia Decker, who always make sure we are grounded in the nuances of the discourse. Many aspects of this book look different than they would have if I had not known and listened to their counsel, even if they didn't know they were giving it.

Last, I want to thank my family for everything, but mostly for just being my family. My wife, Griselda, who tolerates me when I'm at my most obsessive about work and who has supported my work and my life. You are my anchor, and I thank you for everything. But this book is especially indebted to Ethan and Olanna, my Taiwo and Kehinde, who are too young to understand why their father must leave for weeks at a time. Every moment I spend away from them makes me understand that my work is for them. My absences are for them. Everything I have done since they were born is for them. Thank you for being there. I hope that when you're old enough to understand this, you know that when I am there for you, I am there for you. When I must leave for a while, it is still for you.

BIAFRA

INTRODUCTION

THE NIGERIAN CIVIL WAR HAS been known by several names: The Biafra War, The Nigeria-Biafra War, and each of those names has a certain political meaning behind it. I call the war the Nigerian Civil War for the sole reason that it was not a successful secession. In most secessionist wars, when the losing side is reabsorbed into the country it attempted to secede from, the war becomes known as a civil war, such as the American Civil War and Sri Lankan Civil War. When they are successful, they become wars of independence or liberation, such as the American Revolution, Irish War of Independence or Bangladeshi Liberation War. One notable exception to this naming convention is the Second Sudanese Civil War, which led to South Sudan's independence. Two reasons for this are that the war was largely a continuation of the First Sudanese Civil War, and South Sudan did not gain independence directly from this war but only six years later. Thus, my use of the term is simply one that acknowledges the war's outcome rather than a political statement on the validity of secession or any other meaning that this usage implies.[1]

The war began at the end of May 1967, though open hostilities did not start for over a month. The war was the culmination of a protracted crisis triggered by the structural issues of the postcolonial state and the corrupt government that inherited the régime at independence. This government exacerbated ethnic tensions, while using the mechanisms of government to preside over a system of nepotism and corruption that purportedly sought to correct the imbalances that supposedly benefited Christian Southern Nigeria at the expense of the Muslim north. This book is about the crisis that began on the night of January 15, 1966, when a group of mostly Igbo military officers staged a coup that ended the northern dominated First Republic, setting the country on the road to secession and civil war. The war ended exactly four years later on January 15, 1970, when the leaders of Nigeria and Biafra embraced in Lagos, ending a war that cost, by most estimates, a million lives.

This book attempts to explain some of the war's main questions by focusing on the war as a war. In general, military history has had a fraught relationship with the continent's historiography, and postcolonial conflicts in particular suffer neglect for several reasons. Though African Studies as an academic discipline and African history with it had a long history within black intelligentsia dating at least to Samuel Johnson, W. E. B. Dubois, and C. L. R. James, in the 1950s it emerged into White American academia through the works of Melville Herskovits, Simon Ottenberg, and others who founded the African Studies Association. This emergence coincided with the end of colonialism and the political turmoil that accompanied independence in places like the Congo, Nigeria, Ghana, and Zanzibar. Many historians were thus hesitant to engage in military history, fearing it would perpetuate the trope of "broken" Africa, preferring instead to leave military matters within the purview of political scientists such as Rupert Emerson and his protégé Crawford Young. In Africa, the same period saw the emergence of a new type of historian that sought to create a national identity for the newly independent postcolonial states. Centered at the University of Ibadan, this historical thrust became known as the Ibadan School. Spearheaded by scholars like Kenneth Dike, Ade Ajayi, and others, the Ibadan School and its East African counterpart in Tanzania would assert outsized influence in shaping Africa's past. This nationalist writing sought to use the past to build a future for African countries, and as such subverted military history in a way that made it a tool of state creation.[2]

As a result, the military history of Africa has long been a neglected niche, with trailblazers like Adiele Afigbo and his work on the Anglo-Aro war being a noticeable exception to the nationalist historiography.[3] Since the 1980s, there has been a resurgence of scholars willing to engage with Africa's military past, with authors like John Thornton leading the way in his military histories of Atlantic Africa and subsequent work.[4] Though a thorough historiographic survey of Africa's military history in the past few decades falls outside the scope of this book, authors such as those mentioned above and others like David Killingray, Timothy Stapleton, Michele Moyd, Godfrey Uzoigwe, and Bruce Vandervort have expanded our understanding of African military history, especially during the colonial period.[5]

If colonial military history presents us with a challenge in writing the history of the African military experience using European sources almost exclusively, postcolonial military history suffers from a dire lack of sources in general. While most western wars leave an immense paper trail of operational reports, personnel files, procurement and disbursement records as well as personal accounts from people of every rank in the military and civilian experiences at home and on the front, African conflicts suffer from a dire lack of this kind of source material. As such, reconstructing and interpreting the military aspect of the war is especially difficult because of the lack of source material endemic to African military matters in general and African postcolonial conflict especially. In the Nigerian and Biafran cases, very few official military records exist or are accessible. In the Biafran case, the shortage is even more acute because the shortage of basic materials such as paper required reusing documents that would otherwise have been archived. A visit to the Nigerian National Archives in Enugu, which houses most of the extant Biafran materials, shows that many of the later documents are printed on the reverse of older ones, a practice necessitated by the wartime shortages, and evidenced in private, civilian, and military communications and publications. In some cases, Biafran news magazines began their life in 1967 with much fanfare on glossy stock paper rivaling the best-produced news magazines in the world and continued to publish throughout the war; however, by 1969 these publications had shifted to school notebooks, with the blue lines very apparent. The lack of source material is perhaps the most important obstacle in reconstructing the war and required the use of news reports both from Nigeria and abroad, memoirs, and media aggregators like *Africa Research Bulletin* to reconstruct some of the basic facts. Even the dates of some operations and battles are unclear or contested and required a painstaking chronology to perfect.[6]

This difficulty has led many of the problems of writing about the war and has helped amplify its uneven legacies. In this book, I employ a largely chronological approach for several reasons. First, writing a chronological history of the war provides us with a foundational text that will help anchor the debate in the war and how the situation in Biafra and Nigeria evolved over the four years of the crisis and nearly three years of fighting. Second, this approach helps to answer two distinct but interrelated questions about the war. The first question is that of genocide. The issue of genocide is perhaps the war's most polarizing and complex legacies. The strife that led to the coups, pogroms, and eventually secession and war did not end with the war. In fact, memory, propaganda, and ethnic conflict have amplified many of the issues, especially the memory of genocide, which continues to fester in Nigerian public discourse. The literature of genocide during the war consists of two broad threads. The first is activist scholarship that largely takes for granted the idea that the war was genocidal in nature, seeking to garner recognition of that genocide as prescribed in the United Nations Convention on the Prevention and Punishment of the Crime of Genocide (UNGC). The second, a more scholarly approach that examines the nuances and effects that the narrative had on people in Nigerian and abroad, seeks to problematize the issues in a complex fashion and expand historical understanding and conceptualization of genocide outside of the legal framework established in international law.

I show that Biafra's Propaganda Directorate planned the message of genocide very early in the war and used language that evoked the holocaust and Jewish sufferings in Europe to pressure the world to invoke Article VIII of the UNGC that requires signatories "to take such action . . . as they consider appropriate for the prevention and suppression of acts of genocide."[7] Moreover, a chronological approach shows how Biafran messaging changed and adapted to the unfolding military situation and changes in global perceptions of Biafra's ever diminishing ability to survive as an independent state.

In particular, Biafra's initial accusations of genocide came to force the Organization of African Unity (OAU) to intervene as early as the OAU Heads of State Meeting in Kinshasa in October 1967. When the OAU intervention failed to sufficiently internationalize the conflict and give Biafra the recognition Ojukwu sought, he turned to global media outlets. With the assistance of American-owned Swiss public relations firm Markpress, Biafra's Propaganda Directorate gained a global audience that forced Nigeria to acquiesce to a series of peace negotiations in 1968. These meetings gave Biafra a patina of legitimacy in diplomatic circles, but neither of the two conferences, in Kampala and Addis Ababa, yielded any tangible results to end the war or alleviate the civilian suffering that had reached a crescendo by August 1968. The failure of the talks led to the world's largest humanitarian airlift since the Berlin Blockade and the largest private one in history, forcing Biafra to retool its messaging to account for the failures and retain global support.

For all its successes, Biafra's message of genocide ultimately failed to secure a halt to hostilities or any kind of protection for relief supplies, which provided cover for the clandestine arms deliveries financed through the black market and with French support. Because of the fluid nature of the war, and Biafra's constant shifting of the focus of their narrative, the chronological approach is the best way to show how the war affected Biafra's attempts to keep their plight at the forefront of global affairs. Programs like the Land Army Scheme in early 1969 and Ojukwu's Ahiara Declaration in May of that year both served as attempts to show Biafra's strength in the face of genocide—a marked shift from the earlier narrative of victimhood.[8]

The war's memory has been so polarized in Nigeria largely because the war itself has been so neglected in analysis of the war crimes that both sides committed, and the contextualization is missing.[9] This book attempts to correct the notable omission of operational histories in many African wars, especially postcolonial ones.

A chronological approach is also the best way to address another of the war's important questions, namely its longevity. When hostilities erupted in July 1967,

Yakubu Gowon, head of Nigeria's Military Government, characterized the conflict as a "police operation" to arrest the perpetrators of secession, believing the conflict would end in forty-eight hours. This limited operation morphed into a thirty-month "total war." Though some have addressed the issue of the war's longevity, and Biafra's shocking resilience in the face of a better-supplied enemy that possessed armor, artillery, and air support that the Biafrans could only dream of, none have done so from a chronological perspective.[10] The chronological approach shows that Biafra's overall arc of the conflict was one of defeat, but also that at many points in the conflict the Nigerians suffered important and humiliating defeats that gave Ojukwu and his decision-makers the notion that they could capitalize on Nigeria's failures. One such moment, the Biafran destruction of Murtala Mohammed's convoy at the famous Abagana Ambush in March 1968, helps explain Biafran intransigence at the Kampala and Addis Ababa peace talks. The near destruction of Benjamin Adekunle's 3rd Marine Commando Division in November 1968 in the Nigerian's ill-fated Operation OAU, a reference to both the disdain Adekunle had for the organization and the operation's objectives, the last major Biafran urban centers: Owerri, Aba and Umuahia, also gave the Biafrans hope that their ill fortune would soon be reversed.

Other factors that protracted the war had to do with supply issues that became more acute for Biafra as their war effort faltered. But even then, a moment of hope appeared, such as in May 1969 when a Swedish Count, Carl Gustaf von Rosen, who had previously figured out how to fly into Biafra undetected by Nigerian air defenses thus opening the airlift, arrived with several light aircraft and formed the infamous "Minicoin" squadron to global acclaim.

Perhaps the most important issue that has long been neglected and explains more than any other single factor the war's nature being that of command issues within both the Nigerian and Biafran militaries. Nigeria's colonial military suffered from a lack of command officers due to the fact that the British who administered the army did not commission Africans until Wellington Bassey was commission in 1949, followed by Johnson Aguiyi-Ironsi, the first military head of state after the January coup, and Samuel Ademulegun later that year. In fact, Nigeria only had around thirty officers at independence. Most were young and very few had any experience in advanced command and doctrinal courses. After independence, many more officers entered service in a problematic process of Nigerianization.[11] Thus, by the time war erupted in 1967, few officers had the experience of commanding anything larger than a battalion, and many of those who did, like Ironsi, had been killed in the January and July coups. For example, Hassan Katsina became Nigeria's chief of staff in 1968 after his predecessor, Joseph Akahan, died in a helicopter crash. Both Akahan and Katsina previously commanded battalions before they became heads of the military, and both were very young for such a position. Akahan became chief of staff at age thirty, while Kastina was only four years older when he took over after Akahan's death. This inexperience was the norm in the Nigerian army's early years because of the legacies of colonial rule and had many disastrous effects. In particular, at no point in the war did Nigeria's army operate in coordination at the divisional level, and much of the decision-making process seems to have been more by negotiation and bribery than by orders. Both Nigeria and Biafra suffered from this, and the strange ascent of Biafran "Colonel" Joe Achuzia, a man with little if any military training who falsely claimed to have been a Sandhurst graduate yet rose to be one of the main commanders in the Biafran army is emblematic of the conflict. It is, however, the Nigerian side that suffered most from this, because if they had proper coordination and a clear chain of command, the war would not have lasted more than a year. This approach shows how this problem evolved and how it affected the war, largely giving the Biafran forces the hope that they could win despite the odds.

It is precisely this kind of work that is missing in most recent accounts that attempt to historicize the war and place its importance on Nigerian Society. Samuel Daly's recent work on the legal history of Biafra makes a bold claim that the war transformed Nigerian corruption and legal tolerances of what was considered acceptable during wartime, but the work lacks a context of what was happening in Biafra at different times during the war and why the need to tolerate certain forms of survival and not others arose within the context of the war. Similarly, Lasse Heerten's excellent work on humanitarianism during the war removes the actual fighting from the humanitarian catastrophe that unfolded. Adding military matters into this, and other recent works on the war would have given nuance and context where it was desperately needed.[12]

This work may seem somewhat conservative in its approach, as a significant portion focuses on both the operational histories as well as the "new" war and society aspects of the war. Much of the focus comes from the fact that discussing postcolonial wars as wars has largely been neglected, with few exceptions, mostly in southern Africa. In many parts of Africa, including in Nigeria, operational aspects of war are largely absent in discussions of conflicts. This has caused much of the writing about postcolonial African wars to be wars without combat. The Congo Crisis with all its global intrigue, which included the murder of United Nations Secretary General Dag Hammarskjold, has very little written about the war itself, even though it inspired films like *The Siege of Jadotville* and has entered the military heritage of the Irish troops that fought there. Similarly, much of the discussion on the conflict in Rwanda naturally emphasizes the horrific one hundred days that began on April 7, 1994, when Hutu extremists in the Rwandan army shot down the plane carrying the presidents of Rwanda and

Burundi. However, precious few works discuss the genocide within the context of the decades-long war between the Hutu government and Tutsi rebels, except as a backdrop for the genocide and as such, the genocide, both in scholarship and in the public imagination simply occurred, and has not been properly contextualized. Gerard Prunier's work is a notable exception to this omission.[13]

Writing a history of the Nigerian Civil War is rife with complicated issues. First and foremost among them is confronting the conflict's many legacies, especially those that time and memory have amplified and decontextualized from the war itself. The issues that led to the coups, pogroms, and eventually secession and war did not end when the war did. In fact, memory, propaganda, and ethnic strife have amplified many of these issues, chief among them the issue of genocide, the memory of which continues to fester in Nigerian public discourse. The literature of genocide during the war consists of two broad threads. The first is activist scholarship that largely takes for granted the idea that the war was genocidal in nature, seeking to garner recognition of that genocide as prescribed in the UNGC. The second, a more scholarly approach that examines the nuances and effects that the narrative had on people in Nigeria and abroad, seeks to problematize the issues in a complex fashion and expand historical understanding and conceptualization of genocide outside of the legal framework established in international law.

There is little denial that the war caused a massive humanitarian crisis, and that both sides committed war crimes and atrocities of varying scale, chief among them the Asaba Massacre described later in this work.[14] The writings of the Asaba Massacre shed light on the two themes that have dominated the broader discourse of genocide. Elizabeth Bird and Fraser Ottanelli's definitive work on the subject does much to highlight both the horrors of the fateful days in October 1967 when Nigerian forces entered the city and killed thousands of innocent civilians in reprisal attacks for perceived collusion with the Biafran invaders across the Niger.

Because of the lack of official military documentation, I have used several methods to reconstruct the military narratives and had to cross-reference them to ensure reconstructions were as accurate as possible. The basis for much of the battle and operational reconstructions come from the various memoirs, but these are not without issue. First, most of the memoirs come from the Biafran side, with very few Nigerian military commanders writing detailed accounts of their own.[15] Second, most of the authors are very lax with dates, making accurate timelines painstakingly difficult to create. One example comes from Godwin Alabi-Isama's depiction of the taking of the Biafran city of Aba in September 1968. Alabi-Isama states that one of his officers, Philemon Shande, "was ordered to attack Aba within seven days."[16] On September 4, Shande began his assault, but because September 4 is the only date Alabi-Isama provides, there is little evidence as to whether he began the assault immediately, how long he took to prepare his offensive, organize his supply lines, etc. These are key questions because they speak to the military preparedness and coordination between the various parts of the Nigerian military command structure.

On the Biafran side, though many memoirs exist, they also seem to be piecemeal and suffer from a similar lack of chronological certainty. During Biafra's first military collapse in October 1967, Alexander Madiebo and Philip Efiong describe the chaotic scene in the Biafran capital, Enugu, as Ojukwu and the Biafran leadership all scrambled to escape the slow envelopment that the cautious Nigerian colonel Muhammed Shuwa commanded. However, both Biafran leaders are very lax in their dates, leaving us with an accurate depiction of the moment, but a challenge in understanding the timeline.

Official histories offer little by way of assisting in the war's military reconstruction, as many of them avoided discussing it in depth. The earliest histories in Nigeria avoided such discussions and at times actively suppressed discussion regarding the war. As a result, many of the official histories are piecemeal at best in relating the military aspects of the war.[17]

Absent the primary sources that military historians are accustomed to, this work relies largely on memoirs, reminiscences and other works of that nature, which create a unique set of interpretation issues. First, many of the memoirs had the future in mind and were not just looking at the past. Saro-Wiwa, for example, published his account just as he was embarking on the environmental agitation that would ultimately cost him his life. He wrote his memoirs to show how much of a loyal Nigerian he was. Others, like Obasanjo, published their works as a springboard into political life, using their military record as justification for their ability to guide Nigeria's future. This type of memoir is especially problematic, as it invited criticism, and other authors such as Alabi-Isama used their war stories to settle political scores. Alabi-Isami uses almost a third of his book to pillory Obasanjo's memoir; that portion alone is nearly one hundred pages longer than Obasanjo's entire volume.[18]

Absent plans, battle reports, and other timely documentation, many of the only accounts of battles comes from these memoirs but must be carefully cross-referenced and examined, not only for accuracy but also for fears of self-aggrandizement. Two glaring examples come from the Biafran side. The first deals with probably the most publicized battle during the war, the Abagana Ambush on March 31, 1968, where a Biafran force destroyed a Nigerian supply convoy attempting to link Enugu with the newly captured city of Onitsha, detailed in chapter 7. Joe Achuzia, a problematic character during the war for several reasons examined throughout this book, claimed to have led the assault against a caravan of over 400 vehicles driving four abreast, flanked throughout with soldiers marching six men deep on either side on what is today the "old" Awka-Onitsha road. While it is unlikely that that road would have been able to accommodate such a massive convoy, Achuzia's description of the convoy likens it more to victory parade than a convoy attempting to traverse enemy territory. Madiebo's account cites the convoy at a more modest ninety-six vehicles, still rather large for this type of convoy, but one corroborated by the documentary evidence. Further, Madiebo claims that Achuzia was not even present at the ambush and only arrived the next day to field questions from the international press corps.

In chapter 8, I discuss Nigerian Colonel Benjamin Adekunle's ill-conceived Operation OAU and the Biafran counterattack that rolled back the offensive and allowed for the Biafran recapture of Owerri. In his memoirs, Madiebo claimed the assault on Owerri, which began in November 1968 and ended in March 1969, was part of a long strategy that took into account the problems of Biafran logistics and was an ingenious way to win the city through a long-term offensive. However, most news reports and other evidence dispute this account, and, while there may be some truth to the ways Biafran commanders could deal with the constant shortages in food, ammunition, and other war matériel, Madiebo's confident assertion seems to be at least somewhat rooted in hindsight.

Thus, I endeavor, wherever possible, to provide a singular account of the operational history based on a synthesis of the best available evidence. However, in places where the narratives are so divergent, as they are in Abagana and Ikot Ekpene, I was forced to separate them but continue the narrative based on the outcome of operation rather than the divergent accounts.

ONE

THE FORMATION OF NIGERIA

LIKE MANY AFRICAN STATES, NIGERIA was born of violence. The violence of the British conquest became the violence of colonialism and colonial resistance, which turned into the violence of the postcolonial state. However, Nigeria's ethnic, linguistic, environmental, and religious diversity made the conflicts that shaped and continue to shape its destiny unique. As such, the transformation of Nigeria from a heterogeneous geographical expression to a single polity is key to understanding the crisis of the postcolonial state's early years, which led to the civil war and the plight of Nigeria since.

By the 1870s, much of the coast of what would become Nigeria was under some form of British control or oversight, with the Lagos colony established in 1861 and several diplomatic interventions, known as "gunboat diplomacy," in many of the riverine regions of the Niger Delta. This would change when the 1884–85 West Africa conference ushered in a new vision for European powers to interact with Africa's complex assortment of polities. Perhaps the most aggressive and egregious of these interventions came in 1887, when the British consul Harry Johnston deposed King Jaja of the city-state of Opobo at the mouth of the Imo River.[1] This was quickly followed by the defeat, in similar fashion, of Nana Itsekiri in 1894.[2]

The second phase of the British conquest was even less diplomatic than the gunboat diplomacy preceding it. In 1897, the British instigated a crisis with one of the most powerful kingdoms in the region, the Empire of Benin, destroyed and plundered it, and exiled its leader, Oba Ovonramwen. The capital was looted, with the majority of the cultural and artistic legacies taken to the British Museum and dozens of museums around the world, where they still reside more than a century later.[3]

In what would become Western Nigeria, the remnants of the Oyo Empire had been engaged in a series of brutal civil wars that began with the sacking of the city of Oyo in 1836.[4] In 1886, the British brokered a peace deal aimed at both establishing trade relations and buttressing British interests against encroachment from the French in the east. After a decisive victory against the powerful Ijebu in 1892, other states, like Ibadan, signed treaties with the British. By 1900, when the Southern Nigerian Protectorate was established, virtually the entire Yoruba-speaking region was incorporated into the Lagos colony.[5]

At the Berlin Conference, the British claimed Northern Nigeria, an area that was ruled by one of the largest polities in Africa, the Sokoto Caliphate. To conquer the region, the British amalgamated the militaries founded by various trading interests, such as the Royal Niger Company's Constabulary, into the West African Frontier Force (WAFF) and placed it under the command of Frederick Lugard (later Lord Lugard). By 1903, the largely African force succeeded in destroying the various emirates that made up the caliphate and, in a final battle, killing the caliph, Attahiru I, at Burmi, where he was attempting to flee to the east.[6]

After the British conquest, Nigeria was administered as two separate entities until 1914 when Lugard, who returned to Nigeria after a stint as governor of Hong Kong, unified the colonies of Northern and Southern Nigeria to streamline the region's finances. He favored Northern Nigeria, largely because the Sokoto Caliphate had a centralized political structure that was relatively simple to maintain, even though it was not economically self-supporting and was in constant need of cash influx from the south and London. Lugard also preferred a more centralized government, which allowed him to consolidate the administration of the diverse polities that made up the new territory.[7]

The outbreak of World War I in 1914 changed British attitudes toward its colonies, and Lugard sought to implement a system of taxation that would both serve the war effort and act as a teaching tool to give financial responsibility to local leaders in Southern Nigeria, who had for centuries, thanks to their trading networks, been able to rule without the need to directly tax their subjects, unlike the Sokoto Caliphate, which had an established taxation system that the British continued to maintain. Nigerian unification meant that half of the country was not required to pay taxes, breeding resentment in the north. Lugard also calculated that the Yoruba, who had a history of central authority that collected levies and tributes, would be easily converted to his new system. He felt that implementing direct taxation in the south would be relatively straightforward, and in 1916 he was granted the authority to extend his Native Revenue Ordinance to the southern areas, such as the Yoruba-speaking areas and the former Benin Kingdom, where he felt there would be few disturbances because the populations had experience with powerful centralized authorities.[8] However, these efforts sparked massive revolts around the colony, especially in Kabba, near the city of Benin, and the fiercely independent city of Abeokuta.

When Lugard left in 1919, his successor, Hugh Clifford, shifted policies. Unlike Lugard, who preferred to use the existing structures of the Sokoto Caliphate and superimpose their administrative structure onto the south, at times creating rulers, who became derisively known as "warrant chiefs" due to the papers they received from the British as their only claim to legitimacy, Clifford preferred to incorporate Western-educated elites into his government and challenged the Muslim rulers, whom he felt "would occasion cruelty, extortion, and abuse of authority."[9] Clifford also expanded opportunities for Western education in the colony, hoping to "aid the enlightenment and development of the local population, rural no less than urban," arguing that Lugard's previous policies "have been designed to postpone as long as possible the dawning of what is regarded as the evil day of general emancipation."[10] However, because of opposition to Western education in the north, most of the new schooling opportunities came in the south and created a population better suited to administering the colony and, later, the independent country.[11]

Additionally, Clifford sought political integration and instituted the first of many constitutions in the colony. Though Clifford's constitution maintained the near total control of British officials, it created a free press and enfranchised Nigerians such as Herbert Macaulay who formed the first political party, the Nigerian National Democratic Party (NNDP). Clifford's successor, Graeme Thomson, reverted to Lugard's emphasis on taxation and oversaw one of the largest tax revolts when he attempted to impose a new tax regime in Eastern Nigeria. This rebellion eventually became known as the Aba Women's War.[12]

Clifford and Thomson's tenures as governor showcase the issues that unifying Nigeria wrought on the colony, leading to secession and civil war when Nigeria became independent in 1960. Because Clifford and his supporters empowered Western-educated elites, they became integral parts of the colonial administration at all levels, including the military. When Nigeria became independent, these elites became the backbone of the newly independent Nigerian government. However, Lugard and those who supported his idea of indirect rule created in Nigeria a structure that was modeled after the Sokoto Caliphate, and they imposed that structure, which heavily favored the north, onto the country as a whole. Thus, when Nigeria became independent, colonial violence, such as the Women's War, became a way to resolve disputes that could have been dealt with through more pacific means.

Conflicting British policies also played a vital role in the arenas where Nigerians were able to challenge the colonial system, from both inside and out. Clifford's constitution gave Nigerians a say in the government for the first time, and the first to seize on the opportunity were the Western-educated elites, who largely came from Southern Nigeria. Macaulay began a process of holding the colonial government accountable when their actions proved detrimental to Nigerians and beneficial to the British administrators.[13] Macaulay inspired younger Nigerians to take part in the politics that centered in Lagos. Chief among them were Obafemi Awolowo and Nnamdi Azikiwe. Awolowo studied law at the University of London and returned to Nigeria in 1944 to work for the influential *Nigerian Times* before founding the *Nigerian Tribune* in 1949. In both papers, Awo, as he was known, played a pivotal role in Nigerian agitation for more political freedom in the aftermath of World War II, especially in the general strike of 1945.

Azikiwe also came to prominence during the general strike. The son of a civil servant, Zik, as he was known, was Igbo, but like many Igbo, he was born outside the traditional Igbo heartland. Like Ojukwu, Azikiwe was born in the northwestern town of Zungeru, then an important administrative center, in 1904, and after being educated in missionary schools he left Nigeria in 1925 to attend Howard University in Washington, DC. Due to financial difficulties in paying for his education, he transferred to Lincoln University in Pennsylvania, where he graduated in 1930 before earning a master's degree in religion in 1932 and another master's in anthropology from the University of Pennsylvania the following year. He returned to Nigeria in 1937 after a short stint in Accra, where he founded his first newspaper, the *African Morning Post*. Back in Lagos, he founded his most important paper, the *West African Pilot*, which he used, especially after the war, as a mouthpiece for his newly founded organization, the National Council of Nigeria and the Cameroons (NCNC). Azikiwe's vocal support for the strike through both the NCNC and his newspaper network garnered him national attention, and he used the labor movement to create a radical leftist organization, which became known as the Zikist movement.

Azikiwe, as leader of the NCNC, cultivated Igbo identity to solidify his position as head of the party. One of the most powerful groups within the NCNC was the Ibo State Union (ISU).[14] The organization quickly became one of the most important groups within the NCNC. In fact, when the ISU was formed, Azikiwe became the organization's president and leader of the NCNC, linking the political party with the newly forming pan-Igbo identity.[15]

Awolowo developed similar ethnic organizations within the Yoruba-speaking areas, both in Nigeria and abroad. While a law student in London, he created an organization called the Egbe Omo Oduduwa, which was dedicated to the preservation and promotion of Yoruba culture.[16] On his return to Nigeria, he promoted the Egbe society, founding chapters across the Western Region. When Azikiwe left the Nigerian Youth Movement (NYM), which was founded in 1934 as Nigeria's first truly nationalist organization, Awolowo was placed in charge of the now largely Yoruba organization, where he incorporated aspects of Yoruba nationalism before founding the Action Group (AG) in 1951 to capitalize on the growing strength of the regional assemblies.

In the north, similar patterns of ethnic political alignments began to emerge. Because the north had a long history of centralized government remaining relatively untouched during British rule, the emerging political group, the Northern People's Congress (NPC), was relatively conservative. Unlike their southern counterparts, NPC officials preferred to work with the existing powerful traditional authorities rather than directly challenge them the way the Zikist movement challenged the warrant chiefs and Awolowo's confrontational stance against the Yoruba elders. Though the NPC was founded by several of the few Western-educated northerners, such as Mallam Aminu Kano and Abubakar Tafawa Balewa, who attended the University of London together, both Kano and Tafawa Balewa sought to counter Pan-Nigerian identities and focus on maintaining northern autonomy.[17] This approach would have fundamental consequences once Nigeria attained independence in 1960, and it created tensions within the NPC. Kano was one of the more radical voices and wanted the party to challenge the conservative leadership. He eventually formed the Northern Elements Progressive Union (NEPU), which allied itself with the NCNC. Because of the emerging regional nature of politics in the country, Kano relegated himself to a fringe party and failed to have much electoral success, whether for himself or other elements within the NEPU.

Thus, all three regions' political structures were quickly dominated by the largest ethnopolitical group in each region. This led to increased unrest from smaller groups in each region. In the Northern Region, the so-called Middle Belt populations that straddled the border between the Northern Region and the Eastern and Western Regions began to agitate for greater political say, within both their own region and the larger federal structure. Similarly, in the Eastern Region, groups such as the Ijo, Itsekiri, Ogoni, and Andoni struggled to cope with what they perceived as Igbo domination. Similar to NEPU's alliance with the NCNC, smaller regional political groups often formed alliances both among themselves and with the dominant parties in other regions.

In 1948, John Macpherson replaced Richards as governor, and two years later he set out to rectify some of the issues that his predecessor's constitution had created. Even more troubling than the imposition of the constitution, Richards's document created three very powerful entities that wielded almost absolute control in their respective regions. These regional governments quickly came to be dominated by the most powerful ethnic group in each region, further marginalizing the smaller ethnic groups. Though Macpherson lauded the 1946 constitution, claiming that it "worked so well," he congratulated himself for taking "the bold—even brash—step of asking the country to tell me what measure of constitutional advance it wanted."[18] What all sides wanted was more local control over internal matters, but all of the "big three" ethnopolitical groups were also jockeying for position within whatever new structure would emerge to ensure they would not be dominated by the others.

What emerged from the Macpherson constitution when it was implemented in 1952 was an unstable political structure attempting to strengthen both the central government and regional and local institutions in Nigeria. Though Macpherson had taken credit for his "brash" idea of asking local leaders for input, he joked "that it was conceived by Nigerians (though I would admit to being a sort of midwife!), and by suggesting that it was only after it broke down that it came more commonly to be called after me!"[19] What the Macpherson constitution did was establish the country as a completely federal entity but without a strong central executive arm. The new constitution created a twelve-member Council of Ministers with four representatives from each region and six ex officio members, presided over by the governor. It also transformed the central legislature, which had existed since the 1923 constitution, into a House of Representatives. To allay northern fears of southern domination, half of the seats in the House were allocated to the Northern Region, with the remaining seats split evenly between the Eastern and Western Regions. In the subsequent federal election in 1954, the NPC won all the seats in the Northern Region while both the NCNC and the AG won absolute majorities in their respective regions, further cementing the tripartite ethnic divide that would dominate Nigerian politics well into independence.

On October 1, 1960, a ceremony in Lagos ended British rule over the territory, and Nigeria became an independent state. With independence, Nigeria inherited many of the instabilities that plagued the colonial state, exasperating the tensions between the various ethnopolitical groups in the country. Despite initial optimism regarding the country's future, the intergroup conflicts bred corruption and political violence and laid the groundwork for a radical attempt to fix the nation's malaise.

Compounding these tensions, the country's economic footing greatly favored the southern regions. In the Western Region, cocoa production created an agricultural economic boom, known as the cocoa boom. In the Eastern Region, oil was discovered in commercial quantities in 1958 and quickly came to dominate the region's economy, eventually becoming the single most important source of Nigeria's government revenue. The discovery of oil further concentrated economic growth in favor of the south. However, Nigeria's political structure favored the north when allocating seats in both chambers of the new parliament. Because of the country's proportional allocation of seats, the north was guaranteed a majority. Northern leaders such as Ahmadu Bello, the northern premier, had only to maintain a majority in the Northern Region to be guaranteed a majority in the entire country's parliament, thus controlling the appointment of the prime minister. In effect, for northern leaders the rest of the country was of little significance in controlling the federal mechanisms of government, and southern leaders could do little to challenge this political reality.

Complicating matters further, the country's complex ethnic composition was simplified by splitting the country into three regions. The "big three" ethnic groups together accounted for nearly 70 percent of the country's population, and each of the three groups dominated their own region. Thus, the Igbo dominated the government structure in the Eastern Region, the Yoruba controlled the Western Region, and the Hausa-Fulani led the Northern Region. This regional structure further complicated both interethnic and intraethnic conflict within the state, with minorities struggling to find a voice for their concerns and having to subordinate their interests to those of the three largest groups, who came to dominate the country's political machine.

The nature of the Nigerian state was that national power rested in the three regions, making the ability to control the national government in Lagos dependent on the ability to control representation in the country's regional structure. Compounding matters, the country's 1960 constitution subordinated national representation to the regional structure and based the allocation of parliamentary districts on regional populations, which were determined by the decennial census. This further subordinated the country's central government to the regional structure and ensured that most political powers remained in the regional capitals of Enugu, Ibadan, and Kaduna rather than the federal capital in Lagos.

Like many newly independent African colonial states, Nigeria struggled to define a national identity. Because of the country's political structure, regional identities often trumped national ones. For most Igbo, Yoruba, and Hausa-Fulani politicians, their main concerns often centered on avoiding domination by the other regions. As a result, most of the smaller ethnic groups, such as the Tiv, Ijo, Ibibio, Ogoni, and countless others, struggled to find their voices within the regional structure without subordinating themselves to one of the larger groups in a patronage system that they found unpalatable but unavoidable after their failure to earn concessions from the British administration prior to independence.

The British took notice of the minority concerns in the run-up to independence and in 1957 established a special Minorities Commission under the leadership of Sir Henry Willink, a former conservative member of Parliament and vice chancellor of the University of Cambridge. From November 1957 until April 1958, the commission traveled all over Nigeria, holding public and private forums before issuing its report in July 1958. The question most attendees raised was how to secure minority rights within the country's existing structure. The commission report stated that "almost all the witnesses who came before us were insistent that nothing but a separate state could meet their problems."[20] In the end, however, it concluded that rather than creating new states, the constitution should be amended to include protections of what they determined to be "fundamental rights." Most of these were copied verbatim from the 1950 *European Convention on Human Rights and Fundamental Freedoms,*[21] with others lifted from other British colonial constitutions, such as the Malaya and Pakistani constitutions.[22]

The Willink Commission's refusal to address the major issue of Nigeria's composition only exacerbated the problems after independence. In particular, the commission's adherence to a singular solution of enshrining rights for all minorities in the constitution did little to address the diverse problems that the different groups in the country faced. For example, the Ijo in the Niger Delta, who were split between the Western and Eastern Regions, faced serious infrastructure issues that could not be fixed without massive expenditure while the main concern of the minorities in the north was religious domination by the Muslim Hausa-Fulani elites.[23]

Despite these issues, some Nigerians did attempt to create an identity that transcended ethnic, religious, and sectional divides. Some literary works attest to this emerging identity. In 1952, Amos Tutuola published his novel *The Palm-Wine Drinkard,* which tells the story of a rich man addicted to palm wine who hires his own personal tapper to climb palm trees and extract the sap for fermentation. When the tapper dies, the man goes into the magical land of the dead to resurrect him. Written in Nigerian pidgin, an amalgam of English and local languages with simplified grammar to make it understandable in the linguistically varied country, the book was an early attempt to use Nigeria's history and customs to tell a story that could be understood and enjoyed by all Nigerians regardless of ethnicity, language, or class.

Nigeria's best-known writer, Chinua Achebe, wrote *Things Fall Apart* in 1958. The first of his three novels explored the changes in traditional Nigerian life under colonialism and Christian evangelism. This book, along with its two companions, *No Longer at Ease* and *Arrow of God,* made Achebe a household name in Nigeria and abroad, where his books became some of the most important works of African literature. He followed these books with *A Man of the People,* which tells the story of Odili, a schoolteacher in an unnamed African country who receives an invitation to join the country's corrupt civilian administration. After several episodes of political intrigue and personal conflict between the book's protagonist and his former mentor turned corrupt politician, the book ends with a military coup. Though published in 1966, the book was completed before the January coup. Because of the similarities between events in the book and those in Nigeria, Achebe's friend and fellow author John Pepper Clark remarked after reading an advance copy, "Chinua, I know you are a prophet. Everything in this book has happened except a military coup!"[24] By the time the book was released, however, the first coup had already taken place.

Perhaps the most important incubator for a national Nigerian identity came from the university system. Though created by the British, Nigerian universities became some of the most important institutions for higher education in Africa and influenced many of the foundational trends for study of the continent. At independence, very few universities existed in the country, either public or private. The two main campuses were University College Ibadan (UCI), the oldest university in Nigeria, founded in 1948 and renamed the University of Ibadan (UI) in 1962; and the University of Nigeria in Nsukka (UNN), which was established in 1955. In the early years of independence, the Nigerian government established several other schools, such as the University of Northern Nigeria (now Ahmadu Bello University) in Zaria and the University of Lagos (UNILAG), both established in 1962. These universities quickly became multiethnic centers and fostered a sense of community and political activism that both reinforced ethnic identities and challenged them.

The famed author and activist Ken Saro-Wiwa, who would later serve as the civil administrator for the city of Bonny during the war, wrote about student elections during his time at the University of Ibadan in the early 1960s. Despite the university's large multiethnic composition, due to its location, it was dominated by the Yoruba. Saro-Wiwa stood for election for student government at UI. He lost badly, stating, "I once contested a student's Union [*sic*] election and crashed out, winning a majority of votes only in the ladies hall. That year, the entire elected Executive was solidly Yoruba. I believed that the Yoruba students were so ashamed of this that the following year they did not contest any post at all, enabling a minority student to win."[25] Saro-Wiwa's observation confirmed that the strong ethnic connections in the political realm could not easily be overcome in the university setting, but there were conscious attempts to transcend these relationships to create something that was uniquely Nigerian.

Universities also played a central role in disseminating cultural awareness. Wole Soyinka, the first Black African writer to be awarded the Nobel Prize for literature, wrote several works, such as *A Dance of the Forests* and *The Swamp Dwellers*. Similar to Achebe's first three works, Soyinka's plays, especially *The Swamp Dwellers,* examine the tensions between tradition and modernity and highlight the problems associated with compromising these two forces to create a new identity. Like many plays in the country, Soyinka's works were initially performed by university theater groups and were thus multiethnic in their composition. Further, because the plays were in English or pidgin, the performances could be easily understood by most Nigerians, an important consideration in a country with a high illiteracy rate.

At the University of Ibadan, pioneers such as Kenneth Dike founded a historical methodology that would become known as the Ibadan School. Dike's seminal work, *Trade and Politics in the Niger Delta*, focused on the resistance to British incursions in Southern Nigeria during the period before the "Scramble for Africa."[26] Dike's work, an amalgam of political and economic history, concentrated on those leaders in the Niger Delta who were able to keep British interests at bay, such as King Jaja of Opobo, whose life merited a chapter. Most importantly, for the first time a professional historian showed how African societies shaped their own futures and reacted in rational ways to European incursions. By focusing on precolonial societies, Dike helped create a nationalist history for Nigerians that showed many of the common struggles and highlighted the varied and rich histories of the country's cultures. Writers like Dike and those who followed him in creating the Ibadan School, such as Ade Ajayi, Adiele Afigbo, and Saburi Biobaku, not only created a revolution in Africa's historical methodology but also strove to create a new type of Nigerian identity by weaving the nation's tapestry into a unified whole.[27]

These attempts to create a cultural and intellectual basis for a Nigerian nation echoed the efforts of Obafemi Awolowo, whose 1947 work, *The Path to Nigerian Freedom*, recognized Nigeria's instability, which he characterized as rooted in the fact that Nigeria was "not a nation, [but] a mere geographical expression."[28] For Awolowo and many other nascent Nigerian nationalists, the question was how to create not only a cultural notion of what it meant to be Nigerian but also a political expression of what could become a unique form of nationalism. However, when this nationalism found expression, it often came into conflict with state power.

One of the most important expressions of this new Nigerian nationalism came shortly after independence in reaction to the Anglo-Nigerian Defense Agreement. In the run-up to Nigerian independence, the British wished to maintain some form of military presence in the country, but this would not be possible without Nigerian consent. The British surmised that the Nigerian military, still undergoing the process of Nigerianization, that is, the replacement of colonial personnel in positions of power, such as the police, military officers, civil service, and others, with qualified local leaders, would not be able to function properly without British assistance. To this end, the British government, under the leadership of Prime Minister Harold Macmillan, conceived of an agreement that would allow for a British presence in Nigeria while giving Nigerian military units the same rights in Britain. The British agreed to train the Nigerian military and assist in helping to develop the parts of the armed forces that were lacking under colonial rule—namely, the navy and air force. Though much of the treaty could be defended as an attempt to meet both parties' needs, from a nationalist standpoint the treaty seemed heavily skewed in Britain's favor. Though the treaty afforded both countries' military unfettered use of the other's airspace and airports, in reality Nigeria did not have an air force that could take advantage of that part of the treaty's stipulation.[29]

Even more difficult to defend was the fact that British soldiers were to be granted visa-free entry to Nigeria and treated as permanent residents while in the country and were exempt from automobile registration or insurance. But perhaps the most egregious aspect of the treaty was the stipulation that Nigeria would lease land to the British for the construction of British bases in Northern Nigeria. Though the last part was dropped from the final draft of the agreement, the fact that it was considered at all gave rise to a flurry of activism that centered at UCI, with student organizations—namely, the Nigerian Union of Great Britain and Ireland and the National Union of the Nigerian Students (NUNS)—leading the protests against the pact. In one instance, students from UCI stormed the Nigerian Parliament in protest, leading Prime Minister Tafawa Balewa to declare that "I am not prepared to succumb to the threats of irresponsible elements because at my age I am quite ready for either peace or war."[30] Later, trade unions and opposition parties, led by Awolowo's Action Group (AG), joined the students in demanding the pact be renounced. Awolowo went so far as to claim that Nigerian leaders had been coerced into accepting the agreement, stating that in 1958 he and the other regional leaders "were bundled to No. 10 Downing Street and were asked to initial this document on the understanding that unless the document was initialed, it would not be possible for Her Majesty's Government to make a declaration fixing the date for our independence."[31] Faced with such staunch nationalist opposition, the government had little choice but to abandon plans for the treaty, which they did in February 1962.

Despite all the efforts to create a cultural, ideological, and political identity that was uniquely Nigerian, the country's structure made regional and therefore ethnic competition all but inevitable. The 1959 elections set the stage for the regional conflict after the transfer of power. The election results crystalized the north-south divide and reinforced the political elite's fears of regional domination and subjugation. One of the main reasons behind this fear stemmed from Nigeria's adoption of the British first-past-the-post (FPTP) election system rather than a proportional representation system. Even further, the fact that electoral districts were allocated to each region based on population meant that the Northern Region received the largest seat allocation. The results seemed to confirm southern fears, with Tafawa Balewa's Northern People's Congress (NPC) receiving one hundred thirty-four seats in the House of Representatives despite winning only 25.5 percent of the vote, the smallest percentage of the three largest parties. Azikiwe's NCNC won eighty-one seats but secured the largest share of the popular vote, with 34 percent. Similarly, the Awolowo-led AG garnered seventy-three seats despite winning fractionally more votes than the NPC.[32]

The government that emerged after the elections was a coalition between the NPC and the NCNC. Tafawa Balewa became prime minister, and Azikiwe assumed the largely ceremonial role of governor general, replacing James Wilson Robertson and becoming the first Nigerian to inhabit the post. Despite the coalition, the NPC embarked on a series of plans that sought to augment northern representation in virtually all levels of national government and service. To this end, the NPC transformed military and civil service recruitment from the colonial system of examination to a quota-based system. This was especially contentious for the recruiting of officers for the Nigerian military. Unlike the enlisted men, who were traditionally recruited from the North as far back as Goldie's Royal Niger Constabulary, officer enlistment had previously required a stringent set of tests. These tests, administered in the British system, heavily favored southerners, who had a longer history of exposure to colonial education and were thus better poised to succeed in the examinations. Ibrahim Tako Galadima, the minister of state for the army, defended the new quota system, claiming it was necessary for the creation of national unity. He claimed that "if any part of the country is not represented in the army, we may harbour some fear that a particular section will begin to feel that it is being dominated."[33] The quota system increased the representation of northerners in the officers' corps. At independence, Nigeria had eighty-one Nigerian officers out of a total of around three hundred, with the rest British. Of the eighty-one, approximately three-quarters were Igbo. By 1966, the quota system enabled the number of officers from the Northern Region to achieve parity with the east.[34] This did not come without criticism, especially from within the officer corps. Though the system recruited some highly qualified officers from the north, many officers commissioned before independence openly decried the quality of most new northern officers. In fact, many officers, such as Ben Gbulie, felt so personally aggrieved by the new system that it became a vital tool for recruiting young officers into the January coup.

Because northern officers were only reaching parity in numbers in the junior ranks, senior appointments were heavily politicized. The symbol of Nigerianization of the military, the general officer commanding (GOC), became a politicized issue. When the post became vacant in 1962 after the end of Maj. Gen. Norman Foster's term, most in the country expected one of the senior Nigerian officers to replace him—namely, the Igbo Lt. Col. Johnson Aguiyi-Ironsi or Yoruba officer Lt. Col. Samuel Ademulegun. Instead, the federal government tapped another

British officer, Christopher Welby-Everard, as Foster's successor. This move prompted vehement condemnation in the south. The *Nigerian Outlook* newspaper published a scathing criticism of the move, asking, "Are we to believe that if either Lt. Col. Ironsi or Lt. Col. Ademulegun was appointed to take over command of the Nigerian Forces that Northern Nigeria would one day be invaded by the South? Or could it be inferred that since one of the most important ministries—the Defense Ministry—is under the control of a Northerner and perhaps there is no Northerner yet qualified to command the Nigerian Forces, then the post of commander must continue to be occupied by expatriates?"[35]

Three years later, when Welby-Everard left his post, he was finally replaced by Ironsi, a career officer who commanded the Nigerian contingent to the Congo during the Katanga crisis and was a natural choice as the most qualified Nigerian officer. However, his Igbo ethnicity made his confirmation a political issue even though most in the country acknowledged that he harbored little political ambition. An editorial in the Zaria-based *Nigerian Citizen* lamented the appointment, saying, "Today I am weeping because the North has foregone all its advantages brought to it by its natural position—majority in population, expanse of land, and majority in parliament. The head of the police force goes to Eastern Nigeria, the Navy also goes East. Where is the Army now? Eastern Nigeria has captured it too."[36]

The NPC government also used the federal mechanism to divert development funding to projects in the north. Government officials called this a necessary corrective, much like the quota system, to address the imbalance that favored the southern regions before independence. In 1962, the country began its first national development plan that was intended to reduce Nigeria's dependence on agricultural output and create a more industrialized and modern economy. Though the plan successfully diversified the Nigerian economy, much of the touted diversification stemmed from a move from agricultural production to the exploitation of oil in the Niger Delta. Oil production increased from forty-six thousand barrels per day (bpd) in 1961 to six hundred thousand in 1967, on the eve of the civil war. Oil thus accounted for almost the entire increase in the mining sector during this period, which rose from less than 1 percent of the country's GDP in 1960 to 4.8 percent by the end of 1966.[37]

Even more troubling for those in the south, especially in the oil-rich Niger Delta, was the fact that most of the large-scale development projects funded by the federal government happened in the north of the country. Even though much of the delta suffered from underdevelopment, a fact that was exasperated by the region's topography, much of the money earned from the petroleum industry went to large-scale infrastructure projects in the north and not in the south.

Though the oil industry would boom in the post–civil war years and become the most important source of foreign investment and government funds, the sector was already growing during the First Republic, though it did not eclipse the agricultural sector until after 1972.[38] One of the most ambitious of these projects was the Kainji dam on the Niger River near the city of Zungeru in Northern Nigeria. Begun in 1964, by 1968 the project accounted for nearly 10 percent of government development spending. Despite these costs, the dam was never properly completed, with only four of the twelve planned power-generating turbines installed, reducing the dam's initial power-producing capacity from 960 to 330 megawatts.[39]

This politicization of the economic system lay at the core of the country's instability and inability to forge a national consensus. The resulting political climate created incentives to bolster regional identities, which were intertwined with the dominant ethnic groups of each region, confirming many of the minority fears expressed to the Willink Commission. Despite the fact that the NCNC garnered the plurality of the votes in the 1959 elections, they served in the coalition government as the junior partner. Azikiwe, though head of state as governor general, and as president after 1963, held a largely ceremonial role, with the real power handed to Tafawa Balewa as prime minister. The Eastern Region's insistence that much of its wealth was going to subsidize the north led Azikiwe's NCNC to begin courting new alliances ahead of the 1964 federal elections.

In the Western Region, Awolowo's situation as head of the opposition AG became precarious. If the NCNC, as the junior member of the coalition, was being shut out of government, the AG's situation as the opposition was even worse. Samuel Akintola, Awolowo's successor as head of the Western Region and main rival in the AG, called for a closer relationship with the NPC in an effort to gain more access to federal funds.[40] Awolowo wished for the Western Region to embrace a social democratic model of development with the aim of making the region economically self-sufficient.[41] The northern premier, Ahmadu Bello, wary of Awolowo's attempts to develop the Western Region, saw the AG as a threat and collaborated with Akintola to neutralize the troublesome Awolowo, destroy the AG in the west, and allow the NPC to move toward removing Azikiwe from the presidency, replacing the NCNC with Akintola in the federal government.[42]

However, control of the region was also an underlying factor in the crisis that began in May 1962, when Awolowo attempted to oust Akintola from the premiership of the Western Region and replace him with a close ally, Chief Alhaji Dauda Soroye Adegbenro. Ostensibly, the crisis began in January 1962 when Akintola, without consulting the AG leadership, increased the fees that schools had to pay to the government of the Western Region, therefore forcing an increase in school fees across the region. This move was intended to help recoup the losses that the government faced after Akintola had previously lowered taxes and after a global collapse in the price of cocoa, the Western Region's chief export.[43] Though Awolowo no longer controlled the AG's party mechanism, he had substantial influence within the party and, more importantly, within the party's newspaper network. Awolowo had tried to use his position as one of the country's elder statesmen to transform the AG from a regional Yoruba party to one that appealed to the growing Nigerian middle class, especially the newly educated elites. But the AG was shut out of the federal government thanks to the NPC-NCNC coalition, and the Western Region remained Awolowo's sole source of potential power. Even more problematic for the national AG party, Akintola's overtures toward Tafawa Balewa threatened to undermine Awolowo's support because the implication behind it was that Akintola would use his influence to curb AG politicians outside of the west, making the AG into another regional party. The issue of the school fees proved to be the catalyst that Awolowo hoped he could use to unseat Akintola.

Awolowo and Akintola first came to loggerheads in February 1962 at the national AG convention in Jos. Awolowo successfully maneuvered the federal AG to oppose Akintola with the aim of removing the premier. He further managed to marginalize Akintola in the national sphere of the party and passed a resolution stating that if any party official "has lost the confidence of the party, the President of the Party shall summon a meeting of the appropriate body which elected him and require the meeting to either affirm their confidence in the person concerned or elect a successor."[44] This amendment allowed Awolowo to convene a meeting of the Western Region's Executive Council to choose a new leader. Chief Anthony Enahoro, one of Awolowo's main allies who would later play a key role for Nigeria during the civil war, demanded Akintola's resignation both as Western Region premier and from his role in the party. When Akintola refused both demands, the stage was set for a final showdown in the Regional House of Assembly.

On May 25, 1962, the House of Assembly met to consider removing Akintola from his position. Almost immediately after the meeting convened, chaos erupted when one of Akintola's supporters began throwing chairs. Another grabbed the ceremonial mace and attempted to hit the Speaker of the House, Prince Adeleke Adedoyin, but missed, instead shattering the mace on the table. Several other pro-Akintola members joined in the chair throwing. Eventually, the police intervened, firing tear gas canisters into the chamber in an effort to clear the House. Several hours later, Adedoyin attempted to reconvene the session but was immediately met with disruption, with Akintola loyalists shouting and pounding their chairs in protest. One member, Chief Samuel Tinubu, sat on the floor next to the Speaker's chair and rang a bell every time Adedoyin attempted to speak. Soon after, chairs and other objects began to fly across the chamber once more, prompting another round of tear gas.

At Akintola's request, Tafawa Balewa declared a state of emergency in the Western Region despite the fact that the only violence that erupted was inside the House of Assembly. For six months, the Western Region was governed under the state of emergency while Akintola finalized his split from the party and created a new one called the United People's Party (UPP). Even more troubling for Awolowo, Enahoro, and their allies, the federal government convicted the AG leadership of treason, diversion of funds, and many other crimes. They were imprisoned until Yakubu Gowon released them on August 3, 1966, shortly after the second coup brought him to lead the country as the military head of state. Alan Rake, one of the most astute political commentators of the period, summed up the situation, saying that "when the AG leaders were imprisoned and their members reduced to an ineffective rump, the Sardauna saw the way open to complete Northern domination of the Federation."[45]

The Action Group crisis ended with one of the country's elder statesmen rotting in a prison in Calabar and underscored how odious the political reality in the country had become. With new political alignments being formed ahead of the 1964 elections, all that remained was the constitutionally mandated decennial census in 1962 that would establish representation in the Senate and House of Representatives. Because both the AG and the NCNC sought to maximize their potential to replace the NPC in the next elections, they manipulated the census to show that the south had gained a majority in population and siphon seats from the north. The census figures were so grossly inaccurate that they showed a 70 percent population increase in the southern regions compared with a mere 30 percent in the north. The NPC government refused to certify these numbers and ordered a second census undertaken the following year. Unsurprisingly, the new census corrected the imbalance in the 1962 census by adding over eight million new northerners. According to some reports, northern census takers counted livestock as people to make up for the difference.[46] Despite NCNC protests, Akintola's party approved of and certified the figures, and the north maintained its majority in population. In later years, the gross inaccuracies of both censuses would make determining the exact number of casualties in the civil war virtually impossible, leading to estimates ranging from five hundred thousand to upward of three million.

The year 1963 also saw the first attempt at restructuring the country by changing the constitution. Part of the nationalist furor surrounding the Anglo-Nigerian Defence Agreement stemmed from the fact that Nigeria was an independent country, but as a commonwealth, the head of state remained the Queen of England. On October 1, 1963, the country transformed into a republic, replacing the

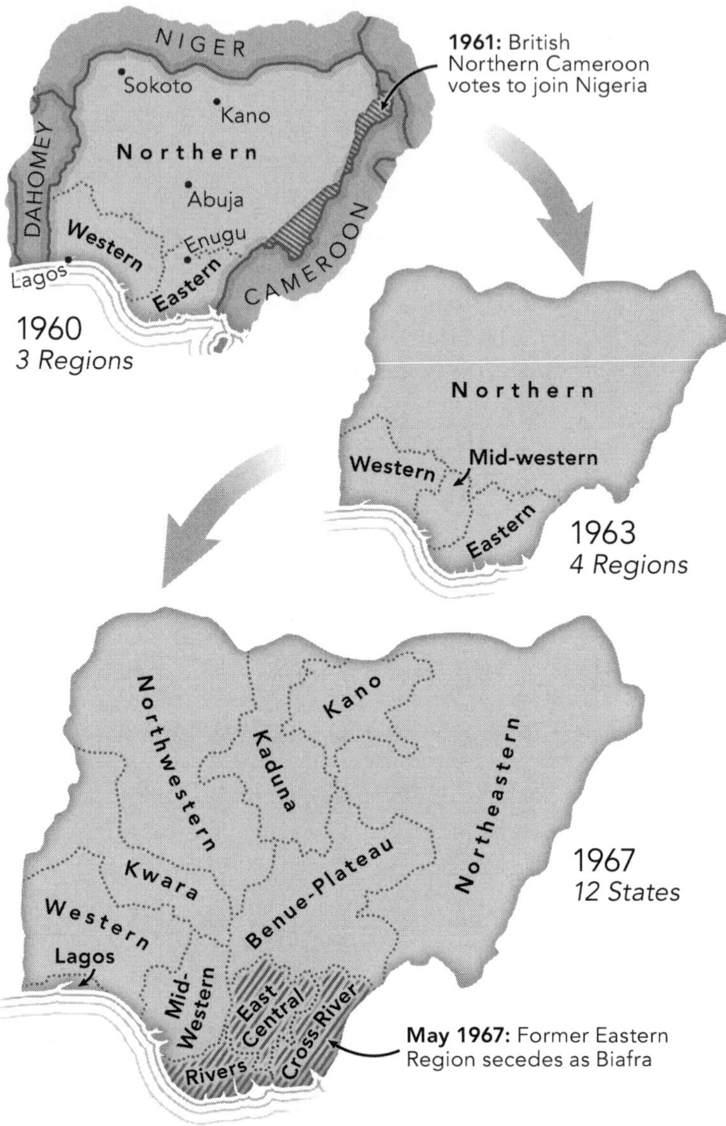

Map 1.1. Evolution of the Nigerian Federal System

governor general with a president as head of state. Azikiwe became the first president of what would later become known as the First Republic, continuing his role as governor general in all but name.

A more important transformation was the creation of the new Midwestern Region from the non-Yoruba areas of the Western Region. The Ijo and Itsekiri in the region had argued for the creation of a state that would free them from

Yoruba domination. The Willink Commission had heard from several groups regarding their desire to create a new state out of the Western Region. The calls did not come from only the Ijo and Itsekiri minorities in the region, who complained to the commission about educational, economic, and representational discrimination; calls also came from the Western Region government itself and a separate delegation from the AG. Despite these pleas, the Willink Commission recommended against the creation of the new state in 1958, stating that "although this area had been neglected in certain respects . . . there was no evidence of deliberate and vindictive discrimination or even culpable neglect."[47] Instead, the commission recommended that the most underdeveloped regions in the Niger Delta be designated a special area and that a federal board be created to address minority concerns of discrimination.[48] Minority agitation only increased after independence in 1960, and when the country's new constitution came into effect, the Midwestern Region was created out of the Edo and Delta provinces of the Western Region, with the capital in the ancient city of Benin. This new region further Balkanized the south, adding new players into the political melee ahead of the 1964 federal elections. This new region further weakened the AG because it created a new regionally based power that was designed to thwart any attempts to organize against a meaningful recovery after the 1962 crisis.

Both the census and the creation of the new region left the NPC in a better position to increase, or at least retain, their power in the federal government. The new census required a reallocation of the 312 seats in the federal legislature. Although the new Midwestern Region gave the NCNC a minor electoral boost and crippled the AG, the prospects for toppling the NPC were almost nonexistent. In fact, the census gave the Northern Region a larger population than the Eastern, Western, and Midwestern Regions combined. As a result, the Northern Region was allocated 167 seats for the 1964 election. All the NPC had to do was ensure that they lose no more than five seats in the north to ensure a majority government that would not need a coalition partner.[49]

With the NCNC and the AG unable to use the census to topple NPC domination and new political alignments coming into existence ahead of the 1964 elections, Azikiwe, along with the remnants of the AG, had little choice but to unite in opposition to the NPC and Akintola's UPP, now renamed the Nigerian National Democratic Party (NNDP). Minority groups who so far had been shut out of the larger political discourse in the country also decided to use the election to leverage some political allies and have their concerns heard above the increasingly bitter contest between the large players. These groups came together in ways that crossed regional lines as they jockeyed for position in the increasingly brutal world of Nigerian politics. Two smaller parties from the Northern Region, the Northern Elements Progressive Union (NEPU) and the United Middle Belt Congress (UMBC), joined together to become the Northern Progressive Front and later allied with the NCNC and the AG to form the United Progressive Grand Alliance (UPGA). The UMBC comprised mostly minority groups from Nigeria's Middle Belt region, particularly the Tiv, Angas, and Birom. Led by Joseph Tarka, the party represented groups that were wary of Hausa-Fulani domination in the north and sought an alliance that would grant them greater power within the country. NEPU were equally marginalized as a small party based in the city of Kano. Both these parties realized they would not be able to share power in the Northern Region in any meaningful way that would challenge the NPC, so their leaders opted to find allies in other regions, with the view that they could at least, if successful in the federal elections, find an avenue in the federal government.[50]

In a similar fashion, the NPC and Akintola's NNDP united with smaller parties from the Eastern and Midwestern regions—most notably, mathematician Chike Obi's Dynamic Party as well as statistically insignificant parties such as the Niger Delta Congress, the Mid-West People's Congress, the Mid-West Democratic Front, and the Igbira Tribal Union—to form an alliance called the Nigerian National Alliance (NNA). The minority parties, whether ethnic or not, desperately needed to ally themselves with one of the larger parties because without the potential to access the corridors of power, their marginalization would continue in virtually every aspect of Nigerian society. Political power meant access to government funds and "that you, your village, tribe, or region obtains all the top posts, the lucrative contracts, roads are tarred, scholarships are provided, wells are dug, and new forms of industry introduced. To lose is to surrender not only the good things but many of the necessities of life."[51] The struggles leading up to the 1964 elections convinced any doubters that politics in the country had become a zero-sum game with the country's leaders willing to do practically anything to maintain their positions. It was thus no surprise that the next election cycle turned violent and corrupt, even by the already low standards set in the previous years.

The oil revenues in the Eastern Region and the industrialization of the country became two of the major issues that sparked calls for new elections. To facilitate national economic planning in Nigeria, the National Economic Council (NEC) was set up, comprising the prime minister, the regional premiers, and four ministers from each region, with the goal of creating a national plan for economic development rather than allowing the regions to develop independently of and often in competition with one another.[52] Shortly after the census figures were certified, the NEC met to discuss the creation of a steel mill and the allocation of the oil revenues from the Niger Delta. Because the NCNC and NPC could not agree on the location of the new steel mill, the project was divided, with part of it in the Eastern Region and the other half in the North, thus undercutting the efficiency of the mill.[53] The oil revenues proved a more delicate issue, as none could argue that the funds came from anywhere except the Eastern Region. The Eastern delegation to the NEC demanded that all royalties remain in the region, but section 134 of the constitution stated that all revenues would be collected by the federal government for redistribution. Half of the royalties were returned to the region of origin—in this case, the Eastern Region—while 20 percent was kept for the federal government. The remaining 30 percent was placed in a distributable pool account and divided into ninety-five units. The Northern Region was entitled to forty units while the Western Region was allocated twenty-four, with the remaining thirty-one going to the Eastern Region.[54] Because mining rents were enshrined in the constitution, the Eastern Region could do little to change the allocation of funds.

Both sides felt embittered by the oil revenue crisis. Northern politicians felt that the south was once again trying to leverage their economic advantages to keep the north underdeveloped. Southerners saw the ploy as another attempt by the north to use the mechanism of the federal government to undermine their region. However, minority groups in the oil-producing regions harbored the same suspicions concerning Igbo domination of the region as the Igbo did regarding the NPC-led federal government. Thus the contradiction was that the Igbo, who politically controlled the oil-producing region, did not actually live on the land where the oil was produced; yet they controlled the mechanisms for distributing the wealth that came from the oil revenue. The Ijo, Ogoni, Ibibio, and other minority groups in the Niger Delta region saw that their wealth was being used to fund projects in other parts of the east with little development in their own regions.

By October 1964 it became clear that elections would be held by the end of the year and that the contest between the major alliances would turn out extremely bitter, even though the outcome was almost certain. Unlike the 1959 elections, which saw the NPC win but come up eight seats short of an absolute majority, this time the Sardauna left as little as possible to the vagaries of the electorate and began a mass campaign of voter intimidation, arrests, and violence. By the end of August 1964, hundreds of UMBC supporters in Sokoto were behind bars, and thousands of UMBC activists suffered the same fate in the Tiv homeland.[55] October saw even more electoral intimidation. In Kano, 297 UPGA supporters were arrested, with all but 68 held until after the elections. On October 17, Tarka himself was arrested on charges of inciting electoral violence.[56] The tactic proved effective, as half of the 174 northern districts saw the NNA candidate unopposed.

Southern parties conducted themselves in much the same manner but on a smaller scale. In the three southern regions, roughly 30 percent of districts were unopposed. As the election neared, it became clear that the NNA would triumph because the country's electoral structure, coupled with the intimidation and violence, made any other outcome virtually impossible. As the election neared, Azikiwe warned the country against the growing dangers of regional sectionalism, imploring the country's leader that "if they have decided to destroy our national unity, then they should summon a round-table conference to decide how our national assets should be divided before they seal their doom by satisfying their lust for office." He concluded with a warning that proved tragically prophetic, warning against secession, claiming that "the experience of the Democratic Republic of Congo will be child's play, if it ever comes our turn to play such a tragic role."[57] Rather than mitigate the crisis, Azikiwe's words had the opposite effect. Ahmadu Bello accused the president of brinkmanship politics, claiming that because the country had no constitutional mechanism for secession, Azikiwe and the NCNC were secretly planning to secede from the country.

In response to the impending electoral catastrophe, the NCNC leadership attempted to stave off the election by calling for a boycott of the entire UPGA. However, for the AG, control of the west was a more immediate priority, and they at first refused to accept the boycott. This tension between the AG and the NCNC ultimately undermined their ability to counter the NNA in the election. The AG agreed to join the boycott only on the day before the December 30 elections, once they realized that they would lose not only the Western Region to the NNDP but also the Midwestern Region to the NCNC. This left the AG, once again, the only national party without control of a regional government. By the time the AG leadership agreed to join the boycott, it was too late to effectively enforce. As a result, none of the election results in the west and only one in the midwest would be challenged and the seat left vacant. The boycott itself proved to be a desperate ploy, and the election results showed how much the NPC had successfully consolidated its control over the federal government by focusing exclusively on the north and allowing the southern parties to squabble among themselves.

When the election results were announced, the NNA candidates won by a large majority. Even more troubling for the UPGA, thanks to the boycott, the NPC secured an absolute majority in the House of Representatives, making their rule even stronger than it was before. Also because of the UPGA boycott, the NPC won a plurality of the popular vote, securing nearly 38 percent compared to the NCNC's 28.5 percent. In the north, the NPC won all but five of the seats, securing for themselves an absolute majority of 162 seats of the 312 in Parliament, making the results in the other parts of the country meaningless. The remaining five constituencies in the north were won by the NPF and Tiv parties. In the east, the NCNC won fifteen of the region's seventy seats, with forty-nine vacant seats due to the boycott. The AG took four seats, and the last two were won by independents. In the midwest, the NCNC won thirteen of the fourteen seats, with the last going vacant. In Lagos, all four of the ridings were left vacant while in the west the NNDP dominated, winning thirty-six of the region's fifty-seven seats, with the AG winning fifteen and the NCNC five.

This election strengthened the NPC's grip on power but also triggered a constitutional crisis when Azikiwe, in his capacity as president, refused to appoint Tafawa Balewa as the new prime minister, citing the many voting irregularities, the election intimidation, and the violence. For northerners, Azikiwe's act reeked of partisanship. Despite the fact that the UPGA's partial boycott invalidated more than fifty results, all were in the south. Further, even though the NPC political mechanism made almost any result other than an absolute victory in the north virtually impossible, the resulting election clearly gave the NPC an absolute majority, regardless of the results of the boycotted elections.

In the standoff, both sides made claims to control the military—Azikiwe in his capacity as head of state and Tafawa Balewa as head of the government. Some scholars, such as Eghosa Osaghae and Billy Dudley from the University of Ibadan, claimed that this conflict began the process of politicizing the military. Dudley claimed that the crisis made the armed forces "aware they had a political role to play and so paved the way for the military coup that followed in 1966."[58] In reality, the military had long been politicized by the elites that used it in their regional political maneuvering. Also, many in the military, especially a cadre of disaffected officers led by the January 1966 coup's leader, Maj. Patrick Chukwuma Kaduna Nzeogwu, had long nurtured a desire to rid the country of the corruption and the brazen opportunism that was emblematic of the First Republic. The crisis that the 1964 election created served only to hasten the republic's demise.

The crisis ended with an agreement between the sides known as the Zik-Balewa Pact, which allowed Tafawa Balewa to form the government with three provisions:

1. Such a government was a "broad based government" and included, wherever possible, representatives of the two competing alliances.
2. The boycotted elections in the Eastern Region were to be rescheduled for March 1965, after which NCNC members would be appointed to the government.
3. There should be elections in the western regional assembly in October 1965.[59]

Though this agreement seemed to avert the crisis, it also laid bare the fact that despite the lofty aspirations of democracy, transparent elections, and national unity, the reality was that the political class had devolved into little more than a fight for access to the "national cake."

Unsurprisingly, when the boycotted elections were held in March, all but two of the fifty-three seats went to NCNC candidates. The remaining two were won by the AG. However, the most contested election would be held in October and would prove to be a violent rematch between Akintola and Awolowo over control of the

Western Region; it would also be the catalyst for the end of the republic the following January, when Nzeogwu's coup transformed the Nigerian political landscape.

Since 1962, the AG had been hoping to wrest control of the Western Region from Akintola, who now controlled the state mechanism and was equally determined to keep control of the region for the NNDP. Though the AG was much more popular, as Akintola was portrayed as a northern stooge, the NNDP controlled the police and the election commission. Akintola's deputy premier, Chief Remilekun Fani-Kayode, reportedly boasted in Yoruba, "*Béẹ̀ ṣe tiwa, béè sì ṣe tiwa, Dẹmọ á wọlé*" ("whether or not you vote for us [or are with us], Demo [meaning the NNDP] will win").[60] Whether this was meant to be a subtle hint at election rigging or simply a preelection boast is unclear. What was clear, however, was that the campaign was marked by violence, with the NNDP using every measure to ensure victory, and though the AG attempted to use the same tactics, the fact that the NNDP controlled the coercive state mechanisms ensured that the AG had no chance at victory. The election had to be postponed for several weeks due to the violence, and it was finally held in November but had little semblance of an orderly or fair election, as both sides tried their best to manipulate the results.

The violence that preceded the election was overshadowed by what followed. On Election Day, both the NNDP and the AG claimed victory, and both sides attempted to use the House of Assembly to swear in their own premier. When the official results were announced, the news of the predicted NNDP victory triggered riots across the region, which were marked by such widespread arson that it garnered the nickname Operation *Wetie,* with unconfirmed reports that some people were lynched by "necklacing," a method where a tire doused with gasoline was placed around the victim's chest and arms and then set ablaze.[61] Because of Akintola's links to the north, Hausa in the region were also targeted in Ibadan and Sagamu, a city some sixty kilometers north of Lagos. In all, approximately two thousand people died in the violence. Unlike the 1962 crisis, where violence was confined to the assembly chamber, the Western Region saw a complete breakdown of law and order. Despite the violence, the federal government refused to declare a state of emergency as it had in 1962, with many pundits citing Akintola's alliance with the north as the reason. Also, many in the federal government feared that army elements would support the UPGA in general and Awolowo in particular, and as a result they refused to summon the military to calm the situation.[62]

Despite the violence, Tafawa Balewa finalized plans for an emergency meeting of the heads of the British Commonwealth to be held in Lagos on January 10–12, 1966, to discuss Ian Smith's declaration of independence in Rhodesia and the establishment of white minority rule in the former British colony. Thus, the situation in the country finally became untenable. Tafawa Balewa's insistence on taking the lead on international matters while neglecting and even encouraging the chaos at home was the final straw for many in the country who wished to be rid of the violence, corruption, and nepotism that had characterized the political establishment in the short five years since independence. Their attempted salvation would come in the form of a small cabal of idealistic army officers whose attempt to overthrow the country would set Nigeria on a path toward secession and civil war.

TWO

COUP, COUNTERCOUP, AND SECESSION

ON JANUARY 15, 1966, NIGERIANS woke to a country in turmoil. During the night, a group of middle-ranked army officers had attempted a coup d'état against the First Republic. The coup plotters became known as the Five Majors because the five main conspirators, Chukwuma Kaduna Nzeogwu, Emmanuel Ifeajuna, Chris Anuforo, Timothy Onwuatuegwu, and Adewale Ademoyega, were all majors. Though the coup failed, the bulk of the country's leadership, including the prime minister, Abubakar Tafawa Balewa; the premier of the Northern Region, Ahmadu Bello; and his Western Region counterpart, Samuel Akintola, were all dead along with many government leaders and key military officers.

Chukwuma Kaduna Nzeogwu, the coup's intellectual leader and mastermind, has been the subject of two biographies, one by his brother and the other by his close friend and comrade in arms, future Nigerian president Olusegun Obasanjo. Like many Igbo, Nzeogwu was born to a family that migrated out of the traditional Igbo heartland and settled in Northern Nigeria. Because he was born in the city of Kaduna, his parents gave him that middle name . Nnamdi Azikiwe and Chukwuemeka Ojukwu—Nigeria's first president and the head of secessionist Biafra, respectively—were also born in the north, in the town of Zungeru. Like Ojukwu, Nzeogwu was committed to the Nigerian ideal and sought a country that developed a true Nigerian identity, not a state whose only goal was to ensure access to the resources in the country, known colloquially as the *national cake*. This determination to reshape Nigerian society was counteracted by the political crises that had rocked the country almost continuously since independence. In trying to understand why his close friend chose to stage the coup, Obasanjo remarked, "The nation was sick" and added that "every national issue since 1959 had led us one or more steps toward the brink of a political precipice."[1] Many in the country echoed Obasanjo's comments. The political situation in Nigeria was so broken by multiple crises that by the end of 1965, it was clear that a more serious crisis would befall the state; in fact, Nzeogwu did not call his operation a coup but rather a rescue operation to save Nigeria from its ruling class.[2]

Nzeogwu's life experiences were largely responsible for his deep concern for the poor and the country's endemic inequality. His younger brother, Okelele, recalled an incident that occurred when the elder brother was only eighteen months old. Their father, James, was fired from his low-paying job at the local power plant after a physical altercation with a coworker who refused to repay a loan. Destitute and desperate, their mother, Elizabeth, took her two children—Nzeogwu and another of his siblings, as Okelele was not yet born—on a four-mile trek to the British plant supervisor's home, where the spectacle of two hungry, screaming children moved the supervisor to restore the father's job. Indeed, the Nzeogwu family suffered many hardships when Chukwuma was a child. Five of his siblings died in childhood, and the family constantly struggled with hunger and deprivation. These experiences instilled in the young man a sense of social justice that came into direct conflict with the manner in which he felt Nigeria was being governed.

If Nzeogwu was the coup's mastermind, the most difficult part of the operation—securing the capital in Lagos—fell to another major: Emmanuel Ifeajuna. He had become an African hero in 1954 when he had won the gold medal in the high jump at the Empire and Commonwealth Games in Vancouver, Canada, becoming the first Black African to win a gold medal at a major sports competition. A natural athlete, he had no formal coaching or training, as this was not widely available in colonial Nigeria. He stopped training altogether during the same year as his triumph when he enrolled at the University of Ibadan. In an unpublished memoir that Obasanjo obtained, Ifeajuna remarked that the coup was designed to end the status quo in Nigeria whereby the ruling elites "sought to absorb you into their ruling group failing which they would seek to destroy you. . . . We were well aware of our actions and we were well aware of the consequences." He continued, "We know the country had been so diseased that bold reforms were badly needed to settle social, moral[,] economic and political questions."[3]

Nzeogwu and Ifeajuna had little difficulty in garnering support for their revolution. Most of the officers they approached had already decided independently that such an act was necessary for many of the same reasons that Nzeogwu articulated. The Western Region election crisis prompted the group to action. Since independence, Nzeogwu had become increasingly pessimistic regarding the political climate in the country, and as the crises multiplied, deepened, and worsened, he appeared adamant about the need for a revolution and became very loose-lipped about his views on the country's future. Thus, when Ifeajuna decided that a coup would be the only option, he immediately contacted Nzeogwu, and the two began to organize.

Only two of the coup's main participants—Ben Gbulie, who was a captain, and Adewale Ademoyega—wrote memoirs chronicling and justifying the coup and their participation in it. In their memoirs, they echoed Nzeogwu and Ifeajuna's frustrations with the corrupt and opportunistic politicians under the First Republic. Gbulie was especially bitter about how the regional structure and proportionality affected the military. In his view, the military became inundated with unskilled officers, many of whom eclipsed him in rank because he was not eligible for promotion during his long stays abroad for training. In one instance, Gbulie recalled a Lieutenant Daniya, whom he encountered at the officers' mess in Kaduna drinking a beer. Not even the base commander, Lt. Colonel Samuel Ademulegun, knew who this new officer was. Gbulie reported with a mix of anger and humor that when confronted, the young Daniya, who could speak English only in a very halting pidgin, told the base commander, "Fremia [premier] no tell you?" The astonished commander did not understand and asked for clarification. Daniya had supposedly been directly appointed by the premier to turn off the lights on the base every night. Yet instead of being a simple laborer, he was granted the rank of second lieutenant.[4] For both Gbulie and Ademoyeaga, this type of appointment was emblematic of the lack of standards that were the direct result of proportional appointments to the military by region rather than by competency. For Gbulie, who remained a captain, the many northern officers who enrolled in officers' training after him and at schools he deemed lesser than Sandhurst, where he had done his training, now outranked him, adding insult to injury.

Some in the north saw this process as a necessary corrective to southern dominance of the civil service, and the military accused the coup plotters of self-righteousness. In response, A. M. Mainasara, a political commentator who claimed to represent northern opinions, said that the coup could be explained only as a sectional or tribal operation because of the disproportionate carnage. In particular, he stated that Ironsi survived "for the simple reason that he belonged to the chosen tribe!"[5] Unlike Gbulie, who saw the ethnic tensions between the various regions as a symptom of a broken country, Mainasara saw the privileges that the federal government bestowed on the north as a corrective to the years of neglect and southern domination. More importantly, Mainasara's work is emblematic of the kind of political accusation game that has pervaded Nigerian politics since the coup and the subsequent civil war. Both Gbulie and Ademoyega framed their actions in perpetrating the coup as an attempt to redefine the nature of Nigerian society and blamed the sectionalism that Mainasara defended as the prime reason why the coup was necessary.

The coup plotters' first known meeting took place in November 1965 at Tarkwa Bay, a pristine beach in Lagos that once housed Lord Lugard's home.[6] According to Gbulie, it was ostensibly a weekend vacation for a group of officers but was used to begin the planning for the coup. The nine men who met that weekend were almost all Sandhurst graduates, and all but Ademoyega were from the East. Ademoyega, the sole Yoruba involved in the plot, was perhaps the most radical of the group and internalized urgency to complete the mission. When addressing the issue of the coup's planning, he claimed to have been meeting separately with Ifeajuna and Nzeogwu since 1961 and that "the seed was sown at that time and needed only to germinate, grow and bear fruit."[7] All of the coconspirators who attended the November meeting were accomplished officers: Chris Anuforo was a well-respected officer who had served with many of his coconspirators in Lagos and Kaduna and with the Nigerian contingent of the UN peacekeeping mission on the India-Pakistan border. Timothy Onwuatuegwu, despite his Sandhurst training, was not part of the radical circle until 1965, when he served under Nzeogwu's command at the Nigerian Military Training College (NMTC), Nigeria's main officer training center. The one officer who was not part of the Sandhurst cohort was Donatus Okafor, who had enlisted in the Nigerian army as a soldier and won his officer's commission by rising through the ranks. Despite the fact that Okafor did not enter the military through the Sandhurst pathway, his personal connections with the other plotters secured their trust, and he eventually became close to Ademoyega in early 1965, when the pair were sent to a course at the British School of Infantry in Warminster. Others included Humphrey Chukwuka, John Obienu, and the only non-major in attendance, Captain Emma Nwora Nwobosi—all Sandhurst-trained officers, with Obienu named the foreign cadet of the year in 1961.

The Tarkwa Bay meeting set the plans in motion that culminated on January 15 the following year. In that meeting the group identified the targets and the means to accomplish their goals. They named their plot Operation Damissa, the Hausa word for leopard, and decided on a takeover of the entire country, splitting their responsibilities along north-south lines, as this was how the military chain of command was organized. They also identified a list of targets they felt were imperative to neutralize. First and foremost, the prime minister, Abubakar Tafawa Balewa, and the four regional governors were of utmost importance. The group of plotters felt that the president, Nnamdi Azikiwe, was not one of the central targets as the president's office, though the head of state, was largely devoid of real power, which rested with the prime minister as head of the government. Also targeted were the top officers in the military, among them Ironsi as GOC; Brigadier General Samuel Ademulegun, who was the highest-ranking Yoruba officer; and Brigadier Zakariya Maimalari, a hard-drinking Northern officer who had previously commanded several of Nigeria's main training centers. In addition to these top targets, the coup plotters drafted a list of persons who could stand in the way of their success and as such had to be dealt with, such as Yakubu Gowon and Murtala Muhammad, two officers who were later to become heads of state.

The first source of contention was how to neutralize the targets. Some of the conspirators, such as Ifeajuna, preferred a bloody coup where all opposition would be killed upon contact. Ifeajuna would make good on his idea and kill more than any of the other conspirators. Others wished for a more pacific and bloodless coup, hoping to employ deadly force only in the case of opposition. In the end, the officers decided that each of them would be responsible for their own actions. This lack of a cohesive policy led to some unnecessary bloodshed and, in the coup's aftermath, helped exasperate some of the Northern political leaders' claims that the coup was ethnically motivated.

The group decided they would transform Nigeria from four large and powerful regions to smaller states, abolishing the regions after putting in place a single unitary transitionary government under the leadership of Awolowo, who was still languishing in a Calabar prison.

When they left Tarkwa Bay that weekend, they did so with the understanding that the coup would take place in January and that they would have to recruit more conspirators for their plot. The latter was a dangerous proposition, as expanding the plot to outsiders whom they could not place complete trust in could put all their lives at risk. Nzeogwu and Ifeajuna approached many officers, and some, like Gbulie, joined the plot. However, both Gbulie and Ademoyega stated that many of the officers who were approached rebuffed the proposal out of fear of the consequences should it fail.[8] Even more puzzling, the conspirators were very open with their plans, and yet not a single officer who declined to participate attempted to stop or arrest them.

At 2:00 a.m. on January 15, 1966, the coup plotters turned their plans to action. The immediate goals of that night were to take control of the regional capitals, arrest the political leadership, and take control of all radio and television broadcasters in the country. The plotters in Enugu, Ibadan, Abeokuta, and Kaduna were to wait for the central group in Lagos to make the broadcast announcing the coup to the entire country.

In Kaduna, the coup proceeded smoothly under Nzeogwu's leadership. Nzeogwu masked his operation by holding a military exercise that night called Exercise Damissa. This was not the first time he had held this battle drill, but this time, as it ended around 1:00 a.m., he announced to his men that he was about to lead a coup "to sweep clean the national stable."[9] He allowed any soldier wishing not to partake in the coup the opportunity to leave, but none did, even those from the north. Whether the soldiers agreed to participate out of loyalty to Nzeogwu or political determination or simply out of fear of consequences can never be ascertained.

Nzeogwu's job was to apprehend the northern premier, Ahmadu Bello, and Makama Bida, the region's finance minister. Nzeogwu's forces quickly approached Bello's compound. According to Gbulie, Nzeogwu recalled the assault later that night, saying that his forces encircled the compound, with one bazooka squad placed to destroy any vehicle leaving the compound and Nzeogwu's own personal unit tasked with entering the mansion and taking the Sardauna, Bello's honorific title. His squad tried to force their way through the gate but were discovered by one of the night security guards, who attacked them with a sword. Nzeogwu shot the attacker at close range. This shot served to both frighten the rest of the night guards and to alert Bello of the assault. Now that Nzeogwu had broken the silence of the raid, speed was of the essence. Nzeogwu threw a grenade over the gate but, in his haste or excitement, forgot to take cover before the blast and was wounded in the neck. Ignoring the pain, he pressed on and entered the mansion looking for the northern premier. In the main living area, his force killed two bodyguards who were waiting in ambush. They then went door to door looking for Bello until Nzeogwu realized that he must have been hiding in the last place anyone would expect to find him—the harem. When they arrived at the harem, they found all the wives huddled together. Realizing that the women were probably not huddled only in fear, Nzeogwu ordered them to disperse. When they refused, he shot and killed one of them. The rest then dispersed to reveal Bello hidden in the middle, pleading for his life. Nzeogwu recalled that he pulled the trigger with disgust, killing the premier almost instantly. The force then continued to Bida's home, but the minister had traveled out of town. When Nzeogwu's group returned to the barracks, Nzeogwu was finally treated for his injuries. When asked how the operation fared, he replied, "Fine. . . . I gunned down the bloody tyrant."[10]

Other groups fanned out to secure the city. Major Timothy Onwuatuegwu set out to arrest the top military leaders who had not committed to the coup: the head of the Kaduna garrison, Brigadier Samuel Ademulegun, and Colonel Ralph Sodeinde, the head of the NMTC. Both raids followed a similar pattern. At Ademulegun's home, the assault force found all the guards either asleep or supportive of the coup and gained easy entry to the building. Leaving the bulk of his men on the first floor, Onwuatuegwu went up the stairs to the brigadier's bedroom and woke him and his wife by turning on the lights and saying, "You're under arrest, sir. Get dressed and come with me, sir."[11]

Ademulegun's wife then stepped between the two officers, yelling at Major Onwuatuegwu while Ademulegun opened a drawer in the dresser beside his bed. Not waiting to see if the brigadier had reached for his clothes or a pistol,

Onwuatuegwu fired his Sten gun, hitting Ademulegun in the chest. The brigadier's wife leapt into the line of fire to shield her husband and was hit in the stomach by another bullet. Both died together.

At Sodeinde's home, the soldiers found the interior doors locked, and before they could force them open, the colonel opened the door, demanding to know the reason for the disturbance. He too was informed that he was under arrest. Like with Ademulegun, Sodeinde's wife appeared asking what was going on. According to Gbulie, Sodeinde, "without uttering a word, turned slowly, rather contemptuously, and started walking away."[12] Onwuatuegwu then fired two shots, one killing the colonel and the other wounding his pregnant wife.

He then apprehended the northern governor, Kashim Ibrahim, bringing the terrified politician to coup headquarters after disarming his police contingent. By 5:00 a.m., most of the carnage was over, and Kaduna was secure.

Meanwhile, Gbulie secured the city's important sites and took control of Kaduna's local and national radio and television stations as well as the important ammunition depot. He then secured the brigade headquarters, making it the base of operations for the coup in the Northern Region. Once the high-profile prisoners were brought to the base, Gbulie wrote a statement that the highest-ranking government prisoner, Ibrahim, was to read. It read in part, "I, Kashim Ibrahim . . . do hereby on this day, Saturday, the 15th of January, 1966, relinquish to the Nigerian Armed Forces all [government] powers, statutory or otherwise, hitherto exercised by my government."[13]

With the city secured, the plotters had two additional steps to take. First, they had to contact officers in other parts of the north whom they hoped would join them and then consolidate the command structure of the northern military units to take orders from Nzeogwu. The first officer approached, Major Hassan Katsina, spoke to Nzeogwu shortly after the assault that killed the northern premier. Katsina was a scion of the house of Ngogo in the northern city of Katsina, and as such, his loyalties to the coup were immediately suspect. However, seeing the results of the assault, and confronting Nzeogwu, who was still armed with the gun he had used against Bello, Katsina immediately pledged his allegiance to the coup, more out of self-preservation than ideology. Likewise, the officers in the city of Zaria—Maj. Alexander Madiebo, commander of the artillery batteries stationed there, and Lt. Col. Wellington Bassey, the first officer commissioned to the Nigerian military, who commanded the ordinance depot—gave their tacit support to the coup.

Further north in Kano, the conspirators attempted to contact Ojukwu, who was commander of that city's garrison. Ojukwu did not commit to the plot but rather reacted to the uncertainty of the night's events by severing Kano's communications links with the rest of the country and imposing a strict curfew on the city and the garrison. He then traveled the city accompanied by the emir of Kano in a show of public unity to assuage any fears about his loyalty. Some of the coup plotters accused Ojukwu of duplicity, claiming that he had pledged his allegiance to Nzeogwu and then spoke to Ironsi, alerting him of the coup, collaborating with both sides until it became apparent which would be victorious.[14] However, it is not clear that Ojukwu was acting as an opportunist. More likely, the confusion of the night led him to isolate his command from the rest of the country rather than risk an open confrontation based on rumors and innuendoes between any men under his command who supported the coup and those loyal to the civilian government. Because the coup in Kaduna was so successful but the operations in Lagos were worryingly silent from both the plotters and the loyal forces, any course of action could have doomed the garrison in Kano.

With most of the north secured, the plotters had only to wait for word from Lagos as to the outcome of the operations in south. In Ibadan, operations were led by Captain Emmanuel Nwobosi, whose orders were to arrest Akintola and his deputy, Remi Fani-Kayode. They arrived at the latter's home first and took him without incident. However, after they left, Fani-Kayode's wife telephoned Akintola and warned him about the coup and his impending arrest. Akintola was ready for them with his shotgun. When the force arrived, they shouted at him to surrender, and he replied by opening fire, wounding Nwobosi and his second in command, Lt. Bob Egbikor, before being shot and killed along with his nephew. Nwobosi then took Fani-Kayode to Ikeja and brought some pieces of heavy artillery to aid the coup. Once the city was secured, Maj. John Obienu, who was supposed to lead the coup in the nearby city of Abeokuta, was to link with Nwobosi to reinforce Lagos.

In Enugu, things proceeded quickly and without bloodshed. A junior officer, identified only as Lieutenant Oguchi, commanded the force in Enugu and took control of the broadcasting station. He then went to the home of eastern premier Michael Okpara and found he had a guest, Archbishop Makairos III, the president of Cyprus, who was in the country attending the meeting of the commonwealth secretariat and had stayed after the meeting to visit with Okpara. Not wanting to start an international incident, Oguchi waited without letting on that he was part of a coup for several hours until Makairos departed. He then took Okpara into custody without incident. Oguchi was also tasked with securing the midwest but could not begin his assault because of the delay with Makairos, and by morning it was too late, as the tide had already turned in Lagos.

Securing the capital at Lagos was the most important part of the coup; without this, the entire undertaking would be doomed to failure. The coup had to be coordinated with Nwobosi in Ibadan to ensure that no hostile forces could arrive from the Western Region capital, scarcely an hour's drive away. There were also several bases in and around the city, at barracks in Ikeja, the naval headquarters in Apapa, and the Dodan Barracks in Ikoyi. All had to be secured from any forces who were not loyal to the coup, otherwise the night could end in failure or a bloodbath that could spark civil war.

The Lagos operation was by far the most complicated and had the highest probability of complication due to unforeseeable circumstances. The evening began with a party at the home of Brigadier Maimalari, who was celebrating his recent marriage. All the major players on both sides in Lagos were in attendance. Maimalari himself would be killed just several hours later. Along with him were Ironsi, Gowon, Larema, who would later be killed, Njoku, and Ejoor. The conspirators Ifeajuna and Okafor were there as well. They decided that their absence would be conspicuous and suspicious. After the party, the conspirators met at Ifeajuna's home to set their plan into action and split the task of securing the capital into two phases. In the first phase, the leaders of the central government would be arrested if possible, and the key buildings, such as the television and radio stations, the telephone exchange, and the Parliament, were to be secured. The plotters were then to return to Dodan Barracks to evaluate the coup's state and to assign tasks for the second part of the operation, depending on how the first phase had been executed. Ifeajuna tasked himself with the capture of prime minister Abubakar Tafawa Balewa and minister of finance Festus Okotie-Eboh. Ifeajuna arrived at the prime minister's residence shortly after 2:00 a.m. and quickly overpowered the police detachment guarding the premises. He then forced the prime minister's staff to lead him to Tafawa Balewa's bedroom. When Tafawa Balewa opened the door, Ifeajuna reportedly saluted him before placing him under arrest without firing a shot. He then instructed all the soldiers present to salute the prime minister.[15] At this point, it was clear that the prime minister was in custody and unhurt. Ifeajuna then went next door to Okotie-Eboh's home and quickly placed the finance minister under arrest.

Ademoyega's first task was to cut the phone lines in the city. He arrived at the phone exchange without knowledge of telephony and tried to force the technicians there to disconnect the lines. The technicians showed him that the main switches were behind lock and key, and no one present had access to them. Without the ability to cut the telephone lines immediately, Ademoyega had to resort to a painstakingly slow method of cutting the individual links to the main control switch. He left some of his subordinates to oversee the job and continued to the Lion Building, the police headquarters, where he told the switchboard operators that the military was conducting an exercise in the city and that they were to stop sending and receiving all communications until further notice. He then went to the headquarters of the Nigerian External Telecommunications Authority, the NET Building, and gave similar orders before securing the grounds of the Nigerian Broadcasting Corporation (NBC), posting soldiers to prevent its reopening in the morning.[16] Having secured the telecommunications blackout, with the exception of the main switchboard, which would be done in what Ademoyega hoped was due time, his team fanned out across the city setting up roadblocks to arrest anyone opposing the coup. He returned to the coup's command center to verify the other plotters' successes and failures.

Major Don Okafor's job was to arrest Ironsi. Okafor knew that his target had been attending the party at Maimalari's house and had expected the general to return to his home afterward. However, when he arrived, he found that Ironsi had instead gone to the port of Apapa to attend a second party on board an ocean liner, the *MV Aureol*, owned by Elder Dempster, a shipping company with deep ties to Nigeria. When Ironsi arrived at the second party, two separate phone calls alerted him to the coup, and he took action to oppose it. Because the general was not at home to be arrested, and because Ademoyega had not been able to cut the city's telephone lines, Ironsi had enough advance warning to muster a resistance against the coup, even though neither he nor most of the officers loyal to him knew the identities of the plotters or their location.

Once Ironsi discovered the coup's existence, he mounted an immediate defense of the republic. Ironsi's job was not an easy one. He quickly returned to Dodan Barracks in Ikoyi and began mustering loyal soldiers. His mobilization was quick and effective. By the time Okafor learned of Ironsi's whereabouts, the latter had effectively taken control of the base. When Okafor arrived to arrest Ironsi, the regimental sergeant major (RSM) had already been briefed and told to take orders from no one except Ironsi personally. Thus, when Okafor attempted to give orders to the RSM, the latter immediately understood that the major was part of the coup and attempted to kill or arrest him. Okafor fled, leaving his entire command behind and under arrest. The battle for Lagos had begun.

After securing Dodan Barracks, Ironsi had to ascertain the identities of the coup plotters and undo their work. On his way from Apapa to Ikoyi, he noticed several of the roadblocks; in fact, when the plotters began to frantically search for Ironsi, one of the roadblocks reported seeing him drive by in his distinctive Jaguar on his way to undo the communications blackout initiated by Ademoyega. One roadblock even attempted to arrest the GOC, but the general exited his car, "stood up straight and roared 'GET OUT OF MY WAY.' They moved."[17]

Having secured the southern part of Lagos, Ironsi moved north toward Ikeja and the airport, to test the loyalty of the 2nd battalion troops there. As soon as he arrived, he informed the officers that a coup was taking place and ordered all of them to assemble. Ironsi then phoned the outgoing commanding officer, Lt. Colonel Hilary Njoku, who was at home, and bluntly asked him, "Are you with us or against us?" and ordered Njoku to report to the base. When Njoku arrived,

Ironsi pointed his gun at the lieutenant colonel, relenting only when he became assured of his subordinate's loyalty.[18]

In the meantime, the plotters, who had made their headquarters at the officers' mess in the federal guard headquarters, also in Ikoyi, were now uncertain of their security, especially as the various groups were returning with their high-profile prisoners. In addition to the prime minister and the minister of finance, they had in their custody many of the top officers in the Nigerian army who were not part of the coup. Because of Okafor's experience at the Dodan Barracks, the conspirators knew they could not remain nearby and keep holding the arrested military officers. They loaded the officers into a three-ton truck and left the guard barracks, still debating what to do with the captives. At one point, Major Anuforo ordered Lt. Colonel James Pam, who had placed one of the phone calls alerting Ironsi of the coup, out of the vehicle with the other officers. He shot Pam as well as Lt. Colonel Walter Unegbe, one of the few Igbo officers killed in the coup; Lt. Col. Abogo Lergema; and Col. Kur Mohammed. The bodies were loaded into the truck as the conspirators decided their only hope for success was to link up with Obienu, who was supposed to arrive with his reinforcements from Abeokuta.

Obienu never arrived, and the group split up. Ifeajuna took the prime minister with him, leaving Anuforo and Ademoyega with the finance minister and the bodies of the dead officers. Anuforo convinced Ademoyega that it would still be possible to link up with Obienu's forces, even if the latter had lost his nerve and abandoned the coup, but they would have to leave for Abeokuta immediately. They could not, however, travel with a truck full of corpses and the still-alive finance minister. Thus, they ordered their force to take the bodies to the bush and bury them on the outskirts of Abeokuta, where they also killed Okotie-Eboh; they arrived around 6:00 a.m. and buried him with the others.[19]

From there the group arrived at Abeokuta barracks, where they discovered that Obienu was nowhere to be found. Ademoyega and Anuforo commandeered four British-made Ferret armored scout cars with their crews and attempted to drive back to Lagos with them. At 11:00 a.m., the convoy returned to Lagos, where they encountered roadblocks manned by troops ordered to arrest any officer considered part of the coup. However, with no idea who the unfriendly officers were, the roadblocks could serve little purpose but to block Ademoyega and Anuforo, who took the Ferrets to Ijebu Ode some ninety kilometers to the east of Lagos with the intention of getting to Enugu to continue the coup. When they stopped to refuel in the town at 4:00 p.m., Ironsi was making an address announcing the coup's failure on the radio. Without a word, the Ferret crews abandoned the majors and drove to Lagos. Anuforo chased them in a car and attempted to block their way, but his vehicle was no match for the armored Ferrets. The captain of the Ferrets rammed Anuforo and threatened to kill him unless the major let him leave.

The rest of the operations in Lagos were similarly falling apart. Because no word came from Nigerian radio or television in the morning, the coup plotters in Enugu, Ibadan, and Kaduna realized that the operations in the capital had gone awry. In Ibadan, Nwobosi attempted to link up with the plotters in Lagos. When he arrived, he split up his command, sending half to the 2nd battalion in Ikeja, and proceeded to Ikoyi to the guard barracks, where he assumed the plotters' headquarters were still located. Both bases were firmly under Ironsi's control, and Nwobosi and his men were arrested upon arrival. Fani-Kayode was released.

None of the coup plotters ever took responsibility for killing the prime minister, and the cause of his death remains uncertain. Whether he was shot on the morning of January 15 or died because of an asthma attack brought on by the stress, the two most likely theories, has never been established. The fact that his body was discovered only on January 23 has led some in his family to claim that he was held until that date before being killed. Because the fate of the prime minister was yet unknown, the government was in turmoil. Further, the coup took such a toll on the political and military elites that many in the establishment doubted that civilian rule could be restored. Several officers began agitating for Ironsi to assume power because any attempt to continue the republic would have kept the mutineers energized to continue the fight. At this point, a series of frantic meetings took place with those in government who were brave enough to meet with the military. In the first meeting, on the morning of January 15, many of the ministers were suspicious of Ironsi, claiming he was part of the conspiracy, but his genuine concern for the fate of the missing prime minister, as well as his anger and sorrow over the death of Ahmadu Bello, convinced the politicians that he had no part in the coup. The cabinet ministers then ordered Ironsi to find Tafawa Balewa and restore the government. By the next day, the situation had reversed. The government ministers learned how successful the coup had been in other parts of the country, especially in the north, and realized that Nzeogwu would potentially march on Lagos if the military did not take power. At the next meeting on January 16, the highest-ranking member of the government present, Transport Minister Zanna Dipcharima, along with Minister of Trade Kingsley Mbadiwe, issued the following statement: "The council of ministers, meeting on 16th January 1966, have asked us to convey to you their unanimous decision to transfer voluntarily the government to the armed forces of the republic and wish the armed forces success to bring about peace and stability in Nigeria, and that the welfare of our people shall be their paramount task."[20] Later that night, Nwafor Orizu, the senate president, completed the transfer of power to the military, and Ironsi officially became Nigeria's first military head of state.

Lagos and most of the south was secure, but the north of the country, with the exception of Kano, was firmly under Nzeogwu's control. Nzeogwu wasted no time; he proclaimed a Supreme Council of the Revolution and declared martial law in the Northern Region. In an address on Radio Kaduna, he suspended the constitution and placed the blame for the coup squarely on the civilian government, claiming, "Our enemies are the political profiteers, the swindlers, the men in high and low places that seek bribes and demand ten percent; those that seek to keep the country divided permanently so that they can remain in office as ministers, or VIPs at least, the tribalists, the nepotists . . . those that have corrupted the our society and put the Nigerian political calendar back by their words and deeds."

He then vowed, "We are not promising anything miraculous or spectacular. But what we do promise every law-abiding citizen is freedom from fear and all forms of oppression, freedom from general inefficiency and freedom to live and strive in every field of human endeavour, both nationally and internationally. We promise that you will no more be ashamed to say that you are Nigerians."[21]

By the next morning, Nzeogwu began planning a military takeover of the rest of the country. His plan was to first establish complete control over the north by invading the cities of Zaria and Kano and then send a strike force south to capture Ibadan and lay siege to Lagos. Ntieyong Akpan, a lifelong civil servant who would later head the Biafran civil service, spoke of the palpable fear of two opposing military governments, one in Lagos and one in Kaduna. Akpan recalled those days as tense, with a real fear of civil war.[22] Ademoyega claimed that had Nzeogwu launched his assault on Lagos, it would have been successful because public opinion supported the coup, and most Nigerians were jubilant that the coup removed the corrupt politicians. Ken Saro-Wiwa, who was then a student at the University of Ibadan, recalled jubilant scenes across the university and the city, with people doing "various things to express their joy—drumming, drinking and dancing. But the note of wild joy was unmistakable."[23]

Within a few days, Nzeogwu agreed to surrender to Ironsi, and the threat of an inter-army civil war was averted. Ademoyega, who was fully convinced of the need for a comprehensive revolution in the country, blamed Alexander Madiebo for convincing Nzeogwu to agree to submit to Ironsi. Ademoyega claimed that Madiebo convinced Nzeogwu that Ironsi coming to power meant that the coup had succeeded and that any continuation of the crisis would be seen as an attempted power grab. Nzeogwu himself claimed that he capitulated because "if I had stuck to my guns there would have been a civil war, and as the official head of the army, he would have split the loyalty of my men. . . . Our purpose was to change the country and make it a place we could be proud to call our home, not to wage war."[24] Nzeogwu was arrested like most of the coup plotters, with the notable exception of Anuforo, who escaped to Ghana.

As GOC of the military, Ironsi was the obvious choice to be placed as head of the new federal military government (FMG). However, unlike many of the other officers in the Nigerian military, he harbored little political ambition or awareness. He was a military man and a very gifted officer with a keen military mind. He faced a difficult challenge in dealing with the conspirators now languishing in prison. Because most of the conspirators were Igbo, and most of the victims came from the north and west of the country, some political activists, both in the army and outside, argued that the coup was an Igbo conspiracy and that because even in failure it catapulted Ironsi, another Igbo, to power, the general himself was a secret collaborator with the conspirators. Coups are dangerous undertakings and can be successful only when the plotters trust each other completely. The plotters trusted each other not because of their ethnicity but because they knew one another from their days in the colonial education system and through their training at the various British military academies.[25]

On the other hand, the coup was immensely popular across the country. To many, the plotters were not criminals but heroes. To execute the plotters, as the law demanded, would have been an unacceptably unpopular move and would have made Nzeogwu, Ifeajuna, and the other conspirators into martyrs and ignited protests across the country. Even more so, a trial—military or otherwise—would have given them a platform to justify their actions in ways that would have resonated with the bulk of Nigerians who supported their actions. Ironsi kept the men in prison but never moved to hold them legally accountable for their actions. The new leader's reaction to the coup was emblematic of the impossible position into which he was placed.

Ironsi appointed military governors to take over the country's four regions. In the Northern region, he appointed Hassan Katsina, the man who'd had to pledge support to Nzeogwu at the end of the barrel of a Sten gun. For the Western Region, he appointed Adekunle Fajuyi, a decorated officer who had commanded Nigerian units in the Congo during the Katanga crisis and earned a Military Cross decoration from the Commonwealth. David Ejoor took command of the Midwestern Region, and for the Eastern Region Ironsi appointed Ojukwu, who had held Kano during the coup, refusing to join the rebels. As his successor as the chief of staff, Ironsi chose Yakubu "Jack" Gowon, another career soldier with limited political ambitions.

As during the coup, Ojukwu's actions in the first months of military rule reinforced his commitment to keeping Nigeria unified and to cleanse it of the corruption and nepotism that led to the first coup. In his inaugural address on January 25, 1966, Ojukwu stated plainly that "it is our intention to stamp out inefficiency, corruption and dishonesty in all facets of public life, to create the consciousness of national unity and to lead the citizens of Nigeria as one disciplined people in purposeful march to maximum realisation of the country's potential."[26] Ojukwu, like many of the officers not involved in the coup, still had a common perception that the coup plotters were, if misguided in their means, at least honest and admirable in their goals.

However, as governor, Ojukwu began centralizing the affairs of the Eastern Region around himself and a cadre of protective advisors. These advisors, whom Akpan felt were overprotective to the point of paranoia, increasingly took over the management of the region's civil service and removed all political appointees, replacing them with people close to Ojukwu. Many of his appointees were his own relatives, despite the fact that they were politicians in the first republic and should have been ineligible under Ojukwu's own rules. With little oversight from Lagos, Ojukwu essentially created a fiefdom that centered on himself with a cadre of personally connected appointees.

Ironsi's choice of military governors, along with his policy toward the coup plotters, proved that he was either unwilling or unable to capitalize on the populist wave that the coup attempt left in its wake. Shaken by the initial success of the coup, Ironsi appointed a council of trusted advisors to help him administer the country in much the same way that he had previously administered the armed forces. However, the advisors he appointed were all Igbo, a fact that only fed the flames of sectionalism and allowed Ironsi's opponents to point at the composition of the military government as proof of an Igbo conspiracy. In fact some, especially in the North, accused Ironsi of being a secret conspirator and believed his taking over the government was the endgame that the coup plotters had sought all along. The leaders of the failed coup also placed the blame for the political deterioration on Ironsi but for very different reasons. According to Ademoyega, the ethnic hatred that emerged during the coup's aftermath was not a product of the coup attempt but rather of the coup's failure, which installed Ironsi, a leader guided by "weakness and non-revolutionary principles," which stood in stark contrast to the "well ordered and well controlled government that was envisaged and could have been run by us if our plans were fully executed."[27]

On May 24, 1966, Ironsi promulgated a decree that once again plunged the country into turmoil and set off the bloody chain of events that culminated in the second coup that ended his rule and life. Ironsi's Decree 34 abolished the regional structure of the country and created a unified administration run from the capital in Lagos. Ironsi's decree was set to create a new political reality in the country by splitting the country into weak provinces that would be administered directly from the central government rather than the four powerful regions that hitherto had dominated Nigerian politics, which many blamed for the political instability that had plagued Nigeria since independence. This system appealed to Ironsi, a military man who understood the advantages of such a hierarchical administrative framework. In fact, he had already created this type of centralized administration that was so natural for a military mind to organize. In his decree, he was simply trying to formalize this administrative style. However, because he saw his system as temporary and administrative rather than revolutionary and political, and he did not foresee the reaction that led to the outpouring of violence that set the country on the road to civil war.

The decree set into motion a series of bloody events that began less than a week later, with the first massacres of Igbo in Northern Nigeria. Though the decree is widely regarded as the spark for the violence, and Northern political leaders used the decree as a pretext to incite angry mobs, the massacres were the result of the long-seated animosity that was simmering under the surface in Northern Nigeria between the Igbo and their host populations, due largely to northern perceptions of the Igbo as Christian invaders who excelled in commercial endeavors that served to impoverish northerners. One apocryphal story that sprung up in the aftermath of the May massacres blamed an Igbo baker in Kaduna. According to this story, the baker was so jubilant over the killing of the Sardauna that he baked a commemorative loaf of bread and used an image of St. George slaying the dragon as the loaf's label. The image portrayed Nzeogwu as the saint, and the dragon being slain was the northern premier.[28] While this accusation had no basis in fact, as it seems to have been created only many years after the events, some Igbo did feel that Nzeogwu's actions were justified. AHM Kirk Greene noted that some Igbo in the north hung pictures of Nzeogwu in their windows and even created songs celebrating the event.[29] The Nigerian edition of *Drum Magazine* featured a mock interview with the Sardauna reportedly "from the bowels of hell," where he reportedly begged for forgiveness for his actions against the country.[30]

Though the coup leaders insisted that they had acted in a revolutionary spirit and that their actions were not motivated by ethnic concerns, the coup's aftermath was shaped by little else than a rekindling of ethnic tensions. Writing shortly after the civil war, journalist John de St. Jorre stated that the ethnic tensions after the coup created a sense of anxiety among many in the north who feared Nigeria's structure would change, thereby robbing them of access to governmental structures and funding.

The massacres of the Igbo in the Northern Region began on May 29, 1966, in Kaduna, Kano, Zaria, and Jos. Unlike subsequent massacres that occurred after the July coup, these appeared to have taken the northern military leadership by surprise, especially that the civilian police forces in the north were actually participating in the riots. Alexander Madiebo, a decorated officer who would go on to become commander in chief of the Biafran military during the war, characterized the unrest as "test riots" designed either to ascertain northern leaders' ability to influence Ironsi to do their bidding or as a test for a much greater upsurge of violence that would accompany the events in July. Madiebo, who was stationed in Kaduna, witnessed the riots and determined that though the military had no hand in planning them, they seemed anything but spontaneous. Even worse, Katsina, whom Ironsi appointed as military governor, did not intervene for over twenty-four hours despite Madiebo's constant pleas both to the governor and to the military command in Lagos for immediate military intervention. This inaction served to exasperate the body count and spread fear and panic among the Igbo and other ethnicities from the Eastern Region.

The massacre's planning soon became apparent to the military leadership. Col. Muhammad Shuwa, who was in charge of the 5th Battalion in Kano and would later command the Nigerian 1st Division during the war, received word that a riot was imminent. According to Madiebo, Shuwa proceeded to the police headquarters and discovered that the chief of police was already aware of the impending riot and was ordered not to intervene until he received a direct order from Katsina to do so. Shuwa then returned to his barracks and ordered his own troops to disperse throughout the city in an attempt to stop the rioters. It was only later in the day on the thirtieth that Shuwa received authorization from Katsina to employ the military in the way that he had already done.[31]

While the attacks were definitely planned, Katsina's response to them led to much of the same kind of rumor mongering that the January plotters enabled when they killed both Bello and Tafawa Balewa. Because Katsina did not immediately intervene, he was cast as allowing and condoning the violence. In reality, his weak military response had a concrete political grounding. Many in the north already viewed the military as being increasingly under the control of the southerners, in particular the Igbo. For Katsina to employ the military to protect them as a first resort would only reinforce that perception. Further, Katsina's father was the emir of Katsina and held much political clout. The emir had already opened his palace to the Igbo in the city who were escaping the unrest, and Katsina hoped that the emir's actions would halt the violence. However, the mobs in the city attacked the palace and inflicted heavy casualties. Zaria and Jos suffered the worst of it, as there was no military stationed in either of the cities, and as a result the massacres lasted for three days and ended only "when the rioters were tired of rioting."[32]

The riots were a sign of what was to come, and the casualties were high, with an estimated figure of about six thousand dead.[33] When the riots subsided, a mass exodus of Igbo began from the Northern Region to the Igbo heartland in the east. It was during this outbreak of violence that northern leaders began using the term *araba*, an act that would foreshadow their future plans. Many writers on the civil war have claimed that the term was the Hausa word for secession, but it seems an inaccurate description and most likely was attributed to the word in the war's aftermath to give a more sinister aura to the July coup. In reality, the word *araba* is most likely a variation of the word *jaraba*, meaning misfortune or doom, and comes to the language as an Arabic loan word from the root ح ر ب, meaning war.[34]

To assuage fears and reinforce his region's commitment to Nigerian unity, Katsina made two important moves. First, he approached the traditional rulers in the North, those that many in the east accused of planning and inciting the riots, to address the issue of their perceived inequality in the wake of the coup. He blamed the traditional elites, accusing them of having a serious hand in maintaining the north's backwardness in educational attainment and, as a result, the inability to compete with southerners in obtaining highly skilled jobs without a quota system. He promised to address these issues and proposed creating "a crash program for education and training."[35]

Like Ironsi, Katsina was treading a fine line between appealing to those who sympathized with the coup plotters' ideals and those who supported northern political elites. Due to the nature of the coup, in the north the latter far outnumbered the coup's supporters, who were mainly restricted to university campuses and those who were out of favor with the traditional emirs. He thus reached out to Ojukwu and Ironsi to heal the rifts between the Hausa and the Igbo. Despite, or perhaps because of, his actions during the riots, Katsina was, like most of the military rulers, still deeply committed to Nigerian unity. Along with Katsina, Ojukwu and Ironsi provided assurances that the Igbo who fled the North could return to their homes and their security would be assured. Ojukwu personally urged easterners to return to the north in a speech at the University of Nigeria, Nsukka, where he appeared in a public display of solidarity with the university's chancellor, the emir of Kano, whom Ojukwu appointed to the academic post as another sign of the eastern governor's commitment to national unity.[36] Ojukwu later pointed to his message as proof that he had wholeheartedly believed in Nigerian unity and that he bore personal moral responsibility for the deaths that occurred in July–September of that year because he willingly sent people back to their ultimate deaths.[37]

Northern leaders, now armed with the very credible threat of mass violence, responded to the appeals for calm and overtures for unity with a set of ultimatums to the Ironsi government. First, they demanded a repeal of Decree 34 because they felt that any implementation of it would lead to deterioration of the north's clout in Nigerian politics. Second, they wanted immediate prosecution of the coup plotters who had been in prison without trial since the end of the coup and had not been dismissed from the military for their actions. Last, they ordered the government not to launch any investigation into the May riots.

Ironsi's response to the demands was to do nothing at all. Though he realized the gravity of the situation, he refused to cancel his decree of creating a unitary government. Instead, he sought to ameliorate the crisis by meeting with the traditional rulers on a tour of the country, culminating in a summit on July 29, 1966, in Ibadan. However, by the time the meeting was called, the northern political elites had become increasingly bitter of what they saw as an Igbo takeover of the federal government. Similarly, northern officers saw the lack of prosecution of the January conspirators, especially Nzeogwu and Ifeajuna, as irresponsible at best and evidence of collusion at worst. In a 2008 interview, one of the July conspirators, Capt. Theophilus Yakubu Danjuma (later chief of staff), expressed the army's widespread sentiment regarding Ironsi's treatment of the January plotters, saying, "[The conspirators] had television, they had everything there despite being detained and nobody was talking about court marshalling them."[38] For Danjuma, like many officers (even those in the south), the issue was not that they had eliminated the Sardauna, the prime minister, and much of the northern political class but that the January plotters had also turned against their brothers-in-arms by killing officers. In the coup's aftermath, the dead northern officers had to be replaced, and Ironsi selected easterners to fill many but not all of the positions. Nzeogwu, Ifeajuna, and the rest of the plotters spoke about how their actions were designed to end tribalism, but in the eyes of many northern officers, ethnicity seemed to be reinforced in the coup's aftermath, as southerners concentrated their control over the military's highest ranks.

Because Ironsi was never a politically aware officer but a professional soldier, he sought to replace the slain officers with the most capable military men available rather than move to alleviate tensions with more politically sensitive appointments. What's more, through the military's Nigerianization project, northern officers achieved parity in number with the south by the end of 1965. As a result, most of the northern officers were of junior rank, and having them leapfrog their seniors in rank to maintain parity in the top positions would have repeated the pattern that Gbulie lamented as why southern officers felt disgruntled in the years leading up to the January coup. Ironsi appointed Northern officers where possible, most notably naming Gowon his successor as GOC despite many qualified officers having seniority over him, such as Brig. Gen. Babafemi Ogundipe, the second-highest ranking officer in the Nigerian armed forces after the coup. Additionally, Ironsi's choice for police inspector general was Alhaji Kam Salem. Thus, placating the southern officer corps meant alienating northern officers and vice versa.

After the May riots, it became clear that the fissure between Ironsi and northerners could not easily be mended, even with the overtures that the military leader made to the northern government. As long as the core demands of both the northern officers and civilian rulers would not be met, especially the prosecution of the January plotters and the repeal of Decree 34, Ironsi could not afford to antagonize them further. According to Madiebo, this led to a breakdown of discipline in the army ranks and made the situation ripe for a countercoup. In fact, northern officers felt so emboldened that one major, who was in the United States at an artillery course, wrote to Madiebo promising to ensure a countercoup when the major returned to Nigeria.[39]

Even more troubling for Ironsi, by the end of April, Nigerian officers and civilian politicians were holding so-called secret meetings that were not well concealed. With northern politicians accused of stockpiling weapons and ammunition, northern newspapers running inflammatory articles calling for jihad, and Ironsi unable to stop the May riots because of northern intransigence, many in the country feared the worst. Madiebo "saw the handwriting on the wall. Indeed, no one could have failed to recognize the signs of impending disaster."[40] De St. Jorre saw the military as ready to rebel, claiming that "at the end of July, the army was like an overwound spring; it had lost its normal tensile flexibility and had passed the point where a normal unwinding operation would have saved the mechanism."[41] Thus, unlike the first coup, which was led by a group of idealistic young officers with a clear vision for the future, the second coup would be both reactionary in nature and lacking a clear vision other than to enumerate the various abuses that the post-coup Igbo-led regime had supposedly inflicted on the north.

In a last-ditch attempt to ameliorate the tensions, Ironsi decided to hold a series of meetings with regional leaders, beginning with a large conference in Ibadan. The evening before talks were set to begin, the countercoup struck. The operation, which some dubbed "the return match" and was later named Operation Araba, had the goal of ending Ironsi's rule and life and restoring the regional balance that the first coup had interrupted. While some of the coup plotters, most notably Murtala Muhammad, argued for the north to leave Nigeria, this goal did not appear to ever have been part of the military's initial plan, nor of Northern politicians who encouraged much of the violence. The coup proved a bloody affair from the start, with the junior officers taking part executing not only Ironsi but also any Igbo solider they could find.

In the early hours of July 29, a group of northern officers took control of the army garrison in Abeokuta while the garrison commander, Philip Efiong, was away in Kaduna for a military staff meeting. The northern officers killed the Igbo officers that Efiong had left in command. With the garrison secure and ready to strike at Ibadan, where Ironsi was about to meet with the traditional rulers, the plotters sent word to Ikeja, where another group of conspirators seized the international airport. Thus, after securing any hope of reinforcements, the plotters, led by Danjuma, surrounded the government house in Ibadan where Ironsi was a guest of western governor Adekunle Fajuyi and arrested both men. Either before or after his arrest, Ironsi was able to phone Gowon to inform him of the coup and ask for a helicopter to evacuate him from the lodge. By the time the helicopter arrived, sometime before 8:30 a.m., the lodge had already been deserted.

Danjuma informed Ironsi that he was under arrest. Fajuyi, who was initially set free, refused to leave Ironsi's side and was also taken into custody, along with the military ruler's aide de camp. The three were stripped, cuffed with wire, beaten to the extent that the captives' bodies were severely swollen and bloodied, placed in separate vans, and taken out of the city. The beatings continued after they arrived at their destination, a nondescript footpath somewhere outside of Ibadan. There, they were beaten so severely that they "were almost dead by now," then each was "separately finished off by a few rounds of machinegun fire."[42] Ironsi's death was not made public for many months, which only increased the tension between Ojukwu, who still considered him missing and as such the legitimate head of state, and Gowon, who became the head of state after the coup.

Gowon's role in the coup has been questioned because he was supposedly loyal to Ironsi but emerged at the end of the coup as the head of state. In reality, Gowon was part of Ogundipe's attempt to counter the coup and restore Ironsi's regime. However, the military had become so fragmented by Ironsi's response to the January coup and the political machinations of northern political leaders to foment the May violence that military discipline had broken down along ethnic and regional lines as well as lines of political opportunism. It was into this climate that Ogundipe dispatched Gowon to Ikeja to restore military order in the wake of the chaos. As it turned out, Ogundipe had sent Gowon into the vipers' nest, where all semblance of military order had deteriorated to the point where northern soldiers took to the streets to exact revenge on Igbo soldiers and civilians across Lagos. In one instance, soldiers hijacked a VC10 airplane belonging to the British Overseas Airways Corporation (BOAC) at the international airport and ordered the crew to carry family members to the relative safety of Kano.[43] The pilot, Alan Kerr, reported that the families boarded the plane with virtually all their belongings and that the soldiers were "terribly polite."[44] It was this flight and Kerr's radio communications that first alerted the world that something was taking place in Nigeria.

When Gowon arrived at the Ikeja barracks, he found the base firmly in the hands of the plotters. He was persuaded to become the soldiers' spokesman and was forced to shift his allegiance to the coup and away from Ogundipe, who was still attempting to mobilize his supporters and take control of the state in the name of Ironsi, who was still considered missing. By the morning of July 29, it became clear that Ironsi had been abducted, but news outlets both in Nigeria and abroad could not ascertain his or Fajuyi's fate, though it was clear that the mutineers were northern officers. The most outspoken of them, Murtala Mohammed, voiced a set of demands, which began with a demand to split the military along ethnic lines and ended in the early afternoon with a call to establish a "Republic of the North," which would amount to secession from Nigeria. Ogundipe's first response came at two thirty that afternoon, when he broadcast on Nigerian Radio a call for calm, declaring a state of emergency in Ibadan, Lagos, and Abeokuta. He then tried to retake control of the Ikeja barracks but was repelled, suffering heavy losses. It was only then that he realized the precariousness of his situation. He sent a second patrol to the streets of Lagos to retake the garrison, but this time his troops were led by a northern officer who sympathized with the conspirators. This officer, while he did not defect, went out of his way to avoid contact with the enemy and returned unscathed. When confronted about the unit's cowardice, one sergeant who was part of the patrol suddenly showed his bravery, brandishing a machine gun at the brigadier, bravely notifying Ogundipe that "I do not take orders from you until my captain comes." He then took Ogundipe to two junior officers who forced the general to write a letter of resignation from the army.[45] Thus, Ogundipe realized that he could not thwart the coup in a similar manner to Ironsi's success in January. As a result, the coup was successful both in securing the capital and in eliminating the military leaders of the western region and the federal government. Even more troubling for Nigeria's future was the complete breakdown of the military's chain of command. If a sergeant could refuse an order from a brigadier general because of ethnic origin, any soldier held in his hands the means to spark another coup.

Meanwhile, in the north, Colonel Madiebo was in Kaduna for a military council meeting and was preparing to move his artillery headquarters to Lagos due to the tense situation. He'd had some advance warning of the coup: Colonel Anwunah had received a call alerting him to the coup the day before. However, Madiebo, along with many southern military officers stationed in the north, such as Philip Efiong who was also in Kaduna on that fateful day, attempted to defend the brigade headquarters against the mutineers. Anwunah knew that the situation between the rival factions within the military was becoming tenser. Once the coup began in Lagos, the officers in the north who were not part of the conspiracy found it difficult to obtain any reliable information, largely because the telephone lines between Lagos and the north had been cut shortly after the coup began. However, all involved realized that time was of the essence, and any indecision in fighting back, joining the plotters, or fleeing to the south would endanger their lives. Even more problematic, Madiebo, as one of the senior officers in the north, had no way to ascertain if the coup had been successful. He was able to reach Lagos on the radio and spoke to a northern officer who assured him there was no trouble in Lagos and all that had taken place was that a group of drunk soldiers had gone out of the barracks and caused panic among the civilian population.[46]

Madiebo knew that something was amiss in the capital, and the radio officer's complete denial was proof enough that at least some elements of the military were in the conspirators' hands. By the next morning, it became even clearer that the situation in Kaduna was about to erupt as northern officers were refusing to disarm their soldiers and openly defying their southern superiors. By the afternoon of the twenty-ninth, Efiong's home in Kaduna was under surveillance, and the other officers in the north were caught in a dragnet, with coup plotters actively attempting to find the officers loyal to Ironsi. In one instance, Efiong's brother had to pose as a gardener to avoid detection when he stumbled across the guards surveilling the colonel's house. However, the haphazard nature of the coup's execution in the north, coupled with the time it took for the plotters to mobilize in Kaduna, gave the loyal officers an opportunity to plan and execute fairly simple escapes from the attempted dragnet, which mainly consisted of stationary roadblocks on the main roads leading out of Kaduna. Madiebo was able to escape by leaving the city on foot and was picked up at a village twelve kilometers outside Kaduna; he went on the run for several days while being hunted by the plotters, who were searching for eastern officers all across the country to enact revenge killings for the January coup.

Unlike the January coup, the July plotters had little forethought in what they hoped to accomplish after the mutiny. This was especially problematic, as unlike in January, the coup succeeded in bringing the plotters to power. The result was tension throughout the country over the uncertainty of things to come, unlike the scenes of jubilation after the first coup. In contrast, the lack of concrete information, coupled with the rumors regarding the BOAC aircraft (one of the few verifiable stories from the first two days of the coup), gave the general impression that the country was close to disintegration. Many in the south took the news that the plane was flying out the families of northern soldiers as proof that the northern secession was imminent. Saro-Wiwa, still at the University of Ibadan, conveyed the general fear in Ibadan those first days when "the soldiers at the barracks at Ibadan had become absolutely impossible, and indeed notorious for the brutal way they in which they treated civilians. They went berserk, ransacking night clubs [*sic*] and behaving like mad dogs." Like many in the city, Saro-Wiwa decided that "discretion indicated that one was best indoors."[47]

Though most details about the few days immediately following the coup are difficult to ascertain because of the lack of information and rampant rumors, in all likelihood, Gowon's defection to the mutineers countered Murtala Mohammed's demands for northern secession. Nigeria's future was bitterly contested in the days after the coup, mostly behind closed doors, with the main questions being both the shape of the country's future and who would emerge to lead it. Though Mohammed was adamant about secession, "there was no careful thinking behind a northern secession, nor any detailed planning to put it into effect."[48] Rather, the idea for secession was born out of the opportunity that the successful removal of Ironsi brought about. According to de St. Jorre, in the end, it was Mohammed's toxic personality that swept Gowon to power and saved Nigerian unity, but only after a tense weekend where local, national, and global players influenced Mohammed to eschew secession. Hausa, Yoruba, Tiv, and other leaders accepted the coup and the change of government with the condition that Gowon be appointed to succeed Ironsi. In the end, all the regional leaders except Ojukwu, who still remained loyal to Ironsi, agreed to accept Gowon as the head of state.[49] By the end of the weekend, on August 1, Gowon was unveiled as the new leader of Nigeria, stating in part:

> As a result of the recent events and of the previous similar ones I have come strongly to believe that we cannot honestly, and sincerely continue this wise [*sic*] as the basis for trust and confidence in our unitary system of Government has been unable to stand the test of time. I have already remarked on the issue in question. Suffice it to say that putting all considerations to the test, political, economic as well as social, the basis for unity is not there, or is so badly rocked, not only once, but many times. I therefore feel that we should review the issue of our national standing and see if we can help stop the country from drifting away into utter destruction.[50]

Just as haphazard as the threat of northern secession appeared to be, the announcement of Gowon's installation as military head of state fanned the rumor mill surrounding the coup. Frederick Forsyth, a British author and staunch Ojukwu supporter during the war, wrote a defense of Ojukwu's actions in *The Biafra Story*. Forsyth questioned the grammatical structure of Gowon's speech, observing that "after a phrase like 'so badly rocked, not only once, but many times' one would expect the word 'that' followed by an announcement of the consequences of the rocking. Moreover it is nonsensical to suggest that the peroration of stopping the country from drifting to destruction would be likely to cause disappointment and heartbreak to all true lovers of Nigeria. In fact, before editing, the speech *was* to have announced the North's secession."[51]

For Forsyth, as well as others, the second coup's ability to maintain a unified country was part of the marathon discussions on the weekend after the coup, details of which have never been fully disclosed, and the language of the announcement is testament to that fact.[52] In the end, Nigeria remained unified only because of backroom dealings that involved civil servants from all over the country as well as the American ambassador and British high commissioner, and mostly because Gowon was a more palatable leader than Murtala Mohammed.[53] Forsyth went so far as to claim it was the July coup that divided Nigeria into two separate entities—the first consisted of all but the Eastern Region and was loyal to Gowon, and the second was the Eastern Region, led by Ojukwu, which did not recognize Gowon's leadership and was thus the last part of the country to still be loyal to Ironsi's government.[54]

The coup was accompanied by a purge of the military, with Igbo officers and soldiers targeted in revenge for the January killings. After the dust settled on August 1, Hassan Katsina issued an order for all soldiers to return to their barracks. However, many of those who obeyed the order were immediately arrested and summarily executed, especially soldiers and officers from the Eastern Region. Though Katsina did not issue the order for their execution, because the coup had inspired an almost total breakdown of military discipline, many soldiers and junior officers took it upon themselves to act against their so-called enemies with complete impunity.[55] Efiong was able to escape Kaduna only by calling on a Peace Corps volunteer who connected him to an expatriate missionary group to smuggle him out of the city and onto a train bound for Lagos, where he hoped to appeal to Gowon to stop the bloodshed. In all, the Eastern Region claimed that over two hundred soldiers of eastern origin were killed in August.[56]

The killings were not confined to the military. Like in May, civilians from the Eastern Region, especially Igbo, were targeted in an organized reprisal campaign that lasted, through several rounds of violence, until September. Unlike in May, this time the killings amounted to widespread massacres that killed thousands and triggered a mass internal migration of easterners from all parts of the country to the relative safety of the Eastern Region. The massacres themselves were especially brutal, involving gangs of men with the assistance of soldiers, especially junior officers and noncommissioned officers (NCOs). Katsina, who, along with Ojukwu, had offered guarantees of safety for Igbo who fled the riots in May, was taken aback by the scale and viciousness of the killings, stating in October that "the events of recent weeks in this Region were unprecedented in both their scale and their form. It is a matter of deep regret that the orderly progress of the Region should be disturbed on so large a scale in this way."[57] Ojukwu later admitted that the massacres were not ordered by the high echelons of the military command, stating that "I will swear on anything that is brought before me today, and I know in my heart that Hassan never ordered anybody to do anything to an easterner. . . . It is what the people underneath did."[58]

What the people underneath did amounted to nothing less than wholesale slaughter. Colin Legum, reporting for *The Observer,* described some of the horrific scenes he encountered when the refugees who fled the violence arrived in Enugu:

> A woman, mute and dazed, arrived back in her village after travelling for five days with only a bowl in her lap. She held her child's head which was severed before her eyes. Another woman stepped off a refugee truck, her face battered. By her side was her little boy, one of whose eyes had been gouged out, and her little girl who had severe scalp wounds. "What," she kept repeating, "has happened to my baby?" It had been tied to her back before she was knocked to the ground. Men, women and children arrived with arms and legs broken, hands hacked off, mouths split open. . . . The scene in the Eastern Region continues to be reminiscent of the ingathering of exiles into Israel after the end of the last war. The parallel is not fanciful.[59]

Legum was not alone in depicting the horrors. Shortly after the July coup, the Eastern Region's government press ran a series of pamphlets with titles such as "The Problem of Nigerian Unity" and later a series called Nigerian Crisis. The third pamphlet in that series was called "Nigerian Pogrom: The Organized Massacre of Eastern Nigerians."[60] The volume recounts many of the horrors including the slaughter of Igbo attempting to board airplanes at Kano Airport, a fictionalized account of which appears in Chimamanda Ngozi Adichie's *Half of a Yellow Sun.* The October 7 issue of *Time* magazine told of a plane from London that landed in Kano on the way to Lagos. The passengers deplaned, and "a wild-eyed soldier stormed in, brandishing a rifle and demanding '*Ina Nyamiri'*—the Hausa for 'Where are the damned Ibos?' There were Ibos among the customs officers, and they dropped their chalks and fled, only to be shot down in the main terminal by other soldiers."[61] The pamphlet contained graphic images of refugees who corroborated Legum's reporting and eyewitness accounts of people who survived the massacres. One Igbo soldier told how he and his fellow easterners were singled out when a sergeant berated them for the murders of Ahmadu Bello and Tafawa Balewa and told them to "give our names and addresses and send any messages we have for our people because we were going to die." The Igbo soldiers were then driven outside of Katsina, where they were summarily shot. The witness was the only survivor, having "felt my leg shattered and I fell down. . . . I managed to crawl into the bush."[62]

Witnessing the killings, especially the purges within the military, a troubled Gowon issued a decree on August 9 that all military personnel should be repatriated to their region of origin. Though Gowon hoped this would ease the tensions and help put a stop to the bloodshed, this move had the effect of segregating the military along ethnic lines while offering an easy target for the marauding northern soldiers eager to continue exacting revenge on their Igbo counterparts, who, now unarmed, were even more vulnerable on the trains, buses, and trucks headed to the Eastern Region. To make matters worse, this further eroded discipline in the ranks, as soldiers mutinied against their superiors. Two such cases showed how military morale and discipline eroded to the point where sections of the Nigerian army could no longer be classified as a military force but rather simply a band of armed thugs. Soon after Gowon issued the decree to segregate the military along regional lines, on August 19, in one much publicized instance, members of the 4th Battalion, a unit of primarily northern soldiers stationed in Ibadan, attended a funeral in Benin. The soldiers learned that some of the conspirators from the January coup were being held in a prison in the city. The soldiers then decided to raid the prison, where they found both northern and Igbo soldiers being held for their parts in the January coup. The northern soldiers were released while the Igbo were tortured to death.[63]

Later, on October 1, in what would become the bloodiest of all the events during the massacres, members of the 5th Battalion stationed in Kano staged a mutiny against their commanding officer, Maj. Abba Kyari (later brigadier), when he addressed them in advance of an operation to escort police to the town of Nguru, some 250 kilometers northeast, near the Nigerien border. The mutineers then raided the garrison's armory, killed the battalion's second in command, and rampaged through the streets of Kano, arming local criminal gangs and attacking Igbo who were trying to flee the city. They raided the airport and train station, killing indiscriminately. Though they targeted mainly Igbo, they killed anyone they felt was trying to assist their victims, including airport personnel and train staff.[64] The events of that day instilled so much fear into officers, even northern ones, that when Katsina called several senior officers to help quell the mutiny, they refused, fearing for their lives.[65] A *Daily Sketch* editorial, in a plea to rescue the country, asked, "Will no one save Nigeria? Is there no one whose love for Nigeria transcends love of tribe or personal safety, who is willing to come forward and seek others like himself to nurse this sick nation? If there be a man, let him come forward. Today, for God's sake!"[66]

Though the massacres instilled terror and created a massive influx of internal refugees into the Eastern Region, the number killed has long been a source of dispute and tension within the country. Because of the contested nature of the 1963 census, the real numbers of people in the country and in each region will never be known. Further exasperating matters was that throughout the war, the claims of the number killed in 1966 never ceased to increase. In the "Nigerian Pogrom" pamphlet, the eastern government placed its official number killed at 7,000, a number that the British high commissioner felt was already inflated, stating that Ojukwu met with the Italian ambassador and "speaking in a manner that made it plain that he was consciously exaggerating, Ojukwu said the number killed . . . was as high as 7,000. . . . If the true number had been 'between

10,000 and 15,000,' he would have told the Italian Ambassador 25,000."[67] A few months later, at Aburi, Ojukwu stated 10,000. By the outset of the war, the number had increased to 30,000 in Biafran publications, only to rise to 50,000 in Ojukwu's Ahiara Declaration of 1969.[68]

Though the actual number of people killed in the 1966 massacres will never be accurately assessed, the firm belief remains among many in Nigeria that the highest number is the correct one, even though the original statement, even by Ojukwu, was most likely closer to the lower end of the spectrum. No one can ever know due to a lack of data. There are several reasons for the discrepancy in numbers. Most likely, the numbers, like many others throughout Nigeria's history, were simply inflated for propaganda purposes during the war. However, though the massacres were widespread across the north, they were extremely localized in their carnage. The scope of the massacres was not altogether clear, as the reporting, both in Nigeria and abroad, showed. Ojukwu's number of 10,000 at the Aburi meeting was probably based both on information on the massacres and on propaganda at a time of serious political disagreements and bitterness.

Regardless of the accuracy of the numbers, the campaign succeeded in instilling such terror that the refugee crisis was very real, and the numbers of between 1.5 and 2 million internally displaced people was quickly accepted by all parts of the Nigerian government and the international community. The terror the massacres inflicted on the population was very real, and none of the perpetrators had any cause to deny the inflated numbers, as it suited their goal of frightening any potential returnees and preventing the Igbo from returning as they had in May. As one of the early writers on the war, Zdenek Cervenka, commented, "Whatever the number, it was sufficiently large to create a trauma of considerable proportions, because it affected so many families and stretched right down through society."[69]

Ojukwu's eastern government's reaction to the massacres quickly coalesced around the word *pogrom*, traditionally associated with the persecution of the Jews in tsarist Russia in the late nineteenth and early twentieth centuries.[70] By calling the massacres pogroms, the eastern leadership began the process of equating the plight of the Jews in Europe to that of the Igbo. The Igbo had long been considered the "Jews of Nigeria" for several reasons. First and foremost, like the Jews, ethnic stereotypes had long portrayed the Igbo as adept businessmen. Ojukwu's father, Sir Louis Ojukwu, was the first Nigerian millionaire and the first to own a Rolls-Royce, which Ojukwu drove in Enugu after he was appointed military governor in January 1966. Like the myth of the "wandering Jew," the Igbo were well known in Nigeria for setting up communities across the country. These stereotypes were so entrenched in the public imagination of the Igbo that Roger Morris, a member of Henry Kissinger's American national security staff, mentioned in a memo to President Nixon that "the Ibos are the wandering Jews of West Africa—gifted, aggressive, Westernized; at best envied and resented, but mostly despised by the mass of their neighbors in the Federation."[71] Ojukwu's nascent propaganda machinery's goal was to establish a link in the popular imagination between the plight of European Jews in the Second World War and the plight of Nigeria's "Jews" who were suffering a new genocide barely twenty years after the Holocaust.

Activists, missionaries, and pseudo-scholars had long posited linkages between the Igbo and a possible Judaic ancestry. The first verifiable analogy came from Olaudah Equiano, who, in his famous narrative published in 1789, when discussing his childhood home in West Africa, surmised that there existed a "strong analogy which even by this sketch, imperfect as it is, appears to prevail in the manners and customs of my countrymen, and those of the Jews, before they reached the Land of Promise . . . which alone would induce me to think that the one people had sprung from the other."[72]

So strong was the belief that the Igbo had Jewish ancestry, or that there existed a lost tribe of Jews in West Africa, that the ill-fated 1841 British Niger expedition carried two letters from prominent London rabbis in the hopes of encountering the lost Jews that Equiano wrote about. Though the expedition found no Jews, they found that the practice of circumcision was widespread, which led many, including Samuel Ajayi Crowther, who was a member of the 1841 expedition and would later be the first African to be named a bishop of the Anglican church, to believe that some connection existed between the Jews and the Igbo.

Later missionaries continued to seek connections between the Igbo and the Jews or other Semitic peoples. In 1900, a member of the Church Missionary Society (CMS) named George Thomas Basden lived for twenty years as a missionary among the Igbo. His subsequent ethnography, *Among the Ibos of Nigeria: An Account of the Curious & Interesting Habits, Customs & Beliefs of a Little Known African People, by One Who Has for Many Years Lived amongst Them on Close & Intimate Terms*, speculated on the similarities in customs between Igbo and Jews but never went so far as to explicitly state that they shared an ancestry.[73] Nonetheless, some Igbo readily embraced the idea that their people's origin lay outside of West Africa. One Igbo writer, Ike Akwelumo, of whom not much is known, penned a pamphlet sometime in the 1950s asserting that the Igbo were of Jewish origin, claiming that the word *Ibo* was a corruption or contraction of the word *Hebrew*. Adiele Afigbo, the pioneering African historian, studied these claims in depth and raised questions about their authenticity. If the origins were widely held beliefs, Igbo oral traditions should have reflected that belief. However, Afigbo found no evidence that oral traditions corroborated any hint of Igbo Jewish origins. For Afigbo, the myths of Jewish origin most likely originated with Christian missionaries through which "educated Igbo young men became acquainted with the wanderings and tribulations of the Jews, as well as with the fact of the 'loss' of the ten tribes, and thus with the 'likelihood' that one of these could have 'wandered' into what is now Igbo land."[74] His conclusion, as well as that of most historians and archaeologists of West Africa, was that "it is now generally believed that this tradition is worthless as an account of Igbo origin, and indeed as an account of the origin of any other West African people. Not only is there no concrete evidence in its support, but it is in conflict with what archeological and linguistic evidence we do have."[75] Despite the evidence, these beliefs persisted and lent the narrative of genocide a modicum of global credibility that would be extensively exploited throughout the war.

The brutality of the coup's aftermath, especially toward the civilian population, instilled in most Igbo, and in many non-Igbo easterners, the notion that they would be safe only in the Eastern Region. While Legum's report focused mainly on the Igbo refugees fleeing from the north, many easterners left their homes in the west and in Lagos, the country's capital. Saro-Wiwa initially mocked those who fled, insisting that, unlike in the north, those who left Lagos and Ibadan were "weak-minded" and "needed only a word of encouragement and they were instantly on the move back home." Eventually, Saro-Wiwa himself proved to be one of those he accused of being weak-minded, as he boarded one of the many vehicles headed east with "women, their lifelong belongings packed up in shabby bundles, children tied to their backs," who all clambered onto the vehicles taking people to the relative safety of the Eastern Region.[76]

Ojukwu felt personally betrayed. Since the January coup, the Eastern leader made several overtures that cemented his commitment to Nigerian unity. The violence against the Igbo that followed the July mutiny, coming so quickly after he, Ironsi, and Katsina, the Northern Region's governor, gave assurances for people to return to the north in May, most likely finalized Ojukwu's resolve that the country could not continue as one. With the aforementioned Nigerian Crisis pamphlets, the Eastern Region government began a campaign using eastern government offices to agitate against other parts of the country in preparation for future secession. This first attempt to craft an official narrative for the crisis laid the foundations for Biafra's Propaganda Directorate, which proved successful in prosecuting the public information aspect of the war until very late in the conflict.[77]

Ojukwu not only began to build a formidable propaganda arm for Biafra. He also began smuggling weapons into the Eastern Region. Because of the political tension that the July coup and subsequent pogroms created in the country, any action taken by either side was framed squarely within the regional balance of power. Thus, when Gowon purchased a large cache of Italian weapons that were stored in Kaduna, known as the Appolo Arms Deal after an officer known only as Major Appolo who brokered the deal, Ojukwu claimed that these weapons were to be used exclusively by northern troops. Gowon responded that the weapons were for the entire Nigerian army and would be distributed once the situation normalized. By this point, Ojukwu would not accept Gowon's assurances for security or equity in administering the country and initiated a clandestine weapons purchase program, which went horribly awry.[78]

Due to their inability to openly purchase weapons, which would be subject to international regulations, Ojukwu's officials had to resort to the black market and rely on smugglers to obtain the weapons they would hope to use to defend themselves against the rest of the country. To this end, Christopher Okigbo, a poet and former Cambridge University Press representative turned eastern government official, set out for Europe, where he contacted several gun smugglers and black market dealers. Okigbo made contact with a German smuggler who was acting as a middleman for French arms dealer Paul Favier for the purchase of a cache of weapons left over from the Second World War. While Favier was working with arms smugglers, he had the tacit support of some high-level officials in the French government led by Jacques Foccart, the architect of much of France's policy in postcolonial Africa, who would later play an instrumental role in shaping De Gaulle's policy toward Biafra, especially in the later stages of the war.

With Foccart's blessing, Okigbo was able to purchase the arms and arrange delivery by a DC-4 aircraft piloted by American mercenary pilots Hank Wharton and Orvis Nelson. Though Wharton claimed to own the aircraft, it had a sketchy past and had been impounded by the Italian government after its previous owner, Swiss smuggler and mercenary recruiter Heinrich Heuer, was imprisoned for embezzlement, fraud, and mercenary recruitment. Wharton arrived in Italy after claiming to have purchased the plane from Heuer and told the Italian authorities he was going to test the engines. Instead, he took off to Rotterdam, Netherlands, to load the first of the arms shipments, which consisted of 960 British Lancaster submachine guns and over 2,000 magazines. The shipment also included hundreds of chargettes, small cranks to load the magazines after depletion. Wharton filed a flight manifest that would take him to Birmingham, England. Instead, he flew to Las Palmas in Spain and from there to Hassi Messaoud, a small town in the Algerian Sahara. After refueling, Wharton and his crew left for one final scheduled stopover in Fort Lamy (now N'Djamena, Chad)—and that was when disaster struck.[79]

Wharton's copilot, Nelson, got lost on the way to Fort Lamy before continuing on to Port Harcourt to deliver the weapons. They discovered their predicament because, as the arrival time to the Chadian capital approached, none of the crew was able to locate Lake Chad, still a large lake at this time and not suffering the effects of desertification. Running low on fuel, Wharton had no choice but to make a crash landing near the town of Garoua, Cameroon, some 450 kilometers south of Fort Lamy. Though none of the crew was killed, Wharton suffered a severe concussion, and Nelson broke his leg. Wharton later claimed that upon his return to Europe, Ojukwu agreed to replace the aircraft. He met Paul Favier in Paris, and the pair went to Madrid, where Favier produced a cigar box with

US$140,000 for a new plane. Wharton would fly to Biafra through most of the war, both as an arms smuggler and for the Red Cross and Joint Church Aid. These early attempts to purchase weapons largely contributed to Biafra's desperate shortage of arms and ammunition, especially at the beginning of the war. The weapons were recovered in Cameroon, but Ojukwu never claimed them as his own, and the incident became a major source of contention at the Aburi meeting in January 1967.[80]

Last, the eastern regional government began retaliatory deportation of non-easterners from the Eastern Region, though it couched this expulsion in the language of safety. In fact, eastern propaganda pointed out how the deportees were escorted out of the region only for their own safety and that "Emeka's ability to control his own police force and a few soldiers contrasted dramatically with Gowon's complete inability to do anything to protect his fellow Nigerians in his own home region."[81] Forsyth recounted a story of a train of northerners on the way to their region being stopped and attacked by a mob of angry Igbo only to be saved by the police. Though several were injured, none were killed.[82]

Despite the rhetorical and practical preparations that both sides were taking in preparation for a confrontation, the second coup's aftermath still needed legal redress. Ironsi was still legally the head of state, and though he was killed in the coup, he would not be officially declared dead until the following January. As a result, Gowon's ascendency to military leadership, argued some, was not technically legal or legitimate. The anti-Gowon group argued that though Ironsi had come to power in the aftermath of a coup, his role as military head of state came only after a legal move where the senate gave him the reins of the state. Making matters worse, Gowon was not the most senior officer, and his installation as head of the military and government ruffled some feathers. Ogundipe was one of the most senior officers, yet he was sidelined during the coup. Equally, the eloquent Ojukwu, with his Oxford education, was senior and regarded Gowon an intellectual inferior, unfit to be his superior.

To ease the tensions and remedy the questions of his legitimacy, Gowon made two important moves. First, at the end of August, he released some of the political prisoners, including Awolowo and Enahoro. Because Awolowo was the closest politician who could be construed as a national figure, and his appeal largely transcended the growing ethnic divide, Gowon hoped Awolowo could help ease the ethnic tensions that were now exposed and manifesting themselves in horrific violence.

Second, Gowon called for an ad hoc constitutional convention that was to be held in Lagos beginning September 11. On the eve of the talks, the last phase of massacres was unleashed on the remaining easterners in the north. Details of the ad hoc convention were never made public, and any progress was overshadowed by the violence. In fact, the killings started the evening before the conference was set to begin, as the eastern delegates were preparing to leave Enugu for Lagos. The riots were so well coordinated, with buses and military vehicles taking the perpetrators from town to town, that "spontaneous" protests erupted across the north and within hours engulfed the entire region and even spread to the west.[83] The 5th Battalion's rampage in Kano, mentioned earlier in this chapter, was part and parcel of this terror campaign, designed in no small part to scupper the talks. The campaign proved a partial success, as when the eastern delegates were preparing to leave for Lagos, news of the violence reached them, and they refused to leave, delaying the conference for a day while Ojukwu scrambled to convince them to attend. Ojukwu's efforts came even as he lost his father the same day. Though the convention did eventually convene, it was suspended after several weeks and abandoned in late November, when the eastern delegates refused to return, citing the insecurity in Lagos.[84]

Though the convention amounted to little, it showcased the emerging tensions within Nigeria's civil service. Because the Eastern Region's delegates refused to fully participate, no real agreement would have been possible. This did not stop delegates from the other regions from attempting to fill the power vacuum. Taking the lead, civil servants from the country's Middle Belt attempted to redefine the country's structure, which was dominated by the "big three" ethnic groups, to give themselves a greater stake in the decision-making process.[85]

With the failure of the constitutional convention, Nigeria's crisis deepened to the extent that it was unclear whether the country could go on in any form, even as the loosest of confederations. What was even clearer was that because of the lack of personal security, there could be no place in the country that the factions could agree upon to hold more meetings. Thus, on January 4–5, 1967, at the behest of the Ghanaian military leader, Joseph Ankrah, the heads of the federal government, and the regional leaders met at Peduase Lodge, the presidential retreat built by Ghana's first president, Kwame Nkrumah, in the resort town of Aburi, forty kilometers north of Accra. Also present at the meeting were Comm. Joseph Wey, the head of the Nigerian navy, and the inspector general of the police, Kam Salem, and his deputy, Timothy Omo-Bare. At Ojukwu's insistence, Gowon was not referred to as head of state, military commander, or any other title that would imply that he was the de facto, if not de jure, head of the government but rather as simply the representative of Army Headquarters—Lagos. This point of contention would be the central sticking point around which much of the meeting's tension would revolve. Ankrah opened the meeting with a short speech where he expressed his hope that the Nigerian military leaders would be able to come to an agreement because "in the whole annals of history, we have not seen failures with military statesmen and when military personnel do take over the reins of government they have proved their worth. . . . But if you think like the politicians do, that they want fame or they want to be heard of and neglect your people, then of course, I am quite sure that we soldiers will live to regret it."[86]

This would be the last time the regional leaders and Gowon would all meet, and the minutes from the meeting provide insight into both the difficulties facing the country and their relatively unguarded personalities when dealing with each other. All these officers had spent considerable time training with each other in various military schools, both in Nigeria and abroad, and had worked closely with each other in the years leading up to the cataclysmic events of 1966.

Despite Ankrah's pleas for a spirit of reconciliation, Ojukwu immediately began the meeting with the question of the Appolo Arms Deal, and when questioned about Wharton's crash in Cameroon, he claimed that the arms were en route to Kano, not Port Harcourt.[87] The group then agreed to monitor weapons buildup in the regions—a tacit concession that they all knew that weapons were being smuggled, purchased, or otherwise unequally distributed within the country. However, the monitoring was to be done on the basis of the regions, as Wey pointed out when he determined that the oversight would be inherently flawed as the Eastern Region officials would be reluctant to venture outside the east and "Hassan's [Katsina] men, too, would not go to the East." Wey then began his attempt to play the calming figure at the meeting, suggesting that the difficulties could be overcome by military honor, stating that "if anyone is dishonest, the truth will come up."[88]

Ojukwu, who had prepared for the meeting, attempted at the very outset to deflect any criticism and accusations of arms buildup. To this extent, he proposed a very innocuous-looking proposal:

> We, the members of the Supreme Military Council of Nigeria, meeting at Accra on the 4th of January 1967, hereby solemnly and unequivocably [*sic*]
>
> 1. Declare that we renounce the use of force as a means of settling the present crisis in Nigeria, and hold ourselves in honour bound by this declaration.
> 2. Re-affirm our faith in discussions and negotiation as the only peaceable way of resolving the Nigerian crisis.
> 3. (This probably will be open to question.) [included in original] Direct that a copy of this declaration be deposited with the secretariat of the Organisation of African Unity (OAU).[89]

Clearly, none of those in attendance could object to this seemingly innocent declaration, and it was unanimously approved on the condition that the third point be deleted. Though Ojukwu's proposal to involve the OAU, albeit in a very tangential fashion, was his first real attempt to internationalize the conflict, it represented a theme that would be a centerpiece of most of Biafra's diplomatic and public campaigns throughout the war. The fact that he agreed to remove the paragraph without discussion most likely meant that he still held out some hope that the crisis could be managed in an internal manner.

The meeting then shifted to the crisis within the military and the civil service, especially with regard to the regionalization of the military, which Gowon feared would create de facto independent armies within the country. The issue arose very early in the meeting when discussing who would control the military but quickly became sidelined when the question of Gowon's legitimacy emerged.

Robert Adebayo, the western military governor, voiced a concern that militarily the weakest region would naturally be the Western Region, as it was overwhelmingly Yoruba and, as such, had the smallest number of military personnel, both commissioned and enlisted. When he referred to Gowon as the Supreme Commander, Ojukwu interrupted him, saying, "Please do not refer to that here," leading Mobalaji Johnson, the Lagos administrator, to begin a discussion about Gowon's legitimacy, a point that Ojukwu was not willing to concede under any circumstances. This animosity between Gowon and Ojukwu would be one of the major escalating factors of the crisis.

At Aburi, Ojukwu explained his distaste over how the power transfer occurred. For Ojukwu, Gowon's appointment was a direct contravention of the chain of seniority, and he voiced that opinion to Gowon, stating that "you announced yourself as supreme commander . . . by virtue of the fact that you head or that you are acceptable to people who have mutinied against their commander, kidnapped him [at this point Ironsi's death was not yet officially announced] and taken him away; by virtue of the support of officers and men who have in the dead of night murdered their brother officers; by virtue of the fact that you sit at the head of a group who had turned their brother officers from the Eastern Region out of the barracks which they shared."[90]

However, the other regional leaders did not wish to discuss the matter. David Ejoor, the Midwestern Region's governor, lambasted what he characterized as Ojukwu's insistence to address the past rather than move forward to resolve the crisis. When confronted, Ojukwu replied, "If a room is dirty you do not sweep the dirt under the carpet, because whenever you raise the carpet the dirt is there," setting off another round of accusations and recriminations that ended only when Katsina stated what all in attendance most likely already knew about Ironsi's fate: "They [Ironsi and Fajuyi] were kidnapped, they were dead."[91] This was the first public confirmation of Ironsi and Fajuyi's deaths, and it prompted Ojukwu to request a private meeting with Gowon to ascertain what had happened and how Ironsi would be honored. Gowon and the regional governors then adjourned to a private room where they would not be recorded. There, Ojukwu was given the full account of Ironsi's death. More controversially, Ejoor claimed that at this private meeting, Ojukwu "accepted Gowon as head of state and agreed that Nigeria should remain one country."[92] In reality, there were two private sessions, one on each morning of the meeting. The first formally established Ironsi's death and laid plans for the funeral. The second, on the morning of January 7, affirmed the Supreme Military Council as the governing body for the country for as long as it was under military control. Because these were the only parts of the Aburi meeting that were not recorded, there was no record of Ejoor's claims in the minutes, nor did any of the other leaders present at the private meetings echo Ejoor. However, the tone of the meeting shifted after the second private session and led to the agreements that gave hope that the crisis would be resolved and civil war averted. Indeed, the meeting's minutes recorded laughter and jocularity after the second private session adjourned. In one instance, Ejoor commented that the regional governors would have exclusive control over the internal matters of their regions, at which point Gowon interrupted with "which will be a thousand years?" Gowon's comment was followed by laughter all around. Katsina also joined in on the joke, saying, "I want to make [a] suggestion. We all resign tonight."[93]

The first matter agreed to was that a meeting of regional solicitor generals would take place in Benin on January 14, 1967, to examine all of Ironsi's decrees and annul them if necessary. All in attendance agreed that Ironsi's Decree 34 lit the fuse that culminated in the July coup, so all other decrees were suspect. Additionally, no other decrees or edicts could be implemented that affected the entire country without the consultation of the Supreme Military Council. This issue would be paramount because it would either confirm a spirit of cooperation or bode ill for the future if used only for obstruction.

Though the leaders found time for cheerful banter, the military issues continued to concern them all. Once the matter of the political leadership was sorted, Adebayo returned to the issue of the Western Region and the imbalance of the military situation. The issue was twofold and was accentuated by the fact that Yoruba, unlike the Igbo and other easterners and the various ethnic groups in the north, did not enlist in large numbers in the military, and those who did were usually tradesmen like electricians, motor pool mechanics, and other support personnel. This type of soldier was indispensable and could not be easily concentrated in one region. As a result, the bulk of the general duty (GD) soldiers stationed in the Western Region were from the north. Because of the behavior of the troops in Benin, Adebayo did not fully trust in the military's ability to control the ill-disciplined soldiers, especially as it was clear that their ethnic loyalties lay above those to Nigeria or their superiors. Similarly, many of the higher-ranking officers, as well as the highly skilled technical soldiers, came from the east and had, by January, returned there. One such officer, Colonel Ejike Aghanya, would later distinguish himself as the head of the Research and Production (RAP) directorate. Several other Biafran officers would lead other Biafran wartime directorates and be instrumental in Biafra's ability to sustain their war effort.

The solution, therefore, was to further segregate the military and, even more troubling, to give each region the ability to recruit, train, and arm soldiers independently of one another. Because the only major training center was in Zaria,

Adebayo suggested that the garrison in Abeokuta be transitioned into a training depot for soldiers from the three southern regions. Ojukwu objected, stating that his men were equally unsafe in the west because most of the soldiers stationed there were northerners. The rest of the governors relented, and Ojukwu was given the authority to open his own training facility in the east. The Ghanaian Ankrah, who was present for the entire meeting but mostly kept silent, felt inclined to interject here, pointing out the obvious danger in this policy, that without interregional cooperation, transportation, and logistical support, "I cannot see how you can merge [the various regional militaries] up properly. If you do not do so, by the time you realize it, one [region] will be recruiting 10,000 troops and the other will be recruiting 4,000."[94] Gowon, however, was satisfied with only a framework agreement and decided to defer discussion on the details of the matter to a later date, at the next meeting of the Supreme Military Council. Perhaps he was more interested in detailing all the agenda items in the short time they had available, or perhaps he felt that Ojukwu would cooperate in the future. Either way, it seemed a minor concession and one that the circumstances necessitated.

Because Ojukwu came to Aburi prepared with a list of demands that would ensure his future autonomy, he managed to get an important concession that allowed any of the regions to opt for confederational status. At the very end of the meeting, Wey, sensing that the agreement was skewed in Ojukwu's favor, attempted to add a provision that would ensure Nigerian unity. Ojukwu was unwilling to compromise, perhaps because he was already planning secession or, most likely, because accepting the provision would have taken away one of his most important bargaining chips in any future negotiation. His tense exchange with Wey is as follows:

> Wey: Gentlemen, I have something here which I do not know whether the council will agree that it should be included in the communique. "That Nigeria should remain under the constitution as one indivisible political entity and that any major constitutional changes should be brought about only by the process of negotiation."
>
> Ojukwu: No. This is quite different. That is a point we have not discussed, the question of indivisible unity.
>
> Wey: To be decided by the people.
>
> Ojukwu: No. We have not even discussed it. To just slip this in at the end of everything is just something to flare up the whole thing again.
>
> Salem: Is there something wrong with it?
>
> Ojukwu: Yes.[95]

In fact, the agreements reached at Aburi could have done much to defuse the crisis and begin to build the trust that was so badly eroded. More critically, the talks exposed the main fissure between Ojukwu and the other participants. Ojukwu's main concern was the security of the Igbo within Nigeria, and there is little doubt that the pogroms that took the lives of thousands and created the refugee crisis in the east were paramount in his decision-making process, which questioned whether any type of arrangement, other than autonomy or independence, could safeguard the security of those from the east. Gowon and the other regional leaders, who still thought Nigeria could be repaired, asked how that process could be handled. For Ojukwu, however, the question was not how but rather whether any type of reconciliation was possible. While the other leaders used the Aburi accords as a way to try to rebuild the country, Ojukwu's interpretation of the meeting's agreements—indeed, his entire reason for attending—was to secure the concessions that would allow him to halt any forced reintegration or redefinition of the country.

The main agreement between the sides was therefore that each region had de facto autonomy in its own affairs and, more troubling, that any issue concerning the entire country required the consent of the entire governing council. This meant that one region could hold the rest of the country hostage in implementing any aspect of the Aburi agreement that did not fit with their interpretation. As a result, when the parties returned from Ghana, these two differing interpretations of the accords emerged. For Ojukwu, the agreements reached at Aburi constituted the transformation of the country to a confederation of loosely associated regions, each capable of complete autonomy and military independence. In a final attempt both to reach out to Ojukwu and to finalize the rules by which the country would operate, Gowon called a meeting of the Supreme Military Council on March 10, 1967, in Benin City, the one venue where none of the attendees could claim insecurity. But despite the security precautions, Ojukwu did not attend the meeting. His absence was viewed as a way to attempt to hamper any progress regarding Nigeria's future and was met with admonition from the other members of the supreme council. At the meeting, the group, without Ojukwu, promulgated Decree 8, which officially transferred the legislative and executive powers of the Nigerian state to the military council. Ojukwu's attempt at obstructing the procedure set the stage for a showdown with the east. In a rebuff of the eastern leader, the decree established that though the regions would have substantial autonomy, national laws were placed above any regional ones, thus reaffirming the country as a federation and not a loose confederation, as Ojukwu interpreted the Aburi accords.[96]

Ojukwu immediately rejected the decree, claiming that it violated the Aburi agreement in that any decree that affected the entire country entailed the agreement of all the members of the council. However, Ojukwu's refusal to even attend the meeting was seen as an obstructionist tactic, and Gowon claimed that because the country was in a state of emergency, he could issue the decrees with the consent of only three of the four regional leaders. This interpretation of Aburi effectively removed any leverage Ojukwu had to be able to exert power over Nigeria's future. Though Ojukwu did not attend the meeting in Benin, he arrived two days after to meet privately with Ejoor, who informed him of the meeting's outcome. In his memoir, Ejoor portrayed himself as the leading voice of compromise and a devotee of a federal Nigeria. He claimed that though he "entirely believed in one Nigeria . . . I could not go on unless I gained support [from leading figures within the Midwestern Region]," otherwise "I saw the Midwest as no more than a bride being wooed by 'big' suitors. What would become of the bride after the solemnization of matrimony did not look particularly attractive[?]"[97]

Thus, when Ojukwu came to visit Ejoor, the latter claimed it was an attempt to cultivate a notion of southern solidarity against northern domination. However, Midwestern Region leaders were more concerned about domination from other parts of the south, especially as "the Midwest had once been part of the West. We knew what we suffered then." Even more troubling for Ejoor was the fact that his region contained a significant Igbo minority that was agitating for increased cooperation with Ojukwu, "making the position of the rest of us extremely irksome."[98] Thus Ojukwu's realization that other leaders were creating a vision of the country without his approval, and without allowing him to obstruct future cooperation, led Ejoor to conclude that Ojukwu "reached the conclusion that we were all anti Ojukwu. I formed that distinct impression that Ojukwu left me resolved to sever links with the rest of Nigeria."[99]

Whether Ojukwu decided to secede after the July coup or the March meeting, or whether he made the conscious decision to do so at all, and whether Biafran independence was a product of failed brinkmanship will likely always be a subject of intense debate in Nigerian politics. Regardless of intentions, Ojukwu's reaction to Decree 8 set into motion the final showdown that culminated in Biafra's declaration of independence three months later. While the rest of the country moved to implement the Aburi accords in their fashion, Ojukwu demanded that the Aburi accords be implemented in full before the end of March, otherwise the Eastern Region would move to implement them unilaterally in the region.

As many feared that Ojukwu would secede when the end of March arrived, a frantic international effort ensued to solve the crisis.[100] Once again, the Ghanaian leader and British high commissioner attempted to mitigate the crisis, with Ojukwu and Gowon flying separately to Ghana to meet with Ankrah. The pair would not meet again in any attempt to defuse the crisis. The meeting ended with Ojukwu calling a fiery press conference where he once again lambasted the northern elites whom he claimed did not necessarily object to the Igbo but rather to any alternative that would grant Nigeria an effective government.[101] Despite the rhetoric, Ojukwu did not declare independence at the end of the month but rather imposed fiscal restraints on the transfer of money out of the region (except for oil revenues, which were paid directly to the federal government) and regionalized the state-owned industries in the region. Though this act was much less than secession, it caused Nigeria to lurch further toward the brink of civil war, and Ojukwu's actions arguably made the situation intractable.

Since the end of the war, many questions have arisen over the nature of the crisis and how both circumstances and personalities drove the country to the breaking point. Because of the nature of the rapid Nigerianization of the armed forces, many officers who inhabited high-ranking and key positions within the military were very young and inexperienced and, as a result, arguably more ambitious and less willing to compromise than a more senior officer would have been. Gowon, when appointed chief of army staff after the January coup, was thirty-one years old, making him one of the youngest men ever appointed to command a national military. His American counterpart, Harold Johnson, was fifty-one when appointed to his post, and Richard Hull, the chief of the defense staff of the British armed forces, was fifty-eight at his appointment. Even in similar postcolonial nations, a young officer assuming such a position was virtually unheard of. In Israel, Yitzhak Rabin was appointed chief of staff in 1964 at the age of forty-two. Even Joseph Ankrah, the Ghanaian leader who came to power in the wake of the coup against Nkrumah, was appointed to chief of staff at the age of fifty-two.

Similarly, Ojukwu was only a year older than Gowon while both Nzeogwu and Murtala Mohammed were twenty-nine when they led their respective coups. While age alone could not account for their failure to mitigate the crisis, "the failure to halt the Igbo killings across the country can be blamed on the very inexperienced government of Gowon, who, unexpectedly thrust into executive power, was momentarily confused as to what action to take." Likewise, Ojukwu's youth may have contributed, along with his upbringing and education, to his sense of self-importance as a shaper of Nigerian history, and his actions during the crisis came from "his moment and chance to make history and carve a country for himself."[102]

Though the leaders' youth undoubtedly contributed to the deepening of the crisis, the entire crisis could not simply be blamed on a group of headstrong young men whose egos made compromise impossible. Many interest groups, especially the ethnic minorities that had been previously excluded from access to power, attempted to use the situation to carve spaces for themselves within the country. These groups renewed the calls that they had previously voiced to the Willink Commission, claiming that the only way to ensure their security within the country was to have a political voice that did not depend on the largesse of the three dominant groups. As they worked largely behind the scenes, their demands for greater autonomy, along with Igbo security fears and the violence, contributed to dooming the ad hoc meeting.

Nigeria's geography also served as a major contributing factor. For the Yoruba in the west and the Hausa-Fulani in the north, the concessions to minority groups could not be viewed as an existential threat. Indeed, the Midwestern Region had been created out of the Yoruba-dominated Western Region with relatively little controversy. This was not the case for the Eastern Region. Though the Igbo were the largest group there, the Eastern Region was the most heterogeneous in the country. Complicating matters further, the bulk of the oil industry, though controlled by the Eastern Region, lay outside the Igbo heartland. As a result, minority loyalties played a key part, and Gowon did his best to woo them from supporting Ojukwu's region. Last, the massacres had left the Igbo feeling extremely vulnerable in Nigeria.

Adding to the fears, the Igbo heartland was surrounded on all sides by other ethnic groups. While the smaller groups, such as the Ijo and Ogoni in the Niger Delta and the Ibibio and Efik in the southeast, consistently lobbied for greater political power within Nigeria, Igbo fears were exasperated because any such gains would come at the expense of the Eastern Region, potentially cutting off Nigeria's borders from the Igbo. These fears gained additional credibility when Gowon responded to Ojukwu's actions in the wake of the March meeting in Benin. Because Ojukwu effectively commandeered the entire federal state apparatus in the Eastern Region, Gowon ceased all cooperation with the region. The federal government imposed stiff sanctions on the east, freezing all money transfers to the region and stopping the postal service. As in many former British colonies, the Nigerian postal service also served as one of the major banks in the country and was widely used to pay government salaries. As a result, most federal employees, including the non-Igbo, in the Eastern Region had their pay effectively frozen. Last, and perhaps most damaging, the Nigerian navy imposed a blockade on the region. Ostensibly, the blockade was intended to prevent illegal arms imports, but virtually all imports and exports were halted by the action, and Nigeria was brought even closer to the brink.

Because the two headstrong young officers seemed almost determined to push Nigeria into civil war, it fell to Awolowo, the recently freed elder statesman, to attempt to reconcile the east with the rest of the country. On May 1, 1967, he convened a convention of Western Region elites aimed at alleviating the tensions that the differing interpretations of the Aburi accord and Gowon's Decree 8 had created. However, the subsequent resolution that the Western Region adopted served only to increase the uncertainty regarding Nigeria's future. After stating unequivocally that the federal government do all in its power to ensure that the East remained within the federation "even if it means a constitutional arrangement that is looser than hitherto," the western chiefs decreed that if the east secedes, the west would declare that "the federation as we know it shall cease to exist and Western Nigeria shall automatically become independent and sovereign."[103]

This last line raised fears in the north about a possible southern alliance should another crisis pit the regions against each other. Indeed, fears of Ojukwu's secession were not the first time that such matters were voiced and even attempted. In February 1963, an Ijo police officer in the Niger Delta, Isaac Adaka Boro, citing grievances with both the federal government in Lagos and the Eastern Region, created an organization called Niger Delta Volunteer Force (NDVF). His short-lived rebellion was quashed after twelve days, and he and his cohort were jailed for treason. Gowon later granted them amnesty; Adaka Boro fought in the Nigerian 3rd Marine Commando Division and was killed in action on May 9, 1968, during the battle for Port Harcourt and its environs.[104]

However, this alliance would not occur, largely because of Ojukwu's insistence on proceeding alone and his manners toward the elder Awolowo. After the meeting of the Yoruba elites, Awolowo traveled to the east to meet with Ojukwu to foster reconciliation between the eastern leader and the federal government. Contemporary reports suggested that Ojukwu was unwilling to compromise, even with the relatively amicable Awolowo, who arrived with assurances that Gowon would ease the economic restrictions on the east. Despite these offers, Ojukwu had his reasons to be distrustful of Awolowo's move and was unwilling to negotiate on terms that he saw as unfavorable to the Igbo.[105]

However, many in the north grew even more wary of these overtures and attempted to back the federal government. Largely because northern officers now controlled government mechanisms in Lagos, northern elites argued for a stronger central government, ironically moving to implement in some form Ironsi's decree that had sparked the events that led to the July coup. In that spirit, the northern elites hoped to isolate the Igbo within the east and sway the smaller ethnic groups, who together comprised a third of the population and controlled both the oil-producing regions and the areas that surrounded Igbo territory, to withdraw their support from Ojukwu and the Eastern Region. In fact, northern emirs met on May 4 and supported the federal government, stating that "the North is irrevocably committed to the creation of more states whether or not they are created elsewhere as a basis of stability in the North."[106] Thus, the northern emirs were willing to create new states, essentially implementing the path that minority groups in the country had been agitating for since at least the Willink Commission. They hoped that if the minorities in the north received their autonomy, those in the east would be more loyal to Nigeria if they were removed from Igbo domination in the east, especially the people of the Niger Delta, where the memory of Adaka Boro's revolt symbolized their ambitions.[107]

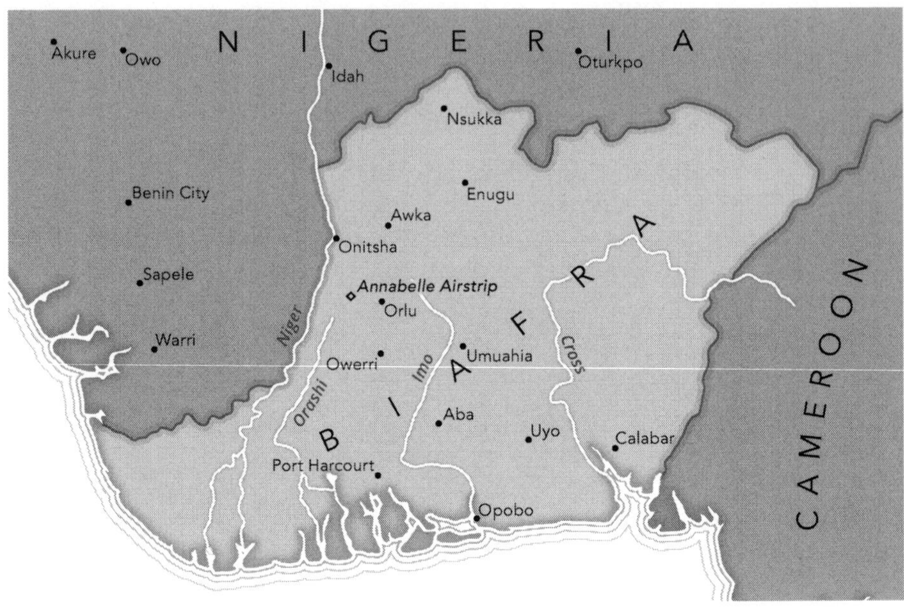

Map 2.1. Biafra at Independence

Once it became clear that Ojukwu would not agree to any compromise that did not involve implementing his interpretation of the Aburi accords, Gowon acted to create twelve states out of the four regions. On May 27, Gowon publicized his decree creating a new political landscape in the country. Most of the states were carved out of the Northern Region, which was separated into six states: Benue-Plateau, Kaduna, Kano, Kwara, and the Northeastern and Northwestern states. The Eastern Region became three states: East Central, Cross River, and Rivers. The Midwestern and Western regions remained largely intact, with the exception of the creation of Lagos State, which consisted of the federal capital and its environs out of the Western Region. With the creation of the twelve states, Gowon attempted to isolate the Igbo by giving the other ethnic groups what they wanted. Joe Achuzia, who would later head the Biafran militias, claimed that "this was a masterstroke by Gowon affecting the future course of the war, and it addressed two of his objectives, one that it would undermine the East's power base and two that it would help his administration's power by giving support to more minorities within the country."[108]

The move incensed Ojukwu, who, in anticipation, called for a meeting of his Advisory Committee of Chiefs and Elders in Enugu on May 26 to discuss their reactions in the wake of Gowon's creation of the new states. The next day, once the new states were officially announced, the assembly mandated Ojukwu "to declare, at the earliest practicable date, Eastern Nigeria a free sovereign and independent state by the name and title of the Republic of Biafra."[109] At 9:11 that night, Gowon declared a national state of emergency.[110] Three days later, on May 30, with the consent of the assembly, Ojukwu declared independence, thus finalizing Biafran secession.

Throughout the crisis, both the federal military government and the Eastern Region portrayed their moves as a way of protecting their people from domination from the other side. Though the dominant narrative was the conflict between the east and the north over control of the federal government, this tells only a portion of what led to the war. In reality, the postcolonial state's structure played an important factor in the road to civil war. Because the Igbo and the Hausa-Fulani were so irrevocably at odds over their respective roles in the country's administration, smaller ethnic groups such as the Tiv, the Ijo, and others attempted to use the conflict to better position their respective voices within the country. From the ad hoc commission until Gowon's creation of the twelve states, smaller ethnic groups, vying for greater roles within the country, managed to maneuver their interests and, much like in the First Republic, caused the larger groups to court their support. As such, the ethnic groups altered the balance of power in the country, eventually pushing the eastern region toward secession.

With the creation of the new states, Gowon hoped that the minority ethnicities in the east would favor the federal government, especially the Ijo, Itsekiri, and Ogoni in the Niger Delta and the Ibibio and Efik near the Cameroonian border, and would thus destabilize Ojukwu's regime and force him to renounce his plans for independence. Ojukwu hoped for the opposite. He hoped to harness the fears that many in the Eastern Region harbored against the federal government, now firmly in northern control. Though the Igbo had borne the brunt of the assaults during the preceding year, all of the ethnic groups from the Eastern Region had been targeted to varying degrees in the attacks that swept the country. To the minority elements in the Eastern Region, Ojukwu and most Igbo, however, did little to transcend the ethnic barriers. The strong allegation was that apart from some lip service, the regional government allowed some of the most egregious elements within the Igbo nationalist sphere to take liberties and at times brutalize the non-Igbo populations within the newly founded Biafra. Thus, from the very first day of the creation of Biafra, it had acquired its own minority problems that allowed the Gowon government to create states that undermined the seceding republic. The question of whether Biafra was an Igbo project or one that could address the problems of ethnicity that had plagued Nigeria since independence was of utmost importance as to whether Biafra would survive as a nation.

THREE

THE WAR BEGINS

BIAFRA'S DECLARATION OF INDEPENDENCE DID not signal the immediate beginning of military hostilities. Instead, both the Biafran and Nigerian sides evaluated how best to pursue the upcoming conflict. The Nigerian government, dedicated to maintaining the country's unity, vowed to squash what they called the rebellion and bring Ojukwu and his "criminal gang" to justice. On the other side, prominent easterners, mainly Igbo, flocked to the Biafran cause. Chinua Achebe became one of Biafra's staunchest supporters and activists and played an important part in the country's public media campaign around the world. He was never officially part of the Biafran government's Propaganda Directorate, but like many Igbo, he felt that they had no future in a united Nigeria. Even Nigeria's first president, Nnamdi Azikiwe, declared his allegiance to Biafra. Unlike Achebe, Zik became an integral part of the Biafran government and acted as advisor to Ojukwu and even penned the Biafran national anthem, adapting the music from Jan Sibelius's *Finlandia*. Around the world, prominent easterners pledged themselves to Biafra. Dick Tiger, the former middleweight and erstwhile light heavyweight boxing champion, shifted his allegiance to Biafra and directed his promoters at Madison Square Garden to play only the Biafran anthem at the beginning of his fights. He also donated the bulk of his fortune to supporting Biafra's war effort and was given an honorary commission in the Biafran army.[1]

Despite Biafra's resolve to follow through with secession, the reality was that the country was ill prepared to fend off any Nigerian attempt to reunify the country. Because of the haphazard nature of the clandestine arms procurement before the declaration of independence, the Biafran military was severely lacking in even the most basic of military equipment. However, most Igbo officers, who comprised the bulk of the senior and middle ranks in the Nigerian army, defected to the Biafran armed forces, making it awash with skilled personnel, many of whom had suffered the reprisals of September 1966 and were thus motivated to secure a future for themselves and the Igbo. Most importantly, the Biafrans could ill afford a prolonged war; however, like most secessionist groups they had the advantage that they did not need to defeat Nigeria but rather simply not lose the war. For the Biafrans, a military stalemate would be as good as a victory because it would preserve the integrity of the fledgling country. On the other hand, the longer the war lasted, the less likely it became that a stalemate could be achieved.

The Nigerian army was little more prepared than the Biafrans for a prolonged war and envisioned any conflict between the two sides to be short and relatively bloodless. After the events of July 1966 that killed many and drove the rest of the eastern officers out of the army ranks, the Nigerian army numbered roughly seven thousand men. This, for a country with a slightly larger land area than France and Germany combined and an estimated population of fifty-two million, was rather small.[2] However, global political and economic realities would force both sides into a shooting war much quicker than either side was militarily ready.

At first, Gowon thought the economic sanctions that the federal government imposed on the Eastern Region would force the Biafrans to renounce secession. However, the increased tension crippled the fledgling oil industry, which had become one of the most important sources of government revenue and the largest growth industry in the country. The main problem lay with the fact that the bulk of the oil reserves lay in the east, in what was now Biafra, a fact that complicated which side would collect the royalty payments from the multinational corporations drilling for oil in the region.

Though commercial exploitation of petroleum resources began in 1958 with the discovery of commercially viable deposits at Oloibiri, a small community about one hundred kilometers west of Port Harcourt, near the town of Brass, global commercial interests had been searching for oil in the region for the better part of the twentieth century. A British firm, the Nigeria Bitumen Corporation, discovered an oil deposit in November 1908 at Lekki Lagoon in the first attempt to find oil in the country. However, technical difficulties made commercial development of the site impossible, as the engineers could not effectively cap the well, leading to the first documented oil spill in the country. Early oil prospectors in the region were small scale and, as such, "lacked the financial and technological resources to explore for oil successfully in the challenging Nigerian environment."[3]

The second stage of exploration began after the First World War, when several large oil companies began to prospect for petroleum in the Niger Delta region. By the 1940s, several multinational oil companies had begun exploration in the southeast of the country. The D'Arcy Exploration Corporation, a subsidiary of the Anglo-Persian Oil Company (which would become British Petroleum [BP] in

1954), which had some small-scale interests in the country dating to 1918, joined with Royal Dutch/Shell to form Shell/D'Arcy (later Shell/BP) in the mid-1930s, most likely to circumvent the laws governing foreign ventures in British colonies.[4]

Though Shell/D'Arcy initially obtained an exclusive charter to explore for oil in the region, by 1940 the company had abandoned its operations in Nigeria because of the disruptions caused by the Second World War. When they resumed operations in 1946, they were met with stiff opposition from the nascent nationalist parties that emerged, led by Azikiwe's NCNC, and, more potently, with editorial resistance from his newspaper, *The West African Pilot*. Due to Azikiwe's agitations and resulting protests, Nigerian labor unions were able to extract some concessions regarding the future of petroleum development in the country and the impact on local property rights. More importantly, Zik's activism and the colonial government's reactions emphasized how important the oil industry would be to Nigeria's future. The colonial government thus created a mechanism of revenue allocation for future oil profits. When the Oloibiri well began production in 1958, other companies, such as the Italian Azienda Generale Italiana Petroli (AGIP—a subsidiary of ENI) and the American firms Gulf Oil and Mobil, were granted concessions in the country.

The British, in an attempt to both maintain control of their investments in the country and create a stable source of revenue for the future independent Nigeria, promoted the new industry. For the British, securing a stable oil supplier was of utmost importance, especially in the wake of the disastrous Suez Crisis in 1956, which soured relations with the Arab world and severely affected the import of oil to Britain. As a result, oil in Nigeria became both an economic imperative for the newly independent state and strategically important in global geopolitics. However, at the time of independence, agriculture remained the most important export during the "Cocoa Boom." Cocoa was the dominant source of economic growth and accounted for more than half of the country's national output. Oil, on the other hand, accounted for only 7.6 percent of Nigeria's economy in 1960, rising to 11.1 percent by 1966.[5] Despite the dominance of the agricultural sector, few in Nigeria doubted that oil was key to the country's economic future. However, it was not until after the war that oil eclipsed agriculture as the largest sector of the economy.

Despite this, oil has been cited as a casus belli by some and by others as a major component of the war. While few would subscribe to British photojournalist Don McCullin's claim that Biafran secession was a "connivance by the Igbo tribe to break away and become independent because they were sitting on all the oil," there is little doubt that oil featured prominently in both sides' thinking about how to effectively prosecute the conflict.[6] More problematic were some attempts to untangle the oil industry's involvement in the war. Though production had not yet matured by the time Biafra declared secession, the oil companies had invested heavily in prospecting and infrastructure development, and they were beginning to extract profits from their investments. These profits also created revenue for the federal government, which had exclusive rights to collect rents and royalties from the companies and distribute the funds throughout the country. Thus, in March 1967, when Ojukwu uncoupled the Eastern Region's budget from that of the federal government, he also demanded that all such payments made to Lagos should now be paid directly to Enugu. Ojukwu's demand proved troubling for both the Nigerian government and for the oil companies, who could not afford to alienate the federal government yet could also not afford to lose their investments in the Eastern Region. The situation deteriorated once Biafran secession was realized in May as control over oil and revenue became the center of diplomatic activities.

For Biafra, oil was the key to its economic future, both in any viability as a state and in sustaining the revenue necessary to prosecute the war. At the war's outbreak, due in no small part to the federal economic embargo, Biafra had a very small currency reserve, equivalent to roughly NG£20 million. Compounding matters, because of Biafra's status as an unrecognized country, the government could not obtain credit normally available to nations to make purchases, for example of weapons. The result was that any arms purchases had to be made in cash, and, as Hank Wharton's attempt to smuggle arms in 1966 showed, these purchases were rife with incompetence, corruption, and theft.

As mentioned in the previous chapter, most of the oil in Biafra was in the Niger Delta and not in the Igbo heartland. As the Eastern Region marched toward secession, Ojukwu's tone became increasingly ethnocentric, alienating the non-Igbo populations in the east, many of whom, like the Ijo, Itsekiri, and Ogoni, inhabited the Niger Delta. Gowon's declaration of the twelve states effectively drove a wedge between some non-Igbo leaders and the Igbo-dominated government in Enugu. N. U. Akpan, the head of the Biafran Civil Service during the war, was one of the highest-ranking non-Igbo in the Biafran government. Yet even he was not immune to the sentiment that the crisis created in the east. As the country lurched toward secession, "The molestation of members of the minority groups increased. Non-Ibo-speaking people could not move freely, without insults and embarrassments, through the different checkpoints manned by civil defenders. My own family experienced serious difficulties when they were traveling home from Enugu to my village. If such was the experience of the family of the chief secretary to the government at the time, then the position of others can be imagined."[7]

Akpan did not blame official policy for this ill treatment. Rather, he cited the poorly trained and hastily assembled civil defense forces for abusing their limited authority to mistreat the minorities in the east. Ken Saro-Wiwa mockingly referred to these forces as "simple defense" because of their perceived low intelligence and inflated sense of power.[8] However, Ojukwu's own words did little to assuage minority fears before the war began. In a speech in the town of Uyo, some fifty kilometers east of Calabar and in the Ibibio heartland, he equated the relationship between the Ibibio and the Igbo to that of a husband and wife, imploring the Ibibio to behave as good wives to the Igbo.[9] Biafra's treatment of the minority groups, especially those in the Niger Delta, showcased one of the obstacles preventing unity—namely, that the territories the Igbo did not control were immeasurably important for the new country's viability, yet the inhabitants of said territories felt alienated from the project that was Biafra. Biafra needed the Niger Delta for oil and maritime ports and access to the Cross River region, which bordered Cameroon, but could not give the people who lived in those regions enough incentive to remain loyal to Enugu. It would be little surprise that once the hostilities began, these regions would be among the first to fall to the Nigerian offensive.

Before the shooting began in July 1967, all through June, both the Biafran and Nigerian governments attempted to persuade oil companies to pay them the royalties that were due in July. Because Shell/BP had the most developed infrastructure in the country, the company was in the most precarious position. Shell's Nigeria headquarters were located in Port Harcourt and Enugu, and the company employed over four hundred staff in both cities and had invested over GB£300 million in the country.[10] In late June, Ojukwu ordered all foreign oil companies to pay the royalties directly to the Biafran government and not to the Nigerian federal government in Lagos. Shell, having anticipated the crisis in May, sought legal counsel on how to deal with the conflicting payment demands. In a legal memo circulated in May, the company stated that the payments should go to the side that exercised "effective control" over the contested area, stating that the company "has no alternative but comply with such authorities' directions and requirements, irrespective of the status of international recognition afforded to such authorities by other countries."[11]

Some historians eager to find collusion between government and multinational corporations, such as Chibuike Uche, maintain that the oil industry, Shell/BP in particular, influenced the British government to adopt a position that favored Nigerian unity.[12] Uche's assertion, however, is based on a misreading of the evidence, especially considering that at this early stage in the conflict Shell's main objective was safeguarding their significant investment in the region, and as such they were willing to deal with both sides, despite attempts from both Nigeria and Biafra to coerce the firm into dealing exclusively with them. The day after Ojukwu demanded that all oil royalties should go to the Biafran government, Gowon threatened a blockade against any company that paid royalties to Biafra. On June 29, Enahoro met with the oil company executives and implored them to continue to abide by their agreement with Nigeria. He even went so far as to threaten the oil companies that should they attempt to placate both sides and pay a double royalty payment, the federal government would insist on the "higher payments to one governmental authority once the dispute is settled."[13]

At first Shell attempted to placate Biafra by proposing a GB£250,000 payment, which they justified because the Biafrans held effective control over the oil fields. However, Biafra did not control the means to export the crude oil. Shell was unable to complete the payment for several reasons, both political and technical. Shell angered Biafra by asserting that the demand for payment came directly from Ojukwu and that the company was providing the payment under duress, implying it was a type of extortion rather than any kind of de facto recognition of Biafra. Further, because Biafra was not a recognized country or political entity, no bank would accept a deposit without Nigeria's permission, which it clearly would not allow.[14] Shell also attempted to place the funds in a Swiss account but could not do so because the laws governing foreign exchange transfers required the British government's approval, and they refused the transfer.[15] Compounding matters, Nigeria imposed its naval blockade and on July 3 seized a Panamanian freighter after the Nigerian navy alleged it was leaving the oil depot of Bonny.[16] With this action, Nigeria effectively displayed that the Biafrans, though in control of the oil fields, could not ensure export and, as such, could not exercise "effective control."

Because the political and diplomatic situation in the first month of secession was so tense, Shell did not make the payment, despite the fact that their concern for their investments and personnel in Biafra were paramount to the offer. However, despite assertions that the oil companies "played a much more important role in the determination of the British attitude to the war than is usually conceded,"[17] the opposite is a more accurate assessment of the situation. Shell was more than willing to comply, at least partially, with Biafran demands if it meant securing their assets in Biafra. However, in subtle ways, such as stopping the foreign transfer to the Swiss escrow account, the British government was able to halt any type of assistance to Biafra. With this action, the British government hoped, in the words of David Hunt, the British high commissioner, that Shell would "clamber hastily back on the Lagos side of the fence with cheque book at the ready."[18]

Loss of the oil revenue was not Biafra's only initial setback. On June 20, Cameroon closed its border with the secessionist state, effectively severing Biafra's only land border to a country other than Nigeria. Ostensibly, the Cameroonian government's action came about for two reasons. Their border could have been used as a major smuggling route into Biafra, as evidenced by Wharton's crash in October 1966. As a result, closing the border made it clear that the Cameroonian authorities would not tolerate clandestine arms smuggling, which would destabilize Western Cameroon, with its significant Igbo population. Additionally, Nigeria had intervened in Cameroon during the Bamileke Rebellion, with Ojukwu himself playing a small but significant role in ending it.[19] Cameroon's policy, which ensured that the war would not spill over into the country, coupled with the Nigerian naval blockade made any import of goods, including war materials, increasingly difficult. As a result, especially in the early stages of the war, Biafran soldiers were ill equipped and poorly trained with wooden replicas of rifles because there were not enough guns to fully equip all the fighting soldiers and trainees.

Despite some small-scale skirmishes, the first large-scale Nigerian invasion started on July 7, only a week after the oil royalties were due.[20] Though the agreements the country signed with the various companies allowed for a grace period before paying the fees, the first Nigerian offensive was timed to remove any doubt regarding Biafra's inability to control their territory and lay to rest any attempts to extract petroleum royalties. The early battles, those over the towns of Nsukka in the north, Ogoja near the Cameroonian border, and Bonny in the Niger Delta, epitomized the early phase of the war. Biafran soldiers, determined yet woefully underequipped, faced a Nigerian army comprising largely ill trained but better equipped green recruits.

When the Nigerians announced their invasion, they touted it as a forty-eight-hour "police operation" to apprehend the "criminal gang" in charge in Enugu. Nigeria's main problem in the war's early stages was that they had only one even partially battle-ready division, the 1st Division, which was formed out of the 1st Area Command, based in Kaduna. The division commander, Mohammed Shuwa, was perhaps the least flamboyant and most professional of all the Nigerian commanders in the war. Shuwa had joined the Nigerian military in 1958 and completed his training at Sandhurst in July 1961. A cautious officer, Shuwa was initially in charge of the notorious 5th Battalion in Kano, whose exploits came after he was unceremoniously removed from his position, ostensibly because during the July countercoup, Shuwa and his deputy, James Oluleye, ordered the battalion's armory to be locked and the key placed in the commander's safe. Unlike some of the other commanders, Shuwa was a meticulous planner who rarely gave in to impulsive gestures and placed his men's safety as one of the top priorities in his operational planning. This made many of his advances very deliberate, and he was at times criticized for not acting quickly and not placing victory in the war as his main objective. As we will see, his cautiousness was instrumental at times in ensuring the Biafrans would not be able to capitalize on their successes in other theaters of the war, especially during several impetuous moments where the other divisions seemed on the verge of collapse.

Because of the shortage in manpower and materiel at the beginning of the war, the 1st Division consisted of only one operational brigade, the 1st Brigade. In the weeks leading up to the war, the Nigerian army ramped up its recruitment and training. As a result, the brigade was able to field three operational infantry battalions: the 4th, 21st, and 22nd Battalions. Supporting the battalions were a field artillery battery as well as an engineering squadron and a mechanized reconnaissance (recce) squadron. More-seasoned soldiers were split up among the new recruits across the battalions. Some of these older soldiers had seen combat in the Congo, and others had been deployed to the India-Pakistan border as peacekeepers. However, at best, only a third of the solders in the brigade had seen any operational duty at all, and even fewer had been in combat.

The first Nigerian objective was the conquest of the university town of Nsukka, as it was just north of Enugu near the Biafran northern border and a natural point on the way to arrest the Biafran leadership. While the 4th and 21st Battalions reached their objectives at Obollo Afor and Enugu Ezike on the northern outskirts of Nsukka with little resistance, the 22nd Battalion under the leadership of Capt. Isa Bukar met stiff resistance when attempting to capture the town of Ibegwa-Ani on the western fringes of the city. After three days of fighting, the Biafrans retreated to regroup, allowing the 22nd Battalion to enter the city on July 9.

Exercising caution, Shuwa ordered the battalions to coordinate the second phase of the assault and reinforced each of the battalions with armored Ferrets and land rovers. They waited a week to continue their advance on Nsukka, which gave the Biafrans time to assess their situation. The Biafran defense of the city was organized by Nzeogwu, who was released from prison by Ojukwu along with the other plotters of the January coup. He made the city's capture extremely difficult. On the morning of July 14, as the 22nd Battalion was preparing for their push, their headquarters came under an intense bombardment. Bukar described the mortar attack:

> All of a sudden two shells dropped near the battalion H.Q. The last I remember was that my hand was in the air trying to order the men to take cover. I was later woken up confused and frightened by the noise of another shell. I rolled myself into a ditch without rifle and jungle hat. I felt a sharp pain in my back which gradually increased as more blood rushed out and . . . [I] became numb in the legs and waist. About 20 feet away, was what used to be my runner—dead with two other soldiers. At about 1830 hours, shelling ceased.[21]

Bukar was taken to the hospital in Kaduna, where he recovered from his wounds. His second in command, Capt. (later Gen.) Abdullahi Shelleng took over command. During the battle, a green soldier in the 22nd Battalion panicked when confronted with the Biafran defense for the first time. The man, a Ferret gunner, opened fire indiscriminately, killing eleven of his comrades and wounding a further seven. He was quickly arrested and shipped to the forward headquarters for court-martial.[22]

Though the Nigerian forces entered the city by nightfall of July 14, the first day of their assault on the city, they did not fully secure it until two weeks later. One of Nigeria's most renowned poets, Christopher Okigbo, a close friend of

Chinua Achebe, joined the Biafran army and, despite lacking any military training whatsoever, attained the rank of major and took command of a squad of Biafran soldiers to defend the city. Okigbo boasted about how he destroyed an armored car with a shoulder-fired rocket, telling his audience on one of his furloughs from the fighting, "Look, when you fire those things, you've got to stand very firm, or otherwise you go with the rocket!"[23] A few days after Okigbo's comment, Achebe was driving from Enugu to his village in Ogidi when the radio reported that his friend had been killed in the defense of Nsukka. Only days earlier, he had learned that Nzeogwu had also been killed. The latter was leading a reconnaissance squad in Nsukka on July 26 when he encountered a roadblock, which opened fire, wounding the major. According to Shelleng, Nzeogwu "fell on the ground and then started shouting, 'Please don't kill me, I am Chukwuma Kaduna Nzeogwu, I know you are looking for me, please don't kill me.'"[24] However, Nzeogwu died of his wounds before Shelleng arrived on the scene. By the time Shelleng arrived, Nzeogwu's body had already been mutilated and his eyes plucked out. His body was flown to Kaduna, where Gowon ordered the major buried with full military honors.

Unlike other military leaders, Bukar praised the Biafran fighters, both trained and untrained. Nzeogwu was one of the best military minds in the country, and he organized the defense of the city in a remarkable fashion, considering the lack of arms and ammunition. What the Biafrans lacked in arms, they more than made up for with ingenuity. The Biafran air force consisted of a pair of B-26 Marauders—medium-range World War II–era bombers, slightly smaller than the iconic B-17—that were clandestinely bought from the French with the help of a former German SS officer, along with six Alouette helicopters and several cargo planes: two DC-3s, a DC-7, and a Super Constellation.[25] These planes became the backbone of the early Biafran air force, and the entire air force was led by a Polish mercenary named Jan Zumbach, who previously had flown for the Katangan air force during the Congo Crisis.[26]

Zumbach was one of many foreign fighters who served in the civil war on both sides. On the Nigerian side, most of the foreigners served as pilots, mainly from East Germany, Egypt, and, after the summer of 1968, Czechoslovakia.[27] During the war, the Nigerian air force received several Russian fighter jets, but the Soviet Union would not allow Western pilots to fly them. The Biafran military made more extensive use of foreign soldiers, with men like the ex–French Foreign Legionnaire Rolf Steiner, South African Hugh "Taffy" Williams, and Dutch mercenary Marc Goosens commanding Biafran infantry in battle.

In addition, the new Biafran air force's armament was largely improvised. In one instance, the Biafrans fitted a tripod-mounted machine gun to the nose of one of the B-26s that had been retrofitted for meteorological duty after the war, and the nosecone window had been replaced with a metal nose to house the weather instruments. Lacking internal radios for the crew or any electric method for firing the machine gun automatically, a gunner was stationed in the nose with a rope attached to his arm. As the gunner could not see his targets, one tug on the rope signaled the gunner to begin firing, and two tugs meant cease fire. Similarly, the Biafrans lacked bombs to drop on their enemies. Reportedly, a former fireworks manufacturer named Willy Achukwe fashioned improvised bombs, called Willy Bombs in his honor. Zumbach described the ingenious construction as "a base containing phosphorus suspended in an insulating liquid. A Bickford fuse ran from this compartment through a partition plugged with wax, into a second stage. This compartment contained gunpowder. The third was crammed with scrap metal. Two big nails protruded from the base of the thing. The impact of landing drives the nails into the base of the bomb and pierces the first compartment. The insulating liquid runs out of the resulting punctures and the air gets in. It sets the phosphorus alight, the heat melts the wax and the Bickford fuse detonates the gunpowder."[28] Because these improvised bombs could not be fitted to the B-26, they were simply thrown out of the open bay doors by soldiers strapped to the plane's fuselage.[29]

It was not only in the air that Biafran engineers created fearsome weapons and other innovations to make up for the lack of imports. Many of the Biafran antipersonnel devices had colorful names, like the Biafran Beer for a makeshift hand grenade consisting of a glass bottle filled with explosives, gunpowder, shrapnel, and chemicals. When agitated and thrown, it would cause a chemical reaction that ignited the explosives and gunpowder, creating "a beer to be thrown to the enemy to drink and die."[30] Several other weapons, such as the Footcutter and Ojukwu's Bucket, were improvised devices with remote wired detonators that resembled claymore mines in their operation and effectiveness. In fact, practically every aspect of life in Biafra was subject to some local improvisation, especially as the war dragged on and Biafrans needed fuel for their vehicles, food to eat, clothing, shelter, and even alcoholic drinks.

The Biafran defenders could not hold the city of Nsukka and instead withdrew to the outskirts, where they harassed their enemies with artillery, mortars, and air support from the B-26 and Alouette helicopters. Alexander Madiebo, the Biafran military commander, realized very early in the battle that "the first days of fighting had shown quite clearly that we would get into serious trouble soon, unless the Nigerians stopped their attacks or a miracle happened in our favor."[31] Madiebo organized the defense of the city with the help of Nzeogwu and Gbulie. On July 19, they staged a successful counterattack in Obollo Afor, which is perhaps how the rumors of Nzeogwu's death there originated. In a coordinated assault from the east, the 1st Battalion of the 51st Brigade dislodged the Nigerian forces in the market, suffering only minimal casualties. In fact, the highest casualty rate came

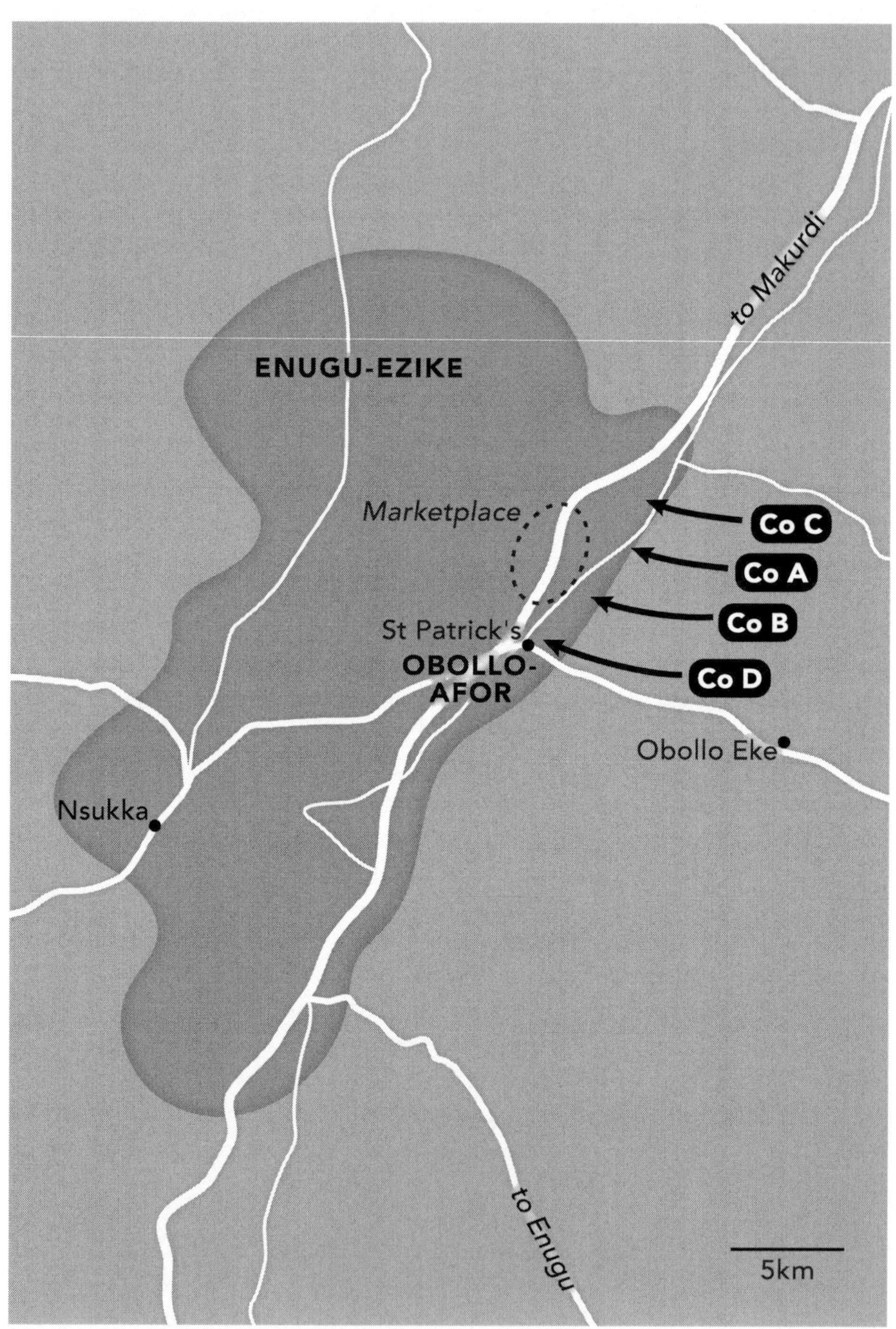

Map 3.1. Battle of Obollo Afor

in a friendly fire incident when the battalion's D Company, sent to clear a major intersection (near where St. Patrick's Catholic Church stands today) in a flanking maneuver, was mistaken for Nigerian reinforcements. That the Biafrans were able to achieve this victory was underscored by how pitifully they were equipped to conduct an assault. The brigade, under Madiebo's personal command, lacked the most basic military equipment, including ammunition pouches. As a result, when a soldier ran out of bullets, he had to rush back to the forward headquarters for resupply and then run back to the front fully loaded with his fresh supply.

However, on July 30 the miracle Madiebo had hoped for finally occurred. After the defeat at Obollo Afor, the Nigerians regrouped for an assault on Madiebo's headquarters in Obollo Eke, a further twenty kilometers east of Nsukka. Sending untested new troops, Shuwa hoped to rout Madiebo's headquarters. In the early morning of July 30, the federal artillery commenced a bombardment so heavy that "movement within the battalion area was virtually impossible for the first thirty minutes."[32] The area commander, Patrick Amadi, ordered his two Finnish-made Tampella mortars to fire their last ten remaining rounds in the area that Amadi thought was the logical point for the Nigerians to mass their troops for the infantry assault. Shortly after the mortars returned fire, the Nigerian bombardment ceased. Amadi prepared his men for the infantry assault, but it never came. The Nigerians had apparently been told that the Biafran troops in Obollo Eke lacked any kind of heavy support or even rifles. When the ten mortar shells fell on them, they panicked and ran, leaving behind most of their equipment, which the Biafrans desperately needed to resupply their own diminished stores.[33]

Though the Biafrans lost Nsukka, they were quickly able to adapt and stabilize the northern front in the Igbo heartland. Even more so, they realized that the Nigerian soldiers were poorly trained and, unlike the Igbo soldiers defending Biafra, had little will to fight or die for their country. To press their advantage, the Biafrans launched a series of air raids on Nigerian cities including Kaduna, Kano, and the capital, Lagos. Though the raids caused little real damage, the Kaduna raid killed a West German officer who was training the Nigerian air force to fly recently purchased Dornier Do-27s and Do-28s.[34] More importantly, the raids sowed panic across Nigeria and called into question Nigeria's ability to win a war they had initially touted as nothing more than a forty-eight-hour police operation.

The relative success in defending Enugu masked a fatal flaw in Biafra's ability to wage war. In the first days of the war, they were unable to depend on Efik or Ibibio support, and as a result the areas in the far east surrounding the town of Ogoja quickly fell to the Nigerians. At the same time that the assault on Nsukka began, the Nigerians launched an assault on Ogoja, roughly one hundred kilometers from Abakaliki. The entire area was secured within forty-eight hours, allowing Shuwa to redeploy his troops from the area to support the assault on Nsukka, which had unexpectedly emerged as a difficult front in the war. One non-Igbo Biafran soldier from the region described how he attempted to persuade his illiterate mother to support Biafra. When Biafra declared independence, he

> switched off the radio set and went to the kitchen to tell my illiterate mother that she is no more a Nigerian but a Biafran. When the old woman heard of this she looked at me with uncomprehending eyes and said "what do you mean, my son?" To answer her question I had to tell her the whole story in our language. She sighed and said "do you mean that another war like the one the Hausas and Ibos were fighting will be fought here amongst us?" I simply said "I don't know, mama." Well, poor woman, to her, like most peasants in the Eastern minority areas, what they abhorred most was a Hausa-Ibo war being fought on their land. Otherwise being Nigerians and Biafrans made no difference.[35]

Similarly, Ken Saro-Wiwa echoed the sentiments of many minorities who did not share the same enthusiasm for independence from Nigeria that infected the Igbo. In his 1989 memoir, he noted that he had always wished for a country

> where all groups would be fairly treated, where all groups had self-determination. Biafra was not the country, for even in the very process of initiating secession when conciliation and fair mindedness should have been the beacons, Ojukwu, the would be leader of the nation, was already quibbling and using the same tactics which past leaders had employed in subjugating the minorities. On the other hand, Nigeria of the twelve states offered a glimmer of hope and I clung to that hope. I must also add that I found Ojukwu even at that time, unattractive. I was impressed by the schools he had attended, but there was something about him, an indefinable quality which made me think him not to be genuine.[36]

Saro-Wiwa developed his animosity toward Biafra and Ojukwu and would later blame the war entirely on the Biafran leader, "whose masturbatory egoism, intransigence and political illiteracy was to wreak so much horror on the peoples of Eastern Nigeria."[37] Though some minorities did join Biafra while others supported Nigeria, the vast majority simply wished to avoid the violence and joined whichever side promised the best chance of a return to normalcy. As outlined in the previous chapter, Igbo attitudes and treatment of non-Igbo minorities did not help their cause in persuading the smaller ethnic groups to join them, though they did make some overtures, even if they were only lip service. The Biafran news magazine *The Spectator* published an editorial in its August 1967 issue imploring all ethnic groups to join together and said that "personal and sectional considerations must give way to a common front, in defence of right, of freedom and justice; in defence of Biafra."[38]

In the far south, the Biafrans faced a very different situation. Once again, the Biafrans had to depend on the support of several minority groups, such as the Ijo, Itsekiri, and Ogoni, and had to fight a naval war, which posed a very different set of challenges to the secessionist forces. If the Biafrans had trouble arming and equipping their army, the challenges of maintaining a navy were almost insurmountable. At the beginning of the war, the Biafrans were able to take control of one of Nigeria's main warships. On May 30, the NNS *Ibadan*, anchored in Calabar, was ordered to return to Lagos. The ship's commander, P. J. Odu, refused the order, and the ship was quickly rechristened the BNS *Ibadan*; however, H. B. Momoh, who authored the Nigerian military's official operational history of the war, claimed that the ship was stolen by another Igbo officer, Lt. Ubitu Ukiwe.[39]

Because of the regionalization of the military in the wake of the July 1966 coup, the majority of the ship's crew was either Igbo or of other eastern ethnicities. However, unlike ground forces, the navy required a level of specialization within the crews that made total regionalization practically impossible. Odu allowed those officers and crew who wished to return to Lagos to do so, and several of his men accepted the offer. Odu was dismayed that his first lieutenant, O. P. Fingesi, left for Lagos despite being an easterner from Okrika, a small, mainly Ijo island community on the southern outskirts of Port Harcourt.[40] Fingesi's move to join the Nigerian navy underscored some of the fissures between the Igbo and the other ethnic groups in Biafra, which manifested early during the war, resulting in significant losses in the non-Igbo areas and the development of the characterization the minority groups who did not commit to Biafra as saboteurs and traitors. Odu also claimed that the Nigerian navy allowed any Igbo officers to quietly leave and return to the east, and many did so, including Wilfred Anuku, who became commander of the Biafran navy. Momoh, however, claims that the Igbo officers fled the Nigerian navy after sabotaging their ships.

Like in the northern sector of the war, the southern sector lacked an effective fighting force in the early stages. On the Nigerian side, the entire south of the country had only one effective battalion, the 6th Battalion under the command of Lt. Col. Benjamin Adekunle. Unlike Shuwa, Adekunle, who was nicknamed the Black Scorpion, seemed to relish creating a persona of ruthlessness. The son of a Yoruba father and a Bwatiye mother, Adekunle had joined the Nigerian military in 1958. Like many of his contemporaries, he went to the officer training school in Sandhurst before serving in the Congo in 1960. In 1964, he was sent to the Defence Services Staff College in Wellington, India, before assuming a company command post in Enugu. When the military was regionalized, he was posted to Lagos and named head of the 6th Battalion.[41]

In the weeks before the fighting began, the 6th Battalion was enlarged into a brigade, and the 7th and 8th Battalions were created. Adekunle was named brigade commander, and Maj. (later Lt. Gen.) Gibson Sanda Jalo was named the new commander of the 6th Battalion while Maj. A. Akubakar and Maj. Anthony Ochefu commanded the 7th and 8th, respectively.

Unlike the Northern sector, any military action would require unprecedented cooperation between the army and navy, a feat no African military had yet been able to accomplish on a large scale. After the early setbacks in the north, it became clear that the war would not simply be a short police action and that it would last longer than Gowon had hoped. Joseph Akahan, the newly appointed army chief of staff, began to plan coordinated amphibious landings to broaden the war in the south. The first location chosen was the oil depot town of Bonny. Located at the mouth of the largest tributary in the westernmost part of Niger Delta, Bonny controlled the waterway into Port Harcourt, Biafra's major port. Because the Nigerian navy possessed only a few warships, the blockade that had been in place since May was only partially effective. The town was also an important site as it housed several oil terminals including Shell/BP's export installations. For Gowon, taking Bonny would hopefully lay to rest any concerns regarding Biafra's ability to control the oil-producing regions and lay a legitimate claim to the royalties.[42] The political situation within Nigeria also complicated matters. When the fighting began, David Ejoor, the governor of the Midwestern State, initially refused to allow federal troops to start a second front. Not wanting to push Ejoor into supporting Biafra and threaten the Western Region (now a state under Gowon) to break from Nigeria, cementing the north-south divide, the decision was made to conduct an amphibious assault.[43]

Last, the Nigerians needed to take control of the minority areas as quickly as possible for several reasons. First, the Igbo heartland was surrounded by non-Igbo peoples, and to take control of the southern Ijo, Ibibio and other communities would increase the stranglehold on the Igbo, who were putting up a dogged resistance defending Enugu. Second, and equally important, these smaller ethnic groups could have been persuaded to accept Biafran sovereignty if the Nigerian government proved incapable of delivering the promised new states. As Jalo later reminisced, "you have to build the confidence of the minority in that place if they have to continue to go with you."[44]

Preparations for the assault were hampered by the fact that the navy had only one landing craft, the NNS *Lokoja*, which was in disrepair. Thus, most of the training for the assault was done inside a gymnasium in the Lagos neighborhood of Ikeja. Jega stated that the soldiers were ordered into the gymnasium and the gym's doors were opened and closed to simulate the landing craft.[45] Shortly before the assault, the *Lokoja* was repaired but could support only a single battalion. Two merchant ships, the *Herbert Macaulay* and *Bode Thomas* were commandeered for use as troop carriers before transferring the soldiers to the *Lokoja* for landing in waves. Compounding matters further, very few soldiers had ever been to sea before, and many suffered from seasickness, and few could swim. When the *Lokoja* was repaired, the army and navy conducted joint exercises in preparation for the assault at the beach in Tarkwa Bay, on the southern edge of the channel connecting Lagos Lagoon to the Atlantic Ocean. When Adekunle's brigade was enlarged into the 3rd Marine Commando Division, Tarkwa Bay transformed into the division's training center.

Because of the lack of credible military intelligence available to them, the Nigerian navy, in charge of finding the landing zone and identifying the defenders, did not know that the Biafrans had moved most of their forces north to defend the Enugu sector, leaving behind only a company to defend Bonny. The Biafrans assumed that because of the complexity of an amphibious assault, the Nigerians would be incapable of conducting such a maneuver with less than a month's preparation and with the limited equipment available. More concerning for the Nigerians was the location of the BNS *Ibadan* and the unknown number and dispositions of small gunships that the Biafrans possessed. These small vessels could harass the Nigerian flotilla and induce panic in the fresh recruits, who were far out of their element on the high seas before the landing.

When the Nigerian fleet departed for Bonny, it consisted of eleven ships. In addition to the *Lokoja, Herbert Macaulay,* and *Bode Thomas,* the fleet included the frigate NNS *Nigeria*; four SDBs (sister ships to the *Ibadan*), the NNS *Kaduna*, NNS *Sapele*, NNS *Benin*, and NNS *Bonny*; the survey ship NNS *Penelope*; the gunboat NNS *Ogoja*; and one more unnamed landing craft.[46] The flotilla set out from Lagos and rendezvoused at the Escravos river, a tributary of the Niger Delta on the far western side near Warri. The initial plan was to arrive at Bonny in time for a dawn raid on July 26, but because the slower ships could not exceed eight knots in the ocean, they arrived long after dawn, and the commanders decided to wait until that night to proceed with the amphibious assault.

Bonny Island's old city faced north toward a creek that housed the old port from the days when it was a slave trading port, and directly south of the old city was the sprawling Shell oil depot, which consisted of a terminal and several large storage containers. The decision was made to land on the city's beach, thus circumventing Shell's installation out of fear that it was mined or otherwise booby-trapped.[47] While the 6th Battalion was preparing to land that night, the weather suddenly brought a torrential downpour so heavy "that we could hardly see one ship from the other."[48] Adekunle quickly made the decision to use the rain as cover and proceed with the landing. The 6th Battalion under Jega's command landed on the beach and quickly overpowered the Biafran defenders. The navy had identified the city's post office as the Biafran command post, and after some support fire, the beach and main road behind it were quickly secured. In the meantime, the 7th and 8th Battalions quickly landed at the Shell installation, and the next day the 6th made a flanking maneuver to secure the installation from land. Initially, the navy's support bombardment mistook Jega's battalion for the enemy because the army and navy radio sets were not compatible. Jega quickly directed his battalion's fire in the same direction as the other Nigerian forces, and the naval officers realized their mistake. Despite this setback, only one man was killed in the initial assault, and seventeen were wounded, including Jega, who was wounded in the stomach.

Once the assault began, the Biafrans attempted to thwart it by bringing in the *Ibadan* and several small gunboats. However, the gunboats arrived only after the *Lokoja* had delivered the first wave to the shore, and they were quickly spotted by the Nigerian navy, who opened fire, sinking one of the gunboats and forcing the others to retreat. The *Ibadan* attempted to intervene but was also sunk after a short chase from the *Ogoja*.[49] Like in other minority areas, the local population, in this case the Ijo, largely welcomed the Nigerian troops. Jega stated that "the people were jubilating. In fact, I can recall one incident—there was one chief . . . he was saying 'What is it?' 'If na Gowon na him say he go save us' . . . when he started hearing the bombing."[50]

Thus, the end of the first full month of fighting showcased many of the issues that both sides would face throughout the war. The Nigerians found that they were facing a very determined enemy who was, despite their shortage in equipment, highly motivated to defend the Igbo heartland. The Biafrans discovered that their ability to defend the parts of Biafra that were not Igbo was extremely limited. However, the Biafrans also found an enemy that was not prepared to fight. Ojukwu decided to stake the war's future on that fact, and on the morning of August 6, 1967, he changed the nature of the war with a stunning invasion of Nigerian territory.

FOUR

THE MIDWEST OFFENSIVE AND THE TRANSFORMATION OF THE WAR

IN THE EARLY HOURS OF August 9, 1967, the war changed. Before dawn, a convoy of military vehicles, private cars, and trucks of virtually every type crossed the bridge linking Onitsha to Asaba across the River Niger after the roadblocks on both sides had been carefully dismantled. More troubling for Nigeria, the soldiers on the western side of the river that now constituted the border between Nigeria and Biafra appeared to have had advance notice of the impending invasion and had either fled their posts or actively collaborated with the invading Biafran forces.

Within a day, the entire Midwestern State came under Biafran control and was later proclaimed the independent Republic of Benin.[1] The move cemented the aura of "Biafran invincibility" that Ojukwu had cultivated since the beginning of the conflict, relying on the string of successes and a formidable public relations campaign that convinced Biafrans that the Nigerian military was no match for their superior military might. With the exception of the amphibious assault on Bonny, the Biafrans were indeed able to hold their ground against the invading Nigerian forces. Despite the loss of much of the far east and the city of Nsukka, the Nigerians were unable to quickly overrun the Biafran positions and put an end to secession, even with Gowon's confident assertions that the conflict would be a limited police action to arrest Ojukwu and his coconspirators.

In fact, if the first month of warfare proved anything, it was that the Igbo would put up a dogged defense of their heartland, but Biafra's hold on the country's non-Igbo areas was tenuous at best. The successes on the battlefield, especially as they came against an ill-trained and panic-prone enemy, led many in the Biafran administration to cultivate an aura of superiority. Ojukwu took special interest in creating the narrative of Biafrans as a modern nation-state trapped in a political union with a backward and superstitious Nigeria.[2] Nowhere was this clearer to him than in the military capabilities of both countries. Despite their advantages in numbers, equipment, and international legitimacy, the Nigerians simply were unprepared to fight the Biafrans. Ojukwu determined to use the early military successes to promote a narrative that despite inferior supplies, the Biafrans were superhuman soldiers who could withstand any onslaught.

The Biafran air force was the first place where Ojukwu sought to press his advantage. When Zumbach arrived in Port Harcourt with the B-26 he had smuggled into the country, he was appointed as a civilian advisor to create the new arm of the Biafran military. Very quickly, he helped train the crews of Biafra's new makeshift air force and led the bomber on several runs, including the assault on the airfield at Makurdi. His memory of the assault is incorrect, especially as he claimed the raid killed Joseph Akahan, the Nigerian chief of staff, when one of the makeshift bombs hit his helicopter.[3] In reality, Akahan died a year later in a helicopter crash. Despite this error, the raid was a great success and a significant morale booster for the Biafrans. When he returned to Port Harcourt, he was greeted with a hero's welcome but was quickly written out of the official narrative of the raid. By the following evening, he recalled, "Ojukwu rewrote the history of Makurdi raid almost immediately," leaving him out of the narrative entirely and helping to augment the growing mythology of the "invincible Biafra."[4] This myth would be put to the test when Ojukwu expanded the war, crossed the River Niger, and invaded the Midwestern State in what became known as the Midwest Offensive.

Leading the assault across the Niger was Col. Victor Banjo, a Yoruba officer who aligned himself with Ojukwu after being falsely imprisoned as a conspirator in the aftermath of the first coup.[5] One of the most experienced officers in the Nigerian military, Banjo had enlisted in the Nigerian army in 1953 and was one of the first Nigerian officers to be commissioned from within the ranks. When the war began, he was commissioned into the new Biafran army, even though his ethnicity raised questions about his allegiance to Biafra. Banjo was one of the few senior officers in Nigeria before the war, and his joining the Biafran side emphasized the familiarity that officers from both sides of the conflict had with each other.

In his memoir, Madiebo published a photograph of himself in training at Sandhurst with Gowon and Anwunah beside him on the obstacle course. These close ties meant that military intelligence at the onset of the war suffered from lax security and that information easily passed from one side to the other. Complicating matters further, Banjo was an electrician who served as the head of the Electrical and Mechanical Engineering Corps and was not a combat officer in any way. Banjo's elevation to command an assault force was further evidence that the 1966 coups, especially the July coup, had so sorely depleted the military's command structure on both sides that officers had to be moved to areas where they had little experience.

Ojukwu and Banjo also demanded complete secrecy over the operation's planning stages. Hilary Njoku, who was at the time Biafra's chief of staff, did not hear about the operation until after it started, and Madiebo, who was army chief, found out about it only when Banjo came to him asking for troops to reinforce the forces deploying for the mission in Onitsha. According to Madiebo, the offensive was designed to take control of all of Southern Nigeria and hopefully the capital in Lagos. Banjo was forming a brigade of three battalions to cross the Niger. Once across, the force would split into three formations. One would move north in an attempt to cut off the supply routes to the Nigerian forces entrenched in Nsukka and presumably preparing for a new assault on the Biafran capital in Enugu. A second small force would head to the Niger Delta and thwart any further amphibious landing in Warri or Ughelli and thus prevent a repeat of the assault on Bonny. The main force, which Banjo would personally command, would capture the city of Benin and then quickly continue west on two axes toward Ibadan and Lagos.[6] Madiebo admitted that he was very hopeful about the plan, but he later lamented that Banjo's operations "were clouded with unnecessary secrecy and mystery and invariably failed totally."[7] Similarly, Philip Efiong, at the time Madiebo's second in command, found out about the offensive only a day after Madiebo and only because a group of officers who were to participate in it asked to requisition ten jeeps for the cause. Once Efiong understood the plan, he immediately called Ojukwu and asked, "May I know why I was not informed about the operation, particularly because of the logistical requirements of such an operation?"[8] Unlike Madiebo, Efiong claimed that he immediately realized that the supply lines would be too long to sustain a push to Lagos and that the entire operation was doomed to fail from the start. Banjo assured him that the supply lines would be of little consequence because the surprise of the attack would force the Nigerians to the negotiating table before any supply issues arose.[9]

It was clear that the offensive would have to be quick so that the federal side would not have a chance to mount a defense in the west. Thus, when Banjo's 101st Brigade crossed the Niger, they met with no opposition, and by midmorning on August 9, the brigade reached Benin hardly firing a shot. The two auxiliary forces to the north and south also reached their objectives in a similarly quick and easy fashion. Rather than immediately continue on to Western Nigeria, Banjo remained in Benin for three days and even went on Benin Radio to address the city after its "liberation." His address, in which he claimed to be at the head of a "Liberation Army," was designed to ease the fears of the local population and stated in part:

> Some of you might have woken up to the sound of minor firing in the Capital city of Benin as well as in some other areas of Mid-Western Nigeria and thought it was in the process of being invaded by Northern troops. I am happy to reassure you that you have not been invaded by hostile troops. As some of you may have found out within the last 48 hours, the soldiers amongst you are disciplined troops of the Liberation Army from Biafra which I command. . . . This action is consistent with the desired intention of Biafra to assist in the liberation of the people of Nigeria from domination by the Fulani-Hausa feudal clique.
>
> It is my hope that by our presence, the people of the Midwest will, in complete freedom from any restraint either direct or implied, be able to seek their rejection of the fiction that peace in Nigeria is only possible under the conditions that the entire people of Nigeria should be dominated by the Fulani-Hausa feudal clique.[10]

Banjo's message was fraught with ambiguities. First and foremost, the cause of the Liberation Army was problematic at best. While Madiebo, Efiong, Ademoyega, and others who wrote about the war clearly viewed the offensive as a Biafran one, it seemed that Banjo had different ideas. Banjo's sister, Felicia Adetowun Ogunṣhẹyẹ, the first woman to become a professor in Nigeria, has claimed that Banjo was not part of the Biafran military structure per se, but he agreed to join Biafra with the understanding that Ojukwu would help him to liberate the rest of Southern Nigeria. Despite not being part of the January 1966 coup, Banjo harbored many of the same ideas that the conspirators held. Ademoyega, who accompanied Banjo on the Midwest Offensive as his second in command claimed that Banjo was a victim of the tension between the revolutionary cadre that perpetrated the first coup and still wished for revolutionary change in Nigeria as a whole and Ojukwu, whom Ademoyega claimed was a reactionary who preferred separation and a loose confederation if absolutely necessary.[11] Ojukwu, on the other hand, seemed to believe the Midwest Offensive was nothing more than a Biafran tactical move to force the Nigerians to negotiate a settlement. He believed that the Nigerians "did not have sufficient troops to be engaged on so many fronts at the same time."[12] Thus, from the beginning the offensive was mired in political wrangling that ultimately doomed it.

As a result, instead of capturing the objectives in the midwest and immediately continuing to Lagos and Ibadan, Banjo halted the offensive and ordered his troops to regroup. This order baffled Madiebo because Banjo had apparently emphasized the need for speed to prevent Lagos from reorganizing and mounting an effective defense. Madiebo blamed politics for the halt, claiming there was no military need to rest forces that had not engaged in meaningful combat.

He claimed that the battle over who would be appointed to lead the region, which was quickly declared the newly independent Republic of Benin, was the main source of the delay.[13] In the end, Albert Okonkwo, an Igbo medical doctor and major, became the governor while Banjo retained control of the military. At the same time, he reportedly telephoned the Western State's governor, Robert Adeyinka Adebayo, to inform him of the impending conquest. Banjo also used his new position to declare that he was "fighting for a Nigeria in which no people will be dominated by any other," claiming to be a loyal Nigerian rather than part of the separatist Biafran military.[14] As a result, Banjo did not continue the offensive until August 12, three days later, "during which he could have occupied Ibadan without firing a shot."[15]

Compounding the political pressures, as Efiong feared, Banjo's forces were ill equipped to complete the ambitious task assigned to them. Ademoyega surveyed the troops and found none of the battalions had any support weapons such as mortars or recoilless rifles, and of the three infantry battalions, the 11th, 12th and 19th, only the 12th had enough weapons for all its fighting men. The 19th could arm only one of its companies, and the 11th had only three machine guns and hardly any ammunition. At one point, Ademoyega appointed a new officer, Lt. Col. Henry Igboba, to the 19th Battalion; Igboba quickly returned to Benin, where Ademoyega was stationed, and claimed that the battalion "was simply a rabble."[16] It took Ademoyega almost a week to scrounge a single 81mm mortar and deliver it to the 12th Battalion to fully equip it so it could continue its advance to Ore. He was also able to find some rifles and distributed those to the other battalions.

Igboba quickly continued the offensive and, using his sole mortar, launched an offensive at a Nigerian position in Siluko, about halfway between Benin and Okitipupa. As with the military miracles mentioned in the previous chapter, it supposedly took only a single mortar round that landed in the middle of the Nigerian camp to induce a panic. The Nigerians fled to Ore, leaving most of their munitions and supplies, and told their company commander of the attack, convincing the entire company to abandon their position at Ore and fall back north to the city of Ondo. The Biafran plan was to continue to Ife and then head west to take Ibadan. However, because of the weeklong delay, the Nigerians had a chance to reinforce their military presence in the west and launched an effective counterattack that eventually pushed the Biafransback across the Niger.[17]

On the Nigerian side, the Midwest Offensive was especially chaotic, as the assault took almost everyone by surprise. One officer, Maj. (later Brig. Gen.) Godwin Alabi-Isama, arrived on the Nigerian side of the Niger in Asaba in late July, ostensibly to be close to his mother. From the beginning, Alabi-Isama claimed to have suspicions regarding the Igbo officers stationed in the midwest, primarily with Capt. Joseph Isichei, whom Alabi-Isama claimed would regularly travel to Enugu for reasons unknown. Further emphasizing the laxness of Biafran discipline, he claimed he had advance notice of the assault and that he was personally targeted for elimination during the raid when one of his lovers, who lived in Onitsha, was able to cross the Niger in a boat to warn him. In his account, his lady friend, whom he never named, claimed he was the sole obstacle that could lead to the failure of the Midwest Offensive. In a dramatic scene at the river, as she was returning to the boat to ferry her back across the Niger, she "turned back, held my hand, and dragged me to a corner and told me that I, Alabi-Isama, was their only problem. I was to be killed and not to be captured." She then ran to the boat, and the boatman took her to the other side of the river. Shortly thereafter, inexplicably, two other women appeared from Onitsha and told Alabi-Isama that the Biafrans were massing for their assault across the bridge.[18]

Alabi-Isama claimed that he single-handedly delayed the Biafrans in Asaba by stalling them there and thus not allowing them to reach what he claimed was their goal of arriving in Lagos the following morning by 6:00. His description of events during the initial invasion reads like the script of an action film, with him single-handedly evading capture while killing or defeating all the Biafran soldiers and their collaborators in the Nigerian military stationed in Asaba who dared confront him. At 10:00 p.m. on the night of the invasion, for some mysterious reason, despite his advance warning, he remained in his house when two Igbo soldiers knocked on his door and opened fire. From Alabi-Isama's writing, it is impossible to determine whether they were Biafran or Nigerian, as the Biafran invasion had not yet begun. Regardless, the heroic warrior, with a single grenade, killed his assailants and escaped to his car. Later that night, he decided to phone his mother, so he risked life and limb to go to the Posts and Telegraph (P&T) station, where he found Biafran soldiers cutting the lines. One of the soldiers decided to give chase, and Alabi-Isama once again dispatched his pursuer with a grenade. Satisfied with his victories, he recalled, "I had achieved my aim of not allowing the Biafrans to arrive at Benin City at midnight and so they could not arrive at Lagos by 6am."[19]

While the events that Alabi-Isama recalls in his work could well be an accurate depiction of what transpired on the night of August 8–9, 1967, his action-packed account elicits some skepticism. Like many memoirs written so long after the war, Alabi-Isama's has several problems that emblemize much of the recent writing on the conflict. Though memoirs written immediately after the war suffer from inconsistencies due to imperfect information and memories, those written decades later, like Alabi-Isama's as well as Obasanjo's and Saro-Wiwa's, suffer from inaccuracies due to faded memory and political expediency. Equally important, Alabi-Isama's memoir, like the memoirs of other actors such as Godwin Onyegbula, attempts at times to offer prophetic pronouncements usually tied to the author's spirituality and express beliefs in overt divine planning of the events as they occurred.[20] Patrick Anwunah's analysis contains similar tropes. In one instance, he questions Biafran capacities during the war, concluding bluntly in a lengthy passage on the war's conduct:

> At this point, all easterners (as well as all Nigerians) should be advised to continue to dispose their hearts to hear the word of God in order to be able to do good for themselves and for their fellow men. Had it not been for the saving grace of the Almighty God, it could not have been possible for two Biafran platoons to rout two enemy Nigerian battalions at the first battle of the civil war at Garkem, in spite of the fact that the Nigerian enemy was supported by three ferrets, one saladin armoured vehicle and a concentration of artillery. How was it that they shelled themselves, thereby creating confusion, in the mx-up of which, the Biafrans started running down south while the northerners started running up north? Who was in control? **It was not Ojukwu or Gowon or Madiebo, it was Almighty God.** He however used Ojukwu, Gowon and Madiebo to work out those miracles for us to see.[21]

Perhaps most importantly, most memoirs written so late contain overt political agendas, and the authors used their war experiences to position themselves for their future work in Nigeria. In addition to Saro-Wiwa, Obasanjo wrote *My Command* in 1981, perhaps to help in his transition from military ruler to civilian life. However, his transition turned to opposition when Muhammadu Buhari seized power in 1983, only to be overthrown by Babangida in 1985. Obasanjo opposed Buhari and his successors, Babangida and Abacha, and spent time in prison when Saro-Wiwa went to the gallows in 1995.

Gowon's response to the Biafran offensive, though hampered by the open collaborations and defections of his officers in the Midwestern State, was to broaden the scope of the war. He no longer considered the conflict a mere police action to contain and arrest Ojukwu and his cohort but declared the conflict a "total war" and began an unprecedented military buildup aimed at ending the offensive and laying the groundwork for what he hoped would be a victory against the secessionists. In an August 11, speech, Gowon declared "an all-out drive until the rebellion is completely stamped out," adding that "no mercy will be shown to the rebel clique and their collaborators anywhere"—a nod to the fact that portions of the Nigerian army and government had proved loyal to the Biafrans, especially in the early days of their assault across the Niger.[22]

Gowon ordered an expansion of the army, creating a new 2nd Division under the leadership of Murtala Mohammed to confront the Biafran invaders and stop them from reaching Lagos and Ibadan. Banjo's hesitation to press the assault gifted the Nigerian command in Ibadan precious time to reorganize their forces to meet the threat. However, creating a new division would take time, and with the Biafrans waiting only a week before renewing their assault, the Lagos Garrison created several new haphazard battalions in the hopes of defending the city against the pending Biafran assault. Thus, a new 7th Battalion was created from new recruits en route to join the Nigerian forces in Bonny who were augmented by members of the Lagos police force and a company from the 1st Division's 3rd Battalion, which suffered heavy losses at the battle of Obolo Afor. Additionally, the Western Region's governor, Adebayo, enlisted the help of the region's civil engineers to blow up the bridges at Ore, thus preventing the Biafrans from advancing.[23] Furthermore, the new 9th Battalion was ordered to defend the route to Lagos and Ibadan and met the Biafrans at Ore, where they halted the rebel advance on August 21, setting ablaze the only tank the Biafrans had available in the region.[24]

In the meantime, Mohammed was busy forming the new 2nd Division. The 6th Battalion, which had previously spearheaded the amphibious assault on Bonny, formed the core of the new division as the battalion had already relocated to Lagos in preparation for an assault on Calabar. Meanwhile, Mohammed, Obasanjo, and virtually every other senior officer in the city scrambled to requisition reconnaissance vehicles for the fighting units, trailers for use as mobile command headquarters, and virtually everything else the new division would require to repel the Biafran invasion. Thus, creating the new division that drove the Biafrans across the Niger took a significant amount of time, just as Banjo's properly equipping his own troops hindered him from pressing the advantage that the surprise Midwest Offensive afforded him.

In addition to creating a new division to defend the west, the northern and southern brigades also became divisions. The north, under Shuwa's command, officially became the 1st Division while Adekunle used his flair for the dramatic to create a new division. Not content with his command being named the 3rd Division, he named it the 3rd Marine Commando Division. Adekunle's forces landed in the Niger Delta, supported the successful capture of Bonny in July, dislodged the Biafrans from the main towns in the region, and by September 4 had reached as far inland as Urhonigbe, some thirty kilometers south of Agbor on the Asaba-Benin road, the Biafrans' main supply route. Meanwhile, the 2nd Division's 6th Brigade advanced from Okene just north of the Midwestern State into Igarra and then to Auchi before arriving in Benin from the west through Ehor. The 2nd Division's newly formed 7th Brigade advanced from Ore to Benin and then to Agbor, where all the forces linked up shortly after September 21 for the final push to Asaba. To slow the Nigerian advance, the Biafrans blew up every bridge as they retreated, the most important being at Abudu to the east of Agbor and the large bridge over the Niger. Thus, the Nigerian Midwest counterattack came from three sides, and in a series of very slow and deliberate movements, the

Nigerians effectively cut off the already stretched Biafran supply lines, thus eliminating the need for any large-scale battles to dislodge the invaders. Aside from the skirmishes in Abudu before the Biafran retreat, the only major battle of the Nigerian counteroffensive came in Benin City, when a Biafran column, unaware of the federal presence in the city, drove into the federal forces and was promptly destroyed. On the morning of September 20, just as the Nigerians were entering Benin, Okonkwo declared the Midwestern State the independent Republic of Benin. By the end of the day, the new republic had ceased to exist, by which time Okonkwo had already fled to Asaba.[25]

The rapidity of the Biafran assault on the midwest, coupled with its sudden and quick collapse and retreat, reinforced the Biafran aura of military superiority and at the same time hardened the suspicions of many in Biafra as to the loyalty of many of their citizens, especially the non-Igbo. Banjo's behavior in the field, especially his military hesitation and political pronouncements, reinforced the notion that saboteurs and infiltrators prevented a quick Biafran invasion of the west and the defeat of the federal government in Lagos. Madiebo claimed that the Nigerians infiltrated Biafran units and spread rumors questioning the officers' loyalties, and to support his claims he pointed to an incident where Col. Festus Akagha's entire command headquarters was destroyed, leaving the colonel stranded. According to Madiebo, "The ambush was organized and executed by our own forces acting under somebody's instructions."[26] Madiebo's claims that Nigerian infiltrators caused Biafran troops to disobey orders are somewhat suspect because later in the war claims of saboteurs, international conspiracies, and other acts of subversion became a key element in Biafra's propaganda campaign to galvanize and unite the Igbo once all that remained of Biafra was the Igbo heartland.

Talk of saboteurs also permeated the upper echelons of the Biafran military. Maj. Philip Alele, a civilian who became a political officer due to his uncanny ability to motivate flagging morale during the siege of Nsukka, was at the center of starting the idea of saboteurs. Madiebo credited Alele for creating the narrative of what the former termed "'sabotage' politics" when, during the siege, Alele broadcast a message on Radio Biafra that "there were top ranking saboteurs in Biafra."[27] For many in the Biafran leadership, the problem, which Anwunah termed "Saboteur Syndrome," added to Biafra's military woes. Most military leaders were at least as fearful of running afoul of political operatives in the Directorate of Military Intelligence as they were of the enemy. Anwunah recalled one instance where, fatigued from the defense of Enugu, he was granted leave, whereby he "took a quick decision and disappeared into Port Harcourt . . . without really telling anybody where I was." When Ojukwu sent word for him to return immediately, he was fearful of the worst, despite the fact that "I had not committed any act of sabotage or betrayal of the Biafran armed forces or people either openly or in secret."[28] Madiebo expressed similar fears during the defense of Enugu. When terrified civilians came to him with rumors or demands to understand the intricacies of the siege they were under, Madiebo "required a lot of patience . . . to listen to everyone religiously. What was more, I had to dispatch troops required for fighting to investigate each report to ensure I did not lose my own head for being a saboteur."[29]

Once the Midwest Offensive stalled and the Nigerian forces began to retake the Midwestern State, several top Biafran officers and civilian leaders allegedly hatched a plan to end the war. Major Ifeajuna, one of the January coup conspirators, along with Alele, attempted to recruit both Madiebo, who had replaced Njoku as head of the armed forces, and Anwunah to convince Ojukwu to step aside and allow others to negotiate a settlement with Nigeria that would, while renouncing secession, allow for some concessions. When asked if the group was plotting a coup, Ifeajuna replied that he had already been involved in one coup and was not ready to hatch another. However, due to the climate of fear that shrouded senior military officers, Madiebo must have been suspicious that it was Alele who approached him, perhaps in an effort to expose him as a saboteur. Details of what transpired and ended with Banjo, Alele, and Ifeajuna's trial and execution remained vague for decades after the war, until Nelson Ottah, a prominent Nigerian attorney, published an account of the events in 1981.[30] Since then, others, especially Banjo's sister Ogunsheye, helped shed some light and context on the first serious challenge to Ojukwu's grip on Biafra. Alele met with Banjo, Ifeajuna, and Samuel Agbom, a career diplomat who was the only civilian actively involved in the January 1966 coup. Together, they authored a memorandum imploring Ojukwu to look for avenues to achieve his goals other than secession. Because Banjo was close to Ojukwu and the most experienced military commander in the young Biafran army, he tasked himself with attempting to convince Ojukwu to either renounce secession or at least recognize the mistakes he had made early in the war. Banjo claimed he had previously garnered Ojukwu's trust, claiming "he [Ojukwu] told me that he needed me here [in Biafra] because he needed someone who could talk to him without ceremony, someone in a position to give blame to him for his mistakes."[31] Thus, when Banjo returned to Enugu on September 19, he thought his personal relationship with Ojukwu would make the latter open to accepting a strategic change.

However, Ojukwu used the confrontation to arrest the four as coup plotters and quickly tried and executed them. Ojukwu had seen Banjo as a friend and trusted military commander in the early days of the war. What's more, the early stages of the Midwest Offensive had given many in Biafra a strong sense of superiority and hope that they would soon emerge victorious from the war. When the assault stalled and later ended at Ore, most everyone in Biafran military circles understood that the assault had failed and that the west and midwest would not follow the Eastern Region into a revolt against the north. More damning for Banjo, his earlier remarks that he was not an integral part of the Biafran military but part of an associated "liberation army" made him an easy target when Ojukwu needed a scapegoat to blame for the failure of the offensive not as a tactical overreach but on account of saboteurs. Ironically, one of the victims, Alele, was the man who came up with the idea of blaming Biafra's failures on internal subversion.[32]

After his arrest, a quick trial took place on September 21, during which Banjo gave impassioned defenses of all his c-defendants, claiming all of them were innocent and all had previously enjoyed Ojukwu's full faith and trust. As such, they felt they could openly approach him with their concerns without needing to heed protocol in such a precarious time. They approached him with their concerns that they should explore alternate ways to press the limited advantages they enjoyed during the assault on the midwest, with Banjo claiming that "while we had control of the Midwest we had a good political bargaining power within the context of Nigeria" and encouraging Ojukwu to use that power to negotiate a settlement.[33] Failing that, "Ojukwu had to be told to step down on that day because we could not afford to waste the time of an impatient enemy anymore."[34] Having been found guilty the same day, Alele, Ifeajuna, Agbom, and Banjo were executed the next morning. Thus began a pattern that would last for most of the war, where Biafran military leaders were at least as afraid of being branded traitors, saboteurs, or deserters as they were of the enemy. Indeed, Philip Efiong became at times both executioner and fugitive under Ojukwu.

Though the Biafran expedition to the midwest aimed to exploit ethnic rifts and presumably to unite all Southern Nigeria against the north, the offensive largely had the opposite effect as it galvanized much of the Yoruba leadership to rally to the federal cause. Obafemi Awolowo, the Yoruba elder statesman, was among the first to cast his lot with the federal cause, urging the Yoruba to unite in their support of Gowon's federal government. However, not all Yoruba heeded Awolowo's call. Wole Soyinka, the acclaimed playwright and future Nobel Prize winner, traveled to Enugu to meet with Ojukwu during the offensive, prompting the Nigerian government to detain him on August 17, 1967, though they did not admit to his detention until nearly a month later, citing security reasons. Soyinka did not support Biafran secession but rather called on all sides to cease their fighting, saying that "there will be no victory for anyone in the present conflict, only a repetition of human material wastage and a superficial control that must one day blow up in our faces and blow the country to pieces."[35] Despite protests from activist and author groups around the world, Soyinka would remain imprisoned for most of the war. Gowon's government released him only in late October 1969, when Biafra's demise was all but complete.[36]

More sinister, the Biafran assault on the midwest unleashed more of the hatred against the Igbo that had been simmering since it erupted in violence less than a year previously. With the Nigerian advance came evidence of fresh massacres against the Igbo populations living on the western bank of the Niger. As the Nigerian forces moved into Benin, reports of looting and reprisal attacks against the Igbo emerged. Many of the reports that have surfaced in the years since the war ended are largely anecdotal and, like the numbers of the 1966 massacres, likely inflated. There can be little doubt that in some instances Nigerian soldiers committed atrocities and in others either could not or would not protect civilians despite pleas and orders from the ranking officers in charge of the Nigerian offensive. Samuel Ogbemudia, who became the governor of the Midwestern State upon its recapture by Nigeria, reportedly attempted to calm matters by warning soldiers and civilians alike that "anyone found looting will be severely dealt with. Unnecessary harassing of defenseless civilians should stop and no one should take the law into his hands."[37] Others claimed not only that the military rank and file perpetrated these massacres but that the military command organized them. Madiebo, in a passing comment, claimed that the 2nd Division was engaged in a wholesale slaughter of all the adult men in Asaba, giving Col. (later Gen.) Conrad Nwawo enough time to organize the defense of Onitsha, just across the Niger from Asaba.[38]

Fear gripped the Igbo communities between Agbor and Asaba as federal troops advanced. Many sent their leaders to meet the advancing troops. In some cases, such as in Issele Ukwu, roughly halfway between Agbor and Asaba, cordial and friendly relationships developed between the Nigerian forces and the Igbo communities. In fact, Issele Ukwu became a center for the federal troops, thanks in part to the work of Nwadie Martin, the first African to serve as an officer in the US military and reportedly the first Nigerian to graduate from an American university.[39] Other Igbo villages and towns did not fare as well. Almost directly on the other side of the Benin–Asaba road lay the town of Ogwashi Ukwu. There, an unnamed Nigerian commander accused the local *obi*, or village chief, of secretly supporting the Biafrans despite the obi's insistence that he supported a united Nigeria. Later that day, after a ceremony celebrating the Nigerian capture of the town, Biafran troops ambushed the Nigerians, killing the commander and igniting a manhunt that reportedly went door to door looking for the Biafrans. However, one Nigerian captain, Sunday Usunbor, maintained his soldiers' discipline, "preventing the ambush fallout from degenerating into a witch hunt."[40] Clearly, some Nigerian officers were able to prevent wholesale slaughter and avoid civilian casualties wherever they could.

By October 7, Nigerian soldiers entered Asaba, officially ending the Biafran offensive. The fighting in Asaba introduced one of the more colorful figures of the conflict, Joe Achuzia, who gained the nickname Hannibal during the waning days of the offensive. Achuzia usually seemed more interested in self-promotion than in fighting and winning the war. Madiebo claimed that Achuzia appeared from nowhere, "said to be wearing the rank of Lieutenant Colonel," and took advantage of the confusion in the Biafran command structure to take over the defense of the city.[41] As the Nigerians closed in on the city, the Biafrans began to suffer from a lack of ammunition and other supplies, including water. Achuzia recalled in his memoir that "the number of casualties had increased terribly and that something must be done to obtain vehicles." However, "every vehicle that I saw was loaded with people and household properties, each heading towards the bridgehead [between Asaba and Onitsha]."[42] That night Achuzia, with the rest of the Biafran forces, crossed the Niger bridge into Onitsha and the next morning detonated the charges that had been readied under the bridge's support pillars, leaving a gaping hole in the center of the span. According to Emmanuel Okocha, one of the most prominent writers on the effects of the war on the Igbo in the midwest, the bridge's destruction killed many who were on the bridge and enraged the Nigerian military, prompting reprisals from "a frustrated army that had been denied its march to its primary objective."[43] Okocha's book, *Blood on the Niger,* contains harrowing accounts of massacres all over Asaba. While the accounts are horrifying, most place the blame on "vicious Benin and Urhobo speaking Nigerian soldiers who without orders killed a lot of innocent people, burning most of the houses."[44]

In other instances, Okocha notes that many of those saved from execution were saved by soldiers and officers, including Chris Ali, who would later become the chief of army staff under Sani Abacha in 1993.[45] However, as Wole Soyinka noted from prison, "the western Ibos . . . required ten positive acts of loyalty to one of the rest of the nation to prove themselves human beings."[46] Despite the fact that the killings were not planned in advance and not orchestrated in a systematic fashion, the fact that they occurred barely a year after the mass killings in the north of the country helped cement the notion that the Nigerians, especially the northerners, were out to exterminate the Igbo. Thus, for many Igbo in Biafra, the only way to ensure their future was to fight until the end for independence. This theme would become central to Biafra's propaganda campaign, both at home and abroad, beginning in early 1968. Recently, S. Elizabeth Bird and Fraser Ottanelli published a book on the Asaba massacre that has proven to be the definitive work on the subject and on the civilian experience in western Igbo societies during the war in general.[47]

After the last of the Biafrans had been routed from the midwest, Murtala Mohammed devised a plan to cross the Niger, capture Onitsha, establish a bridgehead, and pour troops into Biafra to end the war. His plan called for an amphibious assault across the river and directly into the city, which would be secured, and then his forces would link with Shuwa's 1st Division that was in the process of conquering the northern areas of Biafra including Enugu. Mohammed's plan turned into a disaster when the ill-prepared force crossed on the night of October

7–8. Mohammed gambled on speed and surprise as he landed three battalions in the city market under cover of night. The Biafrans, who did not expect an assault three days after the last of their troops had been forced to cross the Niger, were caught by surprise. Mohammed himself led the invasion, utilizing a single ferry that transported him and his men across the river. By morning, they had established a beachhead and attempted to ferry reinforcements to the city. The Biafran forces, though not ready for an assault, had prepared improvised antipersonnel mines and other munitions such as a particularly nasty device called the footcutter, consisting of little more than a ninety-degree metal pipe with its base in the ground. The pipe, filled with gunpowder and shrapnel and positioned toward the enemy, would be ignited with either a tripwire or a manned firing point, sending the shrapnel at approximately knee level at the enemy, like a blunderbuss.[48]

However, once morning came, the Biafrans realized what had happened and quickly regrouped to counter the assault. After the successful first wave, Mohammed returned to the Asaba side of the Niger to organize the rest of the offensive. As the Nigerians had only one ferry and several canoes to transport their men and supplies into Onitsha, the Biafran defenders picked their targets easily. Indeed, on the first attempt to resupply the three battalions in Onitsha, a Biafran sniper killed the ferry pilot, stranding the boat in the middle of the river. Because of Onitsha's topography, which slowly sloped toward the river, the Biafrans held the high ground and continued to pound the Nigerians below, who now ran low on supplies and ammunition. With two of the battalion heads, the last remaining commander, Col. (later Gen.) Geoffrey Ejiga, attempted to contact division headquarters, located some seventy kilometers away in Umunede, almost halfway to Benin City, where Mohammed had returned to, thinking his invasion had succeeded. Ejiga later claimed, "All we got was a walkie-talkie which we found out did not have the range to get [to] Asaba, not to talk about Umunede where the Divisional Headquarters was located."[49] With communication breaking down and the Nigerians unable to resupply the battalions or evacuate the wounded in Onitsha, Ejiga had no choice but to leave his command and personally find Mohammed.

The Nigerians made three attempts to reinforce the battalions stranded in Onitsha and. when that failed, attempted to evacuate their forces. This was no easy task considering the ferry crews had disappeared, making the operation more difficult, as the division could use only smaller vessels to move the troops back across the Niger. Mohammed's rash decision ultimately cost many Nigerian lives, and the deterioration of discipline and morale in the division heavily contributed to the massacres in Asaba. Eventually Mohammed succeeded in capturing the city the following March under equally controversial circumstances.

Once the Nigerian forces pushed the Biafrans out of the midwest, they resumed their attacks on the northern and southern fronts. In the north, the Nigerians resumed the push south from Nsukka, taking the capital, Enugu, on October 4. Four battalions drove south from Nsukka and captured the towns of Abor and Eke, roughly thirty kilometers west of Enugu's city center, despite some stiff resistance from the Biafran forces at Ekwegbe. Though the Biafrans were quickly routed, the Nigerian 5th Battalion led by Captain Abubakar Gora gave chase and advanced on the route of the 22nd, almost resulting in a disastrous friendly fire incident.[50] Although the assault on the city went almost exactly as planned, Shuwa, the cautious commander that he was, failed to end the war by capturing Ojukwu or pressing the advantage. Meanwhile, Ojukwu hatched a desperate plan to defend the city. He sent for thousands of volunteers with no military training and told Madiebo that the force was to assemble at Udi, to the southwest of Enugu, armed only with machetes and a few Dane guns, muzzle-loaded flintlocks built to the specifications of the guns traded to Africans during the slave trade, "and from there, swarm the enemy at Abor on two axes, singing war songs and matcheting [*sic*] all enemy in sight." Predictably, the assault failed miserably. Madiebo noted that "by 0300 hours the crowd moved in vehicles to Eke and before long it was clear they had begun to advance because the sound of their war songs and yellings were audible from many places. Before 0430 hours, the enemy released a tremendous volley of shells in all directions. The yelling and war songs ceased and the warriors dispersed in fright, some straight to their faraway villages and others to Enugu."[51]

On September 26, with the impending fall of Biafra's capital and the enemy only nine miles from the city, Ojukwu fled Enugu, leaving Madiebo in charge of its defense. His instructions were to defend the city for as long as possible and create a unified headquarters for what remained of the army, air force, and police. Two days later, the Nigerians began entering the city in a slow, systematic conquest that would remain the hallmark of Shuwa's 1st Division throughout the war. Though the slow advance ensured the city's capture with minimal chance of the breakdowns in command and morale that had plagued the Nigerians in the initial months of the conflict, it also allowed the Biafrans time to organize their defense and evacuation of the city. Precisely for this reason, Ojukwu was able to flee the city, leaving a defense that was beginning to collapse. In fact, Shuwa later lamented that his forces did not know the terrain well enough to blockade the city effectively and did not possess accurate maps of the area. Ojukwu's escape was only possible toward Onitsha along the old Enugu-Onitsha road through the town of Ngwo, which was adjacent to Abor, where the Nigerians had their troops massed and where Ojukwu's ill-fated civilian assault took place. However, the Nigerian officer in charge, Theophilus Danjuma, did not have maps of the area, and when he arrived at the hospital that would later be the University of Nigeria Teaching Hospital, he mistakenly blockaded that road rather than the actual highway, allowing Ojukwu his escape route.[52]

Even more questionable, after the city fell, Shuwa made little effort to press his advantage against a Biafran military in complete disarray. Biafran leaders recognized that their army was on the verge of collapse. They had only one battle-ready brigade, the 52nd, which had been held in reserve to the south of Enugu. Even this unit was fatigued, and its commanding officer successfully lobbied Ojukwu to keep the brigade out of action during the retreat from Enugu. The situation was so desperate that Madiebo acknowledged that the "army had ceased to exist as an organized force."[53] Anwunah credited Madiebo for rescuing the military from total collapse with his ability to shield his officers from the saboteur hunters and create new formations in times of crisis, which this no doubt was.

Shuwa's cautiousness stemmed from his recognition that at the early stage of the war, hardly any of his soldiers were battle tested and as a result, he had to ensure they were properly equipped and supported to avoid collapse. Compounding matters, Shuwa's division was the only one that fought from the beginning of the war until the end through the Igbo heartland. As he was quick to remind his critics who thought he should use more brash tactics, like those of Murtala Mohammed and Benjamin Adekunle, "they were fighting in friendly area, I am telling you. Midwest was friendly area; Ikom and the rest were friendly areas."[54] As such, they did not require the same kind of security on all the supply, communication, and evacuation lines. Though Shuwa protected his forces and seized the city, even the Biafrans claimed that had he acted more rapidly and with greater efficiency, he most likely would have been able to seal the city and capture Ojukwu, thereby ending the war.

In the far east of Biafra, Adekunle's 3rd Division renewed its amphibious assault along Biafra's south coast, taking the port of Calabar in what became known as Operation Tiger Claw on October 17–19. Though the operation lasted a scant three days with very little resistance, the Nigerians claimed, for the first time during the conflict, that the Biafrans had employed European mercenaries in the defense of the city.

Though the Biafran Midwest Offensive shocked Nigeria, it ultimately was little more than what Efiong would later call "a flash in the pan" that resulted in Nigeria's military government's decision to escalate the war to a hitherto unprecedented scale. Though the war mostly settled into a stalemate that lasted from November 1967 until the early the next year, Biafra's already slim prospects for independence began to look even bleaker. Biafra's military capabilities, which had been stretched thin by the Midwest Offensive, now seemed on the verge of collapse. Even more problematic, the Nigerian navy and 3rd Division had effectively turned the rump of Biafra into a landlocked enclave with no viable means to resupply the besieged forces. The next chapter shows how Biafra's only hope was to appeal to a world that was largely indifferent to their plight.

FIVE

THE WORLD REACTS

AS THE NIGERIAN CRISIS UNFOLDED, the world's major powers followed the developments as the country tore itself apart. Because Nigeria's political and economic tapestry was so complex and diverse, ideological imperatives competed with business interests within the British, American, French, and Soviet arenas and even smaller powers such as Israel, the Arab world, and Czechoslovakia. Adding to the complexity, the racist white governments in South Africa and Rhodesia added to the chaos that was developing in Nigeria. The crisis also came on the heels of the Katanga Crisis in the Congo, another protracted secessionist conflict. In the wake of Katanga, African nations formed the Organization of African Unity (OAU) to, in part, prevent such power politics from playing out in African conflicts again. However, the OAU's ability to block debate in international forums, such as the UN, may have helped prolong the conflict and undoubtedly hardened Nigeria's position in any negotiations, as the Biafrans would have no recourse to global intervention, which they desperately attempted to provoke.

As the Nigerian crisis deepened and turned into Eastern secession, most Western powers viewed the crisis with unease, not least because the outcome was uncertain. Later in the war, Biafran public diplomacy thrust the conflict into the global spotlight, especially the humanitarian disaster that unfolded in 1968, which the Biafrans characterized as a continuation of the brutal killings that began in 1966 and culminated in the Asaba Massacre during the end of the Midwest Offensive. Because of Biafra's effectiveness in developing the atrocities into a narrative of calculated genocide, a great deal of the literature on the global dimensions of the war focus on the debate over genocide.[1] In the very early stages of the war, none of Biafra's official propaganda arms used genocide to characterize the war fought against them. However, when hostilities erupted in July 1967, the world's powers, even Nigeria's closest allies and trading partners such as the United Kingdom, reacted slowly to the crisis, and many adopted a "wait and see" posture, refusing to openly support Gowon for fear of alienating Ojukwu in case his bid for secession was successful. It was precisely this moment of hesitation that defined the global diplomacy for the rest of the war, and as a result, this initial phase of the world's reaction to the uncertainty is instrumental in understanding why a "police action" developed into a thirty-month confrontation.

From the beginning of scholarly inquiry into the war, one of the most studied aspects has been the international sphere. Unlike other aspects of the war, where government documents scarcely survive, sources regarding the international aspects of the war are much more common in archives not only in Nigeria but also around the world. Additionally, newspapers and official publications from Nigeria, Biafra, and the myriad of organizations involved in humanitarian relief as well as activist groups have found their way into archives, with many digitized for future use. As a result, secondary literature abounds, with the foundation being John Stremlau's *The International Politics of the Nigerian Civil War.*[2] Though his book was published in 1977, before much of the archival materials became available, Stremlau interviewed many of the actors involved with the global dimensions of the war and, as a result, produced a nuanced and detailed discussion of the war's international diplomacy. Several other early authors wrote case studies about various countries' involvement in the war as well as that of NGOs and individuals.[3]

In recent years, interest in the war has grown after years of academic neglect, both inside and outside of Nigeria. In a relatively short period, several major academic journals dedicated volumes to the study of the war. After Chinua Achebe published his memoir on the war, *There Was a Country*, the *Journal of Asian and African Studies* dedicated its December 2013 volume to the book's release.[4] The following year, the *Journal of Genocide Studies* dedicated a double volume to the study of the war. The latter volume focused on many of the international aspects of the war, including articles on the UK, Israel, and global entities such as the Red Cross, the United Nations, and the relief agencies that ferried supplies once Biafra had been reduced to an enclave.[5]

For Britain, Nigeria's closest ally and former colonial ruler, the crisis necessitated a delicate balancing act. Throughout 1967, Gowon was in close contact with the British high commission in Lagos, though internal communications between London and Lagos show a British government concerned with its standing in the country and with its leadership throughout Anglophone Africa. Highlighting the problems in Britain's balancing act throughout the crisis, an April 26, 1967 letter from the Commonwealth Office regarding Gowon's decision to impose the naval blockade on the Eastern Region makes clear that the British government would instruct its ships to comply but also that "the Federal Government's enforcement of a blockade would confer belligerent rights on the Eastern Government."[6] The

British thus feared that withholding complete support for the Nigerian blockade would encourage Ojukwu, as it would imply tacit approval for his moves toward secession and encourage him to escalate the crisis.

Ojukwu's May 30 declaration of independence complicated matters further for the British on several levels. Even though Wilson's government remained committed to Nigerian unity, it also opposed the use of force and, early on, urged Gowon not to resort to armed conflict to reunify the country. A June 12 telegram from Lagos high commissioner David Hunt to the Commonwealth Office criticized the policy, saying that the "only way therefore of preserving unity of Nigeria is to remove Ojukwu by force; and if Gowon were to decide against this I think he might himself be removed by force." Hunt seems to have cultivated a disdain for Ojukwu, even at this early stage of the conflict, stating bluntly, "Eastern secession is due less to great impersonal forces than to personal ambition on [the] part of Ojukwu, who has stirred up Ibo feeling." Hunt was quick to stress that the situation was extremely fluid, but there was still a possibility for some kind of return to unity.[7]

Once hostilities broke out in July, the conversation in London began to change, and the myriad of competing interests began to complicate the British position on how to approach the conflict, which still amounted only to Gowon's "police action." When Gowon approached London and Washington with a request to purchase arms on July 1, the British hesitated for several reasons. First, the request amounted to a significant increase in the war's scale. Gowon requested several jet fighters and fast patrol boats in an effort to end the conflict. Gowon also requested antiaircraft guns to deal with the B-26 raids that the Biafrans had been conducting.

Second, the Nigerian government had imposed a blockade of the Biafra coast, which included oil tankers. For Shell/BP, the largest company invested in oil in the country, this presented a serious predicament. As previously mentioned, the company had struggled over the ultimatum regarding which side should receive its royalties. Even the token payment the company made to Biafra angered Gowon and Anthony Enahoro, his commissioner for information. When the latter met Wilson and Hunt on July 17 in London, Enahoro and Wilson sparred over the export of oil. Enahoro stressed that the only way to ensure the uninterrupted export of oil was to allow the Nigerians to purchase the weapons they required to end the war. Wilson felt that the oil blockade came as a retaliation for Shell's payment to Ojukwu and that supplying the patrol boats would only help the Nigerians enforce the blockade that threatened to starve Britain of the petroleum imports. The economic imperative and the possibility of a negotiated settlement became important issues in the initial phase of the war and added to Britain's hesitation over assisting Nigeria to wage a full-scale assault on Biafra.

In the United States, the Lyndon Johnson administration followed the events in the country with growing unease. US interests in Nigeria exposed the complex nature of global involvement in the country. Central to American policy in Nigeria, as elsewhere in the world, was the threat of the communist bloc taking advantage of the crisis to make inroads into the country. Before the January coup, most in the Johnson administration felt that the electoral crises of 1964 and '65 amounted to little more than democratic growing pains and that because of the strength of the Nigerian economy, especially the newly developing oil reserves, "the way ahead in Nigeria is relatively hopeful."[8] Prior to the January coup, the CIA and other intelligence agencies sought to enhance American prestige in the country and safeguard installations such as a NASA tracking station in Kano as late as November 1965. In the November briefing, the administration concluded that "neither the level of radical or pro-Communist activity, nor of the Regional rivalry, now appear to be major threats to Nigeria's internal security."[9]

The events of January 15, 1966 caught the American government completely unaware. After the initial shock of the coup ended, Johnson's aides and intelligence officers realized that Nigeria had entered into a long and protracted crisis and carefully monitored the situation. The CIA, which operated a Foreign Broadcast Information Service (FBIS) station in Kaduna, issued several reports during Ironsi's regime, chronicling the deteriorating situation and Ironsi's inability to ameliorate the tensions. Various communications within the administration and CIA reports made clear, as an April 28, 1966 CIA memo stated, "The Nigerian Government appears to be sliding into a crisis."[10] As the crisis unfolded, Walt Rostow, Johnson's national security advisor, reacted to the problem that arose from Ironsi's declaration of a unitary state. He, along with his advisors, concluded that Nigeria was heading for "trouble for some time to come, with little USG [United States government] leverage to influence the situation."[11] On the eve of Biafran secession, Ed Hamilton, a member of the National Security Council (NSC), laid out American options for the future. In his assessment, the American influence could only be severely limited and ran the risk of alienating all sides to the conflict if the administration made "some sort of grandstand diplomatic play." Hamilton ultimately advised Rostow, "Thus, painful as it is, my advice is that we sweat it out and prepare to deal with whatever configuration of autonomous states emerges. . . . We should take no action which would indelibly identify us with any of the factions."[12]

Five days later, when Biafra declared its independence, the Johnson White House appeared to make this official policy. Like the British, the initial American concern centered on evacuating its citizens from the afflicted areas. However, while the British seemed more concerned with the effect that any evacuations would have on future relations with either Nigeria or Biafra, the Americans removed many of their citizens, especially dependents of official personnel, such as at the consulate in Enugu, on June 4–6, 1967. The administration's main concern was that Gowon simply lacked the ability to control his armed forces. Though that assumption proved incorrect on the operational level, the intelligence analysis, basing its conclusions on the 1966 massacres, proved tragically correct during the reconquest of the Midwestern Region, especially the widespread massacres in Asaba.

When the fighting erupted, Gowon sent messages to both Johnson and Wilson, asking for military support. Gowon requested the immediate sale of twelve fighter jets, six patrol boats, and two dozen antiaircraft guns. The antiaircraft guns showed how afraid the Nigerians were of Biafra's air force, which consisted of only a single combat-ready B-26 and several helicopters, all of which were out of commission by the end of the year. Biafra would not build any new air capabilities until 1969, when Swedish count Carl Gustav Von Rosen created his MINICoin fleet. However, Nigeria's request for a relatively large-scale arms purchase was met with concern, especially as Gowon's request made clear that "if the U.S. and UK were unable to supply these weapons, he would be forced to get them from any source which would make them available—an obvious reference to the Soviets and/or Eastern Europeans."[13] However, Hamilton and Rostow felt there was little chance that the Soviets would succeed in influencing Nigerian politics toward realignment because the internal situation was simply too chaotic. Furthermore, several congressional representatives were already beginning to take a pro-Biafran stance, led by Congressman Joseph Resnick. Resnick and his allies in congress were well placed to block any potential deal to allow the Nigerians to purchase arms and could use their leverage to block other international aid programs, such as the United States Agency for International Development (USAID). Last, Hamilton expressed concern that American support for Israel in the 1967 Six Day War already exposed the administration to global criticism, and appearing to take sides in yet another conflict would have even more polarizing effects on American influence in global affairs. As a result, Johnson's government refused to allow Nigeria to purchase American arms, fearing that acquiescing to any Nigerian request for support "would ruin us forever with the Easterners, and it would set us up for a very hard fall with Gowon if, as I strongly suspect, we couldn't deliver."[14] Thus, the Americans, following Britain's lead, largely refused to supply the Nigerians with arms that the latter believed instrumental in obtaining a quick and decisive end to the conflict.

With the major Western powers hesitant to intervene on Nigeria's behalf, Gowon approached the Soviet Union for assistance. In July, Enahoro traveled to Moscow and signed an agreement that gave Nigeria the airpower it desired, and they relinquished very little in return. Most importantly, the supplies began arriving in Kano in mid-August, just as the Biafran Midwest Offensive began to stall. Soviet military assistance proved instrumental from military and political standpoints. When the first two MiG-17s arrived at Kano on August 8, 1967, they halted much of the Biafran Midwest Offensive and became instruments of terror, although according to Stremlau, they most likely helped galvanize support for Ojukwu and secession when they first appeared.[15]

Gowon's acceptance of Russian aid gave him an important bargaining tool against future concessions when dealing with Western powers, especially Britain. Because Nigeria could obtain much of their materiel from the communist powers, Britain and the OAU had little capability to force any kind of compromise by threatening to withhold supplies later in the war. This ability to leverage international diplomacy proved extremely important in the following years, when the humanitarian crisis brought intense pressure on Wilson, Johnson, and, later, Richard Nixon to intervene to end the starvation.[16] The Soviets hoped that the deal with Nigeria would enable deeper cooperation with Lagos, though they had little hope of shifting Nigerian alliances to the Eastern Bloc.

Both Nigeria and Biafra viewed the West's hesitation to support either side openly with disappointment but also saw avenues for future hope. For Biafra, Britain's failure to unequivocally support Nigeria and throw full support behind the Nigerian Federal Military Government (FMG)'s military option gave rise to a hope that secession could be achieved, but only if they successfully internationalized the conflict and swung global support toward their cause. For Nigeria, Britain's and America's refusals to supply anything except light arms and some antiaircraft cannons forced Gowon to look to the Soviet Union for support. Soviet assistance provided Gowon an important political option in case the British turned decisively toward Biafra. Most importantly, Soviet materiel allowed Nigeria to continue to prosecute the war regardless of Western opinion, which in the coming months would swing decisively in favor of the beleaguered Biafrans. Even more, for Gowon, any kind of dealings with Biafra by outside governments could be construed as de facto diplomatic recognition, threatening Gowon's insistence that the war be treated purely as an internal conflict.

With the Nigerians insisting on handling the crisis militarily and Nigeria's traditional allies unwilling to fully support the Lagos government, some feared the situation could degenerate and become reminiscent of the Congo Crisis. Many officers on both the Nigerian and Biafran sides of the conflict had served as peacekeepers in the Congo. Gowon's murdered predecessor, Ironsi, had served as the last commander of the UN mission in 1964. As such, the military leadership knew very well how the situation could degenerate. Many in Washington and London felt that the only leaders who could help end the conflict were those of other African states who could mediate between Ojukwu and Gowon without giving the Biafran leader the recognition he craved. However, some questioned whether anyone would be able reconcile the two. Joseph Ankrah had attempted such mediation, hosting all the Nigerian military leaders in Aburi in January 1967. Though that meeting ended in an agreement, it was never fully implemented and in the end served only to deepen the crisis. Ankrah made another futile attempt to mediate, but Nigerian concerns that he was too close to British interests to act led Zambia's Kenneth Kaunda and Tanzania's Julius Nyerere to begin to mediate in June 1967.[17]

Ojukwu, desperate for any kind of political recognition, made extensive overtures in East Africa. Unlike the extremely formalized diplomacy Biafran officials encountered in Europe, Biafran envoys to Zambia and Tanzania had little trouble accessing the upper echelons of power there. Helping Biafra further was the fact that some of Nigeria's top Igbo diplomats before the crisis defected to Biafra, taking their contacts with them.[18] In addition, because Gowon was busy courting American, British, and Soviet diplomats to supply arms, he neglected his African counterparts, allowing the Biafrans to build their case for independence to an already receptive group of friends. Augustine Okwu, a seasoned diplomat who defected to Biafra, had maintained a close friendship with Nyerere since he had opened diplomatic relations between Nigeria and Tanzania in 1962.[19] By the time the Nigerians sent a delegation to East Africa to counter the Biafran attempts at recognition, Kaunda's government had already announced an East African summit to discuss the crisis in Nigeria. When the leaders of the four major Anglophone countries in the region (Tanzania, Zambia, Kenya, and Uganda) met on July 8, 1967, the shooting war had just erupted two days prior. Thus, the first item on the agenda was an appeal to halt the hostilities and allow a peace delegation to mediate the crisis. Gowon refused this request, mainly because he thought the military operation would be swift and short.[20]

Though the leaders of the four countries had varying degrees of sympathy toward Biafra, they could all agree that, as Nyerere said, "preventing the United Nations or the big powers from intervening in Nigeria" was imperative in not allowing the crisis to deteriorate into a repeat of the Katanga Crisis.[21] Naturally, Tanzania was sympathetic to Biafra, owing to Nyerere's friendship with Okwu. Zambia's Kaunda was also favorably disposed to Ojukwu.[22] Uganda's president, Apollo Milton Obote, also in the throes of a secessionist crisis in the traditional Kingdom of Buganda, strongly supported Nigeria and opposed any form of secession.[23] Kenya's Jomo Kenyatta, the most cautious of the leaders at the summit, acted as a bridge between these competing aims, and thus, in the final communique, the four leaders offered their assistance to end the conflict.[24]

Complicating matters, Gowon remained adamant that any type of consultation had to come from an established organization such as the OAU and refused to consider any attempts to resolve the conflict through mediation or negotiation so as not to allow Biafra any kind of de facto recognition they could then attempt to leverage. The OAU was scheduled to hold a summit in Kinshasa, Congo, in early September, and Mobutu Sese Seko appealed to bring to it the issue of the war. Gowon was confident he would be able to block any resolution that would be favorable to Biafra or that even acknowledged that the crisis was anything but an internal Nigerian matter. As such, he took few precautions in allowing the war to be part of the agenda.

Ojukwu, on the other hand, saw the summit as his first real opportunity to elicit support and recognition on an international level. As such, Biafran public diplomacy efforts intensified in the buildup to the summit. On August 29, the Biafrans issued a memorandum that became known as the Biafran White Paper, signaling their vision for a future association with Nigeria.[25] Recognizing Mobutu, Obote, and others' fears that secessionism would spread across the continent, the Biafrans appealed to historical precedent, claiming that "too often it has been assumed in certain quarters that the detachment of Biafra from the Federation of Nigeria might lead to Balkanization and therefore instability in this part of Africa. This assumption is not borne out by any objective reasoning. . . . Paradoxically, the political structure of the Nigerian Federation was such that it was a source of the political instability," adding that "only by political disengagement and the promotion of ties that are purely economic, social and cultural can a healthy and fruitful relationship be developed between its various component parts."[26]

The white paper continued by enumerating a future vision for cooperation between Nigeria and Biafra. The detailed proposal, which included a customs union, complimentary citizenship, a unified education system, and a unified authority to oversee cooperation, seemed very similar to the loose confederation that Ojukwu had championed earlier in the year. It is, however, significant to note that despite the close ties that the paper advocated, it made no mention of the oil revenue nor of any plan to share it.

Gowon responded to the white paper in his usual blunt manner. In a September 2 speech, he emphatically stated, "The Federal Military Government will not negotiate with Ojukwu as the rebel leader."[27] He further established two preconditions for any negotiations: an immediate renunciation of secession and an acceptance of the twelve-state structure. Gowon's speech also sought to assuage American fears of Soviet infiltration in Nigeria. For the Nigerians, any future American attempt to mediate could not be simply ignored or rebuffed, and Gowon emphasized that Nigeria was not accepting Russian aid but that all the arms shipments and technical assistance came on a strictly commercial basis, with Nigeria paying in either cash or commodities.

Biafra's white paper proved to be only the first salvo of their public diplomacy blitz. As the meeting began in Kinshasa, Biafran officials, much to Nigeria's chagrin, circulated a memorandum outlining the Biafran position on the crisis despite not being allowed to send a delegation or observers to the meeting.[28] Though the document essentially reiterated the Biafran arguments for independence, Ojukwu's stance on Gowon's illegitimacy as the country's head of state, and the historical interpretations of secession, the document is notable for its introduction for one important reason. In the introductory paragraphs, where the Biafrans claim that Northern Nigerian elites looked at Eastern Nigerians with disdain and hostility, the memo stated:

> In this connection, the remorseless slaughter by Northerners of several thousand [note that the Biafrans do not give an exact number here] unarmed Eastern Nigerians in May, July and September, 1966, was merely the worst round of a continuing genocide unleashed in Jos in 1945 and followed up in Kano in 1953 against [people] of Eastern Nigerian origin.[29]
>
> However, in spite of the bitter experience of the immediate past, the Government of Eastern Nigeria hoped and tried even in the middle of the pogrom of 1966 to salvage whatever common bonds still remained in the Federation.[30]

This was the first time the Biafrans used the term *genocide* in a public forum. Though the term became synonymous with the war, thanks in large part to the intense Biafran public campaign that began in 1968, this attempt to influence a small group of African leaders did not yet signal a shift in Biafra's overall campaign for international intervention. An accompanying piece published in the *African Monthly Review* in September to coincide with the OAU summit returned to the imagery of equating Biafra to the Jewish people's plight. Though the article stopped short of calling the Biafran situation a genocide, it made several overt references to the Jewish crisis during the Second World War and the subsequent foundation of Israel. It claimed that as the Nazis began their persecution of the Jews,

> the world reacted with the usual lukewarm attitude and said, "It was their domestic affair." Pregnant women were murdered; children and elderly people were killed. Their only sin was that they were Jews. It took the world more than twenty years after the war to realize that it was, after all, not Hitler's internal affair. But then it was too late to cry when the head was off.
>
> Likewise, when Israel gained its independence in 1948, they continually fought for their right to exist against the Arab states that "tried three times to wipe out Israel from the Earth, but their efforts were on each occasion abortive."
>
> The Eastern Nigerians thus faced a similar threat, when, after the pogroms of 1966, they had no choice but to create a new nation that, like Israel, had come under assault. As with the Jews, "Once again, the world repeated its history and brushed aside this unprovoked crime of murder in Nigeria and said, 'It is Nigeria's internal and domestic affair.'"[31]

Placing the blame directly on the OAU's secretary general, the Guinean Diallo Telli, the article criticized the OAU for accepting Gowon's position that the war was an internal Nigerian matter.

The issue of genocide remains one of the most important legacies of the Nigerian Civil War. Both in Nigeria and abroad, the images that flooded the world and created a global outcry against the war left a lasting legacy, and as a result the war has become synonymous with genocide. At this juncture, both sides sought a quick end. The Biafran appeal at the OAU summit invoked genocide largely because of the moral and legal issues that accepting the argument would entail.

As the Biafrans well knew, the term *genocide* originated during the Holocaust. Raphael Lemkin, a Polish Jew, escaped the German occupation in 1939 by fleeing to Lithuania and from there to Sweden before arriving in the United States in 1941. In 1943, he coined the term by combining the Greek *génos* with the suffix *–cide*, to mean the murder of a race or people. The term first appeared in his 1944 work *Axis Rule in Occupied Europe: Laws of Occupation, Analysis of Government, Proposals for Redress* and became the basis of international law in 1948 when the UN created the United Nations' Convention on the Prevention and Punishment of the Crime of Genocide (UNGC). The convention defined genocide as:

> Any of the following acts committed with intent to destroy, in whole or in part, a national, ethnical, racial or religious group, as such:
> (a) Killing members of the group;
> (b) Causing serious bodily or mental harm to members of the group;
> (c) Deliberately inflicting on the group conditions of life calculated to bring about its physical destruction in whole or in part;
> (d) Imposing measures intended to prevent births within the group;
> (e) Forcibly transferring children of the group to another group.[32]

Subsequent articles in the convention deal with the prosecution of genocide and, more importantly, stipulate that any party to the agreement is morally and legally obligated to appeal to the UN to take action "as they consider appropriate for the prevention and suppression of acts of genocide."[33]

Despite the memorandum and the references to genocide, the tactic was ultimately unsuccessful. Very few African countries were signatories to the UN's genocide convention. Though most of the North African states had acceded to the convention in 1950s, they did not attend the summit because of the unlikelihood of a resolution condemning Israel for the 1967 Six Day War. Only Ethiopia and Liberia were original signatories to the treaty, and by 1967, only Congo, Ghana, and Upper Volta acceded.[34]

Before the conference began, the council of ministers who set its agenda agreed to Nigerian demands that the crisis would not be included. However, once the summit began, there was little guarantee that any of the heads of state in attendance would refrain from bringing up the issue, especially Kaunda, one of Biafra's staunchest supporters. Though the Nigerian external affairs commissioner, Okoi Aripko, successfully shut out discussion, Gowon was unable to attend the summit because the Midwest Offensive had not been completely defeated yet.

When the summit began on September 11, Gowon sent a high-profile delegation led by Awolowo. Gowon tasked Awolowo with ensuring that Ojukwu's appeals for an OAU-sponsored peace conference based on the Biafran leader's memorandum would not come to fruition. However, because Awolowo was not a head of state, he could do little in the closed-door sessions, especially when Kaunda raised the issue at the summit. Awolowo repeatedly defended Nigeria's right to handle the conflict as an internal affair, even threatening the other states, stating bluntly, "Every one of the members had its own skeleton in the closet and we would not hesitate to raise it. No one had a right to question the internal affairs of another state. If Biafra succeeded all Africa would suffer."[35]

Several other developments added to the confusion regarding the summit's outcome. First, the Arab states boycotted the meeting, fearing that the summit would not condemn Israel for the 1967 war. Second, the francophone organization Organisation Commune Africaine et Malagache (OCAM) met ahead of the summit and devised a plan to raise the Nigerian crisis. When Kaunda introduced a resolution, supported by OCAM, that called for an immediate ceasefire and that negotiations begin with the aim of recognizing Biafra in all but name, Awolowo's worst fears were realized. He responded by adhering to the OAU charter, which explicitly stated in Article III that the members would show "respect for the sovereignty and territorial integrity of each State and for its inalienable right to independent existence."[36] Awolowo even threatened that Nigeria would begin supporting secessionist groups in other countries should OAU support for Biafra materialize.

In the end, Awolowo's harsh diplomatic tactics, along with Mobutu and Ethiopian emperor Haile Selassie's ability to restrain Kaunda and replace him with Obote during a tense caucus meeting, allowed the OAU to save diplomatic face. The OAU resolution issued at the end of the summit recognized the conflict as a Nigerian internal matter yet at the same time named a delegation of six heads of state to act as a consultative mission. Though Kaunda and other leaders pushed for a mediation mission, Awolowo eventually convinced Gowon to agree to the wording of the mission as *consultative* to allow the OAU to play a role in the conflict without compromising Nigerian sovereignty or appearing to grant Biafra any form of recognition as a separate party to the dispute.

Ojukwu responded with his usual wit and venom. In a September 29 speech where he urged his compatriots to defend Enugu as it fell to the federal forces, he lauded the OAU for sending the mission despite Nigeria's objections, taking care to chastise Awolowo and the Yoruba elites "who have made themselves tools for the caprices of a mentally sick Gowon."[37] Ojukwu found in the OAU's statement a first step toward international recognition. Despite the fact that the organization had reaffirmed Nigeria's unity, African leaders had taken a step, however small, toward internationalizing the conflict—one that Ojukwu would hope to capitalize on later. Biafran officials saw that the wording of the statement was designed not to anger the FMG, but the substance gave them hope that such a high-level delegation would force Nigeria into some form of negotiation.

For Gowon's government, the deal ensured two important diplomatic victories. Though forced to accept some form of international oversight for the conflict, Gowon ensured that the OAU and not the UN would lead any future peacemaking attempts. Second, any goodwill that Nyerere and Kaunda felt toward Ojukwu and Biafra had been stifled by the diplomatic maneuvering. Tanzania and Zambia did recognize Biafra but would not do so until the middle of 1968.

When the OAU summit ended on September 14, 1967, Mobutu declared that the mission would arrive in Nigeria within two weeks. However, weeks stretched into months, and the visit from the six heads of state that was supposed to happen by the end of September became four heads of state on November 23. Giving Biafrans a much-needed morale boost, boxer Dick Tiger, who had come out of retirement the previous June with the explicit aim of representing Biafra on the world boxing stage, defended his light heavyweight belt in a November 17 fight against American Roger Rouse. Tiger's twelfth-round technical knockout of Rouse became *Ring* magazine's round of the year in 1967. The November 24 issue of the *Biafran Newsletter* carried a striking image of Tiger in a classic fight pose promotional shot with the caption "T.K.O. TO GOWON!" In the accompanying article, it was noted that Ojukwu reportedly cabled the fighter, stating, "Tiger's retention of the crown has provided a ray of jubilation to all Biafrans and inspired our determination in the current war for the survival of our nation."[38] Coming so close to the OAU mission, Tiger's victory no doubt gave many in Biafra added resolve to continue their resistance despite the many setbacks on the battlefield, including the collapse of the Midwest Offensive and the fall of the capital at Enugu.

When the visit from the OAU finally arrived, the Biafran situation had worsened considerably compared to September, when Mobutu had first announced it. The committee dwindled from six to four when Mobutu declined to participate, as did Liberian president William Tubman, who resigned from the committee after the *Morning Post*, a Nigerian government-owned newspaper, insulted him in an editorial.[39] With Emperor Selassie chairing the commission, Ankrah,

Malian leader Modibo Keïta, and Cameroonian leader Ahmadou Ahidjo arrived in Lagos and were greeted by a hostile Gowon, who in his welcoming address reminded the four that "your Mission here is not to mediate" before telling them that Nigeria would not stop military operations until the Biafrans renounced secession and removed Ojukwu from power.[40]

Though all the members of the mission accepted Nigeria's position regarding secession, they also expressed concern regarding the mounting toll of the conflict. Nigeria's makeup as a postcolonial state, though an extreme case of ethnic turmoil, was by no means unique on the continent. Virtually every African country, regardless of ethnic makeup, harbored the same tensions between political groups due to the makeup of the postcolonial African states that largely kept the colonial boundaries.[41] Complicating matters further, the mission pressured Gowon to allow them to communicate with the secessionists, which Selassie referred to as "the other side which is conducting hostilities" so as to not confer any type of official recognition on Biafra by even mentioning it by name in a formal setting.[42]

In the end, the mission published a rather tepid report where they expressed support for Nigeria's unity and, despite appeals during the visit that the organization be allowed to play an active role in resolving the conflict, agreed that "the secessionists should renounce secession and accept the present administrative structure of the Federation of Nigeria."[43] With this, the OAU effectively closed the door to any contacts that would lead to a peace conference or any other settlement short of what the Biafrans could consider complete capitulation.

The early months of the war, both on the battlefield and in the global diplomatic arena, were extremely fluid yet also set the stage for the rest of the war in several important ways. The Biafrans would never enjoy a moment of tactical success in the field as they had during the Midwest Offensive and would spend the rest of the war in a largely defensive state, more like their predicament after abandoning Enugu. In addition, their attempts to penetrate the global diplomatic world failed largely due to the structure of international diplomacy, which maintained the primacy of the nation-state. As a result, throughout the war, the Nigerians and Biafrans would continue in much the same manner. The Nigerians would insist that the conflict was entirely an internal matter while the Biafrans would attempt any maneuver to internationalize the conflict. Though the first round of this battle ended with a decisive Nigerian victory, the hesitation of the Western powers to throw their support fully to the Nigerian side created some hope that the Biafrans would later attempt to exploit. Soviet influence would become a major source of concern, even though Moscow understood early in the war that Nigeria would not align with the Warsaw Pact world against its NATO adversaries.

When 1967 ended, most of Biafra's connections to the outside world had effectively been severed. The country's only major entrepôt, Port Harcourt, though under Biafran control, was under effective blockade as the Nigerian navy controlled both the waterways into the Niger Delta and the port of Bonny, which commanded the main tributary into Port Harcourt. This blockade, coupled with the stalemate in the fighting that emerged after the capture of Enugu, left Biafra woefully underequipped and its population on the brink of starvation. The Biafrans would use the siege waged against them as a political weapon and assert that the siege, meant to starve the entire country, could be one only thing: genocide. At the end of 1967, and even more effectively into 1968, the Biafrans would develop the idea into a full-frontal public relations assault that transformed the conflict and left the most lasting legacy of the war.

SIX

GENOCIDE

PERHAPS THE SINGLE MOST CONTROVERSIAL and charged issue of the Nigerian conflict was the question of genocide during the war. The argument, which the Biafran government advanced from the early stages of the conflict, had its genesis in two important factors. First, the early defeats on the battlefield left the Biafrans essentially unable to claim, especially after October 1967, that they possessed a viable state. Second, their inability to penetrate the global political discourse and force the world powers to treat them as a state entity left them with few options to pressure the international community and internationalize the war.

The question of genocide has long been a complicated issue with no easy resolution. First, the sheer magnitude of human suffering during the war makes an easy case for those whose memory of the war centers on it being genocidal in nature. Compounding this fact, the war's aftermath and Nigeria's ethnic component further entrenched the idea of genocide as an Igbo phenomenon when the reality of the ethnic politics has proven to be much more complex. Both these issues make the debate regarding genocide even more difficult and intractable. As a result, despite some attempts, the scholarly literature on the war has never really progressed beyond the question of whether the war was genocidal or not.

More importantly, the debate over the nature of genocide in Biafra divorces the narrative from its historical context. Throughout much of the time leading to Biafran secession, both the federal and eastern governments attempted some sort of reconciliation that would have been more difficult if the eastern government had directly accused the federal side of genocide. Once Biafra seceded, the initial goal was to show the country as a bastion of modernity. It was only when Biafra's military situation became untenable, accompanied by their inability to be part of the diplomatic discussion for a solution, that Ojukwu's regime undertook desperate measures—namely, framing the war as explicitly genocidal.

When Enugu fell in early October, many in Ojukwu's inner circle began to feel that the war had entered a more ominous new phase for Biafra. With much of the southern coast and the Cameroonian border under FMG control, the breakaway state was little more than an enclave surrounded by hostile forces. Until May 1968, Port Harcourt remained under Biafran control, but even there, the Nigerians controlled the waterways from Bonny that led into the port city. Although less strategically important, the fall of Enugu devastated Biafran morale, and without Madiebo's skills at reorganizing the Biafran military, the entire war effort could have collapsed.

The Biafrans relocated the capital to Umuahia, where it remained for most of the remainder of the war. There Ojukwu built his bunker, where much of Radio Biafra broadcast from until 1969.[1] With the relocation came a major reorganization of Biafra's military, political, and economic structures to meet the siege that was now imposed and that threatened military supplies as well as civilian necessities. To this end, Ojukwu largely superseded the various ministries of the Biafran government with wartime directorates that had broad executive control over their jurisdictions and consisted of dedicated experts in their field, many of them returnees from the 1966 riots in the north.[2]

These directorates had almost total control over every aspect of Biafran life and included special areas for food, housing, clothing, transport, and fuel. The two most important were the Research and Production Directorate and the Propaganda Directorate—both critical to the war effort.

The Research and Production Directorate (RAP) assumed control of the creation and production of war materiel like those that had proved so effective in the early stages of the war, such as the improvised bombs dropped from the B-26. It also managed the creation of Biafran armored vehicles. Much of this innovation consisted of salvaging metal parts and welding them onto existing vehicles. The directorate learned from various failures in the operation of the war and was able to renovate and redesign their armored contraptions as the engineers and welders learned of new needs. In one instance, the engineer in chief designed armor plating for existing Caterpillar tractors and called the design the Uzummuo, named after the Igbo spirit of blacksmithery. When they discovered that the treads were not able to resist impact from enemy fire, they adapted their design and extended the armor plating to cover the weak spot. Despite the adaptations and upgrades that RAP implemented, they did not have the ability to significantly change the base designs of their chassis, a fact that affected their designs and limited the usefulness of their improvisations.

One early innovation that demonstrated both the directorate's strengths and its weaknesses was the armored car developed in Port Harcourt in early 1968. This car, outfitted with extensive armor plating, could withstand most Nigerian weapons, including the powerful 106mm recoilless rifle. The armor plating not only made it more effective in combat, but its improvised nature also offered a morale boost despite its significant shortcomings. The armor's weight taxed the engines of the industrial vehicles that bore the load, making the vehicle prone to overheating and other problems associated with stressed engines. As a result, the vehicle could not operate at speeds above ten miles per hour and had to be turned off every half hour to cool down. Despite these limitations, the armament's ability to withstand attacks, coupled with the fact that it was designed and built under siege, made it such a source of pride that it became known as the Genocide.

The Propaganda Directorate oversaw an important part of the war effort. Biafran propagandists had a twofold mandate: disseminating Biafra's message to the world and at the same time conveying a message to those at home that the privations of war were necessary to ensure their long-term survival. This herculean task became more difficult as the conflict dragged on. One of the unintended consequences of Biafra's wartime plight is that official archival material is fragmentary at best.

Perhaps Biafra's most potent outlet and one that they utilized in the most effective manner was their radio station, Radio Biafra. Though only a few remnants of Radio Biafra's work exist in sound recordings and scripts, some of their messages survive through news aggregator services like the *Africa Research Bulletin*, Markpress releases, and various activist publications and conference proceedings that used Radio Biafra's broadcasts as tools. Toward the end of the war, the station had to be easily portable to avoid the advancing Nigerian troops, yet through the war, the station broadcast even though silencing it was one of Nigeria's main tactical goals.[3]

The Propaganda Directorate took care to train their operatives in the most extensive manner possible. One of the few surviving manuals is their *Guide Lines [sic] for Effective Propaganda*, published in early 1968.[4] It was also known as Plan #4, as it came as part of a series of plans to train propaganda operatives and organize Biafra's public propaganda push. The other plans in the series have since been lost.[5] The two-part manual first engages the prospective "propaganda man" with the core tenets of effectively conveying a message. The plan's first part explains in detail how to create propaganda, drawing heavily on lessons from the two world wars as well as advertising ideas. The plan stresses that "the presentation of propaganda materials around whatever phenomena should be so striking as to be memorable."[6] To this end, the authors incorporated ideas taken from Josef Goebbels, Hitler's chief propagandist, and juxtaposed them with slogans such as "Freshen up with Seven Up!" Thus, no matter the subject, it should be simple enough to leave a lasting impression and could also be easily remembered.

Radio Biafra programs survive not only in the form of scripts but also as the internal critiques that approved or rejected them for broadcast. In fact, Plan #4 directed all possible propaganda work be submitted directly to an appraisals committee that evaluated each piece to ensure it adhered to the direction the directorate chose and appropriateness for the audience in question. The directorate understood that all messaging had to be tightly controlled, stating that "this practice may be different and rigorous but it is the only way to sharpen the tip point of the propaganda arrow."[7]

The plan also gave writers several guidelines on how to create the most effective scripts and how to avoid giving information away to the enemy. During the war's first few months, several Biafran outlets publicized that the town of Nsukka had been recaptured when in fact it had remained firmly in Nigerian hands from the beginning of the war. Though creating false stories could be an effective way to demoralize the enemy, the directorate was keen on avoiding publishing easily demonstrable falsehoods because "arising from the proximity of the war fronts to the home audience, propaganda of falsehood cannot be effective because the true facts soon reach the audience through eyewitnesses who travel from the war zones back to the centre of population. Propaganda of falsehood thrives only where the verification of the facts cannot be verified. This may in fact, explain Nigeria's lying propaganda. Our propaganda should thus be very cautious about faked stories which are false though aimed at achieving desirable psychological results."[8]

This did not prevent them from publishing false stories that could withstand scrutiny. One surviving appraisal from mid-1969 praised the authors for using an ambiguous report that exploited Yoruba losses on the battlefield while the Yoruba heartland was in the midst of the Agbekoya Parapo Revolt, a tax revolt that began with cocoa growers and later spread throughout Western Nigeria. The propagandists exploited Yoruba ignorance on the exact nature of the battlefield, claiming that the Yoruba losses at the battles of Uzuakoli and Owerri had been disproportionately greater than those of other ethnic groups. "This may well be true," the appraiser stated, "but if it is not true, the Yorubas cannot find out; it is an effective propaganda technique."[9]

The second part of the plan dealt with Biafra's specific predicament as a nation at war, giving advice on how to negotiate the unique obstacles relating to the differing populations their message had to serve. Because the Biafrans portrayed themselves as "progressive blackmen," they took care to show that face to the world. The Oxford-educated Ojukwu's eloquent speeches became the public face of Biafra, and any Biafran interviewed spoke equally flawless English. The situation in the secessionist country, however, was much different, and the Propaganda Directorate adjusted its messaging accordingly. The plan estimated that 70 percent of the country's population was illiterate, and that meant the directorate had to adjust their messaging to reach those who could not be reached by printed publications. To reach these people, the plan suggested that propaganda men go to the markets with batteries (a scarce commodity during the war) and offer them to merchants if they tuned their radios to Radio

Biafra. They also created traveling theater groups that performed plays in rural areas where illiteracy rates were most likely higher than in the urban centers.[10]

Wartime scarcity proved to be one of the most difficult problems to surmount, and because some of the solutions to the high illiteracy rate required significant transportation needs, it became imperative to develop innovative techniques to surmount. However, the Propaganda Directorate deferred most solutions to the other directorates, and the plan bluntly stated, "One of the greatest problems which the Propaganda Directorate has to contend with is that of general immobility in the country. The immobility arose out of the shortage of vehicles and lately of petrol and diesel oil. . . . The problems of blockade and transport cannot be solved by the propaganda machinery. The primary concern of the Directorate is with the mental attitude of the people."[11]

Even though the Fuel and Transportation Directorates were tasked with solving the issues of mobility in Biafra, the Propaganda Directorate urged its people to travel with the military, partly because they received priority in fuel allocations but also because the military could act as a medium to reach the populations most difficult to serve through print or radio. Because of the war's defensive nature, it was largely fought in proximity to the people being defended, and the soldiers would be able to augment the message. Second, the military itself "would benefit from the propaganda for the civilian population, but only as an argumentation of political indoctrination and the special morale services for the armed forces."[12] Thus, civilian populations would benefit from military indoctrination and vice versa.

Understanding how the Propaganda Directorate controlled every aspect of the messaging of Biafra's public voice, both at home and abroad, makes it easier to evaluate the narratives they created and quickly modified to adapt to the changing military and political situations. One of the most complete records that survives is the *Biafra Newsletter*. Though the paper claims to have been printed in Enugu, it was most likely produced in the United Kingdom or the United States for dissemination abroad. Most Biafran documents state Enugu as their place of publication, but given that the city had been in Nigerian hands since October 1967, this claim is an impossibility; the propagandists continued to disseminate it even though it contradicted their own ideas on publishing easily verifiable falsehoods.

The *Newsletter*, unlike other publications, targeted foreign readership, and the articles often appealed to international sensibilities. Many of the themes discussed in the *Newsletter* mirror those of internal outlets, albeit from a different perspective, due to the tight control the Propaganda Directorate maintained over the messaging. During the first months after Biafra's secession, the Biafran papers, both at home and abroad, tried to appeal to panethnic unity within the new country—a unity that struggled to coalesce as non-Igbo territories in the east and on the southern coast quickly fell to the Nigerian forces with little or no resistance. The front page of the *Biafra Newsletter*'s first issue screamed, "WHY

WE ARE FIGHTING" and listed the grievances that southerners living in the north of the country suffered, emphasizing how "Nigeria had reached the depths of degradation in her inhuman treatment of Biafrans."[13] Early Biafran messages sought to minimize the ethnic aspect of Igbo suffering and instead painted the conflict as more ethnoreligious. Thus, when the Biafrans launched a counterattack against the Nigerians in the Bonny sector, the *Newsletter* reported that Emmanuel Aguma, a Rivers politician and later agriculture minister in the Second Republic, expressed hope that the city of Bonny itself would soon be in Biafran hands again.[14] Similarly, military operations in non-Igbo regions, whether real or invented, garnered much attention as the Biafrans attempted to show the world that southern ethnic groups had united squarely against Nigeria.

Local papers in Biafra mirrored the *Newsletter*, albeit with a focus toward keeping the new nation from fraying at the edges. To this end, the Biafrans spared no expense in creating several magazines that rivaled the American *Life Magazine* in quality. Printed on glossy stock, and replete with photographs and in-depth articles, magazines such as *The Spark*, *Biafra Time*, and *The Spectator* ran articles espousing Biafran unity, imploring Biafrans to unite against Nigeria because "personal and sectional considerations must give way to a common front, in defence of right, of freedom and justice; in defence of Biafra."[15] Similarly, *The Spark*'s first issue in September 1967 touted the conquest of the Midwestern Region and extolled Banjo's military prowess. Following the narrative of Biafran military and moral superiority, the article extolling the liberation of the midwest included interviews with "ordinary people," one of whom said, "Man, Biafran soldiers are gentlemen. See how they move about without molesting anybody. If it were Hausa soldiers, our shops and properties would have been looted and our womenfolk assaulted."[16] For Biafran propaganda early in the war, Biafran military invincibility brought with it morality and safety regardless of ethnicity, unlike the Hausa, who created the opposite.

However, even during the euphoric early days of the war, and despite protestations otherwise, Biafra aimed most of its media offensive in the country toward the Igbo. Early issues of *The Spark* and *Biafra Time* contained significant amounts of advertising that targeted mainly people living in the Igbo areas—the bulk of the ads came from businesses in Aba, Owerri, Onitsha, and Port Harcourt. As the war dragged on, the advertisements largely disappeared, and the magazines shifted from a glossy paper stock to school notebooks, with the lines for writing still visible on the pages, when they could be printed at all. The *Biafra Newsletter* did not suffer any major lapses in publication nor from a deterioration in printing quality—another indication of its foreign origin.

Once the military losses began to mount, the Biafran mood shifted from invincibility to survival. However, for the Propaganda Directorate, the task of galvanizing Biafrans became much easier. Because very few non-Igbo remained in Biafra's shrinking territory by early 1968, there was little need to appeal to broader sensibilities. Instead, Biafran propaganda began a process of Igboization wherein the propogandists designed a narrative to appeal to Igbo feelings. This process became so effective that for many in Nigeria during and after the war, Biafra and Igbo became synonymous. To this end, the propagandists developed a narrative based on the massacres of 1966 and the subsequent displacement of nearly two million people into the Eastern Region. For the Biafrans, this horror could be summed up in one word: *genocide*. Though the Biafran government used the term in their letter to the OAU summit in 1967, by the end of the year, they began experimenting with it as a rallying cry at home and abroad before fully embracing it by February the following year.

One of earliest public appeals to genocide came in the *Biafra Newsletter* published on November 24, 1967. On the issue's last page, a scathing editorial by Arthur Nwankwo, who would later go on to found Fourth Dimension Publishing, set the stage for much of the Propaganda Directorate's tone and arguments for the rest of the war. Nwankwo's piece reiterated many of the horror stories of the 1966 massacres, when "wives were forced to witness the slaughtering of their husbands and children and compelled to drink their blood," among others, before concluding that these atrocities occurred "for no other reason than that the victims were Biafrans." For Nwankwo, the Biafran plight was no different from the Jews in Europe who faced extermination "for the same ethnocentric reason . . . **This is Genocide**."[17] Concluding that the Biafran case was no different from the German extermination of European Jewry, Nwankwo demanded that the Nigerians face a tribunal similar to Nuremburg.

Nwankwo's writing touched on all the subjects that would later become the cornerstones of Biafra's media push, both inside the enclave and abroad. Other than accusing Nigeria of genocide, he named Britain and the USSR as complicit by providing military and logistical support. "We want to remind Britain and Russia," he stated, "that genocide is an international crime. Aiding and abetting the Nigerian criminals will only worsen matters."[18] Both the killings and the refugee crisis that ensued would be on the world's shoulders because unlike other similar crises, Biafra received no international support from the United Nations Refugee Agency or, at that point in the war, from any international organization. However, owing to the Biafran spirit, "we have not broken under the burden." Nwankwo concluded his editorial with what he saw as the only hope for Biafra's future: "Recognition of Biafra will arrest the continuing GENOCIDE."[19]

Though Nwankwo's article paints Nigeria as a genocidal monster with Gowon as the "number one accused having organized and directed the killing operations," it is unlikely that the Propaganda Directorate immediately saw the value of using genocide as a device in the propaganda campaign.[20] Most of the accusations against Nigeria came from other sources, but there were few written accounts that made a compelling case for genocide before Nwankwo, who weaved the threads of mass killings, the refugee crisis, and international abetment into one single narrative with genocide as the linking factor. In fact, during most of the war's early period, Biafran writing focused on three main ideas: securing unity in Biafra, painting Biafrans as a modern nation state in the making, and accusing Nigeria of being both imperialist and communist stooges. Internally, to secure the country's postwar unity, the Biafran leadership went to great lengths to motivate the various ethnic groups to unite under the Biafran flag.

Abroad, the Biafrans were slow to react to the fact that they were unable to penetrate international diplomacy in a meaningful way. To this end, they developed two interwoven narratives. First, Biafra promised to be a beacon of modernity and progressive politics in Africa. Indeed, the front-page article of the November 24 issue that featured Nwankwo's article was titled "Biafra Will Be Modern Welfare State." From the onset of the war, the Biafran leadership had sought to convince the Western powers that unlike the "backward North" of the country, the new nation would be a beacon of progress in a continent that many outside observers perceived to be slowly shrinking away from the optimism of independence.[21] Biafran cartoons also made light of the perceived backwardness of Nigerians, almost always portrayed in northern dress, speaking in a barely legible pidgin English. The March 1, 1968 issue of the *Biafra Newsletter* contained a "Biafratoon," as they were cleverly named, that depicted a map of Nigeria with Biafra broken from it, its sinews and blood still raw. On the Nigerian side, an impossibly large barefoot figure in distinct northern dress attempted to spear the breakaway Biafra, yelling in broken English, "KWOM BACK BIAPRA!" while a miniature Gowon, who reached only the knee of the northerner, frantically gesticulated toward Biafra.[22] These articles and images placed Biafrans as the intellectual elites of Africa who, led by an Oxford-educated leader, would free the deserving Africans, the Biafrans, from the horrors their atavistic neighbors in Northern Nigeria inflicted on them.

The other thread painted Nigeria as an emerging Soviet satellite due to the USSR's quick support. Complicating matters, the Soviets and the British both supported a one-Nigeria solution and placed their backing squarely behind the FMG. Using articles such as "Anglo-Soviet Collusion: An Enigma,"[23] "Russian Bridgehead in Nigeria,"[24] and "Nigeria Becomes Soviet Satellite,"[25] the Biafrans sought to exploit American and British Cold War fears. The Biafran narrative also made veiled references to racial preferences, accusing the British and Americans who fought to keep Communism at bay in Europe of turning a blind eye toward "Soviet incursions into some African states." The result of this policy would no doubt be "that Nigeria would be turned into another *Congo* or *Vietnam*." Thus, the only solution would be to recognize Biafran independence to "rescue Africa from the spread of communist activities and spheres of influence."[26] As previously discussed, both the US and British governments had already independently determined very early in the war that the threat of such a shift in Nigeria's foreign policy priorities was negligible.

At first, Nwankwo's article seemed to make little difference in Biafra's propaganda direction. Despite Nigeria's initial military successes, Biafran news outlets continued to portray themselves as champions of the war. Indeed, Murtala Mohammed's failure in Onitsha gave hope that Biafra's military mishaps would easily be reversed. In the Bonny sector, Biafran counterattacks threatened Benjamin Adekunle's hold on the strategically important oil depot. Thus, much of Biafra's media dedicated itself to military victories, postwar projections, and vilifying Nigeria, the UK, the United States, and the USSR as conspirators in the war against them.

Although the Biafran military staved off complete collapse in the wake of the retreat from Enugu and stabilized the fronts in the north and south of the breakaway republic, Biafra's prospects for longevity became bleaker because of the country's inability to import basic foodstuffs and war materiel. Though the bulk of Biafra's population remained under Biafran control, the influx of refugees from the 1966 pogroms crippled the already strained food supplies and initiated a shortage that the Nigerian offensives exacerbated through their control of virtually every entrepôt into Biafra.

Complicating matters, the Nigerian "total war" on Biafra began to take on nonmilitary aspects as well. In January 1968, the Nigerian Central Bank changed the Nigerian pound banknotes, giving the public until January 22 to exchange the previous notes for the new ones. Once the deadline passed, the old notes became immediately worthless, rendering Biafra's existing stock of Nigerian notes useless and nonconvertible into either the new notes or foreign currency. Indeed, Madiebo stated that the currency conversion was such a traumatic financial moment in the war that he called it "the most important single reason why we lost the war," claiming that "we had lost over 50 million pounds which could have made a world of difference in our favor if properly utilized for the execution of the war."[27]

Gowon became so confident of imminent victory that in a New Year's address he declared that the rebellion would be broken by the end of March. Though Gowon did not intend to make the declaration an exact timetable for ending the war, the Nigerian press saw it that way and set March 31 as the deadline for the war's end, with at least one paper placing a "countdown to victory" box on its front page.[28] Gowon's self-imposed pressure led him to escalate the war prematurely to force a relatively quick victory, leading to the military stalemate. Thus, his fiscal plan was an attempt to assuage his critics and show that he was winning the war.

Although the stalemate gave Biafrans hope that they could hold out long enough to force some kind of settlement, the diplomatic lessons from the previous year taught them that their message had to turn more aggressive if they were to force themselves into the realm of international politics. Several factors led to Biafra's embrace of genocide as the rallying cry for the rest of the war. First, the 1966 massacres and the accompanying internal refugees that flooded Eastern Nigeria left little doubt that a monumental catastrophe had befallen the Igbo and other Easterners. Though the Biafran leadership inflated the number killed, most in the east had no way to verify this, and regardless, the humanitarian disaster affected virtually every Igbo and many others in Biafra when nearly two million refugees flooded into the region, overwhelming most social networks' ability to cope with the influx. For the Propaganda Directorate, framing this tragedy as genocide made sense. It gave easterners, especially the Igbo, an understanding that this was not merely an act of violence but an existential crisis that could be solved only with an independent Biafra.

Second, unlike other wartime crimes, genocide held a category all its own—one that compelled concerted international action to not only punish but also to prevent and halt it. More importantly, Article VIII of the UN genocide convention explicitly places the crime outside the normal diplomatic channels by stating, "Any Contracting Party may call upon the competent organs of the United Nations to take such action under the Charter of the United Nations as they consider appropriate for the prevention and suppression of acts of genocide or any of the other acts enumerated in article III."[29] This meant that should any UN member state consider the acts against the Igbo to be genocide, they could, under international law, circumvent any procedures and come directly to the UN to appeal for assistance.

For Biafra, the ability to inject themselves into global public awareness and international diplomatic circles depended heavily on the ability to convincingly propagate the message of genocide outside of Biafra. Though they attempted to circulate their idea at the OAU summit in Kinshasa, they met with little response, and the organization agreed to Nigeria's demand that the OAU treat the war as an internal matter. To this end, the Biafran Propaganda Directorate created the Psychological Warfare Committee, which directed the messaging throughout the war. From the beginning of 1968 until the end of the war, the committee emphasized three broad themes: the Nigerian atrocities, Biafra's inability to compromise with the enemy, and the Biafran will for survival. The committee's weekly recommendations quickly embedded themselves into Biafra's process for creating and evaluating propaganda scripts and messages, some of which are outlined above and others in the following chapters.

The Propaganda Directorate solved their main international challenge of disseminating their message abroad in a remarkable fashion. Soon 1968 would become one of the most eventful years in the entire post–WWII period. American involvement in the Vietnam War took a major turn on January 30 when the North Vietnamese Army (NVA) and their Vietcong allies launched the Tet Offensive, which included audacious assaults on South Vietnamese targets in Saigon. The Vietcong soldiers even managed to infiltrate the US embassy grounds in the city, though American marines prevented them from taking the building itself. The offensive changed the nature of the war in Vietnam, and though tactically a failure, the assaults, which lasted for much of the year, helped turn public opinion squarely against the war in the United States.

In the United States, the Civil Rights Movement began to take a more militant stance with the emergence of the Black Panther Party (BPP) in 1966, whose numbers surged after the arrest and conviction of BPP founder Huey Newton for the murder of an Oakland police officer, which was overturned two years later. Reactions to the Civil Rights Movement also found many victims, most notably in the assassination of Martin Luther King Jr. on April 4, 1968. Two months later, Robert Kennedy, the former attorney general and civil rights champion then running for the Democratic Party's nomination for president, was gunned down in a Los Angeles hotel while attending a campaign event.[30]

Turmoil was not confined to the United States. The year 1968 also saw student protests around the world, with major epicenters of violence in France and Mexico. In France, students protesting the actions of the administration at Paris University Nanterre (then Université Paris X) met police on May 6, 1968. The police charged the protesting students, who retaliated by barricading themselves on the streets. The police assaults led many in the country to support the students, and the largest labor unions called a strike, during which over a million people marched through the streets in Paris on May 13. The continued unrest nearly brought down Charles de Gaulle's government, with the French president briefly fleeing the country to Germany on May 29.

In Mexico, a group of high school students who got into a brawl after a football match barricaded themselves in the Escuela Nacional Preparatoria, the high school run by the Universidad Nacional Autónoma de México (UNAM). Riot police stormed the building after shooting the door open with a bazooka, killing several students. The following summer, students organized to protest police violence and presented a list of demands to President Gustavo Díaz Ordaz, who responded by sending the army to take control of the city's major universities. Students responded by organizing a mass protest at Plaza de las Tres Culturas (Three Cultures Square) in the neighborhood of Tlateloco on October 2. With the 1968 Olympic Games due to begin in less than a fortnight, Diaz Ordaz ordered a military crackdown that became known as the Tlateloco massacre. Though the Mexican government initially claimed that only four students had been killed in the assault, later estimates placed the number at three hundred to four hundred as the Mexican military ran amok throughout the city conducting house to house searches for student protesters. At the Olympics, at the medal ceremony for the 200-meter dash, American gold and bronze medal winners Tommie Smith and John Carlos raised their hands in the Black Power salute, creating an instantly iconic moment. Australian silver medalist Peter Norman stood in solidarity with the two, even giving the pair his gloves to use for their protest.[31]

In the Soviet sphere of influence, similar events began to expose fissures in the Warsaw Pact. After the Israeli victory in the June 1967 war against Syria, Egypt, and Jordan, Polish officials began an anti-Zionist purge of the government that was widely regarded as antisemitic.[32] The Polish communist leadership used antisemitism as a weapon to purge the party and consolidate control over an increasingly restive intelligentsia and student population. On the opposite end of the spectrum, Alexander Dubcek's elevation to the first secretary of the communist party in Czechoslovakia saw him attempt to liberalize the country through a series of reforms known as the Prague Spring, but Dubcek dubbed it "Socialism with a Human Face."[33] Dubcek's reforms ended in disaster when the USSR led Warsaw Pact forces into Prague in August 1968, ending this experiment in liberal socialism. In the invasion's aftermath, Soviet military leaders forced Czech pilots to fly for the Nigerian air force, in part because Dubcek had previously voiced concern for Biafra.[34]

The tumultuous year compounded Biafran needs to penetrate the global system at a critical juncture in the war. To achieve this, they turned to a young author named Cyprian Ekwensi, who created the Overseas Press Service in January 1968. It was his job to propagate the Biafran message abroad, and he did so in several important ways. First, his office transmitted the same messages that the Propaganda Directorate issued for internal use. The goal was to unify both fronts of the propaganda war to maintain the appearance of a siege and build the groundswell for external intervention. Ekwnesi's office contracted an American-owned Swiss public relations firm called Markpress to handle the bulk of Biafra's communications with global news media. During the war and after, many political pundits claimed that Markpress created and popularized the genocide narrative and blamed the company for prolonging the war. In an August 1968 article, *Time* magazine credited Markpress: "Since January [of 1968], Mark-press has literally waged Biafra's war in press releases—more than 250 of them. They are crammed with news of impending arms deliveries that is designed to embarrass European governments and with stark warnings about starvation. The firm has arranged air passage into Biafra for more than 70 newsmen from every West European nation and transmitted eyewitness reports to their publications."[35] Similarly, conservative MP John Cordle told the House of Commons, "Sincere people in this country believe the propaganda and muck which Markpress has put out about Nigeria.

My heart boils when I compare this propaganda with what the Nigerians say for themselves."[36] Markpress's owner, William Bernhardt, responded to Cordle, accusing him of hypocrisy and stating that Markpress was doing the same work the Nigerians had contracted other public relations companies to do, and the Nigerians had the added benefit of their own official government offices and the British Commonwealth offices assisting their public diplomacy efforts.[37]

Stremlau evaluated Markpress's contribution to Biafra's war effort and found that Markpress's international releases varied only very slightly from those the Biafrans released internally. As such, the voice that Markpress amplified came out of Biafra and supported Bernhardt's claim that his only contribution to Biafra's war effort was as a "mail drop" where Markpress used their connections in the global media world to amplify Biafra's messaging. For Stremlau, most of the voices that attacked Markpress did so to discredit the emerging humanitarian crisis in Biafra but did not wish to confront the various NGOs, church organizations, and other humanitarian sources that would have electoral consequences, especially in the UK and the United States.[38]

A close analysis of the timing and development of Biafra's genocide narratives supports the facts that Markpress did little to frame Biafra's message and served only to amplify it. In fact, Biafran outlets had begun developing the ideas before Ekwensi's external office approached Markpress for assistance. In the months after Nwankwo's article, Biafran outlets such as the *Biafra Newsletter* and newspapers not directly under Biafra's editorial control, like *The Times*, published in Onitsha, made scant references to genocide directly but strongly implied that Biafran independence over all the territories was the only option for Biafran security. The December 8, 1967 issue of the *Newsletter* contained a "Biafratoon" with a Nigerian official rubber-stamping a sheet of paper that read, "WE CONCUR WITH GOWON PLEASE CONTINUE THE GENOCIDE ON BIAFRA." The oversized stamp with *OAU* emblazoned on the shaft had a handle in the shape of Emperor Selassie's bust, implying OAU collusion with Nigeria to continue the genocide.[39] The rest of the issue, though covering the OAU mission the preceding month, had a more muted tone and refrained from accusing the OAU and the emperor of directly abetting genocide. The front-page article denounced the OAU mission for not consulting Biafra, claiming, "The committee demonstrated its lack of objectivity and was doomed to failure from the start when it decided to consult with only one party to the dispute."[40] Even the Biafran government's official response to the mission contained few hints of how central genocide would become to their public face in only a few short months. It simply expressed concern "that the OAU as presently constituted has become a willing tool of reactionary African leaders; and a perfect instrument for imperialist and neo colonialist intrigue," adding that, "the civilized world will neither be fooled nor hoodwinked by this stage-managed conference."[41] Though the Biafrans railed against being shut out of the international diplomatic system and the implicit recognition that came with it, they stopped short of openly accusing either Nigeria or any of its allies of genocide.

The following issue signaled the beginning of the shift toward genocide as the central aspect of Biafra's messaging during the war and came before the approaches to Markpress. The headline of a recurring column called "Letter from Biafra" published on December 29, 1967 read, "GENOCIDE IS THEIR AIM."[42] This article was one of the few that tackled the issue of genocide from an ethnic standpoint, challenging the notion that it was directed only at the Igbo. Most prior and subsequent work intentionally eschewed ethnic categorization, but this article explicitly challenged BBC and other news agencies reports. In one instance, the BBC reported that the Soviet-led air strikes on Biafra targeted the Igbo heartland. However, the *Newsletter* emphasized that all Biafrans regardless of ethnicity remained united in fighting Nigeria and called the BBC reporting of jubilant scenes in Calabar false, accusing the reporter of being "very much on a conducted tour."[43]

Most importantly, this article set the stage for what would become Biafra's evidence to support its claims of genocide across the war zone. Air strikes, coupled with the 1966 pogroms and the massacres in Asaba in October 1967, became the core of the evidence that Biafrans used until the end of the war to support their claims. Though the massacres and air raids had been terrorizing the population and became an important tool in pressuring outside groups to come to their aid, this article was the first to explicitly link them to a calculated genocidal campaign. However, the article's conclusion was not fully developed into the global appeal it would become, as it simply stated, "Biafrans will have the right to boast of the proud part they played in establishing for other oppressed one of the most important of all political truth [*sic*]: that genocide should never be a means of settling disputes and that when the ethnic extermination of a people is imminent they owe it as a right to fight for their survival and to exercise their God-given right to self-determination."[44] The Biafrans were yet to develop the message that engaged the world to halt or internationalize the conflict. Here, Biafran messaging remained squarely in the triumphalist sphere, claiming that the spirit of the people would prevail and Biafrans would provide the world with a new moral imperative.

One of the main issues in the article is that it emphasized mostly Igbo concerns and generalized them as those of all Biafrans. Biafran leaders were concerned about the ease with which the minority areas fell, so quickly and without resistance to the Nigerian incursions, especially as minority easterners joined the Igbo in the flight from the Northern and Western Regions during the 1966 pogroms. However, by the end of 1967, many non-Igbo had either, like Ken Saro-Wiwa, defected openly and publicly to the Nigerian side or simply waited to see which side held the upper hand in the conflict and sided with Nigeria on that account. The Biafrans, desperate to show unity across all ethnic groups, made this attempt to emphasize that "the solidarity shown by all Biafrans with the leadership of Colonel Ojukwu's" meant that all ethnicities wholeheartedly supported secession. Later in the war, the Biafrans avoided overt ethnocentrism in their characterization of their suffering. Especially after May 1968, *Biafran* and *Igbo* became virtually interchangeable terms, and Biafra's message of genocide became less implicit regarding the ethnicity of the Igbo as the victims of genocide.

In February 1968, Biafra's message abruptly changed as the Propaganda Directorate began shifting to a direct accusation of genocide. This narrative would dominate public awareness of the war and harden the idea that Nigerian prosecution of the war was genocidal, which has remained one of the most enduring legacies of the conflict. Across all Biafran platforms, the message of genocide became more accusatory in tone and more steeped in appeals to international law. The *Newsletter* opened its February 16 issue with a forceful and lengthy article that, for the first time, expressed the totality of the Biafran experience as genocide. This change in attitude came directly from Ojukwu, who on January 27 delivered a verbose speech laying out the allegations of genocide. Specifically, he detailed several aspects of genocide that Biafrans had suffered, including the 1966 massacres, where the Biafran leader again inflated the number of victims, from 30,000 to 32,000. Ojukwu's speech, reprinted in full in the *Newsletter*'s same issue, was a meandering affair that touched on virtually every aspect of Biafra's previous propaganda tropes, from OAU inefficacy to Britain's collusion with Nigeria. Ojukwu, however, took care to reframe all the old allegations as parts of a concerted effort to exterminate Biafra that could be categorized only as genocide. Ojukwu even read the first four articles of the UN genocide convention, adding that genocide "is a crime under the United Nations Convention on Human Rights. It is totally condemned by all the Christian Churches. Yet, Gowon claims to be 'a Christian and the son of a Methodist Minister,' a claim calculated to impress foreign churchmen and press correspondents who do not know that he is in reality the leader of a Muslim **jihad** directed towards the annihilation of Biafrans and the Islamization of Biafra."[45]

He ended by concluding that "Gowon stands condemned for genocide—a crime condemned by the civilized world under international law, a crime against humanity, a crime against God."[46] The shift in tone was emphasized in the "Biafratoon" that month, which showed a war-torn countryside with a burning village house. One side of the background was littered with bodies, and the other contained a barren tree with a flock of birds, presumably vultures; in front stood a Nigerian soldier, his face contorted with rage, tossing aside some pieces of paper with "Gowon's Geneva Convention" written on them while using his rifle's bayonet to skewer a small child.

The quick and remarkable shift in the message and its tone reverberated across Biafran publications. The Biafran military newspaper *The Leopard* followed a similar shift but with an emphasis on military morale, which had all but collapsed following the fall of Enugu and subsequent setbacks. The first issues contained articles that espoused Biafra's prospects and urged the soldiers to continue their struggle. However, beginning with the February 16, 1968 headline that read, "NIGERIA'S 'BIG PLAN' REVEALED," much of the tone turned to genocide. In fact, the May 31 issue featured a decapitated body on the cover's top fold, with the accompanying article asking the reader, "Does the picture shown on this page remind you of anything? . . . It is a picture of GENOCIDE! It is the dismembered body of a Biafran (probably your own relation)."[47]

Across the Biafran propaganda system, both at home and abroad, the end of 1967 and the beginning of 1968 signaled a shift in strategy and tactics. The Biafran leadership, no longer confident that the war was winnable, began to shift the focus to internationalizing the conflict. However, to penetrate a system whose rules determined to exclude them, the Biafrans leadership sought to create a groundswell of public pressure, especially in Britain. This pressure, the Biafrans hoped, would force the global community to step in to end the conflict, or at least to provide a de facto recognition of Biafra. Thus, using the very real political pressures that prompted secession, the Biafrans created a narrative that resonated around the world and had very real consequences, both during the war and in its aftermath.

SEVEN

BIAFRA AND NIGERIA'S SECOND MILITARY COLLAPSE AND PEACE TALKS

CONTRARY TO COMMON BELIEF, MARKPRESS had little hand in creating Biafra's message but was essential in disseminating it. Thanks to the company's deep and high-profile connections in the global media, Biafra's plight resonated around the world within a relatively short period. While most media outlets could not accept Biafra's own publications and press releases at face value, the message that the Propaganda Committee promulgated demanded further investigation, and the Biafrans were happy to oblige.

The initial flurry of attention came just as the Nigerian military began to ramp up its efforts to stamp out the secession. Because Gowon had proudly proclaimed that Biafra would be finished by the end of March 1968, he came under increased pressure to finish the job, especially after the setbacks in Onitsha and continuing attacks in the Bonny sector. In Bonny, despite the Nigerian amphibious assault in July 1967, the Biafrans continued to harass the occupiers until the following January, when the Nigerians finally succeeded in pushing them off the island. The young Ken Saro-Wiwa drew the ire of Biafrans hoping for a united front with the smaller ethnic groups when the Nigerians appointed him civilian administrator for the city. The Biafrans singled out Saro-Wiwa, who was quite vocal in his opposition to Biafra, by ransacking his home during their retreat from Bonny through his hometown of Bori in the heart of Ogoni. Not all Ogoni despised Biafra to the extent that Saro-Wiwa did. Ignatius Kogbara, another Ogoni, became Biafra's ambassador to the United Kingdom, where he was instrumental in developing Biafra's negotiation efforts with Britain and Nigeria in the hopes of raising Biafra's international profile.[1]

After several failures between October and November 1967 to take Onitsha by crossing the River Niger, Murtala Muhammed decided to take the city by land rather than amphibious assault. What followed was the single most bloody and lengthy campaign in the war, one that left both the Biafran military and the Nigerian 2nd Division in shambles. Muhammed, in his usual recklessness, decided to move his troops north and attack Onitsha from the east. He crossed the Niger some 150 kilometers north of the city at Idah and continued to Nsukka and Enugu, where he met little enemy resistance. However, Muhammed's forces neglected to notify general command or the 1st Division of their movement, and Shuwa nearly mistook the 2nd Division for a Biafran assault. Only a quick phone call from the police in Idah gave Shuwa enough time to verify that the forces moving through the sector were indeed friendly.[2]

Muhammed continued south, where he advanced to Awka from the east, taking the town with no resistance before continuing west on the Enugu-Onitsha road. Though Awka should have been heavily defended, as Madiebo led the city's military, the bulk of the Biafran leadership in Awka, Madiebo included, "were fighting two wars of survival at the same time—one against Nigeria and the other against the over vigilant Biafran public intoxicated by the 'sabotage' propaganda."[3] Further complicating matters, the Nigerians advanced along the road in a valley, which concealed their movements. Thus, lacking the ability to form an urban defense against Muhammed's division, Madiebo retreated to the Ngene Ukwa River, where he attempted to prevent the Nigerian 2nd Division from entering Onitsha.

The fall of Awka led many in the Biafran civilian elite to lose confidence in the military's ability to conduct the war. Many doctors, economists, and other civilians demanded and received direct command over military units, among them people like Joe Achuzia. Achuzia's biography is difficult to ascertain, with much of it contradictory or impossible to verify. He used much of it for self-aggrandizement and to inflate his credentials. What is known is that he arrived in Manchester, England, in the early 1950s to study engineering. There, he claimed to have joined an infantry unit as part of Britain's National Service requirement. His unit was supposedly sent to Korea, where he earned a battlefield commission and became an expert in infantry tactics but was taken prisoner by the North Koreans. At other times he claimed to have gone to Sandhurst, yet no record of him attending Sandhurst or any military record of him exists.[4] Sometime in the 1950s he returned to Nigeria, where he settled in Port Harcourt with his British wife and opened an engineering firm. When the war began, like many in Biafra, he shifted his production to wartime materiel, focusing on bomb making. One plan that Ojukwu hatched was to sail Achuzia's bombs into Lagos and detonate them in the harbor. Ojukwu abandoned the plan when he realized that much of Lagos would flood. Gould speculates whether Ojukwu's hesitation came because of the property his family still owned in the city.[5]

Regardless of his past, Achuzia became close to Ojukwu due to his munitions work, and the latter found enough confidence in him to place the 11th Division under his command to defend Muhammed's approach to Onitsha from Awka. However, few military officers had the same level of confidence in Achuzia that Ojukwu bestowed. In fact, after the war, the Nigerian military conducted a board of inquest to determine Biafran officers' fate. Achuzia was one of two men, along with Captain C. S. Shadrade, detained for "Sadistic Behavior."[6] Efiong's personal confrontations with Achuzia came in the war's final days. Madiebo, who was in charge of the withdrawal from Awka and subsequent defense of Onitsha reported his dismay at how Achuzia conducted his command, hinting that the former had little grasp of how a high-ranking division commander should conduct his affairs. Even more troubling, local intellectuals, such as an unnamed economist and a medical doctor, were given command over battalions under Achuzia's division. When Muhammed's forces attacked, the Biafrans quickly retreated, largely because of Achuzia's incompetence and general ignorance in military matters. Though Madiebo acknowledged Achuzia's personal courage, he thought that he should not have ever been given command of any formation larger than a company. Because Achuzia's battalion commanders also had no military training, they could not recognize their commander's ineptitude, further enabling his bumbling of command. Achuzia never had operational orders ready for his command. He would personally arrive and give orders on the spot, and until he did so, his subordinates could not function properly. As a result, "his troops fought the best they could, but the enemy pushed them quite swiftly to Abagana, with really no organized resistance or counterattacks. The whole division was by then without an effective commander and the troops were in complete disarray."[7] Because of Achuzia's lack of command experience, Muhammed's forces stood less than twenty kilometers from the city they had briefly yet ultimately unsuccessfully conquered the previous October, poised to take it once again.

In addition to Achuzia, the campaign to defend Onitsha saw Biafra employ foreign mercenaries. Muhammed's troops, rather than use the well-defended main arteries from Idah, instead took smaller roads that required the Biafrans to quickly reorganize their defenses and deploy their passive measures, such as the homemade explosives and mines, in relative haste. One mercenary unit disbanded shortly after losing their captain, a man identified only as Captain Le Rois, while defending the small hamlet of Amadim Olo in December 1967. Le Rois's men retreated to Umuahia and left the country from there, leaving Biafra almost without mercenaries.

One exception came in the form of a German mercenary named Rolf Steiner, born in Munich on January 3, 1933. At age sixteen, he left home to become a priest, intending to become a missionary in Africa. However, he left his studies the following year after an affair with a nun at the school and joined the French Foreign Legion in 1950. While in the Foreign Legion, he fought the Viet Minh and parachuted into the Suez Canal in the 1956 Suez Crisis. Steiner's Foreign Legion career ended when he participated in the Algerian War. He sided with the Pied Noirs, the French settlers determined to keep Algeria in French hands, joining the Organisation Armée Secrète (OAS). He was arrested and spent nine months in prison and subsequently was released from the Legion.

In 1967, Steiner met with one of his former Legion commanders, Roger Faulques, who arranged for him to fly to Port Harcourt and join the Biafran forces. Faulques also had a long history in Africa, where he supported Moise Tshombe's Katanga separatists in the Congo.[8] Steiner arrived in Nigeria just as the federal force had completed their conquest of Enugu. Through Steiner, Ojukwu hoped to create a new commando unit trained in guerilla warfare and other unconventional tactics. Called the 4th Biafran Commando Brigade, Steiner's unit first saw action in December 1967, when Muhammed began his long assault on Onitsha. Steiner convinced Madiebo to supply him with one hundred men, whom the German would train and take on an assault on the airport in Enugu. Steiner's men attacked the airport, destroying several Soviet MiG fighters in the process. Though Madiebo cast doubts on Steiner's actual success on the raid, he conceded that the German "had made his name and the sky was the limit."[9] Madiebo claimed that Steiner took the name Commando due to the raid on the airport, but the 4th Commando was also the name of "Mad Mike" Hoare's unit that many of the mercenaries who joined Steiner served with during the Congo Crisis. Steiner himself claimed that Ojukwu gave the unit the number because it was the Biafran leader's lucky number.[10] From then on, Steiner reported directly to Ojukwu, and his commandos became the best-supplied unit in Biafra's army, much to the chagrin of the African officers, who saw Steiner and the other European mercenaries, a new batch of whom joined Steiner after his successes, as nothing more than greedy sell-swords. Though Steiner never played a part in the Katanga Crisis, many of the mercenaries who joined him did.

Welsh-born South African Hugh "Taffy" Williams joined Steiner in the Commandos in late 1967 and has the distinction of being the last mercenary to leave the country, long after any other; he continued to fight long after the Biafrans were able to continue paying him. Both Williams and Steiner had deep respect for the Biafran soldiers they trained and fought with. Speaking to Frederick Forsyth, Williams expressed his regard, saying, "I've seen a lot of Africans at war. But there's nobody to touch these people. Give me 10,000 Biafrans for six months, and we'll build an army that would be invincible on this continent. I've seen men die in this war who would have won the Victoria Cross in another context. My God, some of them were good scrappers."[11] Both Steiner and Williams saw the Biafran soldiers as some of the best they had worked with, and both, especially Williams, believed in the Biafran cause. Whether this was because of the country's successful propaganda or other reasons is unclear.

Belgian Marc Goosens also began his African career in the Congo, but unlike Williams, Goosens served in an official capacity as a Belgian military officer with the Armée Nationale Congolaise (ANC).[12] However, like Steiner and Williams, Faulques recruited him for service in Biafra, and he arrived in Biafra in mid-1968. Like most mercenaries, his presence failed to affect the war in any meaningful way, and he is best remembered for his death in the Onitsha sector in November 1968, largely because of Gilles Caron's widely published images of Biafran soldiers carrying Goosens's lifeless body through chest-high water.[13]

During the war, Ojukwu seemed to have placed high hopes on the foreigners' ability to impact the war, but these were unfounded. Except for Goosens, none of the mercenaries who spent significant time in Biafra had any command experience, nor did they have much expertise in training regimens for large cadres of soldiers. By the time Ojukwu bundled Steiner and most of his fellow mercenaries out of Biafra in December 1968, the 4th Commando unit numbered more than three thousand men and had become leaderless.

On January 24, once Achuzia's inability to contain Muhammed's advance became apparent, Ojukwu ordered Madiebo to take command of the situation and stabilize it. Madiebo sent his operations chief, Col. Anthony Okoro Eze, to the front. He, along with Biafran air force commander Col. Chude Sokei, led a group of officers who took control of the situation and, according to Madiebo, rendered Achuzia irrelevant. Achuzia, however, claimed to have remained in charge of the defense and that he led the attempts to retake the city after its fall to the Nigerian 2nd Division.

One of the difficulties of reconstructing this campaign from this point, like many in the war, is that any operational reports, if written, were never kept and do not survive. As such, the only sources we have are interviews, memoirs, and other accounts that suffer from the ravages of memory and postwar politicization. During shorter or swift-moving campaigns, creating a chronology of events is slightly easier due to the fluid nature of the war and our ability to track if not exact dates then approximate troop movements and reconstruct operations in that manner. In the case of the defense of Onitsha, the conflicting recollections, along with the lack of dates and the static nature of the stalled Nigerian advance and dogged Biafran defense, make the historian's ability to reconstruct the war much more difficult. As a result, I have tried to create a synergy that most accurately reflects the war's conduct while pointing out the irregularities in the source material used to create the reconstruction.

By the time Madiebo's men arrived on the scene, the enemy had reached the village of Dunukofia, only fourteen kilometers from Onitsha. For the following two weeks, the Biafran forces held their lines despite a chronic shortage of ammunition and supplies. At one point during those two weeks, Steiner and his men executed an unsuccessful assault on the Nigerians at Abagana to dislodge them from their positions. Because of Steiner's success at the Enugu airport, Ojukwu and his high command supplied Steiner with the munitions he needed, and the senior officers took up a vantage point to view Steiner's assault. Forsyth, who would later claim that the mercenaries in Biafra shattered the myth of the "White Giants" that dominated the Congo conflict, appeared on the scene to record the assault in what Achuzia characterized as a "charade [that] smacked of a Hollywood stunt war film in the making. Only this time it was a real battle of life and death for the survival of Biafra."[14] Steiner's men would play an increasing role in the fighting in Onitsha, both in the defense of the city and in the various attempts to retake it.

Though the Biafrans lacked basic supplies, they had been able to halt the Nigerian advance for all of February and well into March. By the middle of the month, with Gowon's deadline for victory looming, the Nigerian military began a new push to take Onitsha and to end the war on all fronts. On March 13, the Nigerian assault resumed with fervor. The Biafrans broadcast through loudspeakers that they had surrounded Muhammed's forces, hoping to sow chaos and end the offensive. Instead, the broadcast sparked Muhammed to order a quick breakout toward Onitsha that caught the woefully undersupplied Biafrans by surprise. The Biafran defense quickly crumbled under Muhammed's onslaught. Further complicating matters, the popular air force commander Sokei was hit by shrapnel that pierced his heart, killing him instantly. Colonel Eze, who always appeared on the scene when the Biafran situation was desperate, was also hit during the same mortar shelling but survived. While he was recovering in the hospital, rumors began to spread that he was a saboteur and had killed Sokei. To stop the witch hunt, Eze was relieved of command and would return to action only in the battle of Ikot Ekpene more than a year later.[15] Thus, the Biafrans lost two of their most capable officers—one to the enemy and the other to the paranoia that was sweeping the country in the wake of the rapid military collapse. In fact, to appease Biafran morale, several officers who had been accused of sabotage were removed from active duty, further depleting the Biafran ranks of capable leaders.

The tough fighting into Onitsha lasted another twelve days. On March 25, Muhammed's troops finally entered the city, finishing the task they had begun the previous October. Though casualty numbers have never been released, both sides suffered heavily in the battle. Arguably, the entire war's most spectacular battle occurred as Muhammed began moving his support equipment and staff from Abagana, just behind the front lines, into Onitsha. On March 31, a major convoy departed Abagana consisting of nearly one hundred vehicles. The convoy set out with two armored cars in the front, an FV601 Saladin, and a Ferret, with two more Ferrets bringing up support in the rear. The Biafran force, led by Maj. Jonathan Uchendu, allowed the lead armored vehicles to pass before destroying the first of the supply trucks, blocking the road for the rest of the convoy. The bulky vehicles could not turn around on the narrow road, nor could the lead and rear vehicles reach the jammed convoy to provide support. Very soon, the Biafrans surrounded the convoy and destroyed the support traveling with it, attempting to salvage the desperately needed supplies while bracing for the inevitable counterattack. The forward vehicles did not even attempt to turn around but tried to speed into Onitsha only to be caught by a second ambush led by Col. Emmanuel Udeaja, who captured three of the five vehicles that escaped the initial ambush.

The Nigerian counterattack from Abagana comprised a company-size force and an armored car. The Biafrans, at this point elated and energized by their success, defeated the assault, but in the process one of the fuel tankers in the now captured convoy exploded, initiating a chain reaction that engulfed many of the ammunition trucks. By the end of the battle, only six of the trucks had survived, but the Biafrans had still captured more equipment and ammunition than they would normally receive in any two-month period of the war.[16]

According to Madiebo, the following morning, Achuzia, who had not participated in the assault and had not even been in the area, led reporters on a tour of the site, explaining how he had led the operation. The impressed reporters gave him the nickname Hannibal, and he became famous as Joe "Hannibal" Achuzia, the hero of Abagana.[17]

Achuzia naturally had a very different account of the incident at Abagana. Achuzia claimed he laid a deliberate trap for the Nigerians by clearing the Awka-Onitsha road, allowing Muhammed to think the Biafrans had left the area. Achuzia then ordered a series of diversionary attacks that made the Nigerians believe the road was clear. Once the Nigerians had become convinced, he claimed, they organized a convoy of four hundred vehicles, as opposed to the ninety-six in Madiebo's account, accompanied by soldiers marching six abreast on either side of the convoy, which had "rows of trailers loaded to the top with boxes of arms and ammunition."[18] Once the assault began, the first shell the Biafrans fired landed "on top of the lead tanker and there was a big explosion and fire."[19] Achuzia left the front and returned to his headquarters to manage the salvage of equipment once it became clear the Nigerian formation was in disarray. In Achuzia's version, Uchendu did not lead the assault but rather left his post in a panic when the convoy left Abagana. He then appeared at Achuzia's headquarters, where Achuzia threatened him with execution if he could not prove he had participated in the assault.[20]

Whichever account of the battle was correct, the ambush was so successful that the 2nd Division ceased from that moment to be an effective fighting force. With divisional morale plummeting, the Biafrans hoped to capitalize on the chaos by launching a series of counterattacks to retake the city and drive the Nigerian forces into the Niger. Once again, Ojukwu pushed Steiner's men into battle to attempt an immediate counterattack, which failed under circumstances that remain unclear. By this time, Achuzia had left to organize the defense of Port Harcourt. Though Madiebo was in the area and provided artillery support for Steiner's men, Steiner's assault petered out very quickly, despite the fact that the German's troops were issued for this one operation with as much ammunition as a regular brigade would hope to see in a fortnight. As for the assault itself, Madiebo simply stated, "I frankly did not know what actually happened, and I still do not know. I guess the operation failed."[21]

The Biafrans did not give up in their attempts to recapture the city until November, when Steiner's division was again sent into battle. However, the German had most likely begun to suffer from post-traumatic stress since his defeats earlier in the year. Nonetheless, Ojukwu ordered Steiner to lead his troops on a frontal assault on the city. Steiner protested that he had trained his men in guerrilla warfare, and as such they were ill equipped for such a mission. Dubbed Operation Hiroshima, the campaign lasted a fortnight beginning on November 15 and ending on the twenty-ninth with Steiner losing roughly half of his men.[22] It was during this campaign that Caron captured his series of images of Goosen's death.

The incident apparently drove Steiner into a drunken stupor and would be his last in Biafra. According to an unnamed Danish journalist, on December 6, Ojukwu summoned the German to his presidential compound in Umuahia. Steiner arrived drunk and demanded a beer. Ojukwu's aides and guards attempted to convince the German to sober up before his meeting with Ojukwu. However, Steiner insisted that he drink before his meeting. When a guard gave him the requested beer, he refused it in disgust, claiming the glass was not cold enough. As soon as he entered Ojukwu's conference room, he accused the Biafran leader of responsibility for the massacre of his men and then, in a stunning display, struck Ojukwu. As Ojukwu's bodyguards prepared to shoot the mercenary leader, Ojukwu stopped them and decided instead to use Steiner as an example. Ojukwu sent him out of the country the next day, saying, "It cuts across everything we believe here, to find our struggle for survival led by white mercenaries."[23] However, both Biafra and Nigeria continued to use mercenaries and other foreign personnel both in combat and in training. While many today might consider Steiner's erratic behavior, which began as early as his defeats in April, a symptom of post-traumatic stress, many Biafran commanders viewed the commando unit's preferential treatment as corrupting military morale. After Steiner's removal, Madiebo made sure to appoint a Biafran to lead the commandos with Brigadier General Nwawo becoming the division's commander, integrating the unit into the formal Biafran command structure.[24]

Though the Nigerians never again lost control of Onitsha, the city's capture proved to be a Pyrrhic victory. After the Abagana disaster, Muhammed left his post and did not play a further part in the war, electing to go on an extended leave in the United Kingdom. None of Muhammed's successors—Col. Ibrahim Haruna, who replaced him, and Lieutenant Colonel Jalo, who was the division's final commander—were ever able to regain control of the division's sagging morale and reform the division as an effective fighting force. In 1969, after Benjamin Adekunle orchestrated a similar and spectacular collapse of his 3rd Marine Commando Division, the 2nd Division moved back to the Midwestern State to guard the oil production from Biafran infiltration as part of a reorganization of the Nigerian war effort.[25]

The campaign for Onitsha became the standard for military campaigns for the rest of the war. Although the Nigerians were able to achieve their military objectives, their victories came at great cost, and the Biafran victories, though only mildly substantial in military terms, became public relations coups that were widely touted and publicized. These victories gave the beleaguered Biafrans hope that they could hold out until either victory was achieved or, failing that, the global community would force the Nigerians to deal with the Biafran leadership, and some kind of political agreement could end the war and ensure some degree of autonomy or independence.

Many of Biafra's hopes for survival relied on the ability to mobilize the international community in the new narrative they developed, expressing their war as a defense against genocide. However, in the language of the genocide convention, mobilizing the international diplomatic community hinged on proving, or at least managing, an effective accusation that the Nigerian government was intent on the physical destruction of Biafrans. Legally and politically, this argument was problematic because even during the war, the terms *Biafran* and *Igbo* were practically synonymous, if not officially then at least in the minds of journalists and the public, both in Nigeria and for those who followed the war abroad.

For Nigeria, framing the war as a battle against a small cabal of criminals who hijacked an unsuspecting population into supporting a devastating conflict became essential in their attempts to deflect international pressure and maintain their insistence that the conflict remain a domestic issue. Complicating matters for Gowon, the March deadline for defeating Biafra had expired, and though the Nigerian military enjoyed a commanding advantage, the Biafran army was by no means broken, nor did the Nigerians have a clear path to decisive military victory.

Far from the battlefields, the Biafran genocide narrative began to garner global attention. While most media outlets and news organizations did not necessarily subscribe to the Biafran press releases, Markpress's vast distribution network made it so reporters and organizations around the world began to assess the situation in the country. The Biafrans were more than happy to assist and sponsored reporters and especially photographers to enter the country and report on the situation to their audiences back home in the UK, United States and around the world. Joining

Caron was award-winning photographer Don McCullin, who had previously covered the war in the Congo and the civil war in Cyprus, for which he was awarded the World Press Photo of the Year in 1964 for his image of grieving Turkish women and children.[26] Both Caron and McCullin captured images of the war that shook the world's conscience and created exactly the kind of public pressure the Biafran government had been seeking. The Biafrans hoped the pressure would force Nigeria to the negotiating table or, failing that, provide some relief in the form of an international presence that would both administer aid to the civilian population and act as a de facto recognition of Biafra.

The horrifying images of burned women in vehicles and, more potently, malnourished children, many with the swollen bellies indicative of kwashiorkor, horrified viewers around the world and caused a mass mobilization in support of Biafra, decrying the genocide they claimed was taking place. March and April saw the beginning of small-scale airlifts, headed by the ICRC and the Catholic relief organization Caritas. Originating in Lisbon, where Biafra centered its logistics network for resupplying arms and ammunition, Biafran flights would reach the Portuguese-controlled island of Sao Tome and the island of Fernando Po in Spanish Guinea, which gained its independence in 1968 and became Equatorial Guinea but continued to be used as a base for the relief efforts and arms smuggling. These efforts laid the foundation for the massive airlift that would begin in August and is discussed later in this chapter. The Nigerians attempted to disrupt the flights, which arrived at three small makeshift airfields in Okigwi, north of Umuahia; at Oturu, north of Owerri; and the most well-known at Uli, which was nicknamed Annabelle. By August 1968, only Uli would remain in service for the length of the war and become the hub of Biafra's relief and smuggling operations.[27]

The conflict exposed British prime minister Harold Wilson's government to intense pressure as the death toll began to mount and Wilson's government attempted to deflect criticism while they formulated a plan to assist in ending the war. In one instance, on March 12, 1968, Irish Catholic bishop of Calabar James Moynagh arrived in London for a talk with Michael Stewart, the foreign minister. Moynagh, who had been in Calabar during the Nigerian invasion and witnessed some massacres against the Igbo, told the minister that the Ibibio had been eager to cooperate in the cleansings. Moynagh accepted many of the points that underpinned British policy in Nigeria during the war—namely, that the British could not stop supplying Nigeria with arms because doing so would ruin any credibility and influence, not only with Nigeria but also in Africa and the Commonwealth as a whole.[28] Indeed, though Britain was Nigeria's main supplier of arms, Wilson's government saw the political need to limit civilian casualties and regularly refused to supply Nigeria with the types of shells and weapons that could cause the most collateral damage. In 1967, the Nigerians requested 33,500 105mm howitzer shells, which were refused. In the first six months of 1968, the British did supply

Nigeria with 42,500 of those rounds but refused a request for 50 flamethrowers and 10,000 German self-loading rifles, most likely Heckler & Koch G3s. During the war's first year, the British did their best to limit the export of automatic weapons, delivering only 800 Sterling submachine guns but refusing to deliver Browning and Bren machine guns, mortars, and tanks, instead allowing only the export of light armored cars such as Saracens, Saladins, and Ferrets, though it is unclear if those were delivered with or without the standard mounted machine guns.[29]

Wilson's government also prepared several hard-line defenses of their policies toward the war. When confronted on why they refused to cut off supplies completely, officials were instructed, in addition to the aforementioned claim of losing global credibility, to claim that such a move would make peace harder to achieve because "the Biafrans would draw the conclusion that we and others were gradually being brought round to full recognition of their claims and that therefore they had no need to make any real effort at negotiation or compromise."[30]

Countries not closely involved in the conflict also faced public pressure to intervene to stop what, by April 1968, had become widely accepted as genocide. In the United States, Biafran propaganda was having a profound effect. Images of starving Biafran children were on the news everywhere, and public pressure to help send relief flights to the affected area was mounting from all sides. One of the Johnson administration's first actions concerning the war was a presidential memo to General Gowon urging him to allow for the creation of a Red Cross airstrip at Uli.[31] Though this still did not represent a drastic departure from previous US policy, it would set the tone for events to come.

The US administration was at first resistant to any direct involvement, despite much pressure from activist groups, concerned citizens, congressmen, and even the mayor of Los Angeles Sam Yorty, who urged the president to take responsibility and send a personalized team to assess the situation in Biafra. As a possible emissary, the mayor suggested Senator Edward Brooke, Supreme Court justice Thurgood Marshall, and several others. Though the administration sent him only a cursory reply, Walt Rostow, Johnson's national security advisor, drafted a long letter explaining the US position on the Nigerian Civil War. In the unsent reply, Rostow stated, "We hope that others may be in a better position to bring about a peaceful end to the Nigerian conflict. We have quietly encouraged efforts of the Organization of African Unity and the British Commonwealth Secretariat to bring the sides together. And we welcome the individual efforts of men of good will. In the last analysis, only the Nigerians themselves can settle their dispute and resolve to live in peace with one another."[32]

The letter from Mayor Yorty was one of the first to arrive at the White House demanding action regarding Biafra. When the scale of the humanitarian disaster became apparent, the administration was flooded with petitions, letters, and photographs from people of every walk of life, and Americans also began to donate money to alleviate the famine in Biafra. The intensity of the letters showcased the public pressure on the Johnson administration to act in Biafra.

A letter from Robert Schulman, the head of the Department of Ambulatory Care at the Albert Einstein College of Medicine, Yeshiva College, said, "Why should these people die—just one—because the rich nations stood idly by when they could have helped, it will be another black mark on the history of mankind . . . and you, Mr. President, will be more to blame than anyone, because all you have to do is pick up a telephone to have the food sent. . . . Will your conscience permit you one moment of peace if you let millions starve? If so then God help you, for no one else can."[33]

While many of the letters to the president had such a strong emotional overtone, not all of them were as aloof and damning to a president who had little ability to act decisively to end the famine. Reverend Edward Riley, a catholic priest from New Orleans who was on his way to teach at a seminary in Ibadan, had a much more sober view of the situation, though he came to much the same conclusion as Schulman. In his letter, Riley stated that he understood the diplomatic difficulties in bringing food to Biafra, but the starving masses could not wait for a political solution. He ended by expressing sympathy for the decisions Johnson must make, not only regarding Biafra but also on Vietnam, civil rights, "and other difficult problems which daily confront you."[34]

Other writers had more practical requests. In a joint letter, several leading religious figures from the Boston area asked why the United States had not offered any logistic means to transport the food.[35] In a similar vein, a letter from Conrad Brown, an editor from one of the publishing houses in New York, wrote, "Let us counter America's bad world image resulting from civilian casualty figures in Vietnam by loading long range bombers with food for the starving children of Biafra."[36]

The Israeli government was also the target of a large number of letters urging the Jewish state to assist the Biafrans. Israel's position was unique, as the Biafrans went to great lengths to tie their suffering to that of the Jews during the Holocaust. In one letter sent to Yitzhak Rabin, then the Israeli ambassador in Washington, Simon Obi Anekwe, a prolific letter writer throughout the war, wrote, "I am left with the impression that neither Israel nor the AJC or other agency has been moved to assist the people who in happier days had been their friends and have extended the welcoming hand. Even over the objections of Nigeria's Muslim leaders. I am puzzled to think that not a bottle of aspirin or a vial of penicillin; not a rubber ball has gone from the state and the people possessed of such military and financial strength that they could stand up to the whole Islamic Middle East: not an ounce of eight to Biafra from those they thought of his friends."[37]

Anekwe concluded:

> The hour is late but not too late for you to reflect on the role you played in the face of Nigeria's attempt to do to Biafra what Nazi Germany did to Jews in Europe. Justice and morality are universal. Genocide is genocide; extermination is extermination, whether by gas or the bullet. I hope when the history of the Biafran struggle is written, it can be said that Israel and American Jews reverted to the kind of role played by Pres. Roosevelt and setting the right course to a people whose plight paralleled today in Biafra was crying out to the conscience of mankind.

In another letter, sent to the Israeli consulate in New York, the president of the Biafra Students Association in the Americas, Godwin Anyaogu, stated that "having been called 'the Jews of Africa,' we are now passing through similar historical process [*sic*] as the Jews of Europe and Israel" and continued by saying, "Our cries for help have gone unheard, and the same forces which have conspired to destroy the State of Israel are seeking to annihilate the Biafran people."[38]

Biafran students studying in Israel also formed student organizations and embarked on a letter-writing campaign to try to sway the Israeli government to its side. A senior Israeli official, Yochanan Bein, was visited by a Biafran, Okey Anyadike, who introduced himself as the publicity secretary of the Biafran Union of Israel. Anyadike gave Bein a letter that read much like the letter from Anekwe, urging Israeli support: "Very often people have pointed out the similarities between Israel and Biafra. . . . Thus, by recognizing Biafra, Israel will gain a true friend among the progressive nations of Africa. We Biafrans are eagerly expecting the government of Israel to recognize our young republic soon."[39]

Bein attached a memo to the letter, which he circulated to the foreign ministry and the Israeli embassy in Lagos, stating, among other points, that "I explained because of its size and struggle, official Israeli recognition might add prestige, but will bring diplomatic harm without any gains to Biafra and Biafra first needs recognition of a large country outside of Africa."[40]

Because the Nigerian press repeatedly accused Israel of actively assisting the Biafrans militarily, the Israeli government was extremely cautious in dealing with the Biafrans and kept its involvement only to humanitarian aid. In all, the Israeli government sent two military medical teams to rebel-held territory, the first time the Israeli government committed any troops to overseas deployment.[41] The Israeli government also donated twenty tons of canned meat to Biafra, which was actually war loot captured from the Egyptian army during the 1967 war. The labels were replaced and sent to Biafra, though the source of the meat was not publicized at the time.[42]

Clearly, the Biafrans hoped to enlist some material help from the Israeli government. However, reluctant to take sides in the conflict, the latter declined to openly assist the Biafrans in any way other than humanitarian aid.

Biafra's propaganda made tangible gains when on April 13, Julius Nyerere became the first leader to recognize Biafra. In his speech declaring Tanzania's recognition of Biafra, he echoed the narrative that linked Biafra's plight to that of the Jews in the years leading to Israel's establishment:

> Tanzania has recognized the State of Israel and will continue to do so because of its belief that every people must have some place in the world where they are not liable to be rejected by their fellow citizens. But the Biafrans have now suffered the same kind of rejection within their state that the Jews of Germany experienced. Fortunately, they already had a homeland. They have retreated to it for their own protection, and for the same reason—after all other efforts had failed—they have declared it to be an independent state.
>
> In light of these circumstances, Tanzania feels obligated to recognize the setback to African unity, which has occurred. We therefore recognize the State of Biafra as an independent sovereign entity, and as a member of the community of nations. Only by this act of recognition can we remain true to our conviction that the purpose of society, and of all political organization, is the service of Man.[43]

Such was the recognition of Biafra's plight that Nyerere was willing to place on hold his vision for a united continent to attempt to facilitate an agreement between the feuding sides. In the next month, three more African states recognized Biafra. On May 8, Omar Bongo's Gabon extended diplomatic recognition to the besieged state. Ivory Coast followed on May 15 and Zambia's Kenneth Kaunda five days later. Despite attempts to secure major recognition outside of Africa, with the overtures to Israel, the only non-African country to recognize Biafra would be Haiti, which extended diplomatic relations on March 23, 1969. None of the countries ever established diplomatic relations or secured any representation in the country, and all of them had been involved in pressuring Nigeria from the beginning of the war. Gabon and Ivory Coast also played central roles in supplying Biafra with war materiel.

These small diplomatic victories would be meaningless if Biafra could not secure its long-term independence, and the Nigerians had been easily stymieing Biafra's access to the UN, OAU, and any other multilateral organization that could pressure the FMG into any kind of negotiated settlement. However, Biafra's campaign to win global sympathies heaped pressure on Gowon's government to end the war, adding to the calls from within Nigeria to end the war that many in the country thought would be over by March 1968. Nongovernmental organizations (NGOs), such as various relief organizations, also began to take an interest in the civilian suffering that was beginning to reach crisis levels in many parts of Biafra.

Foreign interest in the war would thus change the dynamic of the conflict's international scope. Because Catholicism was the major religion among the Igbo, and many of the priests and bishops who served in the areas that now constituted Biafra came from outside Nigeria, the Vatican took an early interest in the war's humanitarian aspects. Thus, the first foreign delegation to visit Biafra came in the form of two monsignors, one of whom, George Rochau, represented Caritas, the church's relief organization. The pair visited Lagos in December 1967, met with Gowon, and asked if he would agree to a Christmas truce that would enable them to visit Biafra and open an indirect and informal communication channel between the two sides. When Gowon refused, they returned to Rome to lobby for a formal visit to Biafra. This visit came the following February when the same monsignors flew into Biafra, landing at one of the airstrips that was used to smuggle arms into the country. As the Vatican emissaries were the first foreign officials to enter Biafra in any capacity, their arrival was greeted with great fanfare, and their meeting with Ojukwu was highly publicized. Though Ojukwu proclaimed that he would be willing to issue a ceasefire and enter into any negotiations, ultimately the Vatican effort failed to achieve anything concrete, and similar visits from various Protestant relief organizations in early 1968 similarly did not yield results in either achieving a ceasefire or securing relief for the besieged Biafran civilians.

Yet the Vatican emissaries' visit did herald a beginning of a softening of Nigerian demands for the crisis to be accepted as strictly an internal matter. Indeed, beginning in January 1968, Canadian Arnold Smith, the first secretary general of the Commonwealth of Nations, urged both sides to agree to a peace conference to be hosted by the Commonwealth. By April both sides had agreed to meet and chose Kampala, the Ugandan capital, as the site for the peace talks to take place. That was where any agreement ended, and the preliminary talks as to the agenda, or even who would chair the meeting and which secretarial service the conference would utilize, became sources of contention between Anthony Enahoro, the Nigerian information minister, and the Biafran justice minister Sir Louis Mbanefo. The preliminary negotiations ended on May 14, 1968, and the sides set May 23 as the date for the conference to begin.

As the conflict dragged on, pressure began mounting on Gowon from within Nigeria. To alleviate it and forestall any Biafran successes at Kampala, Adekunle's 3rd Marine Commando Division launched an assault on the last direct Biafran link to the outside world and Biafra's most important urban center, Port Harcourt. If the months of fighting in and around Onitsha were any indication, the battle for the city would be hard fought and lengthy. However, Biafran resistance, which had several spectacular victories at the beginning of the conflict, was now overstretched and could not cope with the newest amphibious assault on the region's main port and second most important oil facility after Bonny. Since the assault on Bonny the previous August, the division had grown substantially and by mid-1968 could count on a force of five brigades. Throughout March, Adekunle's division had perfected the art of the amphibious assault, capturing several towns in and around Calabar in the Ibibio-speaking regions near the Cameroonian border and along the Cross River. By the end of March, the division had captured Opobo, approximately fifty kilometers east of Bonny along the Imo River, at the easternmost mouth of the Niger Delta. In April, Adekunle's forces began their assault on Port Harcourt, attempting to capture the town of Onne, a small port approximately halfway between Bonny and Port Harcourt. The evenly matched Biafrans and Nigerians could make little headway against each other until a mercenary, whom Madiebo identified only as George and who most likely was Italian George Norbiatto, arrived with a company and within four hours had cracked the Nigerian defense. The Nigerians abandoned their positions, leaving behind significant loot for the Biafran war effort, including three hundred thousand rounds of ammunition, rifles, bazookas, and food.[44] Norbiatto died in the battle when he was shot in the head. Biafran jubilation, which included a special mourning period for the Italian hero, was short lived. Within a month the Nigerians would return with a significant force that included armor, heavy artillery, and air support—a force that the Biafrans could not hope to contain or defeat.

Starting on April 20, the Nigerian 3rd Marine Commando Division massed an offensive that overwhelmed the Biafran defenders and quickly enveloped Port Harcourt from the south and north. They began by landing troops at Kono and Obete along the Imo River, north of their newly captured base at Opobo. Though far from the city, this allowed the Nigerians to safely land their armor and heavy artillery in a place that could easily access Port Harcourt, whereas the areas south along the coast, such as Bonny and Opobo, were inaccessible by land.[45] The forces soon overwhelmed the Biafran defenders, who numbered a company each at Obete and Kono. Despite the odds, the Biafrans launched a counterattack and succeeded in driving the Nigerians out of Obete; however, the latter quickly returned with air support, secured the bridgehead, and unloaded their heavy weapons. After five days of fierce fighting, Ojukwu replaced Colonel Kalu, the commander of the Biafran 11th Division, with the popular but controversial Achuzia.

Though Achuzia's popularity buoyed civilian confidence in Port Harcourt, his lack of military understanding doomed the city's defense, and his boastful cruelty caused morale to crater as he gleefully executed soldiers he accused of insubordination and cowardice. Achuzia was also in the enviable place of being outside the military chain of command. Technically he commanded the militias and as such was answerable to Ojukwu alone. According to Madiebo, when Achuzia arrived in Port Harcourt, he arrived with great fanfare and confidently asserted that he would "destroy the enemy within 48 hours provided no one interfered with his operations and Kalu was removed from Port Harcourt."[46] Achuzia, on the other hand, claimed that when he arrived in the city he met with Madiebo, who told him that he was to take command of the city and that Kalu had been transferred and ordered to return to Umuahia. Whatever the reality, Achuzia took control of the city's defense and had less than an hour for Kalu to brief him on the situation before taking his command, claiming in his memoir that "I felt like crying" before heavily protesting the order that Madiebo claimed came directly from Ojukwu.[47] The disparity in these accounts proves two things. First, the two top commanders in Port Harcourt hated each other with a passion and second, had little respect for each other's ability on the battlefield. While Madiebo acknowledged Achuzia's bravery, he questioned his tactical abilities. In one instance, when the Nigerians had broken through to the north and south of the city, Madiebo claimed that Achuzia entered the command center blaming saboteurs for the collapse in the city's defense. Madiebo, who saw the damage that talk about sabotage could incur, dissuaded him from an action that would collapse all morale and end in a massive witch hunt instead of planning the city's defense. Though Madiebo shared his plans with Achuzia, he later claimed, "I was not sure how much of those orders Major Achuzia understood."[48] Achuzia equally despised Madiebo and all but accused him of cowardice, claiming that Madiebo had "a pathological fear of being caught in an operational command area when action was in progress." He also claimed that as an artillery officer, Madiebo lacked the ability to understand infantry field maneuvering, concluding, "I could not look for operational advice from [Madiebo], and decided to regard him as the SITREP postal center."[49]

Regardless of their animosity, both agreed that Biafran soldiers in Port Harcourt had little will to fight and suffered from lax discipline, with many troops staying in comfortable accommodations in the city while treating their soldiering as if it were a day job. When Achuzia first arrived in Port Harcourt, even before he officially took over command of the city's defense, he came upon a squad that, after a long day of fighting, returned to their barracks in Port Harcourt. Achuzia ordered the troops to prepare for an immediate return to the front, and the exchange continued:

> Then I said "listen to me carefully and all of you. I am going forward to ascertain the enemy's true position. . . . I want to see all of you ready, formed to move, and if you are not ready, you my friend who said you are in charge, I will shoot you down like a dog, and any other soldier that refuses to obey orders. . . . When I came back I met the troops in the same position I left them. They had made no attempt to get ready to move. . . . I walked up to the soldier. I asked him, "Why are you not ready?" He said "I told you we are no more fighting." He was holding his gun in his hand. I told him to hand the gun over to me. He refused. I lifted my automatic rifle from my shoulder. I said "I warned you all before I left. Now I will carry out my threat and anyone still sitting down will be dealt with in the same way." I lifted the gun and shot him where he stood, then I said "everybody get up." They all jumped and I marched them forward.[50]

He then told the men that he would be waiting in the rear until morning, and anyone who attempted to return to the city would suffer the same fate as the insubordinate soldier. Col. Robert Obioha, who witnessed the altercation, reportedly said, "Now I know what they mean by the Achuzia method. I will combine it with my method and see what they can produce."[51]

Achuzia's exchange with soldiers he did not even command illustrates two important problems in the defense of Port Harcourt. First, the Port Harcourt defense was woefully inadequate to repel a major federal invasion. Compounding matters, the lack of discipline necessary to organize and maintain military cohesion made any defense even more difficult. These problems, coupled with Achuzia's lack of military tactical knowledge, doomed Port Harcourt to a quick and ignominious defeat. Further, Achuzia's quick temper and cruelty toward his men, even those he did not command, enhanced his reputation as an authoritarian commander and arguably even justified his imprisonment after the war.

Port Harcourt's defense was thus hampered by factors that compounded and virtually ensured that the city would fall in short order. The lack of discipline, combined with the two top-ranking officers' mutual animosity and lack of professional respect for each other, could not be reconciled because of the Biafran military's convoluted chain of command. Though the army, navy, and air force answered to Madiebo and Efiong as the top-ranking military leaders, the militias, which Achuzia commanded, and the commandos under Steiner until November 1968 answered to Ojukwu directly. As such, Madiebo, and the rest of the Biafran military, could only offer suggestions to Achuzia and not order him to coordinate the city's defense. These factors made Biafra's shortage of materiel even more acute in the face of an enemy force that had now fully mobilized to capture the city before the start of the peace negotiations in Kampala.

The only hope at halting the well-equipped Nigerian advance was to cut off communications and supply lines rather than attempt to halt a frontal assault or, even worse, to initiate one. Thus, once reports filtered in that the Nigerian forces had advanced from Kono as far inland as Bori in the Ogoni heartland, roughly sixty kilometers southeast of Port Harcourt, Madiebo suggested that the Biafrans outflank the advancing Nigerians and attack the bridgehead at Kono, cutting off the supply and communications lines between the advance force and Adekunle's headquarters across the Imo River. If successful, this assault could cut off both the troops advancing from Kono and those who landed further north in Obete.

Not trusting Madiebo's tactical advice, Achuzia instead opted to halt both Nigerian advances with frontal defenses along the axes leading to Port Harcourt, in the north at Umu Abayi and in the south at Bori. Though the Biafrans held the towns for five days, the Nigerians eventually succeeded in breaking the defenses and pushed through to Port Harcourt. Madiebo blamed the defeat on both Achuzia's inept tactics and the overwhelming forces that Adekunle committed to the assault while Achuzia blamed the ever-elusive "saboteurs" for undermining his plans. He also blamed the various directorates for diverting vital resources such as food, vehicles, and fuel from the city's defense, opting to supply the civilians instead.[52]

Though sabotage most likely had little to do with the failure to defend the city, the rest of the factors no doubt conspired to doom it. Though actual sabotage did little to harm Biafra's defense, the fear of the saboteurs and the zealotry in weeding them out compounded the other factors and ultimately, as in other theaters, spawned a host of vigilantes determined to punish those who collaborated with the enemy. Madiebo described the scene: "From then on, Port Harcourt grew rather lawless. Everybody set up his or her own roadblock somewhere in the town, and searched for saboteurs. People had their property seized if it appeared they were leaving town, while others were beaten up for one reason or the other. In other words, the usual atmosphere that preceded the fall of a major town had been created, and no one again talked of the enemy, but saboteurs."[53]

If the Biafran preparation and execution of the defense of Port Harcourt was disorganized and ad hoc at best, the Nigerian 3rd Marine Commando Division's assault had all the hallmarks of a well-planned invasion. In his memoir, Alabi-Isama, who was a brigade-level commander in Adekunle's division, provides what he claims were the excerpts from the Nigerian operational plans; however, whether these were the actual plans or simply his recollections of them is unclear.[54] Regardless, the assault on Port Harcourt was a massive affair for the Nigerians, who had learned the lessons of the chaotic, if ultimately successful, capture of Onitsha.[55]

The Nigerians emphasized two important factors in their assault. First, though the campaign started in April, before the prospect of any peace process, by the beginning of May it became clear that talks of some sort would commence in the relatively near future. It thus became imperative that the campaign to capture the city be concluded before these talks began. If the city, which was the only port still left in Biafran hands, could be captured, the Nigerians could argue that Biafra could no longer call itself a viable state and demand that Ojukwu's regime renounce secession while limiting any concessions to the breakaway republic. Second, the Biafran campaign that charged the Nigerian government with orchestrating genocide had begun to put pressure on the FMG that led to the agreement to hold talks, and it became important that the non-Igbo populations in Biafra decide not to back the rebels, undermining Nigeria's claim that they wished only to liberate the areas under Biafran control. Though some of the so-called minority people like Ken Saro-Wiwa and others in the Niger Delta openly supported Nigeria, largely because Gowon's twelve-state plan gave them administrative independence from the Igbo-dominated Eastern Region, others, alarmed at the violence that Nigerian troops perpetrated, sought unity with Biafra. Even Saro-Wiwa mentioned the rape and destruction that the advancing federal troops left in their wake, writing in his memoir that his sisters had to hide in the forest from the "raping Federal soldiers."[56] One reporter in London's *Sunday Times* wrote on April 26, "I have seen things in Biafra that no man should have seen. Sights to search the mind and sicken the conscience, I have seen children roasted alive, young girls torn in two by shrapnel, pregnant women eviscerated, and old men blown to pieces in an uncontrolled annihilation and mass massacre of Easterners of Nigeria."[57] The reporter was referencing the Nigerian bombing campaigns mainly against targets in the interior of Biafra and largely perpetrated by poorly trained Egyptian pilots who did not have the skills to fly precise missions like their East German and later Czech counterparts. Nonetheless, the reporters who had come to Biafra at the Ojukwu government's behest seemed to confirm the worst aspects of Biafra's propaganda. Images of starving children, charred remains, and other reported atrocities seemed to undermine Nigeria's claims that they were benign liberators seeking only to preserve the country's unity. Thus Biafra's effective message could undermine these claims and send minorities fleeing into the Biafran heartland, complicating matters during the peace talks.

To show the people in the Niger Delta that the Nigerian forces had indeed come as liberators, Adekunle, commander of the Nigerian 3rd Marine Commando Division, created the 19th Brigade, which would spearhead the assault from Opobo, and placed Isaac Adaka Boro as its commander. Adekunle hoped that by commissioning the former secessionist leader into the Nigerian army, he would alleviate fears that the Nigerians were simply invaders and not liberators. Adaka Boro's leadership was only one factor that the Nigerian 3rd Marine Commando Division used to assuage the local and international concerns that Biafran propaganda had been stoking. The second strategy was to establish the states in the non-Igbo areas as quickly and efficiently as possible. According to Alabi-Isama, this was done with foresight and served both tactical and strategic goals. On the tactical level, attempting to overrun the southern coast in a strictly military fashion was near impossible for a force like Adekunle's. Though the division consisted of over forty thousand men, the region's topography made supplying the soldiers a tricky proposition because of the many rivers and creeks that required marine transport the Nigerian military simply did not possess. As Alabi-Isama wrote:

> Let us for a moment assume that we attacked Port Harcourt from Bonny, advancing with over 40,000 troops in hundreds of dug-out canoes. That would have been a disaster on its own, especially with some of our troops from outside our operations area who barely could swim or had never seen such an expanse of water in their lives. At most of our crossings, the dug-out canoes could only take a maximum of six soldiers with their kits. Even a bag of rice or gari was too heavy for the canoes we had. That was why we had to build pontoons at Opobo.[58]

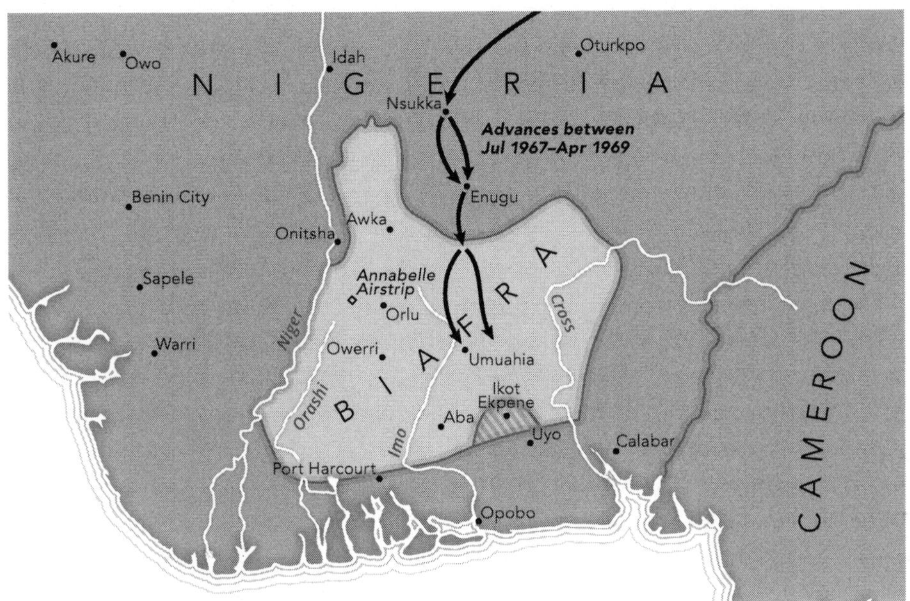

Map 7.1. Biafra ca. June 1968

As both the Nigerians and Biafrans well knew, the lack of effective transport meant that a total assault was not possible, and the Nigerians would be forced to rely on the two bridgeheads that Madiebo hoped to destroy. Second, the Nigerians had captured much of the area that constituted two of the three states that the Eastern region had become, along with the significant and worried civilian populations of those regions. Alabi-Isama hoped that putting the civilian government in place would remove the military's responsibility to supply them and allow the it to focus on military matters.

With the Biafran withdrawal from the city, Adekunle effectively controlled the entire southern region of Biafra, which for the Nigerians constituted the Rivers State. More importantly, the Nigerian offensive captured most of the non-Igbo parts of Biafra, leaving Ojukwu's regime with little more than the Igbo heartland that was overflowing with refugees from all parts of Nigeria and now virtually the entire population of the evacuated city of Port Harcourt. When the peace talks in Kampala began, the Nigerians hoped to use their recent conquests as proof that the twelve-state solution had become a fait accompli and that the Biafrans would now realize their dream of independence was dead.

However, Mbanefo, the Biafran chief justice and head of the delegation for the talks did not even acknowledge that the city had fallen and called any mention of that fact immaterial to the proceedings.[59] For Biafra, the Kampala Conference was the culmination of their propaganda efforts, and now, for the first time, they felt they were being recognized as a sovereign state equal to Nigeria. Enahoro summed up the Nigerian position in his opening address, stating, "The concept of Biafra is now dead," adding that "I suggest we address ourselves here at this meeting to the need to lay a sound foundation for a political solution at a later stage."[60] The Biafrans, led by Mbanefo, could not have been further from their Nigerian counterparts in conceptualizing their position. In his opening address, Mbanefo demanded not only an immediate end to hostilities but also that the Nigerians withdraw to the prewar borders and end the economic blockade.

Stremlau called the Kampala Conference the Kampala Confrontation, and with good reason.[61] Even before the conference began on May 23, 1968, it was clear that getting the Nigerians and Biafrans to agree would be difficult at best. The most fundamental contention, that of Biafran renunciation of secession, could not easily be resolved. For the Nigerians, the first step to stopping the war was "acceptance by the rebels that Nigeria should remain one sovereign united country."[62] The Biafrans had suffered so many setbacks on the battlefield after their failed Midwest Offensive that renunciation of secession became the only real bargaining chip they had left. At the beginning of the war, the British International Institute for Strategic Studies assessed Nigeria's ability to win in a military confrontation and concluded that "the Nigerian Army of 8,000 men . . . was never intended as an instrument of invasion" and that it would be unlikely that Nigeria could defeat Biafra militarily.[63] By mid-1968, the Nigerian military had increased substantially in both men and materiel and had effectively reduced Biafra to the Igbo heartland. Indeed, Shuwa's 1st Division alone numbered some 40,000 men, while the 3rd Marine Commando Division would end the war slightly smaller, with 35,000. In total, the Nigerian Army grew to 250,000 by the end of the war.[64]

Nonetheless, the Nigerian position, as outlined in a twelve-point proposal, called for the Biafran military to "renounce secession, order their troops lay down their arms as from the cease-fire hour, and announce the renunciation [of secession]" twelve hours before the ceasefire. Enahoro iterated the Nigerian point in his opening speech, claiming, "Those now in rebellion must also accept the twelve State structure. . . . One of the root causes of the Nigerian problem was the fear of domination by one region or one ethnic group," adding that "it is only with the success of this exercise that all tribes in the former Eastern Region can co-exist peacefully . . . because now they would be free of Ibo domination, real or feared, and the resentment it engenders."[65] Just as the Igbo's fears of domination from the north were valid, whether or not they were real, the fears that other ethnic groups in the former Eastern Region harbored against the Igbo were equally valid.

The Nigerian demand that Biafrans renounce secession and accept the twelve-state solution was anathema for the Biafran delegation. To agree to renounce secession as a precondition to any talks would effectively force the Biafrans to agree to any Nigerian dictate and leave them with no leverage in establishing a final status within any new Nigerian state. Mbanefo, one of Nigeria's first lawyers and a storied judge who served in an ad hoc position on the International Court of Justice, was aware of international law and versed in the rhetoric that allowed the Biafrans to take part in the Kampala negotiations. Like many Biafrans, he viewed the Igbo's position in Nigeria as exceedingly precarious and untenable. In his opening speech, he claimed "to force Biafrans back into the federation would be like forcing the Jews who had fled to Israel back to Nazi Germany."[66] For the Biafrans, even appearing to agree to a ceasefire or anything that could be considered a surrender without first negotiating security for the Igbo was an impossibility. For the Nigerians, negotiating without a commitment to a united Nigeria was equally unacceptable.

As a result, it was up to Smith as the convener to attempt a mediation that would, if not achieve a breakthrough, at least allow the sides to save face and not end the talks in abject failure. Such a failure would humiliate the Commonwealth and President Obote, and neither could accept failure after involving themselves so heavily in the attempts to end the war. Further throwing the conference into chaos, Johnson Banjo, a low-level stenographer for the Nigerian delegation, disappeared from his hotel while making copies of Enahoro's opening speech. Both sides accused the other of malfeasance for the disappearance, with the Nigerians threatening to abandon the talks unless Banjo returned. The Biafrans countered by threatening to leave the talks if they did not resume immediately. Ojukwu threatened to have his delegation walk out of the negotiations, and after several days both sides agreed to resume negotiations without a resolution as to Banjo's fate. Weeks after the end of the talks, his body turned up in a marsh outside Kampala. Though the case was never officially solved, Ugandan authorities blamed the abduction and murder on Bugandan separatists.[67]

Enahoro attempted to devise a way out of the impasse. He understood that the Biafrans could not simply surrender and that to demand that they accept unity before any final negotiations was demanding just that and would essentially ensure the war continued. However, he could not concede any arrangement other than a commitment to a single unified Nigeria and an acceptance of the twelve-state solution. To negate this point, Enahoro engaged one of the basic tenets of Biafra's propaganda: that the only way to ensure security was through sovereignty. In his opening speech, he accepted that the Igbo had justifiable concerns and attempted to assuage them by separating security from sovereignty and introducing an element of reciprocity into any ceasefire plan. Enahoro's plan amounted to a twelve-point step-by-step solution that would reincorporate the Eastern Region into Nigeria under both federal and Igbo supervision and Commonwealth observers. Enahoro's proposal was as follows:

1. A date shall be agreed upon as Cease-Fire Day.
2. A time on Cease-Fire Day shall be agreed upon as Cease-Fire Hour.
3. Twelve hours before Cease-Fire Hour:
   a. The Rebels will renounce secession, order their troops to lay down their arms as from the Cease-Fire Hour and announce the renunciation and the order publicly and simultaneously.
   b. The Federal Government will order the Army, Navy, and Air Force to cease military operations as from the Cease-Fire Hour and announce the order publicly.
   c. The Commonwealth Secretariat will make the same announcements as at (a) and (b).
4. At Cease-Fire Hour all troops will be frozen in their positions. An Observer Force drawn from a source agreed at this meeting shall take position at the Cease-Fire Lines.
5. Twenty Four hours after Cease-Fire Hour, a Mixed Force shall enter Rebel-held areas for the purpose of disarming of Rebel forces. The Mixed Force shall consist of: elements of the Observer Force, elements of the Federal Army and Police, Ibo policemen from the Police units established in the Liberated Areas. The Mixed Force shall cooperate with elements of the Rebel Forces.
6. Not later than Seven Days after Cease-Fire Day, the Administration of Rebel-held areas will be handed over to the Federal Government.
7. Pending arrangements to bring the administration of the East Central State into line with the rest of the country, the Federal Government will appoint a Commission to administer Rebel-held areas. The Commission shall consist of a Chairman who is Ibo appointed by the Federal Government and a number of other members appointed by the Federal Government, half of whom shall be appointed in consultation with Rebel leaders.
8. Law and order in the Rebel Areas will be the normal responsibility of the Police.
9. The Federal Government will recruit people of Ibo origin and integrate them with the Nigerian Army.
10. As soon as possible, a person of East Central State origin will be appointed to the Federal Executive Council.
11. The Federal Government will, in respect of the organizers of the rebellion, grant amnesty in appropriate cases and will, in respect of other persons connected with the rebellion, grant general amnesty.
12. Prisoners of war held by both sides and hostages taken by the Rebels will be released.[68]

For the Biafrans, accepting the twelve points was tantamount to surrender. Mbanefo agreed that an end to hostilities could entail accepting points one, two, and twelve, and point three without the Biafrans' renunciation of secession.[69] Smith, who, along with Obote, did not want to see the conference end in failure, convened the sides in off-the-record closed-door sessions where, he believed, they were close to an agreement that would bring about "a loose federal solution with safeguards for Ibo rights."[70] Though Enahoro and Mbanefo had made progress at the talks, Gowon and Ojukwu independently set limits that the other side could not accept. For Gowon, no progress could be made until the Biafrans accepted the twelve-state solution. Further, Gowon sent word that directly undercut points five and nine in Enahoro's earlier proposal, stating that no Biafran units would be reincorporated into the armed forces, and no Biafran military or police forces would be allowed to keep their arms.

Similarly, Ojukwu decried the Kampala talks in a speech at Biafra's first anniversary celebration, claiming that the Nigerians wanted only a military solution and that the entire peace process was a sham to deflect from the genocidal campaign they had been waging against Biafra. Ojukwu's speech marked the end of the talks, as later that day Mbanefo announced the Biafran delegation's departure, and they left for London shortly thereafter.

The Kampala failure did not end the attempts to end the conflict, but it heaped pressure on the British Commonwealth and Harold Wilson's government in the United Kingdom to end the war, or at least to stop supplying arms to Nigeria. This put both the British government and the OAU under increased pressure because the very successful public campaign demonized Wilson's government as complicit in genocide and increased public and diplomatic pressure on a way to end the war. After the collapse of the Kampala talks, the OAU, which had until now successfully blocked the conflict's internationalization, took the lead in attempting to broker some kind of agreement between the sides.

Thus the OAU brokered another peace conference in August in the Ethiopian capital of Addis Ababa, under the auspices of Emperor Haile Selassie. OAU officials hoped that the emperor's standing and gravitas would hinder a repeat of the acrimonious outcome in Kampala. Further, before the August conference in Ethiopia, the OAU held a series of preliminary talks in Niamey, the Nigerien capital, to boost the likelihood of some sort of agreement. The Niamey meetings' purpose was to set expectations and ensure that the emperor would not be embarrassed by a surprise confrontation in Addis Ababa.

One often-neglected question regarding Biafra's public diplomacy push is whether the genocide narrative served its purpose in attempting to bring an end to the conflict or whether it further galvanized the Biafran leadership to continue the struggle and prolong civilian suffering during the war. After the diplomatic setbacks in 1967, the Biafrans pushed this narrative to create international pressure that would force Nigeria to accept international mediation and end the OAU's insistence that the global community treat the conflict as a solely internal matter. The conferences in Kampala and Addis Ababa testify to Biafra's mastery of the media narrative, but the failure to reach any kind of agreement to end the war or allow humanitarian aid showed the difficulties in translating the groundswell of public opinion into tangible diplomatic advantages. The Biafrans were simply fighting a global political structure built on the primacy of the nation-state, and achieving any kind of intervention without Nigerian approval, whether from the Commonwealth, OAU, or UN, was simply not feasible. Additionally, as the peace talks continued, the Biafrans, perhaps buoyed by their successes in the public media sphere, understandably hardened their demands. The Nigerian demand that Biafra renounce secession as a precondition to any talks to end the war was a nonstarter, as it was the main concession that the Biafrans could hope to use in any negotiation. For the Nigerians, any success to internationalize the war would be a step toward official recognition of Biafra, and Gowon could not allow this under any circumstances.

Thus, all aspects of the talks in Addis failed. The Biafrans could not negotiate an end to the conflict, arrange for any international presence to alleviate the siege, or set up any relief for the civilians caught in Nigeria's blockade. Once it became clear that the talks in Addis would not result in a ceasefire, the Ethiopian emperor focused his attention on mediating between the two sides regarding a relief corridor into Biafra. Even on this issue, the two sides could not come to an agreement. The Nigerian proposal called for a land corridor where they could inspect all goods going into Biafra to ensure that only relief supplies, and not war materiel, entered through the relief channels. The Nigerians proposed two possible corridors, one from Lagos airport that would enter across Onitsha and the other that would accept flights into Enugu and travel south to Awgu and Okiwe. Ojukwu rejected this proposal, stating publicly that the Biafrans could never accept a land corridor and allow their genocidal enemy to inspect and possibly poison the relief supplies.[71]

The relief issue galvanized the international community, with many world leaders taking a keen interest in ensuring that if a ceasefire or an end to the war was not possible, at least some agreement could be reached to bring much-needed supplies to alleviate the hunger in Biafran-controlled territories. In the United States, the Lyndon Johnson administration took a particular interest in the relief issue and went to great lengths to act as a mediator, with the administration's senior Africa official, Ed Hamilton, offering his assessment, stating, "The US cannot control the situation without major troop commitments. And we are not thinking in any such terms," adding that without an agreement, "no outside force is going to mount a massive relief program necessary to rescue upwards of 4 million people."[72]

The Americans also attempted to mediate between the ICRC and the Nigerian government, since the US had a positive relationship with the ICRC's commissioner, August Lindt, a former chairman of UNICEF and the UN's high commissioner for refugees (UNHCR) as well as former Swiss ambassador to both the United States and the USSR.[73] However, Lindt and Gowon's relationship quickly soured, as Gowon viewed the former to be pro-Biafra. Lindt did little to maintain an aura of neutrality, openly collaborating with Ojukwu on the issue of relief corridors. On August 15, after months of working with Ojukwu on a proposal for relief flights, Lindt unveiled his proposal at a press conference and not behind closed doors, as is customary in delicate negotiations. Gowon could not accept any agreement under such conditions and despite a personal letter from Johnson wherein the American president pleaded with Gowon "to make it possible for relief supplies to move rapidly into the hands of the needy by facilitating the establishment of this relief corridor on an urgent basis."[74] Ultimately, the talks in Addis Ababa did not end in any kind of agreement for a relief corridor, and they soured the relationship between Nigeria and the ICRC, which would only get worse in future months.

As the peace talks failed, the ICRC came under fire, quite literally, for continuing relief flights. On August 12, the Nigerian government declared it would continue its policy of intercepting relief flights in an effort to influence Biafra and the relief agencies to agree to the monitoring of their cargoes. On August 17, Lindt decided to move ahead with the large-scale airlift without Nigerian approval, stating, "The ICRC deplores the fact that the Federal military government has not accepted the solution to the problem of transporting relief supplies quickly to the victims in Biafran held territory."[75] Into this diplomatic morass entered Swedish pilot and mercenary Carl Gustav von Rosen.

Von Rosen was born in 1909 to an aristocratic Swedish family. Despite his familial link to the Nazi parties in Germany and Sweden, he quickly became an anti-fascist fighter. During the 1935 Italian invasion of Ethiopia, he flew missions evacuating battlefield casualties, at one point suffering an Italian mustard gas attack.[76] During World War II, after assisting Finland in the Winter War, von Rosen went to England to volunteer to fight against the Germans but was refused due to his family ties to top Nazi leader Hermann Göring. After the war, he returned to Ethiopia, where he became a flight instructor until 1956, when he left under acrimonious circumstances. In 1960, he became UN secretary general Dag Hammarskjold's chief pilot during the Congo Crisis. He was ill the day of the fateful flight where Hammarskjold's plane was shot down by Rhodesian pilots.[77] He arrived at Sao Tome in early August 1968, shortly after Nigeria's threats caused the airlift to halt.

On August 11, von Rosen flew with one of Hank Wharton's crews to assess the ability to break the Nigerian blockade, not just for one aircraft but in a way that would allow the airlift to proceed and protect the flights from Nigerian air defenses. For von Rosen, the key was flying low enough to evade patrolling MiGs, typically flown by Egyptian and East German pilots, and at the same time avoid detection from the ground. His solution, which he tested the next day, was to drop his altitude to under sixty meters, a tactic widely accepted in "bush flying" circles.[78] Using an Irish priest as his guide, he flew through the riverine regions of the Niger Delta, landing at Uli just after dusk on August 12. He stayed in Biafra, meeting with Ojukwu to coordinate the resumptions of the airlift before flying back the next day, thus renewing the airlift into Biafra.[79] In June 1969, von Rosen would create a new Biafran air force, famously called the MINICOIN or MINICONs.

Von Rosen's flight initiated the large-scale airlift that has been one of the most discussed aspects of humanitarian aid, with the ICRC and Caritas joined by new organizations like the World Council of Churches and Joint Church Aid, initiating the largest private wartime airlift in history and the largest airborne relief supply since the Berlin Blockade of 1948–50. Until recently, the literature on the airlift focused on the political and religious aspects of the project, and not much has been written on the airlift's logistics, except for how the planes arrived.[80]

With the failure of the peace conferences, Adekunle decided to launch an OAU operation of his own, to capture the last three major urban centers under Biafran control: Owerri, Aba, and Umuahia. Like Nigeria's previous ambitious offensives in Onitsha and Port Harcourt, Adekunle's mission would achieve some of its goals but leave his division on the brink of collapse. As with Murtala Muhammed's assault on Onitsha, Biafra's military successes nearly destroyed the 3rd Marine Commando Division but failed to turn the tide of the war. Nonetheless, these successes gave Ojukwu's leadership hope entering 1969 that a change was imminent, and with it hope that holding out would force an end to the war.

EIGHT

BIAFRA'S COLLAPSE AND REBIRTH

WITH BIAFRAN HOPES FOR A negotiated end to the war shattered, they prepared for the inevitable renewal of military action, and Madiebo was especially concerned regarding the southern front when Adekunle, head of the 3rd Marine Commando Division, began massing his soldiers for Operation OAU. Compounding matters, the Biafran military's haphazard command structure with personal ambition often overpowering competence, undermined unit cohesion, placing additional stress on the ill-equipped defenders. Steiner's commandos were emblematic of this, as they ostensibly answered to no one except Steiner and Ojukwu, existed outside of the normal Biafran military hierarchy, and in August 1968 were still under Steiner's command. By the end of August, Ojukwu could no longer depend on Steiner to obey commands, making the mercenary colonel in charge of a well-armed and trained cadre of personal soldiers. Steiner's commando division also had priority in supplies, making them a well-fed, well-armed, and well-rested group while the bulk of Biafra's military struggled to supply even five bullets a day for those soldiers who were lucky enough to have serviceable rifles. The fall of Port Harcourt exacerbated the supply issues, as the only link to the outside world was now the airstrip Annabelle at Uli.

Biafra also had considerable organizational problems beyond Steiner's presence. Some officers, like Achuzia, placed personal ambition above the tactical situation and actively campaigned for promotions and commands. Just before the Nigerian Operation OAU began, Captain Wilfred Anuku, a navy officer, oversaw the Owerri sector and held two brigades, the 52nd and 60th, despite the lack of supplies and reinforcements that reduced the effective fighting capability in the sector to a single battalion strength.[1] In August 1968, when Madiebo decided to create a new division to oversee the sector, he naturally sought to retain Anuku in the position, as the navy captain had graduated from the Royal Navy College in Dartmouth. However, the untrained Achuzia, who planned to be appointed the new division commander, orchestrated Anuku's removal by launching a series of complaints against the latter. Madiebo had little choice but to remove Anuku, who then accompanied Ojukwu to the peace talks in Addis Ababa, but appointed Colonel Ben Nwajei, commander of the 53rd Brigade, Madiebo's second in command during the fall of Enugu the previous year.[2] Achuzia does not mention his attempt to usurp command of the brigade but devotes a short paragraph to Anuku, whom he calls a "'Mamma's Boy,' who took delight in playing a sailor, forgetting he was already one." He had little positive to say about the navy captain, complaining, "I wish his brains were as big as his girth" and that he "was a bully with all the bad qualities of a bully, especially in the area where it mattered, courage."[3]

During the peace conferences, Adekunle's division consolidated their position around Port Harcourt and fortified the towns along the Imo River, intending to move north as soon as possible. Adekunle made no secret about his plans and spoke to reporters as early as May 21, 1968, boasting that he would initiate his Operation OAU and capture the three cities by October 1, Nigeria's Independence Day.[4] The lax attitude toward military secrecy was endemic on both sides, as evidenced by Banjo's invasion of the Midwest and his alleged communications with the Nigerian leadership during the offensive. Adekunle's boastful assertion caught many of his officers off-guard, including Alabi-Isama and Ipoola Akinrinade; the latter would become Nigeria's chief of staff during the Second Republic. Most of the officers' concerns centered on the lack of supplies to undertake such a mission and Adekunle's perceived lack of support for his officers and soldiers, "who advanced, fought, got shot, carried dead and dying comrades, had no food, drank blood-reddened water, had cold, dysentery, malaria and blisters on their feet on the way to Port Harcourt."[5]

Compounding the division's sagging morale, the Biafrans launched several counteroffensives in June and August 1968 with the dual aim of recapturing Onitsha and cutting off the Nigerians in Calabar by pushing south to Opobo. Following Biafra's loss of Port Harcourt, Patrick Amadi, who led the Biafrans at the battle of Obollo Eke in the fight for Nsukka early in the war, replaced Achuzia as commander of the Biafran 11th Division. After constructing a defensive line along the roads leading into the city, he launched a three-pronged attack that ultimately failed but delivered the Biafrans a morale-boosting victory in the form of a soldier remembered only as Corporal Nwafor. On June 30, 1968, the Nigerians immediately countered the attack in the northern sector with their armored cars, British-made Saladins. Nwafor shot the Saladin with his brigade's only antitank rocket, killing the crew but leaving the vehicle relatively intact and salvageable. Adding to Biafra's good fortune, the driver of an armored personnel carrier behind the Saladin panicked and drove into a ditch, overturning the vehicle. The occupants then fled on foot, leaving both vehicles for the Biafrans to recover under fire. Nwafor was killed during the recovery, but how is not recorded. In his memory, the Biafrans named the Saladin the Corporal Nwafor. Later lore claimed that at his funeral, the Nigerians launched an air raid on Nwafor's village, but because most everyone was in the church, they were not harmed. The only casualty was a man who fled the church in fear.[6]

Nwafor's canonization was a badly needed salve for both military and civilian morale following the series of crushing defeats that left Biafra teetering just as the peace conferences began. If Ojukwu embarked on the path to secession to protect easterners and Igbo in particular, by mid-1968 the situation in Biafran-held territories had become increasingly dire. When Biafra declared independence, roughly a million people had fled their homes in other parts of Nigeria and returned to their families and ancestral villages. Once the Nigerians began overrunning the Igbo heartland, beginning with Nsukka and Enugu in 1967, the dynamics of the refugee crisis changed significantly. Both the Biafrans and Nigerians attempted to minimize civilian displacement, but for very different reasons. For the Biafrans, attempting to escape a city as the Nigerians closed in was tantamount to treason, as it conveyed a lack of confidence in the Biafran military. Likewise, Biafran propaganda still maintained a sophisticated mechanism, and residents in the early stages of the war believed the military could ward off any invasion from the Nigerians. In places where they failed, the Biafrans blamed saboteurs, setting off the witch hunts against high-ranking military and civilian leaders. Biafran propaganda was so successful that even those who wrote it believed it to a reckless extent. Believing that Enugu would never be captured, few of Biafra's government organizations took precautions to secure their materials. Madiebo recalled one egregious example where the Food Directorate's warehouses were simply abandoned with "enough food to feed any of the brigades for at least a fortnight. Other stores contained crates of drinks and cigarettes."[7] Madiebo and his driver took as much as they could and fled the city with the warehouse's lone sentry, who was forgotten at his post.

Nigerian propaganda, on the other hand, would routinely claim victories where none existed, lulling many civilians into a false sense of security. One Enugu resident who listened to both Radio Biafra and Nigerian radio from Kaduna claimed that the Nigerians had broadcast their capture of a town on Enugu's outskirts, a fact he knew was false, and as a result he ceased to believe the Nigerian radio and felt that the Nigerians would never enter the Biafran capital. Another survivor, from the Cross River region, said in an interview, "Propaganda sent us into a confused state. Each radio station stood in favor of itself. We did not know which side to believe."[8] At other times, people would flee their homes in what they assumed was a temporary escape from air raids or artillery bombardments and took with them only enough to survive the day before they could return at night. When they returned home, they found the Nigerians had advanced, and thus they could not reenter their villages.[9]

Where Biafran propaganda and persuasion failed, authorities resorted to coercion to keep people from fleeing. Nowhere was this more prevalent than in Port Harcourt. Emmanuel Aguma, the city's wartime Biafran administrator, created a series of checkpoints throughout the city to keep residents from leaving. Only the few people who possessed travel permits that he had personally signed were allowed to traverse through the checkpoints, and he routinely made surprise visits to them to ensure that people were not bribing their way out. When the Biafran defenders eventually abandoned the city, the panic caused most residents to flee with little but what they could carry. Many would never return to their homes.[10]

As a result, when people did flee the war, they did so at the last moment and with very few of their belongings. Unlike the refugees after the July 1966 coup, those fleeing the war had little in the way of assistance for several reasons. First, unlike the prewar refugees who returned to relatively stable familial relations, those displaced by the fighting largely lived in squalid camps or in public venues such as schools, churches, and event halls. These accommodations created conditions of squalor and spread diseases and parasites like bedbugs. As Biafran-controlled territory shrank, the number of refugees increased, further straining Biafran abilities to keep them alive. By the end of 1968, Biafran authorities recorded over 700,000 displaced persons who fled the war and lived in the camps. By the end of the war, that number had almost doubled to 1,220,000.[11] Taken together with Biafra's shrinking territory, some estimated that up to one-third of Biafra's population at the end of the war consisted of refugees.[12]

If fighting the war rested on the shoulders of the men, surviving the war and being able to cope with the food, clothing, and other shortages invariably fell to women. Acute food shortages that led to horrific medical conditions such as kwashiorkor began developing in mid-1968 and continued until the end of the war, and women were at the forefront of adapting households to meet the wartime challenges. Two of the most important roles that women played were trader and smuggler. Egodi Uchendu's unique study of Anioma women during the war is especially illuminating. The Anioma Igbo resided on the west bank of the Niger and suffered the brunt of the Asaba massacres. These women generally smuggled goods by trading for them with the Nigerian soldiers despite commanders' attempts to stop it. They would then carry the goods some fifteen kilometers through the marshes of the Niger Delta to the shore of the Niger River opposite Atani, about ten kilometers south of Onitsha, where the goods would be ferried across the river in canoes. The riverine marshes, which contained much of the oil deposits that the Nigerian and Biafran governments depended on for revenue, also provided cover to Biafran commandoes who would use them to launch raids and plant explosives, sometimes to devastating effect. On May 2, 1968, a commander in the district, Patrick Idahosa, launched an assault on the town of Isheagu, one of the centers of the trade, known as the *ahia attack* (attack trade) or night market.[13] Because of the nature of the trade, the Nigerians were convinced the people of Isheagu were in collusion with the Biafrans. The assault reportedly wiped out the town and killed over three hundred people but did not destroy the trade, as the women involved simply moved their base to the neighboring town of Nsukwa a few kilometers west.[14]

Igbo women on both sides of the lines engaged in the attack trade, though the origin and definition of the term is unclear. Egodi Uchendu does not elaborate on the term's origin, simply stating that it was called so because of the proximity to the enemy and that it was at night. Sydney Emezue goes into detail on the various origins, each of which adds some level of explanation to the trade's dangerous nature. For some involved in the trade, it simply meant trade under conditions where you were in danger of attack, such as those who traded at the Ndoro market between Umuahia and Ikot Ekpene. For others, it meant that if caught by soldiers, they would attack your supplies and take half of them. Others simply saw it as a euphemism for stealing when necessary.[15] Regardless of the term's origins, the attack trade served an essential purpose in bringing supplies into the overpopulated Igbo heartland from the region north of Onitsha and west of Nsukka, the last food-producing region still in Biafran hands, known as the Anambra basin. Biafran military efforts centered on keeping a land corridor open, and control of access routes would be a central motive for launching Operation Hiroshima against Onitsha in November 1968.

While Igbo women under Nigerian occupation were smuggling goods across the Niger, their counterparts in Biafra were busy adapting to daily life under starvation and siege conditions. In many cases, fathers, husbands, and sons joined or had been conscripted into the Biafran military. In many cases, this was double-edged sword, as being a soldier's wife brought a level of prestige and protection. On the other hand, it brought fear and uncertainty because the Biafrans lacked a system of verifying and notifying next of kin when a soldier died. This "led to some people being declared dead (and their funeral being held) who later came back alive and some being reported as being alive who had long been dead."[16] Other women who had men of conscription age in their household who did not enlist assisted them in evading the impressment gangs that would conscript the men and boys into service. In doing so, the women took on roles usually reserved for men, such as tapping palm trees for wine and oils to make soap.[17]

In addition to the added roles as smugglers in the attack trade and the roles that women undertook to compensate for the lack of men conscripted to the front, the war wrought changes that transformed women's abilities in many of the traditional roles they played in society, especially in food production and preparation. Biafra's geography and the movement of refugees into a shrinking and more overpopulated space, coupled with the economic blockade and lack of agreement regarding relief supplies, meant that every type of food, condiments, salt, and other necessities were in extremely short supply. Additionally, relief supplies, when they became available, were usually things like cheese and crackers, which were not part of the region's dietary habits prewar. In some cases, salt was in such short supply that women killed termites and let them ferment in a container, forming a salty paste that was used in cooking.[18] In the refugee camps, when cheeses arrived with the relief supplies, they were generally ignored, as women did not know how to incorporate them into their traditional foods like egusi soup and other local staples. However, once the cheese began to spoil and mold, the smell reminded many women of *ogiri,* a local condiment made from fermented seeds. As a result, moldy cheese became both a popular condiment for soups and an important source of protein.[19]

Women also suffered from various types of violence during the war, ranging from soldiers abusing their power and robbing or extorting the market women and attack traders to rampant sexual violence, especially during the immediate aftermath of large-scale engagements. Most interviews with women after the war reveal they suffered some kind of violence. Emezue, Ahazuem, and Harneit-Sievers conducted nearly two hundred interviews for their *Social History of the Nigerian Civil War* and concluded that violence against women was widespread, especially in federally controlled areas where commanders either encouraged or ignored such trespasses. Uchendu comes to a similar conclusion after conducting over one hundred interviews, almost all to the west of the Niger, which was Nigerian controlled after the Midwest Offensive. Saro-Wiwa echoes these voices but also minimized the horrors inflicted on women, asking, "What's rape in war-time?"[20] Not all soldiers went unpunished for their crimes against women. In Afikpo, one notorious Nigerian soldier, remembered only as Timothy, would routinely rape women quite openly after assaulting or otherwise coercing them in various ways. Timothy, who gained the nickname Kpaberekpe, eventually murdered a young woman who would not submit to him, and for that he was executed.[21]

The relatively meager punishments meted out for the war crimes that ill-disciplined Nigerian soldiers committed had little effect in assuaging Biafran fears of genocide, especially given Adekunle's boastful preparations for his upcoming offensive. In an interview with several reporters dated June 8, 1968, Adekunle emphatically stated, "I want to see no Red Cross, no Caritas, no World

Council of Churches, no Pope, no missionary and no UN delegation. I want to prevent even one Ibo from having even one piece to eat before their capitulation. We shoot at everything that moves and when our troops march into the centre of Ibo territory, we shoot at everything, even at things that don't move."[22] Biafran propagandists both at home and abroad latched onto this statement as evidence of a planned genocide rather than the boastfulness of a commander who wished to use his bully pulpit to press his advantage and instill fear in the enemy population.

Even so, Adekunle's threats of starvation meant that maintaining control of the meager food-producing regions became a top Biafran priority. Keeping the Nigerian 1st and 2nd Divisions from linking along the Enugu-Onitsha Road was of highest importance for the Biafrans to keep the food supply reaching those who most needed it in the Igbo heartland and securing Biafra's airstrip at Uli, approximately halfway from Onitsha to Owerri. Also, to the north of the road lay the Anambra Basin, the last major food producing region the Biafrans held. Losing access would put Biafra's already meager food supplies under more stress. Thus, the operation that resulted in Nwafor's canonization was not a complete military failure. It prevented the two Nigerian divisions from linking, which they would not do until June 1969, and opened an opportunity for a Biafran southern push that could split the 3rd Marine Commando Division and thwart Adekunle's boastful OAU plan.

During the peace talks, Adekunle was busily consolidating his control over the sectors he captured around Port Harcourt in May, and his men were slowly making inroads into the Biafran heartland, especially around the city of Aba. Adekunle was in the midst of a reorganization of the division, which he split into four geographical zones running west to east, with each zone comprising roughly the strength of a brigade. Sector One came under Godwin Ally's command and stretched from the Niger River to the north–south line between Owerri and Port Harcourt. Sector Two, headed by Philemon Shande, went until the Imo River and Sector Three from the Imo to Cross River, commanded by Alabi-Isama. Sector Four comprised the Cross River to the Cameroon border and was placed under the command of Ayo Ariyo. It was during this restructuring that the Biafrans launched their assault on Ikot Ekpene in late July to early August 1968.[23]

Although the battle of Ikot Ekpene was a minor skirmish, it had several important implications for Biafran and Nigerian tactics for the rest of the war. The town is situated approximately halfway between Calabar and Port Harcourt, roughly one hundred kilometers north of the Atlantic coast, and only fifty kilometers from the Biafran capital of Umuahia. It was thus an important junction town, and control of it was key to managing supply lines for the Nigerians as they consolidated their position in anticipation of Operation OAU. The Biafran assault itself was part of a three-part strategy designed to provide a show of strength during

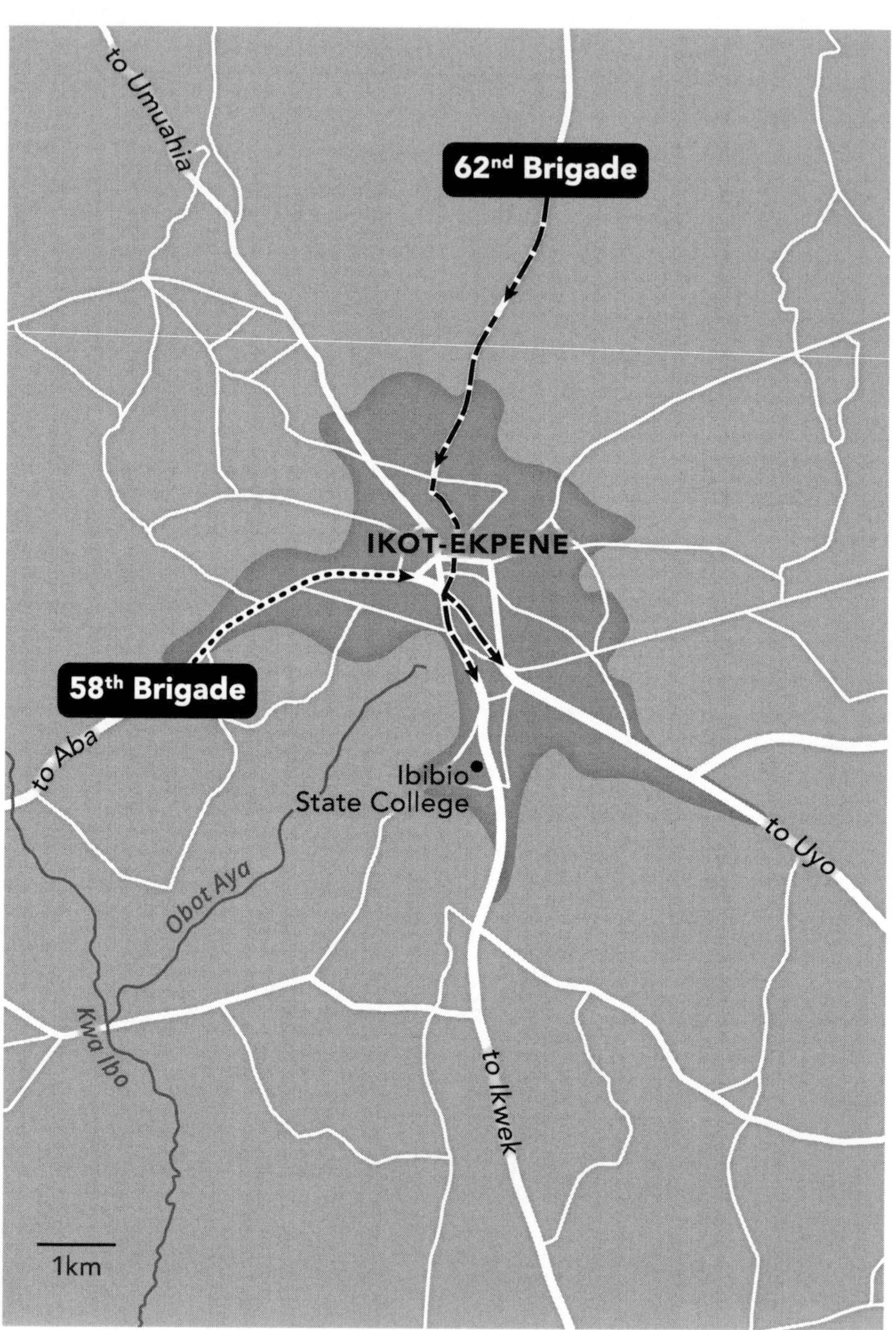

Map 8.1. Battle of Ikot Ekpene

the peace talks, revive Biafran morale after the loss of Port Harcourt, and delay any Nigerian offensives while capturing as much materiel as possible. Because the operation was relatively small, especially compared with the Nigerian operation that was to follow, most memoirs and histories ignore the operation, despite its careful planning and implications for the rest of the war. Philip Efiong, who would replace Ojukwu as Biafran president in January 1970, does not mention the offensive, even though it was his hometown, but dedicates several pages to the town's capture in the Nigerian offensive to take Port Harcourt. Momoh's history of the war likewise does not list it in either Nigerian or Biafran operations. Only Madiebo and Alabi-Isama devote lengthy discussions to the operation, and the analysis of it relies heavily on these as well as a series of reports from British television reporter Peter Sissons, who was embedded with the Biafrans during the early stages of their assault.[24]

The Biafran strategy that led to the short-lived capture of the town was three pronged and included the operations mentioned earlier in the Onitsha sector that involved the capture of the Saladin. In the south, a small force crossed the Niger at Atani, the site of much of the attack trade from the midwest, and raided enemy stores in the region while the Nigerian army was preoccupied with the offensive in Onitsha. The most ambitious part of the plan came from Col. Anthony Eze, commander of the 12th Division. Eze's plan was to create a series of diversionary attacks along the Imo River to draw Nigerian troops into the sector around Port Harcourt in anticipation of a Biafran offensive to retake the city.

Two simultaneous attacks came along the river; the first crossed into Umu Abayi, some forty kilometers west of Port Harcourt, and seized a large supply depot, capturing ammunition, food, and even two antiaircraft guns. The second attempted to push down to the mouth of the Imo River to Opobo, threatening the 3rd Marine Commando Division's supply routes there, and into the Cross River region ports at Calabar and Oron. Alabi-Isama was especially alarmed by the prospect of losing his supply lines during the battle. Ikot Ekene controlled the junction that connected Oron and Calabar with the rest of the division. As such, "Ikot Ekpene axis was a 'no-go' area for Biafran troops," and Alabi-Isama took direct command of the Nigerian forces as soon as he learned the gravity of the situation.[25]

After the diversionary attacks, the Biafran 58th and 62nd Brigades under Eze's command approached the town from the west and north, respectively. The Nigerians, who were not expecting a coordinated attack, scattered quickly, leaving the 58th Brigade to clear the city in its entirety before the elements of the 62nd arrived at their rendezvous points on the roads to Uyo and Ikwek. The Nigerians fled to Oron, leaving a company at the Ibibio State College secondary school in the south of the town. Madiebo lamented that his men did not have the ammunition and supplies to mount a quick pursuit, as most of the ammunition captured at Umu

Abayi was of a different caliber than Biafran guns, leaving the Biafrans with only fifty rounds per person for the assault.[26] Typically, when Biafrans captured ammunition that did not fit their weapons, the Research and Development Committee would extract the explosive elements and turn them into improvised munitions.

As the Biafrans waited for ammunition, Madiebo visited the town, stopping at the Ikot Ekpene prison, where he "saw several hundreds of zombie-like creatures—men, women and children, lying, sitting or squatting in the midst of others who were dead. The living ones were completely reduced to skeletons and could not talk. I was seeing for the first time what I later knew to be kwashiorkor, which was not yet noticeable in Biafra-held territories." Madiebo lamented that those in the prison were not Igbo but "minority" people, the Ibibio. If the Nigerians treated those they claimed would be liberated by the twelve-state system that triggered the war with starvation, Madiebo feared "what would happen to the 'majorities' [i.e., Igbo] at the hands of the Nigerians."[27]

When the situation in Ikot Ekpene turned in favor of the Biafrans, Alabi-Isama arrived nearby in Uyo to coordinate the Nigerian response. It is not entirely clear how long it took from the beginning of the battle until the Nigerian counterattack. Madiebo stated that the Biafrans were waiting for ammunition to continue the push south when the Nigerians counterattacked and drove them from the town. The reports Alabi-Isama received seem to confirm that the stalemate lasted at least two weeks from the end of July until roughly August 11, which corresponds to news reports on the war.[28] Alabi-Isama asked the town's garrison commander, Captain Audu Jalingo, how the town was captured. He reported that the food situation was indeed dire and that several Biafran POWs had told him they had not eaten for days. Further, the local population and refugees had also been suffering from hunger. Jalingo claimed that he had not only fed the prisoners but also allowed food across the lines to feed the Biafrans. There was no official ceasefire, but the talks in Kampala led to a lull in the fighting as both sides wished to focus their efforts on the diplomatic front, rather than on the battlefield. This led to fraternization, and at one point during the stalemate that coincided with the peace talks in Kampala (this was in July, and the talks in Addis Ababa did not begin until mid-August), the two sides held a football match that exploded into violence. During this match, the Biafrans attacked the Nigerians on the pitch after going down 3–0 in the first half. The Biafrans, so enraged at the prospect of losing, captured the entire Nigerian squad and the spectators, thus conquering the town.[29] Madiebo does not mention any fraternization or a football match, and Sissons's report from July 24, 1968 shows the poorly outfitted Biafran troops clearly assaulting the town from the outskirts, not the kind of trap that Alabi-Isama claims.[30] However, both Madiebo and Alabi-Isama concur that starvation was already a factor in the area, though their conclusions were opposite as to who was to blame and who tried to alleviate it. Additionally, an unnamed catholic priest who ran a refugee center in Biafra, whom Sissons interviewed during the battle, had little to say about Nigerian "largesse," stating that many of the Ikot Ekpene refugees preferred to flee into Biafra rather than stay with the Nigerians "that did very little for them."[31]

In fact, the Nigerian officer who reported the football match claimed to be so incensed at the betrayal of his goodwill that he was eager for an immediate counterattack and "vowed he would not take any prisoners."[32] However, Alabi-Isama discouraged a headstrong reaction, instead focusing on collecting intelligence and planning an assault to minimize the likelihood it would end in catastrophe. Most importantly, he withdrew the company stranded at Ibibio State College as bait. He told them to make as disorganized a withdrawal as possible, so it would appear they had panicked, to draw the Biafrans into pursuit. He claimed the Biafrans followed, but Madiebo claimed the opposite—that the Biafrans did not continue their attack because of a lack of ammunition. Nonetheless, the Nigerians did not enter the town but rather opted for a double envelopment with the 13th Brigade. Because the Biafrans had little ammunition to mount a defense, they withdrew "disappointed, but not exactly demoralized."[33] The Biafrans had achieved a victory they claimed was not complete due only to a lack of munitions and managed to capture a large amount of enemy supplies and even a new Russian artillery piece.[34]

The battle exposed the strengths and weaknesses on both sides, and both would continue to make similar errors and exploit them in their enemies. For the Biafrans, the shortage of equipment and ammunition would dictate their ability to prosecute the war. Ikot Ekpene showed that they could not withstand even a small assault without being heavily fortified in defensive positions, as they had been in the June attempts to retake Onitsha. In Ikot Ekpene, they could not press their advantage or withstand the Nigerian counterattack, and the battle amounted to little more than a raid. The Biafrans would not be able to withstand intense pressure nor be able to sustain it on offensives. For the Nigerians, the battle exposed deep problems in the army's command structure, an issue that afflicted both sides, but on the Nigerian side the problems of inflated commanders' egos, growing pressure from within the country to end the war, and international pressure to alleviate civilian suffering made for a complicated situation wherein military planning was not prioritized. Further compounding matters, no effective central command existed to coordinate between the divisions, leaving each commander to his own judgment regarding planning and executions of missions that had consequences for the entire theater.[35] In the battle's aftermath, Alabi-Isama blamed Adekunle for many of the problems that the 3rd Marine Commando Division faced, bluntly stating, "Adekunle was no more fighting for Nigeria but for his own ego."[36] Despite touting his grand Operation OAU, which he later changed to OOAU to include the town of Oguta, his commanders had very few plans and did not receive the promised supplies to prepare for the assault.

By August, it became clear that Adekunle's much-touted offensive was imminent. Nigeria's 14th Brigade and other elements had taken up positions ready to cross the Imo River that snakes around Aba's southern fringes and then takes a northern turn, skirting the city's western peripheries. Other Nigerian elements were massing to the south of Owerri, near the confluence of the Imo and Otamiri rivers, in preparation for their upcoming assault on Owerri and Oguta. The recent fighting at Ikot Ekpene and the diversionary tactics had exhausted Biafran troops in the area and depleted their ammunition supplies. The only well-rested and resupplied unit in the Biafran military was Steiner's 4th Commando Division. Steiner's men had not seen action since their failed attempt to capture Onitsha in April. Madiebo thought it best to bring them to lead a raid to destroy the main bridge across the Otamiri at Chokocho, about twenty kilometers north of Port Harcourt.

However, Ojukwu's insistence on Steiner's independence from the Biafran chain of command began to show its cracks, as the German mercenary created a fanatical unit loyal to him and the other mercenary commanders like Taffy Williams and Marc Goosens. Complicating manners further, by August Ojukwu seemed to have lost control over Steiner and his unit, as when Madiebo approached the Biafran leader to order Steiner into action on what should have been a commando unit's forte, Ojukwu told Madiebo to speak directly to Steiner. When Madiebo arrived, he found Steiner "on his throne in the Commando Officers' mess, surrounded by almost a platoon of fierce looking soldiers." When Madiebo asked the German to join the assault on the bridge, the latter agreed, but only if Madiebo would give him a Mercedes car for his personal use, which Madiebo agreed, not knowing this would be only the beginning of the unit's blackmail.[37]

The initial plan was for the Biafran 14th Division to move south from Umunelu and the 12th Division to cross the Imo River and head west from Owaza. Taffy Williams and his brigade of about 750 men joined the 12th at Owaza while the 2nd commando brigade went to Umunelu with the 14th. However, the Nigerians anticipated the assault at Owaza and, on August 22, launched an attack against the Biafrans massing for their assault. The Nigerian attack, supported by recoilless rifles and heavy artillery, quickly overwhelmed the Biafran troops trying to hold the bridge for Williams's commandos. Williams refused to join the fight, claiming it was "the infantry's" job to hold it for them. By the next day, the Biafrans had been pushed back to Aba with the Nigerians able to cross the bridge and advance to Asa. The Nigerians thus controlled all the southern approaches to Aba in anticipation of their offensives, and Steiner's commandos had refused to fight. Madiebo attempted to organize the defense of Aba, but Steiner and the mercenaries revealed that they would refuse to fight until all their salaries had been paid in full. Exasperated, on August 30, Madiebo tried to mount an assault to clear Owaza and Aba's southern environs to no avail. Without Steiner's well-equipped men, who now numbered about 1,400 in Aba, the city was doomed. Once the assault failed, Steiner and his men left for safer territories and would not see action until Operation Hiroshima in November. Steiner left Biafra under less than amicable terms shortly after.[38]

As evidenced in the defense of Aba, Biafra suffered from a similar dysfunctional command structure as Nigeria, and its supply and distribution problems compounded the military's ability to wage an effective war. The fact that Biafran military units had not coalesced into a singular command structure by the middle of 1968 meant that the military leadership, especially Ojukwu, had not learned the lessons of the previous year of fighting. With militias, regular army, commandos, and the nebulous "liberation army" of the Midwest Offensive all competing rather than cooperating, Biafra's war effort became seriously hampered by infighting and the search for "saboteurs" by Biafran leaders eager to deflect their failures. Biafra's military leaders, like Madiebo and Efiong, had to construct a strategy that would allow them to fight with minimal supplies and deal with interference from the political leadership—namely, Ojukwu—who was determined to personally dictate the war to the smallest detail. In one instance, both men met with Ojukwu, who showered them with medals and decorations. When Madiebo asked Ojukwu who was on the committee that decided these awards, Ojukwu replied, "Mr. Chukwuemeka, Mr. Odumegwu and Mr. Ojukwu," meaning he made the decisions himself, as those were all his names.[39] Efiong would later comment that Ojukwu "skimmed over essential issues like the supply of armaments, and concentrated more on the trappings and paraphernalia of office [such as the various awards and decorations] which had nothing more than a nuisance value at the time."[40]

With the Biafran counter neutralized, Adekunle's ambitious operation began on September 4 with the first stage of his operation: the invasion of Aba. The city was relatively undefended because the previous Biafran operations at Ikot Ekpene and the aborted assault on Chokocho left the Biafrans in disarray, and supply issues prevented any ammunition from reaching the sector until the Nigerian assault began.[41] Thus, the Nigerian 13th Brigade secured the city with little effort, though the region's commander, Col. Philemon Shande, died from a sniper bullet to the forehead and was replaced by Akinrinade. Even though the Nigerians secured the city with little resistance, Adekunle's division was ill prepared for what followed, as for the first time the division would be fighting in the Igbo heartland, where Adekunle's bravado and recklessness would have disastrous consequences.

Like the Nigerians, the Biafran leadership would not internalize some of the lessons that had crystalized at Ikot Ekpene, including political interference in military matters. Though the issue of saboteurs was long established and added a layer of dread to military setbacks, the fall of Aba amplified this as Ojukwu sent a high-level delegation to investigate how a major Biafran city fell without a fight. The delegation consisted of the chief of police and several other top civilian administrators, who claimed that Aba fell because the soldiers had lost confidence in their officers. To remedy that situation, Ojukwu personally ordered the creation of a new unit, called S Division, under Timothy Onwuatuegwu's command, with Achuzia serving as adjutant. The new division was equipped from Steiner's commandos' supplies and had the express orders of recapturing Aba. However, Adekunle's quick victory led the federal forces to push their advantage into the town of Oguta, to surround Owerri from the northwest and threaten Biafra's lifeline: the airstrip at Uli, only six kilometers away.[42]

Oguta was important for several reasons. First, if Owerri was to be taken, the Njaba and Orashi rivers, which converge at Oguta Lake, had to be secured as they ran through Owerri and were essential supply routes. By September, the lake contained the last remnants of the Biafran navy, a single patrol boat armed with a World War II–era Ordnance QF 6-pounder. Although this gun was a land-based antitank gun, the Biafran navy improvised by fitting it on their patrol boats, a testament to the country's Armaments and Research Directorates that many had lauded for their work during the war.[43] Second, Oguta was only six kilometers from Annabelle, the Biafran airstrip at Uli, and was situated along the final approach before the planes would begin their loop approach to the runway. Losing Oguta would doubtless mean either losing Uli entirely or, at the very least, seriously hampering the airlift that supplied civilians and the munitions smuggling operations that would soon increase when France began to openly support Biafra at the end of 1968.

The Nigerian forces, with air support from the Soviet MiG-17 fighters and Ilyushin Il-28 bombers now flown by a host of pilots and not just Egyptians, began to soften the area around Oguta. The Soviets had been reluctant to allow any Western pilots near their aircraft, fearing spies would divulge critical information to the Americans, who were battling similar planes in Vietnam. As a result, much of Nigeria's early use of air power was ineffective and targeted civilian targets of opportunity as the Egyptian pilots gained a reputation for cowardice and incompetence. These pilots preferred to attack easy-to-hit targets from high altitude, such as hospitals with their brightly colored red and white crosses painted on the roofs, rather than military targets that were well defended and riskier to assault. These early sorties helped give credence to the Biafran narrative of genocide, as hospitals, markets, and other civilian targets usually accounted for high casualty rates.[44] Eventually, the Soviets agreed to bring East German and, after the invasion of Czechoslovakia in August 1968, Czech pilots to assist in more targeted attacks on the Biafran military.[45] Later, the Soviets would even allow some British and South African pilots to fly the MiG-17s as long as they were not active Royal Air Force pilots.[46]

Despite the new air support, the Nigerians were unable to cross the bridge at Ebocha, some thirty kilometers to the south of Oguta. Ebocha and the area around it was critical to Biafra's survival, as it contained the only oil field still under Biafran control. The Biafran Fuel Directorate had been refining the oil to supply what they could for military and civilian use. By September 9, the Nigerians had sent several gunboats up the Orashi River toward Oguta to bypass Ebocha and engage the single remaining Biafran navy vessel. In the ensuing battle on the river, the Biafran boat sank two of the Nigerian ones before being disabled and forced back to Oguta Lake. This left the river relatively undefended, and the Nigerians were able to use it to invade the unsuspecting town, quickly overrunning it, bypassing the 60th Brigade that was defending Oguta from the south. Madiebo claims that he understood that the town would not be defended, as the aerial and artillery bombardments made it impossible to "dig trenches because, besides the heavy artillery and mortar bombardment going on, the Russian jets strafed and bombed individuals who dared move around."[47]

As a result, Madiebo did not mount a defense for Oguta, instead opting to plan for a counterattack. The first part of the plan was to contain the Nigerians in Oguta using the 52nd Brigade to fortify the roads leading northeast to Uli. The second phase was to deploy enough men and materiel to retake Oguta. Because of the proximity to both Uli and Owerri, both Ojukwu and Madiebo gave retaking the town the highest priority, but the lack of a clear command structure caused several issues that almost ended in disaster.

The Nigerian 3rd Marine Commando Division suffered its first major setback of the war at Oguta, as it was "the first time in the historic battles of 3MCDO [Third Marine Commando], we lost a town that we could not re-enter."[48] Though Alabi-Isama does not elaborate on the battle, he does state that many of the divisional officers, including himself, Akinrinade, and Ayo Ariyo, warned Adekunle that marching blindly into the Igbo heartland was suicidal. Adekunle decided to rely on yes-men like the recently arrived Godwin Ally, who "had no maps . . . no specific aims for wanting to capture these towns [meaning Oguta and the surrounding villages] except for capturing sake."[49]

Meanwhile, Mdiebo was preparing Biafra's defense. After scrounging ammunition and redeploying troops into the Oguta sector, he set an attack date to retake the town for September 12 in the afternoon. He would later claim:

> I left the area of Oguta at 0700 hours [on the date of the attack] to go and deal with other urgent matters and also to prepare for the operation.
>
> Achuzia, who was also delegated to assist with the operation later came to see me at 1200 looking extremely worn out and dejected. He revealed that the counterattack I planned for Oguta at 1600 hours had already taken place

> and failed woefully. He narrated how Colonel Ojukwu came to the sector at 0900 hours shortly after my departure and ordered an immediate counterattack to be controlled by him personally. Not only had the operation failed and the head of state returned to Umuahia, all the ammunition including 300 rounds of 105 mm artillery shells we had saved up for the operation had been exhausted. . . . Achuzia still maintained that we could clear Oguta.[50]

This would not be the last time that Ojukwu personally intervened in the war's operational level or the last time it would end in failure. At Oguta, the failure did not lead to immediate disaster, as Madiebo reorganized the troops and, even after receiving a message from Ojukwu that claimed retaking Oguta "appear[ed] fruitless," ordered another attack with the depleted forces, which succeeded, eliciting the aforementioned criticism from Alabi-Isama. Within less than two hours, the town had been cleared and the Nigerian forces thoroughly routed, with both the town and the oil fields to the south secured in short order. The Biafrans even captured a Bofors 40 mm antiaircraft gun, no doubt being positioned to threaten the planes arriving at Annabelle. Even Madiebo, whose dislike for the militarily unskilled Achuzia is well documented, could not help but praise his bravery in the operation, though Achuzia did not mention this battle in his memoir, whose war narrative abruptly ends after the fall of Port Harcourt. Madiebo's frustration with Ojukwu's usurpation of command and control is understandable, and he implies that his plan was successful despite Ojukwu's meddling. However, it is entirely plausible that Madiebo's assault was successful because the Nigerians were not expecting a second assault so soon after they had repulsed a major counterattack. Neither Madiebo, Achuzia, Alabi-Isama, nor any other writer on the war gave a detailed account of the battle and why the Nigerians had been so easily routed other than the lack of preparedness and arrogance that Adekunle had allowed to permeate throughout his division after the successful operations in Port Harcourt and Aba.[51]

While the reversal at Oguta was unfolding, Adekunle was busy planning the assault on the next target in Operation OAU, the city of Owerri. The failed assault on Oguta showed the 3rd Marine Commando Division the hazards of operating within the Igbo heartland, a lesson that Murtala Mohammed had learned much earlier in the war. After the Biafrans successfully retook the western flanks of the city, Akinrinade pleaded with Adekunle to either rethink his plans or take precautions to successfully take and hold the city. Adekunle opted to continue unabated, even though his western flank was now completely exposed. His division would soon learn that fighting in the Igbo heartland was much more difficult than in the relatively friendly areas of the Niger Delta and Cross River region, where a significant percentage of the population supported the federal government, if only for the prospect of attaining their part of the twelve-state solution and ridding themselves of Igbo dominance.

As the fighting in the southern region intensified, the airlift largely suspended flights, which not only caused civilian relief to pause but also suspended valuable flights filled with ammunition that the Biafrans desperately needed. Though public opinion around the world was still raising money and putting pressure on governments to help alleviate the suffering and end the war, the war's narrative was beginning to shift, and with it global support for Biafra's continued existence. While the fighting was going on around Oguta and Owerri, the American Committee to Keep Biafra Alive held a large rally in front of the United Nations in New York, with Israeli Abie Nathan, a former RAF and Israeli Air Force pilot who flew missions of mercy into Biafra, as one of the keynote speakers.[52] Nathan's support was a moral boon for Biafra as they hoped to court Israeli support and thus give more credence to their accusations of genocide. The protest in front of the UN was important, as the UN answered a Nigerian and British invitation to sponsor a mission to evaluate Biafra's accusations. Even though the organization did not officially convene the mission, it was widely regarded as a UN mission and as such featured heavily in Biafran propaganda. The team followed the Nigerian army and visited many of the areas shortly after conducting interviews. In all their interim reports and the final report, the observers noted there was no evidence of genocide because they adhered to the legal definition and saw no intent to destroy. This did not mean they minimized the civilian suffering. In fact, during the battle for Owerri, the observers entered the city shortly after the Nigerians occupied it and were, for a short time, trapped in the Biafran counterattack's encirclement.[53]

The Biafrans refused to accept the observer report dismissing it as Nigerian propaganda. In retaliation, the Biafrans convened a commission of their own, which relied on testimonies and affidavits collected from a person identified only as Dr. Mensah, who, judging by the name, was presumably Ghanaian. The Biafran report claimed to have a smoking gun where Northern elites along with British collaborators had "devised a seven-point programme aimed at a complete extermination of the then Eastern Nigerians (now Biafrans)," meaning all Eastern Nigerians, not just Igbo. Despite the fact that this report received little notice or attention during the war, in recent years Biafran activists have used it as the "smoking gun" that proves Nigerians intended to commit genocide in the legal sense in much of the activist scholarship that accuses Nigerians of genocide.[54] However, others have pointed out the problematic genesis and lack of oversight in the creation and dissemination of the document, adding to the problems of using it as unquestionable evidence of genocide.[55]

Despite Adekunle's boasts about not allowing the Igbo to eat before their capitulation, he allowed the international observer team almost immediate access to the newly occupied areas, sometimes even before it was safe to do so, as the Owerri episode illustrated. The colonel himself was more concerned with conquering and capturing than with many of the operational, logistical, and civil administration aspects of conducting a war in enemy territory with a hostile population. The assault on Owerri proved both the high point of Adekunle's assault on the Igbo heartland and the beginning of its unravelling.

Akinrinade led the assault on the city with Colonel Akpan Utuk's 16th Brigade doing most of the fighting in the city. Two other brigades, the 14th and 15th, had been tasked with protecting Akinrinade's east and west flanks, respectively, but both assaults around Owerri failed because of Biafran determination to protect the roads to Umuahia in the east and Uli to the northwest. As a result, Utuk was left in the city with no protection on either flank and no chain of command to request support. Godwin Ally, the sector commander, had remained in Port Harcourt, some one hundred kilometers to the south, while Adekunle had been shuttling back and forth between Port Harcourt and Lagos. Thus, the problem for the Nigerians was not conquering the town but protecting their conquest from Biafran counterattacks that were sure to come.[56]

Adekunle's assault on the Igbo heartland exposed one of the fatal flaws in both Nigeria and Biafra's ability to conduct large-scale operations: the lack of a unified chain of command above the division level and, in Nigeria's case, even within the 3rd Marine Commando Division. As Nigeria's southern division split into the four geographical zones, each regional commander was responsible for his area, and coordination between the commanding officers seemed to have been on a voluntary basis. As the Nigerians were making their way to Aba, Alabi-Isama volunteered to cover Shande's flank, but the latter ended all communication as he began his assault on the city. Despite Shande's death at Aba, the Nigerian capture of the city did not suffer because of the lack of support, but Nigeria's occupation of Owerri would prove disastrous.

While some of the issues were no doubt due to personality conflicts and political ambitions of some of the officers in command, structural and training issues compounded the problems of waging large-scale military operations with a relatively young officer corps. Though many of the officers commissioned in the early years underwent their training at the Royal Military Academy Sandhurst, very few had attended senior officer command and staff training colleges. Gowon attended the British Staff College at Camberley in 1962 but had been in a staff position for only three years before becoming GOC after the January coup and, later that year, head of state. Obasanjo attended the Indian Defense Services Staff College in 1965 but largely played a supporting role in the war until May 1969, when he replaced Adekunle as the head of the 3rd Marine Commando Division after the ignoble end of the latter's Operation OAU. Shuwa, who commanded the 1st Division for most of the war, lamented the lack of training and criticized the other staff officers who, like him, had not been able to attend command and staff schools. In his only interview about the war, which appeared in Momoh's tome, he claimed that while Adekunle used his position for self-aggrandizement and Murtala left the military after his operational failures taking Onitsha, he himself brought books with him on campaign as a form of on-the-job self-training.[57]

Like many postcolonial African militaries, the Nigerian army's process of Nigerianization of the officer corps became tinged with ethnic and religious rivalries, much like the ones that crippled the First Republic. Many officers advanced more quickly than they would have in other circumstances and without much of the training necessary to perform those functions. Following the January 1966 coup, Yakubu Gowon became GOC at the age of twenty-nine and head of state later that year. His successor, Joseph Akahan, was only thirty when he assumed the role and had previously only achieved the rank of lieutenant colonel and had not trained at a staff college. After Akahan died in a 1968 helicopter crash, his replacement, Hassan Katsina, similarly lacked qualifications. Katsina, a northern officer promoted quickly to achieve parity in the Nigerianization process before the war, had previously commanded only a company and a reconnaissance squadron before assuming command of the entire Nigerian military in the middle of a war.[58] It was during his tenure that Adekunle conceived of Operation OAU and was able to execute the disastrous parts of it despite the obvious warnings from his subordinates and others in the Nigerian military.

Complicating matters further, many of the most capable officers lost their lives during the two coups. During the January coup, the plotters eliminated many officers who refused to join the plot and targeted them regardless of ethnic identity. The violence that accompanied the July coup targeted the Igbo almost exclusively and claimed the lives of many officers and enlisted men, prompting the ethnic separation of the military. In an interview, Maj. Gen. Mohammed Magoro, then a platoon commander in the Nigerian 1st Division during the Nsukka campaign in the war's early months, lamented, "The Division commanders seemed to be operating each in their own little warzone, not much of coordination with their neighbor and that, of course, affected the conduct of any operation. . . . They could have come out with a strategy to see what should have been done to end the war as quickly as possible involving if possible all the divisions themselves. . . . Where do we lay the fault? I honestly can't say."[59] These issues hampered both sides' ability to coordinate between and within their organizations. Moreover, coupled with intense political interference, these issues would lead to many tragedies.

Much like the capture of Aba, the assault on Owerri involved little planning. Unlike Aba, which sat at the southern fringe of the Igbo heartland, Owerri lay in the heart of it and was thus surrounded by a hostile population that constantly threatened supply lines. Further complicating matters, the city was flanked by the Imo River on the east, its tributary the Otamiri, which entered the city from the south, and in the west by the Orashi, the river that led to Oguta, and patrolled by the Biafran navy, which by this point in the war had lost its oceangoing capabilities but still maintained a handful of makeshift river gunboats. However, the fighting in Oguta halted Biafra's ability to resupply both the military and civilian population, and despite the reversal and retreat, the Biafran army's depleted resources made it unable to repel the better-supplied Nigerian forces. The Biafran need to hold Oguta also taxed their reserves and ability to muster fresh troops to meet the Nigerian offensive, and the Biafran focus had to make a marked shift. Madiebo saw that he would not be able to hold Owerri, so he turned to halting the Nigerian advances east to Umuahia and north toward Uli and Orlu, which, if captured, would most likely have spelled the end of Biafra.

Though Adekunle's division captured Owerri on September 16, the fighting intensified in the sector as the Nigerians pushed toward Umuahia with the Biafran defenses desperate to stop them. By October 1, the Nigerian 1st Division under Shuwa's command had taken Okigwe to the north of Umuahia, and Ojukwu once again personally intervened in the military's operations, appointing Achuzia to head the Biafran 13th Division, which the superstitious Achuzia quickly renamed the 15th, as 13 was an unlucky number. Ojukwu also ordered all officers who had lost the town demoted by one rank for their perceived incompetence, a sentiment that Madiebo did not share.[60] However, Achuzia planned to retake the town and launched three offensives that all failed due to lack of planning and failed leadership, and he was removed from his command after two months. Madiebo lamented, "The rapid loss of Aba, Owerri and Okigwe all in one month simply broke the will of the Biafran people to continue the war" and that to divert attention from the military losses, "a new group of saboteurs had been discovered," which included most of the senior leadership, including Mbafeno, Azikiwe, and Madiebo.[61]

Despite the losses, the Biafrans held their defenses while Adekunle attempted to capture the capital at Umuahia. Ignoring Nigerian intelligence assertions that "going to Umuahia at that time would be suicidal," Adekunle pressed his assault instead of refocusing his efforts to capture Uli, which was in a more precarious position, especially as the capture of Okigwe essentially left the Biafran airstrip isolated.[62] While few of the major actors detailed the assault on Umuahia and instead focused on the battle for Owerri, news accounts, both printed and filmed, detailed the collapse of Adekunle's division that within a week "had lost virtually all its troops and weapons."[63] Though Adekunle had set a deadline of October 1 for the completion of his objectives, by October 7 the division was on the verge of collapse, which gave the Biafrans an opportunity to counter and stop the despair that Madiebo detailed. More baffling was the lack of coordination between the Nigerian divisions. Shuwa's 1st Division, which had secured Okigwe was well poised to resume its offensive to the south and either attack Umuahia, barely thirty kilometers south, or head west toward Uli and Owerri, block Biafran supply lines, and protect Adekunle's flanks. Why this did not happen is the source of much speculation. Whether Adekunle shunned cooperation for egotistical reasons or Nigeria's central command was simply unable to facilitate such coordination is unclear.[64]

The Biafrans decided to counter the Nigerians on two fronts. The first was to retake Aba and Owerri, and the other was to attempt to recapture Onitsha, which had been in Nigerian hands since March. The latter was code-named Operation Hiroshima and, as mentioned earlier, involved Steiner's commandos, who attacked the city in a full-frontal assault against the fortified Nigerians. This assault, which Ojukwu personally ordered, ended in disaster, as Steiner's men had trained in commando and guerrilla tactics; despite being among the best-supplied and most well-rested men Biafra could muster, they lacked the training for that type of assault. As a result, Steiner's commandos lost nearly half their men, and their commander suffered the breakdown mentioned in the previous chapter. After Ojukwu deported the German commander, he placed the commando division under the Biafran command structure and subordinated it to Madiebo, who appointed Nwawo as its commander, thus reining in the renegade division and placing all Biafran units under one command structure. However, Ojukwu's personal interventions in tactical matters would not end after the fiascos at Oguta and Onitsha and would challenge the military's command structure until the end of the war.[65]

Shuwa used the failed Biafran assault to attempt an advance south and cut the Biafran link to the Anambra Basin that the Biafrans had been tenaciously defending. Loss of the food-growing region north of Onitsha would have meant an even more acute food shortage. The Nigerians advanced south toward Biafran defenses at Agulu on November 25 and overran the Biafran company stationed there before stopping south of Agulu at Adazi Nnukwu. The Nigerian pause gave the Biafrans time to regroup and send two brigades, including Ojukwu's personal reserve force, known as the Umuahia Brigade, as well as Achuzia's 15th Brigade.[66] Because of the sector's importance to Biafra's food supply and the proximity to Ojukwu's home in Nnewi, the Biafran leader once again took operational control of the battle and ordered Achuzia to launch a counteroffensive the following day, even though Madiebo claimed he had planned an assault from the morning of November 27. According to Madiebo, instead of following Ojukwu's orders, Achuzia disappeared from the front with most of the ammunition and fuel, leaving only 150 of the 750 men he had originally planned for the assault.[67] Despite the setbacks in men and ammunition, Madiebo commenced with his assault as he had planned and by that afternoon had routed the enemy. Once the Nigerians fled, Madiebo lamented the breakdown of military discipline, claiming, "Most of the Biafran troops left the battle area and went back to Nnewi to celebrate the victory and it took a pretty long time to get them back to their defensive positions. If the enemy had carried out an immediate counterattack, it could have had disastrous consequences for us." Regardless, Madiebo writes, the success at Agulu convinced Ojukwu to allow for planning and helped him recognize the utility of flanking maneuvers against armored opposition. The Nigerians had at least one armored Saladin in the battle that Madiebo ignored because of his lack of antitank weapons. Despite Ojukwu's actions at Oguta and during Operation Hiroshima, where he allegedly forced Steiner's commandos into the frontal assault, the idea that the Biafran leader, a trained staff officer, would not know these things is more than somewhat questionable.[68] Regardless of the failure of Biafra's operation to retake Onitsha, they succeeded in stabilizing the front, and the Nigerians would not attempt to cut their access to the Anambra Basin for many months, securing some vital food and smuggling routes that had become Biafra's lifeline. The Nigerians would not complete the linkage until the last days of the war, on December 24, 1969. When Shuwa's 1st Division eventually captured Umuahia in April 1969, they completely bypassed the Awka sector, instead traveling south from Nsukka and Enugu, running virtually unopposed until Uzoakoli, less than twenty kilometers north of Umuahia. This is discussed in detail later.

The second phase of the Biafran counterattack came against the remnants of Adekunle's 3rd Marine Commando Division. It began in late November with a failed push to recapture Aba and Owerri and ended the following March with the Biafrans ousting the Nigerians from Owerri, the only time the Biafrans had been able to dislodge the Nigerians from a major urban area larger than small towns like Ikot Ekpene and Oguta. After stabilizing the front along the Onitsha–Awka axis, the Biafrans exploited the confusion in the Nigerian 3rd Division and the lack of effective central control in the Nigerian army to launch a fresh attack on Owerri. Because of the lack of planning, the Nigerians were able to capture the city but had been beaten back on the city's east and west. The result was that the city became a poorly defended bulge protruding into the Igbo heartland. Supplying Utuk's Nigerian 16th Brigade in the city depended on keeping the corridor to Port Harcourt open. The assault would be a drawn-out affair because despite the tactical advantage of attacking a poorly defended salient, the Biafrans lacked the firepower to assault the Nigerian positions in Owerri. However, the disarray in the Nigerians' 3rd Marine Commando Division meant they would be able to lay siege to the city and, through attrition, slowly gnaw at the Nigerian defenses. Madiebo acknowledged, "It was a very ambitious plan based entirely on optimism" due to the uncertainty of Biafran supply chains and the Nigerian division's ability to regroup after the disaster at Umuahia.[69]

By this time, the Biafrans knew that their lack of materiel would prohibit a quick assault against the enemy that had entrenched itself in the city since September. Thus, the Biafrans came up with a three-part plan for a long siege. In early December, the Biafrans began their offensive that would last until March the following year. The key was to show enough strength to the enemy but also project weakness to ensure the Nigerians would not send reinforcements until it was too late. The first phase of the operation was to cut the Nigerian communication and supply lines in every direction but keep the main road to Port Harcourt in Nigerian hands so as not to overly alarm the Nigerian 16th Brigade in the city. The disarray on the Nigerian side meant that the first part of the operation, encircling Owerri on three flanks, was successful after only three days, and Utuk's Nigerian 16th Brigade had been pushed back from the city's environs into the core.

The operation's second phase took considerably longer, largely due to ammunition shortages. Unable to supply all three Biafran brigades engaged in the operation, Madiebo decided to complete this part of the operation one brigade at a time. By now, the troubles in the command structure on the Nigerian side had begun to mount, and it was clear there was no effective way to counter the Biafran moves against Utuk in Owerri. At the end of 1968, the Biafrans stood poised to press their advantage and inflict further misery on Utuk and the entire 3rd Marine Commando Division.[70]

Though Adekunle's Operation OAU was an unprecedented disaster that nearly destroyed his division and cost him his command, Shuwa's careful advance in the north placed Biafra in a dire situation, with the cautious commander poised to lead the final assault on Biafra. However, as 1968 ended, the Biafrans had cause for hope. In a single calendar year they had effectively destroyed two of the three divisions attacking Biafra and forced the Nigerians to allow them some acknowledgment on the international stage. They successfully made their plight a cause célèbre around the world, turning world opinion against Nigeria and those who aided in the war against it. Despite these hopes, the secessionist republic was not only a landlocked enclave; it had also lost almost all the urban areas they once controlled. The only exceptions were the capital at Umuahia and the city of Owerri, which the Biafrans were able to retake during Adekunle's collapse. Even worse, the peace talks in Kampala and Addis Ababa failed to provide for a relief corridor by either land or air, leaving the only option for humanitarian and military resupply coming from the airlift with the constant threat of Nigerian action against it.

As 1968 ended, Biafra's ability to leverage global support into tangible diplomatic successes also ended. If the accusations of genocide throughout 1968 heaped pressure on Gowon and his allies in London to end the war, the failure of the talks in Kampala and Addis Ababa also shifted the tone of political pressure.

Many leaders and pundits saw Ojukwu's lack of flexibility in the talks as bluster with little military support, and calls for the Biafrans to end the hopeless war increased throughout the end of 1968 and into 1969. For many foreign officials and analysts, ending the war was the only way to end the suffering.

Despite public pressure to allow a land corridor for resupply, Ojukwu's insistence on the airlift troubled many world leaders, especially as even at full capacity with daytime and night flights, the airlift could supply only about a quarter of the estimated four thousand tons of food the Biafrans needed. However, allowing daytime relief flights would complicate the smuggling of arms and materiel that Biafra depended on to continue its military campaign.

NINE

THE END (?) OF BIAFRA

THE ASSAULT ON OWERRI WAS probably the most significant battlefield Biafran victory. It was also the last major offensive that they would be able to sustain. Though the Biafrans took the city, it was followed shortly thereafter by the Nigerian capture of Umuahia, which had been Biafra's de facto capital since the fall of Enugu in October 1967. However, more problems began to mount for the Biafrans that would begin to unravel their war effort long before the final Nigerian offensives, Operations Finishing Touch and Tail Wind in October 1969 and January 1970, respectively.

Perhaps Biafra's most important success in 1968 was the extremely well-organized propaganda campaign that catapulted the war to global attention. However, by the end of the year, the lack of diplomatic successes to accompany the public outcry began to generate a shift in the world's attitudes toward the humanitarian catastrophe in the country. Biafra's original goal was to pressure world governments to end their support of Nigeria, especially Britain and the USSR, which were the Nigerians' main arms suppliers. Though the pressure worked in a partial fashion in the UK, with the Wilson government limiting the supply of the more destructive weapons that could cause significant collateral damage, both countries continued to supply Nigeria. The Soviet Union also supplied pilots and support staff to operate and maintain the MiGs that had wrought devastation on Biafra's civilians.

While Biafra's public pressure did not choke off Nigeria's arms supplies, it did force Gowon to accept the peace talks in Kampala and Addis Ababa, an act that the Nigerians had been resisting since the conflict's beginning, as any internationally mediated meeting could give the Biafrans a veneer of respectability and thus recognition. However, both peace talks ended without an agreement either to end the war or to open a supply route to feed the starving population in Biafra.

As a result, world opinion began to shift toward a belief that ending the starvation and stopping the genocide required an immediate end to the war, a prospect the Biafrans were unwilling to entertain.

Thus, in January 1969, the Food Directorate began a new program called the Land Army Scheme.[1] This program was designed to increase food production across Biafra and to use the civilian population to grow food that would be shared between the military and the neediest civilians while also rewarding those who participated. The program was born out of two necessities: First, the war's longevity and Biafra's increasing isolation made extra food production necessary. Second, Biafra had to convince its own people and the world that despite the starvation, disease, and suffering, the fledgling nation could provide for its citizens and thus continue the war, even with the heavy military setbacks. The Land Army program aimed to utilize as much of the areas that Biafra controlled to increase food production and redistribute it throughout the country. The Biafrans were especially active in ensuring people who grew the food would cooperate with the program, so the Propaganda Directorate engaged in an aggressive campaign to promote participation, especially among women, who, because of the war, became even more important in providing a semblance of normality on the home front. One of the few extant documents from Biafra in the Nigerian archives, titled "What Biafrans Know about the Nigeria/Biafra War," most likely created in early 1969, was designed to ascertain the level of engagement with the war effort of different groups within Biafra. It found, in part, that "female youths, as a group, appear least committed to the struggle. . . . This attitude appears quite dangerous at a time when the females, especially the female youths, are being called upon to take over the running of this nation so that the males can move to the war fronts."[2]

The report detailed a string of surveys that the directorate performed across Biafran-held territory and was remarkable in its scope and logistic capability, especially considering the grave situation in the country. The report gave special attention to the Land Army because "a clear knowledge about the pattern of the distribution of the rewards of any project of the society influences their degree of participation and enthusiasm in it and therefore the success of the project."[3] Thus, the Land Army's success depended on the people's, especially women's, willingness to cooperate with the program.

As they did with much of Biafra's public diplomacy and propaganda, the Propaganda Directorate also aimed the public messaging of the Land Army to global audiences, particularly those that were concerned with the food situation in Biafra. In February 1969, an American mission led by Senator Charles Goodell viewed the Land Army as a possible solution to the country's food shortages and recommended tools and expertise be supplied to aid in food production.[4]

The Land Army was not the only project that the Biafran leader created to help prosecute the war in the face of Biafra's mounting troubles. Because of the territorial losses, Ojukwu instructed the creation of a new force that would operate behind enemy lines called the Biafran Organization of Freedom Fighters (BOFF). This new force was designed to act as both a smuggling operation, much like the ahia attack, and a guerilla force behind enemy lines. Though little work about BOFF is available, due largely to the organization's informal nature and the general lack of Biafran documents, some work suggests that the organization mostly targeted Igbo who collaborated with the Nigerian occupiers.[5]

If little literature exists to corroborate much of BOFF's work, the organization's reputation gives it an outsize presence in the war's fiction. One well-studied work, Eddie Iroh's *The Siren of the Night*, written in 1982, uses BOFF as a central plot element. The book's protagonist, Ben Udaja, is a founding member of the organization who defects to the Nigerian side in Enugu in the hopes of shortening the war and ending Igbo suffering. His actions make him the target of reprisals, and he lives in fear of assassination by BOFF agents.[6] Iroh's work is part of a trilogy about the war, and *The Siren of the Night* is particularly important as it shows the growing disillusionment and despair that gripped most of the Biafran population in the latter stage of the war, especially after May 1969.

Although the defection depicted in Iroh's book is fictional, the war brought several high-profile defectors, and as the war turned more desperate, the Biafran leadership reacted with venom to each and worse to those who were suspected of planning to defect. Efiong recounted that in the chaos that surrounded the fall of Umuahia in April 1969, Ojukwu tried to summon him. Efiong, however, was preoccupied with the situation in the city. Once the hopelessness of the situation became clear, Efiong "went away with a friend who took me to a quiet place he had found . . . where I was able to have a much needed rest for a good 24 hours." In his absence, Ojukwu became convinced that Efiong was attempting to flee and ordered the latter's immediate execution. It was only when the general arrived for a meeting with Ojukwu that the death sentence was rescinded. Perhaps no defection harmed Biafra more than that of Nnamdi Azikiwe, discussed in detail later in the chapter.[7]

The Land Army and BOFF were ways the Biafrans tried to stem the growing tide against them at home. Abroad, the Biafrans never gave up the attempt to garner moral, diplomatic, and material support by painting their country with a veneer of viability to global audiences. Throughout the war, the Biafrans appealed to celebrities, sports icons, and other people with popular appeal to boost Biafra's prospects.

In Biafra, the Land Army and BOFF became central aspects of Ojukwu's attempt to rebrand Biafran independence. On Biafra's second anniversary, Ojukwu published what has become known as the Ahiara Declaration, where he set out a new vision for the postwar future. The declaration itself was a mix of ideas such as Black Nationalism, African Socialism, and other ideologies that the authors of the document, a group of scholars from the University of Biafra (formerly the

University of Nigeria—Nsukka) led by Chinua Achebe, sought to imbue their republic with. Ojukwu hoped the ideas would reinvigorate support for Biafra abroad and reenergize the sagging morale at home. In particular, the declaration sought to establish Biafra's revolutionary bona fides by casting the country's plight as "the latest victims of a wicked collusion between the three traditional scourges of the black man—racism, Arab-Muslim expansionism and white economic imperialism."[8] Though the work casts itself as a progressive vision for Biafra's future, it is also shaped by a strong anti-Muslim tone in an overt effort to cast aspersions on Nigeria's northern population as a tool of oppression and as another foreign invasion of the continent. Thus, not only an independent and free Biafra but also a Christian one could withstand these three ills.

The tensions between the declaration's enlightenment ideals and the political realities that Biafra faced in its final year led to many internal contradictions, with the Muslim issue being the most prominent but by no means the only one. As Jago Morrison writes, much of the declaration reads like the "spectacle of a leader casting around for languages with which to articulate some viable idea of nationhood."[9] Ojukwu thought the declaration would reinvigorate global support for Biafra, and when that support failed to materialize he blamed external forces, like the plight of eighteen oil workers that is detailed later in this chapter, as overshadowing his revolutionary document. The Ahiara Declaration was an inconsistent vision of an imagined utopia that could do little to confront the bitter realities Biafra faced after two years of war.

Biafra's fortunes were further hampered right before the Ahiara Declaration when, on April 19, 1969, Shuwa's 1st Division entered Umuahia after a monthlong offensive that began in Okigwe, which Shuwa had taken in his effort to support Adekunle's 3rd Marine Commando Division the previous September. The assault on Umuahia became one of the longest and costliest engagements of the war, lasting nearly a month of continuous fighting from March 27 until the final capture of the city on April 22 with over ten thousand Nigerian casualties and at least as many Biafran. For the historian, the battle is unique, as firsthand accounts survive in the form of interviews and memoirs from participants on both sides, which in some ways makes reconstructing the battle more difficult as the accounts are contradictory.[10]

Knowing that the Biafrans would protect the city at all costs, Shuwa prepared an elaborate ruse, tricking the Biafrans and their BOFF operatives into thinking that the assault would proceed either along the Imo River or via the more direct route through Ezinachi to Umuokpara. However, on March 27, Shuwa assembled five battalions, the 4th, 21st, 25th, 44th, and 88th, for the assault, codenamed Operation Leopard, and headed east toward Ahaba before turning south to confront the Biafrans on the poorly defended eastern end of the city. It was only when the Nigerians reached Uzuakoli, the Biafrans' main refining facility, on April 1, 1969, that the defenders realized that Umuahia was the operation's target and began to organize a stand on the city's outskirts rather than defend Umuahia from inside the capital. Madiebo scrambled the 15th Division to meet the Nigerians, and Ojukwu even sent his personal bodyguards to Uzuakoli to aid in the defense, but the dire situation saw some raw recruits who had not completed even rudimentary training put into action. Madiebo commented that many of the Biafran troops sent to the front were so green that "most of them had never touched a rifle before and none of them had seen before the type of rifle they were issued with."[11]

For the Biafrans, losing Umuahia could have spelled the end of the war, but they internalized the lessons from the previous defenses of Enugu, Onitsha, and Port Harcourt. This time, the Biafrans were determined to avoid an intense urban battle and met the Nigerians at Uzuakoli with their lone French Panhard armored car, the Oguta Boy, named after the battle in Oguta where it was captured. The Biafrans used Oguta Boy to such effect that Nigerian Maj. (later Gen.) Mamman Jiya Vatsa thought he was facing several of them. During the battle's early phases, the Biafrans captured a Saladin and an APC, which added to their ability to hold out and forced the Nigerians into costly improvisations. To combat what they thought was a new threat of multiple armored cars, the Nigerians devised a company-level diversionary assault they nicknamed the *alalaba*, the Hausa word for sneaking. Because the Panhard was tanklike in its capabilities, Vatsa needed to find a way to destroy the multiple armored cars he thought he was facing with a close-range shot to minimize the Panhard crew's ability to identify the team and return fire. As such, he employed a company to confuse the crew and allow the antitank team to set up at close range and hit the Panhard on the first shot.[12] Because the Nigerians did not expect to face armored opposition, they suffered heavy casualties as they developed their new tactic in a trial by fire. The result was a catastrophe for the Nigerian 25th Battalion that led the advance, which lost all but two officers and nearly all its NCOs. With the battalion on the verge of collapse, it retreated into the fold of the 28th Battalion, but Biafran snipers soon began to target the commanders and NCOs, sowing panic in both battalions, which fled further into the eastern outskirts of the town and dug in. Though the Nigerians would eventually devise a maneuver that would prove successful, the soldiers had to learn the diversionary tactics under fire, and only through great losses could they create a tactic that could function effectively.

The Biafran military's desperate stand in Uzuakoli to protect the fuel-production facilities left the rest of the theater virtually undefended. This allowed elements of the Nigerian 28th Battalion to reach their destination in Bende, some ten kilometers south, and prepare for the assault on Umuahia. However, command issues and personal rivalries compounded the problems on both sides and likely led to more bloodshed and prevented either side from pressing their advantages. On the Biafran side, commanders from all over the country rushed to Ojukwu's defense, with Achuzia arriving from across the Niger where he was no doubt working with BOFF operatives or coordinating smuggling activities. However, his chief personal rival, Onwuatuagwu, also arrived with a few hundred men from his S Division to ensure that Achuzia could only share in the glory at best.

On the Nigerian side, command issues prevented coordination between Shuwa's 1st Division and Adekunle's 3rd. Adekunle, though still in command of the 3rd Division, had been unable to return it to a fighting force after his disastrous attempt to take Umuahia the previous October as the final phase of Operation OAU. He would not last much longer in his command, and Obasanjo replaced him the following month, in May 1969. As a result, Shuwa was unable to count on the support of either the 3rd Division or the 2nd, which had been restricted to Onitsha since Murtala Mohammed's Pyrrhic assault more than a year before. Complicating matters further, the Nigerian high command under the inexperienced leadership of Hassan Katsina was either unwilling or unable to make major command decisions, leaving the field commanders to essentially negotiate matters of support between and sometimes even within divisions, as illustrated during the capture of Aba and Owerri in the previous chapter.

—∞—

Though Biafra's global campaign never garnered the tangible diplomatic results of invoking Article VIII of the UN Genocide Convention or otherwise forcing some kind of international intervention, the campaign succeeded in forcing the Nigerians to accept Biafra into the peace talks and thus tacitly easing the secessionists' diplomatic isolation. Though five countries recognized Biafran statehood, Ivorian and Gabonese support was used as a proxy for French clandestine support, especially in arms deliveries, as France indirectly funneled weapons and ammunition through their African client states.

Early literature on the war credits, or blames, French assistance for prolonging the war into 1969, and de St. Jorre's claim that "French intervention decisively saved Biafra from defeat, [and] decisively prolonged the war" is emblematic of the early ideas on French assistance to Biafra.[13] However, later work has shed light on how French involvement was part of a French policy against Anglophone Africa in general and Nigerian dominance of the region in particular. Stremlau expanded on French support in his seminal work on the international politics of the war. Many in France, chief among them the head of the Secretariat for African Affairs, Jacques Foccart, saw in the war a chance to allow France to play a greater role in the region. French support expanded significantly in the months after the failed Addis Ababa peace conference, but by the middle of 1969, it became clear, even to Foccart, that Biafra's prospects for survival were slim and that French interests would be better served focusing on repairing what relationship they had with Nigeria. As a result, most of the arms supplies through Gabon and Ivory Coast greatly diminished, though Gabon's help would be instrumental in one of the most publicized aspects of the war, the return of von Rosen with a new Biafran air force known as the MINICOIN.[14]

In addition to the French, both South Africa and Ian Smith's Rhodesia supported Biafra, albeit in very insignificant ways. For both regimes, destabilizing Nigeria seemed to be a priority, and the Biafrans reluctantly accepted help, with Ojukwu claiming that he would accept aid from the devil if it meant helping Biafra survive. Of the two, Rhodesia provided a regular supply of arms throughout the war but had little impact on the ground. Ironically, because of the Russian refusal to allow western pilots into the MiG 17s, at least one anonymous South African was remembered by relief pilots flying into Uli. In a thick accent, he would attempt to intercept the planes flying into Biafra calling on the radio, "'Ullo, 'ullo, this is '*Genocide*' [apparently his callsign] calling."[15]

French support was not the only factor that helped the Biafrans weather the loss of their capital. In May 1969, the Swedish pilot von Rosen returned to Biafra and helped build a new guerilla-style air force. Months earlier, von Rosen appeared at the First International Conference for Biafra and posited that a small force of light aircraft could be deployed in a way that escaped detection and used to "go in and smash those fighters and attack bombers on the ground which Nigeria has used to kill off the civilian population."[16] Not content simply to present papers on how airpower could win the war, von Rosen spent the next several months arranging the purchase of a squadron of light aircraft—Swedish-manufactured Malmö MFI-9, which he purchased with the help of French and Tanzanian diplomats. Because the Swedish government did not want to supply the Biafrans with arms, the aircraft had to be bought without alerting the Swedes to their ultimate destination. Two stories have emerged regarding von Rosen's purchase of the planes. In one, the Swedish government sold the five aircraft at the behest of a Tanzanian diplomat who claimed the planes were destined for a new government-run flying school. Another story was that a Swedish doctor living in Rome purchased the planes for US$60,000 and created a fictitious leasing company, claiming the planes would be used for aerial ore prospecting.[17] In reality, the planes arrived in France, where the French air force measured one of the planes for underwing rocket launchers. All five of the planes were then disassembled and flown to Gabon, not Tanzania as originally promised.

When the planes arrived in Gabon, crews reassembled them and fitted the rocket launchers. Four pilots, two Swedish and two Biafran, joined von Rosen in Gabon, and on May 22, 1969, the five planes left Gabon for their flight into Biafra, which included an attack on the Port Harcourt Airport that destroyed one MiG-17 on the ground and most likely damaged several others.[18] They followed up with attacks on the airports in Benin and Enugu as well as the power station in Ughelli, crippling the station, which supplied most of the region's power, including the Benin airport's, for nearly six months.[19] Von Rosen dubbed his squadron the Miniature Counter Insurgency Aircraft, or MINICOIN. The name was quickly corrupted in the global media, and the planes became known as the Minicons or, more colorfully, as the Biafran Babies, a nod to the publicity that the humanitarian catastrophe, especially the pictures of starving children, had garnered.

One of von Rosen's main goals for the MINICOINs was to create a quick strike ability against the Nigerians. The use of concealed airstrips where the small planes could be easily hidden, coupled with an operating range of eight hundred kilometers and the fact that they needed only very short takeoff and landing lengths, made them versatile and difficult to destroy, both in the air and on the ground. The Nigerians reacted quickly both to attempt to destroy the new threat and to protect against it. The same day as the Port Harcourt attack, the Nigerians attempted to locate and destroy the planes, which used at least three known airfields, but it took the Nigerians a week to discover any of the airstrips, and their ineffectual attacks on the strips, despite some casualties, did not damage the planes in a meaningful way.

The first MINICOIN assaults garnered important publicity for the Biafrans, whose wartime fortunes had taken another turn for the worse after the fall of Umuahia in April. Approximately a week after the MINICOINs' arrival, Biafra celebrated its second independence anniversary, and the Biafrans desperately needed more battlefield successes to accompany their celebrations. Thus, the Biafrans decided to use the MINICOINs as close combat support and not, as in the previous raids, against static infrastructure. Their new goal was to support the Biafrans who had recaptured Owerri the previous month and sow panic among the remaining Nigerians in the area. However, von Rosen and his team did not find any targets during their dusk raid and returned to base without any success. This also marked the last flight for the three Swedes, as they left Biafra the next day, leaving Okpe as the only operational pilot. Willy-Bruce had apparently suffered from some kind of operational fatigue or exhaustion and did not fly again for some time.[20]

They were replaced by former Swedish air force pilot Rune Norgren, who joined Okpe, and the two launched twenty-one attacks in July. In one raid, they attacked a Nigerian ammunition store but were almost shot down in a friendly fire incident by Biafran antiaircraft batteries who were unaware of the raid.[21]

The Biafrans and their allies were eager to capitalize on the MINICOIN success. With French and Ivorian help, four more MFI-9 were smuggled to Gabon. By September, the Biafrans had four dedicated airstrips for the MINICOINs, but their main problem was pilot training.

The Biafrans had some pilots who previously flew in the Nigerian air force or for Nigerian Airways, but none had any combat pilot training. Thus, in August, von

Rosen returned to help train new pilots, as Okpe was the only pilot available after Norgren left in late July. Von Rosen created a three-tiered training system. Their first round of training was basic flying and rocket launching in Gabon, followed by operational training in Biafra, where the trainees took part in actual missions. At some point, the pilots returned to Gabon for a series of drills involving instrument and night flying. Okpe, Willy-Bruce, and one other Biafran pilot known only as Goody became the first group to complete their training. By the end of the war, the Biafrans boasted ten pilots, not all of whose identities have been clearly established.

These pilots continued their attacks with mixed results. When they attacked static targets such as airports, they had much success, like the October 10 assault on the Benin airport. In this attack, four pilots, a German named Friedrich Herz, and three Biafran pilots known only as Ibi, Alex, and Benny attacked the airport and claimed a huge success with the destruction of at least one MiG-17, a DC-4 cargo plane, and an ammunition depot and the killing of twenty-eight men, including Col. Shittu Alao, the head of Nigeria's air force. However, most of these claims were fabricated, as Alao died five days later in a plane crash. In reality, the damage the Biafrans did was largely to the control tower, where the controller was seriously wounded. At the time of the raid, a Nigerian turboprop was preparing to land. When the aircraft received no response from the airport, the crew simply assumed the power was out, a thought reinforced by the fact that the outer marker, the radio tower that was supposed to indicate that the aircraft was on course to begin its final landing approach, was not functioning. The wounded controller was able to scramble and reach his radio in time to yell "GET OUT! GET OUT GET OUT!" and thus saved the crew from becoming an easy target for the MINICOINs.[22] Oil installations were also a frequent MINICOIN target, and the squadron attacked Mobil and Shell installations as well as several oil tankers and barges.

However, when the Biafrans attempted to use the planes for close air support of ground forces, the results were not as spectacular, as they lacked the coordination to identify their targets quickly, and the light trainer planes they used were incapable of any kind of air-to-air combat, so surprise was the only advantage they had. They thus needed to appear and then disappear before MiGs scrambled against them, leaving them precious little time to identify targets.

Despite their limitations, the MINICOINs garnered publicity around the world, and their use, especially in the weeks following their introduction, helped boost Biafra's sagging morale. Reports in the *New York Times* and the Associated Press, including an interview with von Rosen, helped boost Biafran fortunes at a time when they needed it most.[23]

Shortly before the MINICOINs arrived, on May 9, the Biafrans committed one of their most damaging blunders during the war: a commando assault on an Italian AGIP oil facility on the west bank of the Niger near Kwale. In the assault, the Biafrans killed eleven oil workers, buried them in a shallow grave, and took eighteen foreign survivors prisoner. For two weeks, the Nigerians and a team from the oil company searched for clues before finding the grave that the Biafrans had dug. A few days later, Ojukwu disclosed the fate of the surviving workers, sentencing them to death on June 2 for aiding a genocidal war.

In reality, Ojukwu used the oil workers and the global outcry for their release for several intertwined reasons. First, Ojukwu wished to gain de facto recognition of his government at the highest levels that had previously shut out the Biafrans. Second, Ojukwu hoped to use global concern for the oil workers to highlight the perceived racism of a world that had turned its back on the millions of suffering Biafrans and instead concerned itself with eighteen missing oil workers. Ojukwu famously stated on Radio Biafra, "For eighteen white men, Europe is aroused! What have they said about our millions? Eighteen white men assisting in the crime of genocide. What do they say about our murdered innocents? How many black dead make one missing white? Mathematicians, please answer me. Is it infinity?"[24]

Most controversially, the death sentences that Ojukwu meted out seemed to spur a payment from AGIP and the Italian government, facilitated by the Holy See and Portugal. Though no official confirmation of a ransom exists, new reports and diplomatic sources have quoted a payment of anywhere between three and twenty million dollars that secured the oil workers' release.[25] Regardless of whether Ojukwu secured a ransom, the affair soured Biafra's carefully constructed public relations campaign, had serious effects on Biafra's relations with allies around the world, and gave Nigeria an opportunity to increase its actions against the humanitarian efforts with relative impunity. As Chinua Achebe lamented, "As a people proclaiming victimization at the hands of Nigeria, and rightfully so, we could not be seen as victimizers in any situation or setting, in order to continue receiving the widespread moral and humanitarian support we needed in order to survive. This failure to recognize this fundamental principle, I believe, contributed immensely to the downturn in Biafra's fortunes."[26]

Though Ojukwu bemoaned that the AGIP affair distracted the world from his vision for Biafra in the Ahiara Declaration, the affair was much more damaging to Biafra's war effort. In March, prior to the incident, Gowon had limited the Nigerian air force's ability to operate due to the reports of widespread civilian casualties, but the AGIP affair, coupled with the new threat of the MINICOINs, gave Gowon both the operational justifications and relative immunity from international criticism to renew full air force operations. The Biafrans decried the new raids, but by June 1969, the Nigerians had replaced the ill-trained Egyptians with Warsaw Pact and other mercenary pilots.[27]

The Nigerians reacted swiftly to the MINICOINs, targeting the Red Cross in a growing spat with August Lindt, whose seeming collaboration with the Biafrans had long irked the federal government. Also, von Rosen's ability to skirt Swedish laws about exporting weapons gave the Nigerian air force an opportunity to send a message to both the ICRC and the Swedish government, as von Rosen was also the man who began the airlift. On the night of June 5, an ICRC DC-7 captained by the American David Brown with a Swedish and Norwegian crew left the airport at Santa Isabel (today Malabo) with a cargo of rice.[28] Complete details of the night are unclear, but what is clear is that a Nigerian MiG-17, most likely piloted by either British pilot Mike Thompsett or South African Ares Klootwyk, intercepted the plane as it passed into Nigeria near the town of Eket, about one hundred kilometers east of Port Harcourt. Because airlift pilots received bonuses for multiple flights per night, Brown and his crew would regularly fly three times a night into Uli. Leaving earlier meant being able to squeeze in another flight, with each crew member earning fifty to one hundred dollars per extra flight on top of their salaries.[29] According to Frederick Forsyth, the plane left Fernando Po well before sundown and traversed the 120-kilometer journey to the Nigerian/Biafran coast in barely twenty minutes, about half an hour before sunset, which on that day was at 6:38 p.m. At 6:03, "his voice was heard in the Fernando Po control tower and by other Red Cross pilots on the same run [three other planes were following]. He gave no call-sign, and the voice was high pitched with alarm. He said: 'I'm being attacked . . . I'm being attacked.' His switch went dead. . . . Thirty seconds later the voice came back on the air: 'My engine's on fire . . . I'm going down . . .' Then there was silence. Nothing was ever heard from Captain Brown again."[30]

Though the Nigerians at first claimed the incident was a case of mistaken identity, the attack was a calculated escalation of the conflict between the Nigerian government and the ICRC that went back to Lindt's tacit embrace of the Biafran cause during the peace conference in Addis Ababa. The Red Cross was specifically targeted because unlike the Joint Church Aid or Caritas, the ICRC behaved in a quasi-governmental fashion and would publicize any incident of this kind while the other organizations were more likely to keep silent about them. As Nigeria's air force chief Alao said, "As far as we're concerned, we are hitting at anything flying into Biafra, Red Cross or not."[31] For the Nigerians, shooting down the Red Cross plane proved especially fortuitous, as it was a Swedish Red Cross plane, and half the crew were Swedish. Though there is no evidence that the Nigerians targeted the plane for this reason, many pundits saw this as a response to von Rosen's MINICOINs, with one European officer in Nigeria stating that von Rosen's actions amounted to "the bee sting that made the horse go wild."[32]

The Nigerians had long held that the Red Cross was secretly supporting Biafra by using the air corridor to ferry weapons as well as relief supplies to the secessionist enclave. While the ICRC did not smuggle guns or ammunition, other actors, such as the American Hank Wharton, the Gabonese and Ivorian governments, and many others did use the corridor to bring in weapons and war materiel. However, according to Marie-Luce Desgrandchamps, the issues between Nigeria and the ICRC centered on Lindt's personal control of the relief efforts and his "authoritarian and arrogant" personality.[33] On May 28, Lindt arrived in Lagos and was arrested at the airport, quickly deported, and declared persona non grata, thus ending his role in the conflict. By the middle of June, the ICRC had its status as operations coordinator revoked, and it ceased its operations in the country.[34]

Lindt's confrontational style and attempts to control the ICRC response in Biafra drew anger both from Nigeria and from some younger French ICRC members, who criticized the Geneva headquarters' ineffectual stance against genocide. This tension led to a split within the ICRC, with the French teams in Biafra appealing to their government to publicize Nigerian atrocities. After a series of Nigerian air force bombings in December 1968, a group of doctors in Biafra formed Le Comité international de lute contre le genocide au Biafra to put pressure on the ICRC headquarters to take a more forceful stance against Nigerian acts. These protests from within the ICRC eventually led one prominent doctor, Bernard Kouchner, to form a new humanitarian organization in 1971 called Médecins Sans Frontières.[35]

The early months of 1969 helped the Biafrans stabilize the front, and by May the Nigerians had only one combat-ready division in the theater, Mohammed Shuwa's 1st Division that captured Umuahia in April. The Nigerian command had been reluctant to engage in several key changes to reform the army, chief among which was to remove Adekunle from his command of the 3rd Marine Commando Division following his disastrous and insubordinate assault on Umuahia the previous November. In fact, the Nigerian command structure throughout the conflict contributed to Biafra's ability to prolong the war. The lack of coordination between the divisions meant that the Nigerians had been essentially fielding three separate militaries against the Biafrans, and even within each division, the planning of operations seemed more of a negotiation between commanders than centrally planned offensives. These deficiencies in the command structure caused the implosion of Murtala Mohammed's 2nd Division after the capture of Onitsha and Adekunle's 3rd Division in the southern theater. The Nigerians were able to replace Mohammed due to his resignation, but none of his successors could reform the division into anything resembling a fighting force. Adekunle had no desire to relinquish command, even as his division lay in tatters for the better part of six months after the destruction of his men in the attempt to capture Umuahia and the debacle at Owerri.

On May 16, 1969, the Nigerian high command finally undertook a reorganization of the military to facilitate a final push to end the war. The first and perhaps most important part was the appointment of Olusegun Obasanjo as commander of the 3rd Marine Commando Division, replacing the increasingly ineffectual Adekunle. Obasanjo wrote extensively about his attempts to reform the division in his memoir, *My Command*. It is important to note that his memoir, published in 1980, most likely came as part of an attempt to enter civilian politics in the Second Republic era. Obasanjo, already lauded for his handover of power to President Shehu Shagari in 1979, sought to remake himself as the chief engineer of Nigerian victory in the civil war ahead of his entry into parliamentary politics. His plans were thwarted by Muhammadu Buhari's coup on New Year's Eve 1983, and Obasanjo became a fierce critic of the new military governments under Buhari and his successors, Ibrahim Babangida and especially Sani Abacha. As part of Abacha's reign of terror in Nigeria, he sentenced Obasanjo to life in prison for being part of an imaginary coup, with the other "plotters" sentenced to death, including Shehu Musa Yar'Adua, the brother of future president Umaru Yar'Adua, though most of the death sentences were later commuted to life in prison. Yar'Adua would die in prison in 1997 while Obasanjo was released the following year, following Abacha's sudden death.[36]

The only other major memoir from a Nigerian of the 3rd Marine Commando Division is Godwin Alabi-Isama's *The Tragedy of Victory*. Though some of Alabi-Isama's recollections of events are problematic, his attitude toward Obasanjo is especially venomous, and he seems to hold the former in nothing but contempt. He repeatedly calls Obasanjo a coward and an incompetent leader and mocks him for getting shot in the buttocks during his first battle as divisional commander, claiming he was running away, panicked from a Biafran ambush near Owerri.[37] Even more problematic in his account, Alabi- Isama intentionally changed Obasanjo's writing to portray the latter as particularly incompetent. One glaring example is a passage that Alabi-Isami quotes:

> Just as we were driving back to headquarters, we received the news that an outpost on River Otamiri some eight miles away had been overrun. Efforts to contain the rebels had not been too successful. I seized the opportunity to see, at firsthand, what was happening and what assistance I could lend. By the time we arrived the scene, the battle was raging fiercely under the efficient command of the brigade major. But the situation was getting out of hand. Our men who had suffered heavy casualties were running short of ammunition.
>
> I returned to Port Harcourt to authorize what supply of men, stores and materials would have saved the situation.[38]

As he does in the last part of his book, Alabi-Isama then launches a series of critiques in his "Comments" section, saying in part, "We need to ask about what happened to the reserve of ammunition that he said he used to carry as extra in his vehicle," to support his assertion of Obasanjo's cowardice. However, the above passage omits the following from the original in Obasanjo's account: "Our men who had suffered heavy casualties were running short of ammunition. The reserve ammunition carried by my escorts was ready and handy."[39] He also accuses Obasanjo of leaving the front and driving two hundred kilometers to Port Harcourt to collect the ammunition. However, neither Obasanjo, Alabi-Isama, nor any of the Biafran leaders specify the location of this battle along the Otamiri river or its date, which was most likely near the end of May. The river itself originates in Oguta and travels to Owerri before heading on a southern course until its confluence with the Imo River at Oyigbo, some fifteen kilometers northeast of Port Harcourt. Assuming the battle took place somewhere along the river between Owerri and Port Harcourt, the most Obasanjo would have had to travel was seventy kilometers to reach an ammunition depot and return. Though this section contains one of the more egregious examples of Alabi-Isama's malice, his hatred for Obasanjo taints much of his writing once the latter became the divisional commander.

For his part, Obasanjo characterized Alabi-Isami as "a flamboyant character" who was "by any standards a very intelligent man and would have been one of the best officers the Nigerian Army had ever produced if he had applied his intelligence and ability fully to productive action in the Army."[40]

After Shuwa's capture of Umuahia in April, the 1st Division finally broke the Biafran defenses along the Awka-Onitsha road and linked Onitsha to Abagana, where Murtala had failed so spectacularly over a year prior. This action left the Biafran 57th Brigade stranded in the Anambra basin without a supply route. The ahia attack routes were able to smuggle some supplies to the isolated brigade, but these operations required extensive manpower and were dangerous and time consuming. However, the basin's importance as an agricultural area made these missions necessary so long as the Biafrans were unable to retake the stretch of road between Awka and Abagana. In September, Madiebo organized an operation to reopen the corridor. Because of the importance of the region to Biafra's already dwindling hopes for survival, it was named Operation Do or Die.

Like many of the issues that plagued both sides as the war dragged on, military planning became more of a negotiation process between rivals than a clear-cut operation. Madiebo claims that he requested five hundred guns from Achuzia to support the operation, but the latter did not wish to part with them and instead decided he would supply five hundred men and personally command them. However, the Biafran 11th Division's commander, Brig. Patrick Amadi, refused to accept Achuzia's presence and relented only under threat of court-martial and even then still refused to place the notorious commander into his chain of command. Once the battle plans were laid, Achuzia's objective was to assault the Dumez quarters located on the eastern fringes of Onitsha to prevent Nigerian reinforcements from leaving the city to support the rest of the assault that would take place across a long front from Afor-Igwe to Nkpor. He initially refused because he wanted a more high-profile assignment.[41]

As the battle began, the Biafrans massed one of the largest concentrations of artillery they had in the entire war, but even that was paltry by any measure, consisting of a single 82mm mortar with one hundred rounds, a handful of shells for two antitank guns, and ten rounds for two Marshal mine throwers. Nonetheless, the Biafran assault commenced because, as the operation's name made clear, it was a must-win operation. The Biafran attack took the Nigerians by surprise, and most of the Nigerian forces withdrew along the front, with the exception of a Saladin and antitank squadron at Nkpor junction. This team proved very successful in halting much of the Biafran advances in the area as the Nigerians prepared for a counterassault that displayed Nigeria's marked advantage in men, weapons, and air support. The battle raged for three days and, according to Madiebo, was one of the costliest military engagements of the war. Madiebo especially mentions the MiG-17 raids that wreaked havoc on the Biafran lines and the civilians caught in the middle. In one instance, the jets attacked a funeral procession in Onitsha, killing twenty mourners. In another, the Nigerians used napalm that engulfed an ambulance ferrying Biafran wounded in Obosi, incinerating the vehicle and killing fifteen people inside. Both sides kept poor track of their casualties, a fact that many commentators, including Obasanjo, lamented, as many in Nigeria knew nothing of their loved ones at the front—a cause for much anxiety and unrest.[42] This would be Biafra's last major attempt to regain the initiative before the final Nigerian assaults in October and December–January. Despite Madiebo's claims of victory, the operation was another Pyrrhic victory, as it did not stop Nigeria's military reorganization or give the Biafrans the same clear connection to Anambra that they once possessed.

After Murtala Mohammed's debacle at Abagana in March 1968, his 2nd Division ceased to be an effective fighting force, and his resignation shortly thereafter plunged the division into deeper chaos. Despite several attempts at reforming the division, it remained little more than an occupation force in Onitsha, and Biafra's tenacious defense of the Awka-Onitsha road meant that the division was unable to link with Shuwa in Enugu. Haruna replaced Murtala, but he was unable to stem the division's deterioration. In one case, Haruna ordered the execution of a group of soldiers who robbed a bank in Asaba. Other soldiers in the division were court-martialed for a scheme to collect the pay of dead and missing soldiers.[43] Shuwa later commented on the disarray in the Nigerian army, saying, "There was a difference between me and the other Divisional Commanders. Others used to go to Lagos and collect the money for their division, put [it] in the bank of their own choice and went to pay the soldiers. I never collected a kobo. . . . I would sign to show money was collected and used for the correct purpose."[44] Haruna's ineffectual command ended in June when the division's deputy commander Gibson Sanda (GS) Jalo took command. The division left Onitsha when reassigned to the midwest, with its main mission to secure the oil fields, shortly after the attack on the AGIP facility at Kwale.[45]

After the successful redeployment of the 1st and 2nd Divisions along the front, Col. Iliya Bisalla took over the 1st Division from Muhammad Shuwa in September.[46] Shuwa's command of the 1st Division was perhaps the most consistent and professional that the Nigerians fielded during the war. Though some commenters attributed Shuwa's successful command to circumstance, with the 1st Division being the core of the prewar Nigerian army and with an already established command structure and procedures in place, unlike the other two divisions that were hurriedly created in the war's early months. However, both the newly created divisions were successful in the early part of the war, especially Adekunle's amphibious assaults and the capture of Port Harcourt. Shuwa's command also had the added challenge of fighting the entire war in the Igbo heartland, and not like the other divisions who largely fought in the Eastern region's minority areas and helped to create the promised new states that swayed many Ijo, Ogoni, and other minorities to the federal cause. In fact, if the command structure had nothing to do with the commander, then changing the division's commander would not have had an impact on operational effectiveness, but as Shuwa himself pointed out, his former command "did not move one inch after I left before the war ended."[47] The bulk of the fighting would now be in the hands of Obasanjo's 3rd Marine Commando Division.

As Obasanjo, Alabi-Isama and the leadership of the division reorganized it and returned it to fighting shape, the Biafrans suffered a series of political setbacks that crushed the population's morale. Chief among these was the defection of Nigeria's first president and later one of Biafra's main supporters, Nnamdi Azikiwe. On August 17, 1969, Azikiwe, colloquially known as Zik, arrived in Lagos and met with the Nigerian leader Gowon. On August 28, Azikiwe released a statement where he explained his change of heart in regard to Biafran secession. He urged Biafran leaders to end the war, stating in part, "I cannot be expected to support any policy which is based on the calculated falsehood to deceive the Ibo or the non-Ibo to believe that they are destined to be exterminated," calling Biafra's claims of genocide "palpably false." He ended his plea by saying that Ojukwu perpetrated an "April fool" joke and that "the information [regarding genocide] is a cock-and-bull fairy tale."[48] Soon after, he sat for a lengthy interview with the Nigerian *Sunday Times* that was published on September 21, 1969. In the interview, Azikiwe claimed to have been acting mostly under duress when supporting Biafra, claiming he was given prepared statements to read and that he eventually "escaped" to freedom in London in October 1968. He spent considerable time attacking Ojukwu, calling him a petty tyrant and asserting that "when you get close to Ojukwu you will realise that in spite of his blusters, he is a confirmed coward."[49]

The Biafran propaganda machine reacted with predictable venom, casting the former ally "as dishonest, morally bankrupt, a traitor to his own people and as one that lies against his nation with the express purpose of pleasing his Nigerian masters."[50] The *New York Times* commented on the Biafran reaction to Azikiwe's change in position citing a mixture of outrage, shock, and bewilderment. Further, the paper reported on Biafra's accusations against Azikiwe that he was in cahoots with the British oil industry and "he always ends a crisis by sacrificing the people's interests once he has found a personal accommodation."[51]

Azikiwe's betrayal of the Biafran cause was not the secessionists' only source of concern, as the political and military situations were quickly unraveling. Though few official documents from the Biafran government survive, one particular source sheds light on both how effectively Biafra's propaganda operated and how difficult it was to maintain in the last few months of the war. Though mentioned earlier, Radio Biafra's report, *A Critique of Propaganda Radio Programmes*, published in October 1969, was only one in a weekly series of reports where radio programs for Radio Biafra were read and critiqued. Sadly, the report, numbered the fourteenth, is the only extant one, and the authors apologetically write that it is "by far less comprehensive and less ambitious" than the previous ones. However, it sheds important light on the situation in Biafra, especially one program, *Calling Biafrans behind Enemy Lines*. In the program, the scriptwriters called Biafra's struggle one of Black Liberation, akin to the ideas Ojukwu espoused in the Ahiara Declaration. The authors presumed the target audience would be familiar with the ideas of Pan-Africanism and global politics. The appraisers of the program did not approve of the tone, stating, "Those behind enemy lines are probably mostly villagers, and therefore least educated, the script writer should have made simplicity his watchword."[52]

Even more problematic, the program depicts many of the tropes that Biafra's genocide narrative had been repeating for over a year. However, in the waning months of the war, it became clear to those living under Nigerian rule that the genocide failed to materialize and that the Nigerian military under Obasanjo, Jalo, and Bisalla had strict orders to clamp down on violence against civilians and property. This sentiment, echoed in Stremlau's work, meant that the program was conveying a reality that did not actually exist and was thus out of touch for the Igbo who lived under Nigerian control. Sadly, the critique does not include the appraised scripts, so it is not possible to sample that source material. However, the critique itself shows that the Biafrans were well aware that outside their enclave, life was beginning to return to normal, a fact that seriously hampered their ability to both continue the war and keep the population willing to suffer the deprivations that their brethren were now able to escape.[53]

It was not just Biafra's civilian population that was beginning to lose cohesion. The military was also suffering the strains of fighting a war that by the middle of 1969 looked hopeless. Nowhere was this more apparent than in the collapse of Biafra's 12th Division in the area north of Ikot Ekpene near the Imo River. That sector in particular, one of the few that included a significant number of non-Igbo, saw a rise in what Madiebo, Efiong, and Gbulie recalled as "Spiritual Churches." These churches, which Gbulie likened to "prayer-houses functioning like thriving business ventures in our area of authority," fed on the civilian population and military leadership, in effect offering safety and victory by communing with God—for a price.[54] These churches took hold in the region largely after the April capture of Umuahia severed the area east of the Imo River from the rest of the Igbo heartland, effectively cutting off almost all supplies to the beleaguered 12th Division. Even food was in such short supply that "any soldier who was sure of one good meal in two days was indeed lucky."[55] Ammunition was impossible to come by because of the lack of fuel and oil for the vehicles. The entire division had no more than six serviceable vehicles and did not have the fuel to travel to Owerri, where the main ammunition depot dispensed materiel. As a result, the entire division was in a state of disarray and the spiritualists, supposedly headed by a Doctor Wise who supplied potions and advice to military commanders, seemed to be in charge of the situation.[56] Madiebo reports that the doctor's political connections were so extensive that Gbulie arrested him only for him to secure his own release thanks to a personal intervention from Ojukwu.[57] From that point, Doctor Wise operated with impunity, undermining the already frayed military and civilian structures by injecting himself into the command structure and offering unsound advice and counsel based largely on his mystical "abilities" enabled by his political connections. When Nigeria's final offensives arrived, the division's collapse was almost immediate.

Though much of Biafra's capacity to fight had eroded to the point of breaking, the Nigerian leadership was also facing a challenge of maintaining a war that began as a forty-eight-hour "police action" but transformed into a brutal conflict that lasted for over two years. Gowon's government previously stated that Biafra's ability to fight would be broken by March 1968; the Nigerian newspapers used the date of March 31 as the deadline for the end of the war. When the deadline passed with no end in sight, Nigerian frustration grew and strained other parts of society. In the Western Region, long-simmering tensions between the government and several peasant organizations turned to violence in September 1969 in what became known as the Agbekoya Parapo Uprising.

The peasants in the Western Region, especially the cocoa growers, had long suffered from abuses at the hands of corrupt government officials, and the civil war meant that the western states and the federal government increased taxes substantially. The strain of the war was exasperated by a global crash of the market for cocoa, which was the region's main export. In 1964, the price of cocoa more than halved from US$700 per ton to less than US$300. Though the price quickly rebounded, many of the marketing boards set up in colonial times to ostensibly help the farmers in moments such as this had little ability to assist, and in many cases the marketing boards were little more than tools of arbitrary abuse against the producers.[58] Thus, by 1968, taxes had risen substantially and devastated the poor in the region. The state government imposed a tax of six pounds on anyone earning less than fifty pounds, though some sources place the tax as high as eight pounds.[59] In addition, the federal government increased taxes to pay for the war, further eroding livelihoods of the most vulnerable.

After a long campaign to effect change, the state government reacted with force, first by arresting the leaders of the Agbekoya rebellion and then by sending tax collectors with armed escorts to collect revenue, which often erupted into violence. The protesters in turn responded with violence, destroying government facilities and attacking officials and any leaders who expressed support for the government. By July 1969, the conflict had assumed the level of a guerilla war, with the Agbekoya having raided the prison where their leader was held and killing the *soun*, or king, of the city of Ogbomoso along with five of his chiefs. By September, the federal government intervened, and Obafemi Awolowo, who served as minister of finance, forced the Western State government to acquiesce to the Agbekoya's demands, lowering the flat tax to two pounds and suspending other fees.[60]

Obasanjo assumed command of the 3rd Marine Commando Division with three main tasks. First, the division was to straighten the front line from the Niger to the Cross River. This was no easy task, as the line in May 1969 consisted of several bulges that largely corresponded to the Igbo heartland's demographics. Adekunle's legacy of capturing with little regard for support operations during his Operation OAU led not only to the loss of much of the division in the assault on Umuahia and the loss of Owerri several months later but also to the city of Aba being surrounded on both flanks by hostile troops. To the west, the Biafran bulge extended from just west of the city to just north of the Port Harcourt–Aba road, constantly threatening to cut off the road at Asa. In the east, another Biafran bulge extended south to Azumini and from there east to north of Ikot Ekpene, which was still in Nigerian hands after the battle in September 1968. Obasanjo's division was in such disarray that straightening the line would have been a herculean task, and the other two immediate objectives, the recapture of Owerri and Oguta, were in the realm of the impossible. Bisalla's first division had similar objectives of seizing Ojukwu's hometown of Nnewi and the town of Orlu in hopes of taking the airfield at Uli.

Obasanjo's first battle took place merely four days after his appointment on May 20, 1969, in the town of Ohoba, just west of Owerri. Though details of the battle are unclear, the assault came right before significant Biafran gains in the sector, taking advantage of the recent retaking of the city and an aborted attempt to do the same in Aba. On the date of the assault, Obasanjo visited the troops, many of whom were from the 16th Brigade and still exhausted from their ordeal in Owerri, where they were besieged for over four months before evacuating. Many refused to take part in the assault, and the new division commander pleaded with them to do so. According to Obasanjo, the assault petered out after the Nigerians advanced for a few miles and met with stiff Biafran resistance, suffered "slight" casualties, and returned without capturing their objective. Alabi-Isama, who dedicates the final third of his book to a page-by-page commentary of Obasanjo's *My Command*, paints a much different picture, accusing the future president of cowardice, calling him an absentee commander, and claiming a thousand casualties in the assault, which lasted only an hour. While the truth is likely somewhere in between the two accounts, Alabi-Isama's casualty claims must be read with some skepticism, as the battles in the war, like many in African postcolonial conflicts, generally were not large in scale. Additionally, the number of battlefield casualties in the war is relatively noncontroversial, unlike the number of civilian casualties, which activists continually revise upward. Thus, one thousand casualties would mean nearly 1.5 percent of all casualties in the war came in this one hour of fighting in a relatively minor skirmish. Alabi-Isama punctuates his account with a picture of several vultures, which he claims feasted on the Nigerians that Obasanjo sent to their deaths. At some point during the battle, Obasanjo's convoy came under attack by a Biafran ambush. Alabi-Isama claims that Obasanjo was shot in the rear end and uses that to mock his former commanding officer, saying that "he was not ambushed, he just ran away," which is why he was shot in the behind. Regardless, Obasanjo was able to meet with Alabi-Isama that evening, so any wound sustained could not have been severe, as Alabi-Isama does not mention whether his commander was able to sit down or not.[61]

However, clear to all was that by June 1969, the Biafrans were far from beaten, and the 3rd Division was in no state to press forward. Coupled with the Biafran offensives in the south, Obasanjo's planned straightening of the front could not happen before he solved both operational and morale issues. The issues he faced were great, but not unsurmountable, and his main challenge was to rebuild the division's fighting capability while also curbing the brutality against the civilian populations that had done so much to feed Biafra's propaganda machinery.

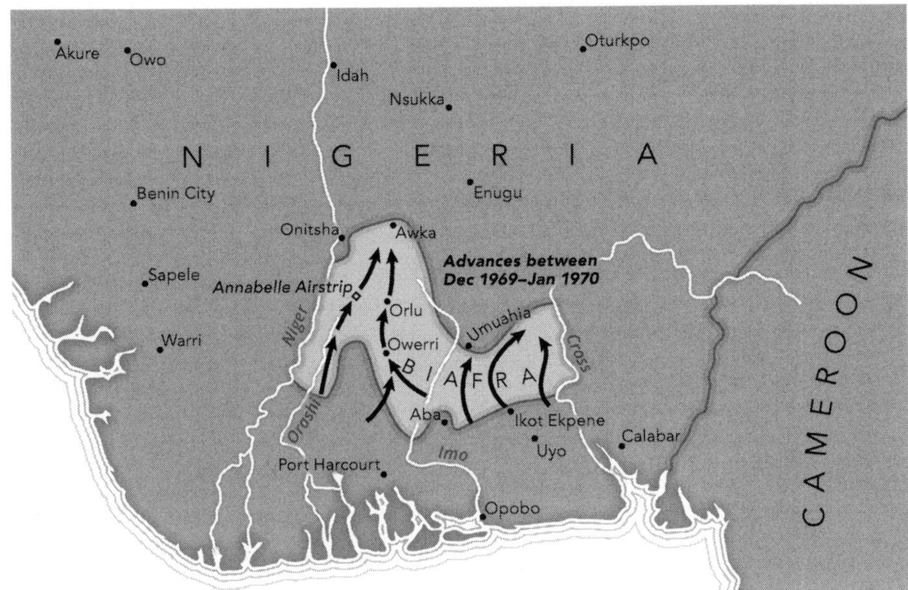

Map 9.1. Biafra ca. June 1969

However, lack of discipline in the division came from several distinct sources, all stemming from command neglect, and Obasanjo remarked on several important symptoms of the breakdown in military readiness.[62]

The primary source was undoubtedly operational fatigue, with some soldiers having been at the front for nearly two years without any kind of extended leave. Obasanjo lamented that many soldiers "set out to inflict injuries on themselves so that they could be evacuated to Port Harcourt, Calabar or Lagos," adding that "more than fifty percent of my casualties were self-inflicted."[63] However, in his first assault as commander, detailed above, he mobilized soldiers from the 16th Brigade who had been besieged for months in Owerri, rather than let them rest after their ordeal. Adding to the soldiers' misery, and perhaps stemming from it, command structures became ethnocentric in nature, with officers giving soldiers of their own ethnic group more lenient punishments for desertion than those of other groups under their command.

Another factor that hurt morale and undermined the division's command structure was the existence of so-called Commando Girls that the ostentatious Adekunle encouraged. In 1968, Randolph Baumann interviewed Adekunle for the German *Stern* magazine in what can only be described as a nightclub setting in his headquarters, with what Baumann called "uniformed go-go girls" and the Nigerian commander playing with his pet goat, which he named Ojukwu, after the Biafran leader.[64] Many of these girls also had relationships with senior officers, causing consternation among the ranks, especially as many of the women were technically enlisted in the military, but as the *Stern* interview suggested and Obasanjo remarked, "were more useful for social functions than army duties."[65]

Perhaps the most important indicator of the collapse of military discipline was when it affected the military's relationship with the civilian populations in both Igbo and non-Igbo regions. Obasanjo saw looting and purchasing goods from locals as the root of much of the problem for several reasons. First, this action undermined trust within the military, as for soldiers engaged in this practice, their own interests would undoubtedly outweigh unit cohesion and undermine the effectiveness of their units. Second, there was no way of ascertaining whether the items that Nigerians took home came from the actual owners or if the sellers even existed.[66]

To remedy these problems, Obasanjo took a singular approach, albeit one that many in his division, chief among them Alabi-Isama, felt was heavy handed at best and counterproductive and criminal at worst.[67] His first approach was to alleviate some of the distresses that had caused a collapse in the division's fighting efficacy. Chief among them, he created a new system of paying salaries and guaranteeing leave from the front. Obasanjo also employed military justice to stem many of the solutions that soldiers attempted to remedy their situation, especially the self-inflicted wounds. After stabilizing and reforming the pay system, the problem of soldiers shooting themselves did not end, and after one day that saw twenty-three soldiers commit the offense, he had them court-martialed and sentenced twelve to death by firing squad. He chose the death sentences as a deterrent, focusing them on areas that had high prevalence of indiscipline. After the sentences were carried out, "only two cases of self-inflicted injuries were reported to me again before the war ended."[68]

Solving the dissent and indiscipline in the officer corps proved a different matter altogether. The first step was to change the relationship between the officers and the Commando Girls that Adekunle had created. Obasanjo relieved the uniformed women of their military duties and converted them to civilian workers. He also ended the practice of the parties that Adekunle was so fond of, like the one Baumann had encountered the previous year. He also sacked one officer whom he called "the greatest bane of the division," promptly sending him to another division. While he does not name Alabi-Isama as this toxic officer, and Alabi-Isama does not acknowledge his departure from the division, the latter ceased to play any part in operations until the end of the war and no doubt does much to explain his grudge against Obasanjo.

Compounding all these issues was the fact that Operation OAU had, for the first time on the southern front, penetrated the Igbo heartland. The collapse of the offensive and the Biafran counterattack in Owerri saw Biafran forces attempt to press their advantage to retake Aba and possibly Port Harcourt. Though both objectives ultimately failed in the May–August Biafran offensives, the Nigerians had to reform their division under fire and work on both operational and morale issues simultaneously while also stemming the collapse of the division, especially the western sector, known as sector one, which had suffered the brunt of the Biafran offensive into Owerri.[69]

The Biafrans waged a series of campaigns in the south that threatened to disrupt much of the 3rd Division's reorganization and "straightening" of the battle line. In addition to the operation in September to retake the link to the Anambra Basin, the Biafrans launched several offensives against both the reconstituted 1st Division and the regrouping 3rd Marine Commando Division. The most ambitious offensive was an attempt to repeat in Aba what had been so successful in Owerri. The Biafran 12th Division under the command of Tony Eze pushed south along Aba's western environs to the town of Owaza, capturing the oil fields there and threatening the Port Harcourt–Aba Road. In five fierce days of fighting, both the Nigerians and Biafrans exhausted their ammunition, with the Biafrans making initial gains that the Nigerian 17th brigade eventually reversed.[70]

Similarly, the Biafrans targeted the oil fields west of Owerri near the town of Ebocha along the Osrashi River that connected Oguta, the town with the last vestige of the Biafran navy, with the Niger Delta. The navy's sole remaining ship fired several shots as the Biafrans routed the Nigerian defenders holding the bridgehead. The Biafrans quickly secured Ebocha and proceeded south toward Ahoada but reached only Omoku and Ogbogwu, about twenty kilometers north of Ahoada, after a five-day campaign. The Nigerians countered with an all-out offensive accompanied by air support, and within a few days the Biafrans, now without the gunboat, which began to leak oil and could not move for fear of the MiGs, withdrew back to Ebocha, where they were beaten back across the Orashi River. Madiebo claimed that the entire populations of the villages they briefly occupied suffered from kwashiorkor and that the Nigerians did not alleviate the hunger and malnutrition as they had been claiming.[71]

Though the bulk of the Biafran harassment campaigns centered on keeping control of Owerri and the oil fields in the Egbema region between the Niger and Orashi rivers, they launched one assault in an effort to disrupt the 1st Division in Umuahia and hopefully sever the supply links to the city. The Biafrans concentrated their 15th Division to capture Okigwe, roughly halfway between Enugu and Umuahia. However, the division lacked basic supplies, with each soldier given only thirty rounds for the operation, and even then, that region of Biafra lacked sufficient food for the soldiers and civilian population. Nonetheless, the divisional commander Linus Ohanehi planned to surround and isolate the town, thus allowing two battalions to enter and clear the Nigerians entrenched there without hope for reinforcement. Like most Biafran offensives, the initial assault caught the Nigerians by surprise, and the defenders scattered in panic. The better-equipped Nigerians eventually battered the Biafrans with artillery and air support, and the Biafrans had to stop to loot the Nigerian camps for ammunition and, above all, food. The Biafrans were so poorly supplied that "two Biafran soldiers collapsed and died from hunger." Even so, the Biafrans gained much in this offensive and weathered the Nigerian counterattacks without losing much of the ground they gained.[72]

The Biafran offensives and Nigerian response made two things abundantly clear. First, the Biafran capabilities, which were already limited in scope by ammunition and materiel shortages, could no longer sustain any offensive capability, and the enemy knew this. On the Nigerian side, Obasanjo's reorganization had begun the process of creating a force that would ultimately end the war in five months. The 3rd Marine Commando Division was once again a force capable of fighting an offensive war. If the Biafrans thought that the division was on the verge of collapse, "they knew better after this encounter."[73]

By September, Biafran supply shortages had become critical. French support had all but evaporated, leaving the black market as their main source of supplies. Compounding matters, the assault and political fallout from the raid on the AGIP facility left the Biafrans with few friends abroad. Though they most likely secured a hefty ransom for the eighteen oilmen, the episode caused the veritable collapse of Biafra's fundraising in Europe for both humanitarian and governmental means. As Jaques Freymond, the ICRC's acting president, lamented, the affair and Ojukwu's handling of the hostage crisis made any more fundraising for Biafra in Europe futile.[74] The only offensive capability that Biafrans retained was the MINICOIN squadron, but even those nine planes could halt the Nigerians only so much.

On the other hand, the reinvigoration of the Nigerian 3rd Marine Commando division and the simplification of the command and supply structures, now with only two divisions east of the Niger, saw the Nigerians poised to complete the defeat of the Igbo heartland and end Biafra's secession. With few friends outside Biafra, Ojukwu could do little but try to slow the Nigerian advance to buy some time to maneuver, but that precious time was running out for Biafra.

Biafra's end began in October, when the Nigerians capitalized on the internal fissures within the Biafran 12th Division. On October 18, Obasanjo launched an offensive on the town of Eberi, on the western outskirts of Aba.[75] The Biafran division's collapse was almost immediate. The political and social issues that the spiritualists exploited to place themselves in a position of authority over the civilian and military leaders in the region buckled and caused the division to fall into almost immediate disarray. By the afternoon of the first day, the Nigerian

12th Brigade had captured the Biafran headquarters almost intact. Some prisoners showed Obasanjo exactly how pitifully equipped the Biafrans had become. One soldier, despite having a relatively new Heckler & Koch G3 rifle, was issued only five rounds, and his entire ration for the day was a piece of boiled cassava.[76]

Chaos reigned on the Biafran side due to a lack of supplies and organization within the division, which had recently lost its commanding officer to hepatitis, and the influence that the spiritualists commanded over military decision-making. With no ammunition, no fuel, and a flood of civilian refugees, the Biafran division had no choice but to leave their dead and wounded in a hasty and disorganized retreat that was complicated by hourly air strikes from the Nigerian MiGs. The only way the Biafrans had to slow the Nigerian advance was to blow the bridges along the Aba–Umuahia Road.[77]

By the end of the month, Ojukwu once again intervened personally in an attempt to stop the collapse. He ordered the 12th Division disbanded and sent his commandoes to arrest the officers and administrative soldiers of the division for dereliction of duty. Many officers fled across the Imo River to seek protection with the Nigerians while others arrived at Madiebo and Efiong's headquarters for the same reason. Ojukwu's action set Biafran against Biafran, and with the Nigerians still pressing, the collapse soon became complete and the Nigerian 12th Brigade was poised to link with the elements of the 1st Division that occupied Umuahia in what became known as Operation Finishing Touch. On Christmas Day 1969, the Nigerian 1st and 3rd Divisions met in Umuahia, cutting what remained of Biafra in two from the Imo River to the Niger. An isolated pocket of Biafran troops occupied the area surrounding the ancient city of Arochukwu, between the Umuahia–Ikot Ekpene road and the Cross River.

By the end of 1969, Biafra was essentially broken, but Ojukwu made no move to surrender. However, without anyone to turn to in the international community, the Biafran leader had few options to continue the fight. Obasanjo understood Biafra's situation and knew that any delay would allow Ojukwu time to regroup, and even before linking with the 1st Division in Umuahia, Obasanjo attempted to coordinate an offensive with the 1st and 2nd Divisions. However, both Bisalla and Jalo could not offer anything more than moral support, and Danjuma, the GOC, thought it best to focus the military's efforts on capturing Ojukwu's hometown of Nnewi. Obasanjo was given the green light to press his plan, and his division broke the Biafran defenses, which, though dogged at first, rapidly disintegrated, allowing him to finish the operation within four days. He recalls that his message to 1st Division headquarters to prepare for his imminent arrival in Umuahia and avoid friendly fire incidents "was received with surprise and disbelief."[78]

As the Biafran army was collapsing, Efiong and Madiebo urged Ojukwu to convene the civilian leadership in the hopes of forcing an end to the war. The

Biafran leader instead invited military leaders on January 5, demanded "the war... continue to the last man," and expressed a delusional plan to send Achuzia with four thousand men to cross the Niger and invade the midwest in a second Midwest Offensive.[79] Three days later, Ojukwu reversed his decision and announced that he would leave the country with his family and top civilian advisors in what he called a "quest for peace" mission.[80] The following day, January 9, the Nigerian 17th Brigade entered Owerri, and the 15th Brigade began a push north toward Oguta along the Orashi River.

Secretly, Ojukwu knew there would be no "quest for peace" and that he was fleeing the collapse of his secessionist state. He called Madiebo, Akpan, Biafra's top civilian administrator, and Michael Okpara, the Eastern Region's former premier and close confidant of Ojukwu, to join him at the Uli airstrip. He designated Efiong as caretaker, telling the general to hold out for two weeks until Ojukwu returned with a plan to end the war. However, Efiong thought Ojukwu knew that the end was imminent, stating that Ojukwu "knew we had lost the war, and he was 'checking out' for good and leaving the rest of us to survive as best we could."[81]

Nonetheless, Ojukwu broadcast a message on Radio Biafra announcing his departure and naming Efiong "to run the affairs of the republic while I go on this mission."[82] Shortly after, the Biafran leader met with Madiebo in Nnewi as they organized their departure. However, the Nigerian 15th and 17th Brigades were closing in on Uli from the south, and as Madiebo met Ojukwu, he noticed that "for the first time during the war, he appeared terrified" as they departed for the airstrip on the afternoon of January 10, thinking they would not be able to escape in time. Ojukwu's entourage arrived at the airstrip at eight in the evening, and the plane departed at three in the morning on January 11, leaving Efiong to decide on Biafra's final fate.

Efiong wasted no time in preparing for Biafra's capitulation but "wanted to avoid any allegation of taking such a major decision arbitrarily." In an interview with *Drum Magazine* several months after the war's end, he reconstructed his meeting of January 11 with his military officers.

> Military Officers: General, when are you making the statement?
>
> Efiong: Which statement?
>
> M.O.: Of course, you know what we are talking about.
>
> Efiong: How do you expect me to know what you have in your mind? Tell me.
>
> M.O.: Are we going to continue like this? We think we should stop fighting.
>
> Efiong: Are you suggesting we surrender?
>
> M.O.: Will that amount to surrender?
>
> Efiong: Of course. Yes.
>
> M.O. Ah! Well, if that amounts to surrender, let's stop fighting all the same. The people are suffering unnecessarily.

Efiong: Okay, gentlemen. Go and put it in black and white, I will be guided in my decision by the greater interest of our people.[83]

Shortly after that meeting, Louis Mbanefo, Biafra's justice minister, arrived to offer his support and help draft the message that Efiong delivered on January 12 at 4:40 in the afternoon. He stated, in part:

> I am convinced now that a stop must be put to the bloodshed, which is going on as a result of the war. I am also convinced that the people are now disillusioned and those elements of the old government regime who have made negotiations and reconciliation impossible have voluntarily removed themselves from our midst.
>
> I have, therefore, instructed an orderly disengagement of troops. . . . I urge on General Gowon, in the name of humanity, to order his troops to pause while an armistice is negotiated in order to avoid the mass suffering caused by the movement of population. . . .
>
> May God help us all.[84]

On January 14, Efiong and his delegation, which included Mbanefo, Patrick Amadi, Patrick Anwunah, and several other high-ranking Biafran military and civilian officials, traveled from Owerri to Lagos to formally end the war. At nine in the morning on January 15, the fourth anniversary of the coup that had begun Nigeria's descent into civil war, Gowon and Efiong, who were old friends, embraced at Dodan Barracks, with Gowon saying, "Philip I am glad we are able to do this on our own." Efiong replied, "Jack, I am happy to be back." Efiong then shook hands with the members of Nigeria's military council and read and signed the official surrender document, where he formally accepted the twelve-state solution and renounced secession.

Biafra was no more.

EPILOGUE

GOWON AND EFIONG'S EMBRACE AT the Dodan Barracks in Lagos signaled the end of the war but not the end of ethnic strife in the country. Many of the tensions that caused the First Republic's demise and set Nigeria on the path to secession and civil war continue to plague the country. In fact, many of Nigeria's currents crises can be traced directly to the war's immediate aftermath and the ways that successive military governments sought to suppress the political and intellectual discourse on the war. This policy of active neglect allowed many of the grievances that triggered the crisis and war to fester and inhabit the country's body politic.

Around the world, the war was quickly forgotten, though its legacies have been equally far-reaching. The conflict shaped global humanitarian relief policies for decades and spawned new ways of dealing with global catastrophes, and new organizations, such as the venerated Médecins Sans Frontières, or Doctors without Borders.

After the war ended, Gowon attempted a political and social reconciliation that he coined "no victors, no vanquished." In attempting to reunify the country, Gowon's policy effectively shuttered any serious discussions on the war, save those that would stress national unity. This policy had the effect of stymieing any reckoning about the conflict, the lingering accusations of genocide, and the perceived marginalization of the Igbo in the postwar order.

As part of the economic embargoes the federal government imposed on the Eastern Region and later Biafra, the government froze eastern assets, denied pay and stopped money transfers to government workers, and froze bank accounts belonging to easterners. When the Nigerian government enacted its currency shift in January 1968, it effectively rendered worthless all Nigerian currency held by Biafrans who were unable to convert to the new banknotes. In addition, the Nigerian government nationalized the accounts of all easterners in Biafra, effectively confiscating millions to ensure that the funds could not be used to further Biafra's war effort. At war's end, bowing to demands to redress the issue, the Nigerians agreed to pay twenty pounds per account to compensate easterners for their monetary losses.[1]

At war's end, Gowon also vowed a return to civilian rule within five years, but instead of working to achieve this, he oversaw the beginnings of a corruption culture that far overshadowed the allegations of abuse and cronyism that Nzeogwu and his cohort used to justify the January 1966 coup. Perhaps one of the most egregious of Gowon's corruption schemes was nicknamed the "cement armada" and proved to be one of the catalysts for his overthrow.[2]

In 1966, Leopold Senghor of Senegal hosted a massive festival of African and diasporic arts and entertainment called the First World Festival of Negro Arts (FESMAN) in the capital Dakar. In 1974, Gowon announced the second such festival in Lagos, called the Second World Black and African Festival of Arts and Culture (FESTAC). One of the issues with this festival was the construction required for building the venues and housing for the festival and its attendees.[3] In addition, the Nigerian military embarked on an ambitious expansion program that entailed building up to forty new constructions a year. However, two of the country's cement plants had been located in the former Biafra and were severely damaged from the war, causing a decrease in the country's ability to produce enough cement for both projects as well as other projects in postwar construction. To alleviate the shortage, the Nigerian government estimated it would need to import substantial quantities of cement. The Ministry of Defence alone would require 2.9 million tons of cement annually, and the Port of Lagos would have been unable to accommodate more than 1 million tons a year. However, beginning in October 1974, Gowon's government contracted over 16 million tons of cement at US$60 per ton, when market rates for cement were estimated to be at US$51–$54 per ton. Predictably, the enormous amounts of cement caused congestion at the port, with ships waiting up to fourteen months to unload their cargoes, with many collecting generous demurrage fees in the process. Compounding the congestion, some ship owners capitalized on the chaos in the port and added themselves to the moorage queues for the sole reason of collecting these fees. By the end of 1975, the average wait time for ships to unload cement was over five hundred days. In 1976, a commission of inquiry found that many government and military officials benefited from both the awarding of contracts and the chaos in the port. Though much of the corruption in Nigeria was endemic before the war, scholars such as Samuel Fury Childs Daly have pointed out that the war both broadened and deepened the corruption culture in the country, and it had not abated in the nearly unbroken military rule that ended only in 1999 (with the short-lived Second Republic notwithstanding).[4]

Despite the criticism of Gowon's lack of engagement in reconciliation, he created a lasting legacy, that of the National Youth Service Corps (NYSC) in 1973. This program, designed to foster national unity, continues to be a requirement for all Nigerian university graduates to apply their newly acquired skills in a part of Nigeria other than their own. Indeed, one of the program's stated objectives was to have young Nigerians work together "with a view to removing prejudices, eliminating ignorance and confirming at first hand the many similarities among Nigerians of all ethnic groups."[5]

The armada scandal, along with Gowon's unfulfilled pledge to return the country to civilian rule, sparked his overthrow on July 29, 1975, in a bloodless palace coup while Gowon was attending the OAU summit in Uganda.[6] Joseph Garba, along with Obasanjo and Murtala Mohammed, announced the coup and replaced Gowon with Mohammed. After the disastrous campaigns to capture Onitsha during the war, Mohammed left the army and the country, taking a leave of absence in the United Kingdom. He returned to Nigeria in 1971, shortly after the war and after completing command and staff college in the UK. When he assumed power, however, his rule lasted less than a year, and on February 13, 1976, he was assassinated in a failed coup attempt, and Obasanjo replaced him as military leader.

Obasanjo's ascent to leadership in Nigeria also came at the end of the first part of military rule in the country. He called for a new constitution in preparation for handing over power in 1979, when Shehu Shagari came to power in the short-lived Second Republic. Muhammadu Buhari overthrew Shagari's government in a coup on December 31, 1983, ushering in a new and more repressive military junta that lasted until 1999, after Sani Abacha died. Obasanjo was then elected president. He served until 2007 and retired to private life.

When Ojukwu fled the country in January 1970, he claimed that he would return to continue the fight, but with Biafra's almost immediate capitulation, he remained in Côte d'Ivoire, where President Houphouët-Boigny granted him political asylum. Shagari granted Ojukwu a pardon in 1982, along with his onetime nemesis Yakubu Gowon, who was implicated in the assassination of Murtala Mohammed, and the former Biafran leader returned to Nigeria and announced his candidacy for senate in the 1983 elections. He remained a perennial candidate for local and national office until his death in November 2011.

Many of the other major actors of the war led relatively private lives afterward, none more so than Mohammed Shuwa, who retired rather than enter the cutthroat politics that accompanied military rule in the country. He gave only one interview on his actions in the war, which was published in Momoh's lengthy tome.[7] He retired to a quiet life in the northern city of Maiduguri, which saw the emergence of terrorist group Boko Haram in the early twenty-first century. On November 2, 2012, he was murdered by suspected terrorists during a battle for control of the city between youths associated with the organization and the Nigerian military.[8]

The notorious Black Scorpion, Benjamin Adekunle, remained in the military after the war, and in 1974 Gowon tasked him with alleviating the congestion in the Lagos port, which was problematic even before the infamous Cement Armada. During his short tenure he was implicated in a drug smuggling network, known as the Iyabo Olorunkoya affair. In it, Olorunkoya, a well-known socialite, attempted to smuggle seventy-eight kilograms of marijuana from India to the United Kingdom. During her trial, she implicated Adekunle and another brigadier general, Folasho Sotomi. Though he was never charged for any crime, his previous associations with Olorunkoya and the fact that she implicated him in her trial in the UK was enough for Gowon's government to remove him from his post and forcibly retire him from the military.[9] He largely led a private life after his dismissal, though unlike Shuwa, he enjoyed speaking to the media and remained a vocal defender of his military record both during the war and after. He died in 2014 in Lagos.

Though Gowon claimed that he would return Nigeria to civilian rule, the military ruled the country from the end of the First Republic until 1999, with the brief interlude of Shagari's Second Republic from 1979 to 1983. Events like the Cement Armada showed the levels of corruption that the military government could descend to, but it was only after the 1983 coup that the corruption was matched by levels of brutality and avarice that had not been seen before.

Perhaps no issue has left a more indelible mark on the war's memory and its global engagement than that of the lingering question of genocide. For many in Biafra who suffered the privations of war and the casual violence that Nigerian soldiers inflicted on the conquered areas, as well as the organized violence such as the massacre at Asaba, the idea that the Nigerians fought a genocidal campaign is self-evident. While there is little doubt that the Nigerian military committed many atrocities during the war, and that many of the actions, especially those in Asaba, would certainly constitute war crimes, there is scant evidence that would trigger prosecutions that rely on the UNGC and hinge on the issue of "intent to destroy." The lack of a reliable number of victims and a verifiable link to any notion of intent from Gowon or the Nigerian leadership has further hindered Biafran claims to a legal recourse. Some scholars have resorted to questionable evidence, such as the Dr. Mensah report mentioned in chapter 8, but these assertions, weakened by the debunked evidence, do little but promote the narrative to the already convinced.

These issues are not simply a legacy of memory and memorialization, but they have far-reaching political repercussions in contemporary Nigeria. The memory of genocide and the Nigerian state and society's inability to pave a path toward reconciliation have spawned several generations of progressively militant Biafran secession movements that use the memory of genocide as an effective rallying point in their messaging.

Because successive Nigerian governments in the immediate postwar period actively suppressed discussion about the war, famously known as Gowon's "no victors, no vanquished" policy, many of the assumptions propagated during the war went unchallenged, and some of the most outlandish assertions have been magnified in the years since. Chief among these is the number that died during the war. As previous chapters note, any attempt to ascertain an accurate number is nearly impossible given the lack of records during the war and the blatant fraud that marred the immediate postwar census. As a result, the claimed number of victims who died during the war has grown exponentially and has been amplified by some prominent authors and scholars. In his final work, *There Was a Country,* the great Chinua Achebe bizarrely claims that over two million people died and Awolowo somehow orchestrated the genocide because "his ambition drove him into a frenzy to go to every length to achieve his dreams. In the Biafran case it meant hatching up a diabolical policy to reduce the numbers of his enemies significantly through starvation—eliminating over two million people, mainly members of future generations."[10] Whether he meant that the war killed so many or that it simply prevented future births, thus culling the Igbo population, is unclear. What is clear is that Achebe's amplification of at least two and possibly up to three million deaths has seen that number largely established as fact in the common discourse about the war, as evidenced by global news networks that now cite the three million claim as a fact when prefacing the war.[11]

Because of the oppression of military governments, especially the brutal Abacha regime, Biafran nationalist activism simmered under the political radar, especially in the face of the brutality of Abacha's crackdown on political opponents like MKO Abiola, Obasanjo, and, above all, Saro-Wiwa.[12] Thus, 1999, the year of the return to civilian rule, saw the emergence of the Movement for the Actualization of the Sovereign State of Biafra (MASSOB), led by Ralph Uwazuruike, the first of the new organizations that have agitated for a return of Biafra's independence. In 2012, another organization, the Indigenous Peoples of Biafra (IPOB), was formed by Nnamdi Kanu. Though both organizations touted nonviolence, the Nigerian governmental responses have been harsh, both legally against the two leaders and against any attempt to organize protests or other activities. The Nigerian government has responded with severe legal action against both MASSOB and IPOB leadership, imprisoning both Uwazuruike and Kanu, whose ordeals in the Nigerian courts have been especially tumultuous, with the IPOB leader fleeing abroad and being extradited from Kenya, after a brief escape to Israel. Nigerian courts ruled that Kanu's extradition was illegal, but the same courts also ruled that he could still stand trial for treason, and as of this writing, he remains in Nigerian custody awaiting trial and has sued both Nigeria and Kenya for his extradition.[13]

Despite both organizations claiming nonviolence, the Nigerian government has cracked down on protests and other attempts to mobilize toward independence. In 2013, Nigerian courts approved a charge of treason against Uwazuruike, but as of 2022, no such trial or conviction has taken place. IPOB has taken a more militant approach to confronting the Nigerian state. In 2020, in response to Nigeria's attacks on peaceful protests, IPOB announced the creation of the Eastern Security Network (ESN), ostensibly to combat encroachment of Fulani herders into the Igbo heartland. However, in 2021, ESN operatives orchestrated a massive jailbreak in Imo state, and despite IPOB's denial of responsibility, the Nigerian government declared the ESN a terrorist organization and urged the UK and US governments to do the same.[14]

Other separatists and reformers of the Nigerian body politic have used the war and the memory of it to advance their own claims, and many groups have advocated for reform and secession and used varying degrees of violence to advance their claims. Nigeria's overly pragmatic response to the war's legacy and memory among the differing populations that suffered it has left an indelible mark on the nation's psyche, and many in the country still relive the war, and use its legacy, especially that of genocide, to further political and military claims within the country. From the horrific insurgencies of Islamic militant groups such as Boko Haram in the north to the various groups that vie for a share of Nigeria's oil wealth in the south, such as the Movement for the Emancipation of the Niger Delta (MEND), to the violent clashes across Nigeria between sedentary agriculturalists and their pastoralist neighbors, the civil war's shadow looms large in how these groups approach their positions with their neighbors and the Nigerian government. Because of the government's fear of secession, successive administrations have equated most any kind of challenge to the central authority in Lagos and later Abuja as a direct challenge to the state's legitimacy, hence the harsh crackdowns on any kind of dissent, regardless of the merits of the dissenters.[15]

Nigeria's inability to deal with the war's legacies is also evident in the broadening and deepening of corruption since the war, a fact that has corroded the state-society relationship in the country and continues to do so. One of the main instigators of the January 1966 coup that set Nigeria on the road that led to the war was the problem of corruption and cronyism endemic in the First Republic. Because the January coup plotters used these issues as one of the main reasons for their coup, it was very popular in the first few days, but as it failed, ethnic recriminations began to take shape that eventually led to the war just sixteen months later.

The war's immediate aftermath, rather than seeing a strengthened military government clamp down on corruption, facilitated a deepening of corruption, self-enrichment, and cronyism that has lasted in the country since. Though the Cement Armada was the most publicized of scandals, it was so largely because of the scale of the ineptitude and self-dealing, but the largest source of corruption in the country since the end of the war has been the oil industry. Though the decades of corruption are well documented, successive governments have been unwilling to change the corrupt practices that have led to the embezzlement of untold billions of dollars. During the decades of military dictatorship, the government imposed a subsidy on the price of gasoline, ostensibly to protect Nigerian consumers. The problems with this policy have been magnified through the decades. However, the result was that government officials in charge of distributing the oil to the gas stations instead allowed the gas to be exported and then reimported on the black market. The result was that most of the fuel available for Nigerians could come only from black market sources. Once the subsidies were eased after the return to civilian rule in 1999 and then again in 2007, fuel returned to the gas stations at prices closer to the market value. However, these changes led to widespread civil unrest and strikes.[16]

One of the catalysts for the beginning of hostilities in 1967 was the payment of oil rents in July. Even though the country entered the war with a relatively diversified economy in 1967, since the end of the war, the petroleum industry has dominated government revenue, accounting for more than 80 percent of government revenue in 2019, despite being only 5.9 percent of the country's gross domestic product (GDP).[17] Nigeria's reliance on oil rents began shortly after the war and intensified, transforming the country into a "rentier state" and creating an impetus for the government to protect oil interests at the expense of its people, with successive governments eroding local control of the oil revenues and oppressing any kind of dissent that could hinder oil payments.[18]

Nigeria's culture of corruption has long been part of its international obligations, especially those involving its military. The early years of Nigeria's independence saw the creation of a well-trained and educated officer corps that participated in international missions such as the United Nations Operation in the Congo (UNOC), where Ironsi became the mission's final commander in 1964. The issues of Nigeria's perceived professionalism have plagued the country since the end of the war, largely due to the corrupt and political nature of the military's involvement in politics until 1999 and even after. Most troubling has been Nigeria's involvement in the ECOMOG intervention in Liberia.

When the civil war in Liberia ended with a ceasefire treaty in 1997, the Economic Community of West African States (ECOWAS) tasked itself with monitoring the ceasefire, creating the ECOWAS Monitoring Group (ECOMOG), in which Nigeria and Ghana played the leading roles. While the mission itself was hailed as a breakthrough in regional peacekeeping, the Nigerian contingent was so plagued with underfunding and corruption that the Nigerian soldiers became notorious for looting, and Liberians mocked the acronym ECOMOG, calling it Every Car or Moving Object Gone because of the levels of outright theft the Nigerian soldiers perpetrated.[19]

Perhaps the best studied of the war's legacies is its effect on global humanitarian interventions, especially in times of crisis and war. While the most famous of the organizations founded after the war is undoubtedly Médecins Sans Frontières (MSF), the war influenced virtually every aspect of humanitarian relief. MSF's foundation claims center on the inadequacies of humanitarian intervention and the disagreement between Bernard Kouchner and his superiors at the ICRC in Biafra. However, Marie-Luce Desgrandchamps's extensive research into both the foundation of MSF and the necessary reforms the ICRC initiated after the war found that Kouchner's grievances had been overblown and were not as profound as MSF lore suggests.[20]

The fact that MSF leaders overplayed the disagreements between them and the ICRC does not mean that the organization was well suited to be thrust into the brutal conflict, and the lessons the organization learned during the war, detailed to some extent in the previous chapters, shaped its future, not least in the need for a media arm that would publicize the work the organization did and ensure a greater revenue stream and, more importantly, an organizational structure that would allow them to deal with unexpected situations that evolve in unpredictable ways.[21]

The humanitarian crisis and global response came as a result of Biafra's successful use of media outlets to globalize the conflict in a way that had not been previously done.[22] Biafra's use of the global media environment to publicize their people's plight and accuse the Nigerian government of genocide was obviously not the first successful use of propaganda during wartime. However, the employment of Swiss firm Markpress to essentially handle international dissemination of their public diplomacy was one of the first instances of a government effectively outsourcing their diplomatic messaging to a private firm.[23] Biafra's successful use of the media began a new trend in governmental use and co-option of media outlets to shape narratives that other countries, organizations, and movements followed.

During the war, Biafra's accusations of genocide successfully galvanized world opinion, a lesson that has continued to influence activists around the world in their efforts to penetrate global media. In some cases, such as the Rwanda genocide in 1994 and the breakup of Yugoslavia, especially the Bosnian War (1992–95), the genocidal aims of the perpetrators was clear. In other instances, like Saro-Wiwa's Movement for the Survival of the Ogoni People (MOSOP) and other places where the UNGC would not apply in legal terms, activists and scholars have debated the idea of genocide outside of the scope of UNGC. To accomplish this, they used similar approaches to those that Biafra spearheaded during the war. The Ogoni case is particularly of note, as Saro-Wiwa learned from his experiences during the war as a young civilian administrator. Despite being on the Nigerian side, he saw the effectiveness of Biafran imagery and his side's inability to effectively counter it. In 1990, when he embarked on the campaign with MOSOP, he shrewdly tied his ideas of environmental degradation and destruction of the Niger Delta to genocide and traveled widely around the world, learning from groups like the Sierra Club and various rainforest-oriented networks before catching the attention of both Amnesty International and Greenpeace.[24]

Many of the legacies that have plagued the memory of the Nigerian Civil War are intrinsically tied to the issues of the way African conflicts, especially postcolonial ones, are studied in academia and how they are perceived in journalistic and other methods of popular consumption. In many cases, wars are treated as backdrops for social, economic, and other kinds of histories. As such, in the study of many African wars, conflicts are perceived as events that influence societies but do not drive them.[25] One notable exception has been Gerard Prunier's work on the myriad of conflicts in the Congo.[26] Prunier's ability to craft a narrative that focuses on the conflicts' ebb and flow has been a welcome change that addresses many of the issues that have been ignored in the study of conflicts across the continent. In many cases, the Nigerian Civil War included, combat and operational histories factor in only when white soldiers enter the fray. In Biafra, mercenaries and pilots have dominated the operational questions, and the book that has come closest to an operation account of the war has long been Draper's account of the air war and airlift.[27]

Conflicts across the continent follow a similar trajectory. In cases like the brutal civil wars in Liberia and Sierra Leone, much of the popular imagination and academic work focused on the barbarity that perpetuated the "broken" and "exotic" Africa tropes that have become endemic in writing about Africa.[28] However, in instances where white soldiers played a leading role, such as the South African Border Wars of 1966–90, military accounts proliferate, and the war is widely understood as a conventional military confrontation. A partial explanation for this is no doubt the recordkeeping in South Africa and the Cuban involvement that gave the war a Cold War relevance that other continental conflicts did not possess. However, the bulk of histories, memoirs, and fiction have come from the South

African side. In conflicts where there is little outside involvement, the voices of the combatants and the ways that the wars are conducted are even further removed from how these histories are told, despite the fact that they are integral to the lived experiences of those who fought and otherwise lived through them.

As the proverb "until the lion learns how to write, every story will glorify the hunter" encourages us to understand the totality of a situation, so does the study of military matters in African history. This book hopefully demystifies and brings more understanding to the events that made the Nigerian Civil War a war, and it is my hope that this trend continues across the continent so that those who perished in Biafra and elsewhere in Africa will not have died in vain.

NOTES

INTRODUCTION

1. The term *civil war* itself originates from the Latin *civilis* ("pertaining to citizens"). The war thus means a war between citizens and not the popular meaning of civil today, which means politeness.

2. For a deeper discussion into the past, present, and future of African Military History, see Charles G. Thomas and Roy Doron, "Out of Africa: The Challenges, Evolution, and Opportunities of African Military History," *Journal of African Military History* 1, no. 1–2 (2017).

3. Much of Afigbo's work centers on the abolition of slavery and the slave trade in the Niger Delta hinterland, and his work on various aspects of the British expedition to Arochukwu places the military aspects of both British power and Aro resistance at the center of his scholarship. See A. E. Afigbo, "The Aro Expedition of 1901–1902 (an Episode in the British Occupation of Iboland)," *Odù: Journal of Yoruba and Related Studies*, no. 7 (1972); "The Calabar Mission and the Aro Expedition of 1901–1902," *Journal of Religion in Africa* 5, no. 2 (1973).

4. Thornton's first foray into the military history of Africa was John K. Thornton, "The Art of War in Angola, 1575–1680," *Comparative Studies in Society and History* 30, no. 2 (1988). This work later evolved into his seminal *Warfare in Atlantic Africa, 1500–1800* (New York: Routledge, 2005). He has remained at the forefront of studying Africa's military past ever since.

5. David Killingray and Martin Plaut, "Fighting for Britain: African Soldiers in the Second World War" (2013); Michelle R. Moyd, *Violent Intermediaries: African Soldiers, Conquest, and Everyday Colonialism in German East Africa* (2014); Timothy J. Stapleton, "No Insignificant Part: The Rhodesia Native Regiment and the East Africa Campaign of the First World War," (2006); *A Military History of Africa* (Santa Barbara, CA: Praeger, 2013); Bruce Vandervort, *Wars of Imperial Conquest*

in Africa, 1830–1914 (Bloomington: UCL Press, Indiana University Press, 1998); G. N. Uzoigwe, "The Warrior and the State in Precolonial Africa: Comparative Perspectives," *Journal of Asian and African Studies* 12, no. 1–4 (1977); *Britain and the Conquest of Africa : The Age of Salisbury* (New York: NOK, 1978); Michelle Moyd, "African Military Historiography," *War & Society* (2022).

6. One of the most important sources for Nigerian news from the period is the Nigerian Institute for International Affairs (NIIA) in Lagos. The archivists there worked tirelessly through the war and after in collating and preserving the newspaper articles and classifying them.

7. "Convention on the Prevention and Punishment of the Crime of Genocide," United Nations Treaty Collection. https://treaties.un.org/doc/Publication/UNTS/Volume%2078/volume-78-I-1021-English.pdf.

8. For important work on Biafra's messaging and the global response to it, see, among many others that deal with the subject, Douglas Anthony, "'Resourceful and Progressive Blackmen': Modernity and Race in Biafra, 1967–70," *Journal of African History* 51, no. 1 (2010); "'What Are They Observing?': The Accomplishments and Missed Opportunities of Observer Missions in the Nigerian Civil War," *Journal of African Military History* 2, no. 2 (2018); Lasse Heerten, *The Biafran War and Postcolonial Humanitarianism: Spectacles of Suffering* (Cambridge: Cambridge University Press, 2018); Roy Doron, "Marketing Genocide: Biafran Propaganda Strategies During the Nigerian Civil War, 1967–70," *Journal of Genocide Research* 16, no. 2/3 (2014).

9. I discuss several of these crimes, perhaps the most heinous being the Asaba massacre perpetrated by the Nigerian army in October 1967. The Biafrans also committed atrocities, though because they were fighting a defensive war, had less opportunity to inflict harm on their enemy's civilian population. Perhaps the most publicized of Biafran excesses was the assault on the AGIP oil facility in May 1969.

10. Several conferences in Nigeria addressed this question, mostly from a thematic approach. The Proceedings they published are Ibrahim Haruna, "The Nigerian Civil War—Causes and Courses" (paper presented at the Nigerian Warfare Through the Ages, Umuahia, Nigeria, 1985). Several chapters in Armstrong Matiu Adejo, ed. *The Nigerian Civil War: Forty Years after, What Lessons?* (Makurdi: Aboki Publishers, 2008), also address this issue focusing on thematic and economic approaches that while useful, limit our understanding as they do not account for time in their analysis.

11. For several studies on the fraught state-society relationship in Nigerian and the military's place in it, see Norman Miners, *The Nigerian Army, 1956–66* (London: Methuen, 1971); Jimi Peters, *The Nigerian Military and the State* (London: Tauris Academic Studies, 1997); Max Siollun, *Oil, Politics and Violence Nigeria's Military Coup Culture (1966–1976)* (New York: Algora, 2009).

12. Samuel Fury Childs Daly, *A History of the Republic of Biafra: Law, Crime, and the Nigerian Civil War* (Cambridge: Cambridge University Press, 2020); Heerten, *The Biafran War and Postcolonial Humanitarianism: Spectacles of Suffering.*

13. See Susan Williams, *Who Killed Hammarskjöld?: The Un, the Cold War, and White Supremacy in Africa* (Oxford: Oxford University Press, 2017); Gérard Prunier, *Africa's World War: Congo, the Rwandan Genocide, and the Making of a Continental Catastrophe* (New York: Oxford University Press, 2012).

14. S. Elizabeth Bird and Fraser M. Ottanelli, *The Asaba Massacre: Trauma, Memory, and the Nigerian Civil War* (Cambridge: Cambridge University Press, 2017); Joe O. G. Achuzia, *Requiem Biafra: The True Story of Nigeria's Civil War* (Asaba: Steel Equip Nigeria Ltd., 1993); Emma Okocha, *Blood on the Niger: An Untold Story of the Asaba Massacre in the Nigerian Civil War* (Lagos, Abuja: SUN-RAY, 1994); S. Elizabeth Bird and Fraser Ottanelli, "The History and Legacy of the Asaba, Nigeria, Massacres," *African Studies Review* 54, no. 3 (2011).

15. Some prominent accounts from the Nigerian side include Godwin Alabi-Isama, *The Tragedy of Victory: On-the-Spot Account of the Nigeria-Biafra War in the Atlantic Theatre* (Ibadan: Spectrum Books, 2013); Olusegun Obasanjo, *My Command: An Account of the Nigerian Civil War, 1967–1970* (Nairobi: Heinemann, 1981); Ken Saro-Wiwa, *On a Darkling Plain: An Account of the Nigerian Civil War* (Port Harcourt: Saros, 1989). Though Saro-Wiwa was not a military commander, he helped secure the riverine regions in the Niger Delta in late 1967, early 1968.

16. Alabi-Isama, *The Tragedy of Victory*, 341.

17. Tekena N. Tamuno, ed. *Proceedings of the National Conference on Nigeria since Independence, Zaria, March, 1983*, 3 vols., vol. 3, National Conference on Nigeria since Independence (Zaria: The Panel on Nigeria Since Independence History Project, 1983). This conference collection details the war but leaves most military aspects untouched, while H. B. Momoh, *The Nigerian Civil War, 1967–1970: History and Reminiscences* (Ibadan: Sam Bookman, 2000) has a rudimentary timeline that ignores many of the pivotal moments of the conflict. Perhaps the most detailed timeline is in John J. Stremlau, *The International Politics of the Nigerian Civil War, 1967–1970* (Princeton, NJ: Princeton University Press, 1977).

18. Alabi-Isama, *The Tragedy of Victory*, 487–653.

1. THE FORMATION OF NIGERIA

1. For the most comprehensive account of Jaja's life and death, see S. J. S. Cookey, *King Jaja of the Niger Delta: His Life and Times, 1821–1891* (New York: NOK, 1974).

2. Toyin Falola and Matthew M. Heaton, *A History of Nigeria* (Cambridge, UK: Cambridge University Press, 2008), 98.

3. Paddy Docherty, *Blood and Bronze: The British Empire and the Sack of Benin* (Oxford, UK: C. Hurst, 2022).

4. For a detailed account of various aspects of the wars, see I. A. Akinjogbin, *War and Peace in Yorubaland, 1793–1893* (Ibadan, Nigeria: Heinemann Educational Books (Nigeria), 1998).

5. Toyin Falola, *Colonialism and Violence in Nigeria* (Bloomington: Indiana University Press, 2009), 12–13. The only exception was Abeokuta, which would retain some manner of independence until 1914, when Lugard would wage a war to incorporate it into the rest of Nigeria. See Harry A. Gailey, *Lugard and the Abeokuta Uprising: The Demise of Egba Independence* (London: F. Cass, 1982).

6. Boyd Alexander, Percy Amaury Talbot, and Arnold Edward, *From the Niger to the Nile* (London: Edward Arnold, 1907), 225.

7. John M. Carland, *The Colonial Office and Nigeria, 1898–1914* (Stanford, CA: Hoover Institution Press, 1985), 93. Nigeria is roughly the size of France and Germany combined.

8. Falola, *Colonialism and Violence in Nigeria*, 83.

9. S. J. S. Cookey, "Sir Hugh Clifford as Governor of Nigeria: An Evaluation," *African Affairs* 79, no. 317 (1980): 532, 535.

10. Clifford to Milner, October 28, 1919, CO 583/78.

11. For a comprehensive, if dated, treatment of the development of British colonial education, see J. F. Ade Ajayi, "The Development of Secondary Grammar School Education in Nigeria," *Journal of the Historical Society of Nigeria* 2, no. 4 (1963).

12. For a full account of the Women's War, see Toyin Falola and Adam Paddock, *The Women's War of 1929: A History of Anti-Colonial Resistance in Eastern Nigeria* (Durham, NC: Carolina Academic Press, 2011).

13. One of the most important cases was known as the Cocoa Pool Incident, where British governors used the "pool," one of the organizations that was ostensibly created to aid Nigerians by stabilizing market prices, to protect British investors. The outcry by Macaulay and other Nigerian political movements ended the practice. See A. Olorunfemi, "Effects of War-Time Trade Controls on Nigerian Cocoa Traders and Producers, 1939–45: A Case-Study of the Hazards of a Dependent Economy," *International Journal of African Historical Studies* 13, no. 4 (1980): 673.

14. As of 2024, Igbo is the accepted spelling of the word used to designate the ethnic group. The "gb" in the word is a digraph unique to the language. Until 1976, this digraph, along with "gh" and "gw," were spelled with only a single letter. In 1976, the current Igbo alphabet came into being, differentiating the various digraphs. When historical records use the previous spelling, I remain faithful to them.

15. For an in-depth discussion of the formation of Igbo identity in Nigeria, see Axel Harneit-Sievers, *Constructions of Belonging: Igbo Communities and the Nigerian State in the Twentieth Century* (Rochester, NY: University of Rochester Press, 2006).

16. The literal translation of Egbe Omo Oduduwa is the Society for the Descendants of the Oduduwa. The Oduduwa is the mythical founder of the Yoruba.

17. They both attended the University of London's Institute of Education, which today is part of University College London (UCL).

18. John Macpherson, "Sovereign Nigeria," *Journal of the Royal Society of Arts* 109, no. 5059 (1961): 530.

19. Ibid.

20. Henry Willink et al., "Report of the Commission Appointed to Enquire into the Fears of Minorities and the Means of Allaying Them," ed. Colonial Office (London: Her Majesty's Stationary Office, 1958), 98.

21. European Court of Human Rights, ed., "European Convention on Human Rights" (Strasbourg: European Court of Human Rights, 1950).

22. Willink et al., "Report of the Commission," 102–3. For an in-depth discussion of the Willink Commission and the effect it had on the early years of Nigerian independence, see Michael Vickers, *A Nation Betrayed: Nigeria and the Minorities Commission of 1957* (Trenton, NJ: Africa World, 2010).

23. Many of these infrastructure problems continue to plague the Niger Delta region as a whole, where roads are very difficult to build and other means of transportation and infrastructure such as water, electricity, and sewage cannot be effectively maintained due to the nature of the swampy delta and constant reconfigurations of the natural waterways. A more detailed discussion of this issue occurs in the epilogue.

24. Ezenwa-Ohaeto, *Chinua Achebe: A Biography* (Bloomington: Indiana University Press, 1997), 109.

25. Amayanabo O. Daminabo, *Ken Saro-Wiwa, 1941–1995: His Life & Legacies* (Buguma, Nigeria: Hanging Gardens, 2005), 32.

26. K. Onwuka Dike, *Trade and Politics in the Niger Delta, 1830–1885: An Introduction to the Economic and Political History of Nigeria* (Oxford, UK: Clarendon, 1956).

27. Paul E. Lovejoy, "Nigeria: The Ibadan School and Its Critics," in *African Historiographies: What History for Which Africa?*, ed. Bogumil Jewsiewicki and Davis S. Newbury (New York: SAGE, 1985).

28. Obafemi Awolowo, *Path to Nigerian Freedom* (London: Faber and Faber, 1947).

29. Jimi Peters, *The Nigerian Military and the State* (London: Tauris Academic Studies, 1997).

30. Cited in "How Long Can Senate President Hold Out?," *This Day*, January 21, 2002.

31. Peters, *The Nigerian Military and the State*, 73.

32. E. O. Awa, "Federal Elections in Nigeria, 1959," *The Indian Journal of Political Science* 21, no. 2 (1960): 110–11.

33. Peters, *The Nigerian Military and the State*, 79.

34. Norman Miners, *The Nigerian Army, 1956–66* (London: Methuen, 1971), 118–19.

35. *Nigerian Outlook*, February 23, 1962.

36. *Nigerian Citizen*, March 3, 1965.

37. Falola and Heaton, *A History of Nigeria*, 163.

38. For an extensive overview of oil's development in Nigeria and the effect on government and society, see Roy Doron and Toyin Falola, *Ken Saro-Wiwa* (Athens: Ohio University Press, 2016), 77–99.

39. For an overview of Nigeria's electricity plans in the 1960s, see E. S. Simpson, "Electricity Production in Nigeria," *Economic Geography* 45, no. 3 (1969). Since its

construction, and despite the installation of four more of the originally planned turbines, power generation has consistently fallen. As of 2013, the dam's production was reported to have dropped to 120 megawatts due to neglect. For more informaion, see Simon Echewofun Sunday, "Kainji Turbine Get First Turnaround Maintenance in 40 Years," *Daily Trust*, October 29, 2013.

40. Though Akintola took over the leadership of the Western Region and the region's AG party, Awolowo remained a powerful figure at the head of the national AG party. Unlike the NCNC and NPC, the AG drew considerable support from outside their region. They were the only political party in Nigeria to have more seats in the federal legislature come from outside the region they governed than from within it.

41. An overview of the development of the different strains of ideology in the Action Group exists in John A. A. Ayoade, "Party and Ideology in Nigeria: A Case Study of the Action Group," *Journal of Black Studies* 16, no. 2 (1985).

42. Alan Rake, "Nigeria after Elections: What Happened?," *Africa Today* 12, no. 1 (1965): 6.

43. Cocoa was so central to the region's economy that the tallest building in the regional capital of Ibadan was named Cocoa Tower.

44. *Constitution of the Action Group of Nigeria (as amended by the Congress of the Party held at Jos from February 2nd to 7th, 1962*, cited in John P. Mackintosh, "Politics in Nigeria: The Action Group Crisis of 1962," *Political Studies* 11, no. 2 (1963): 140–41.

45. Rake, "Nigeria after Elections," 6.

46. Eghosa E. Osaghae, *Crippled Giant: Nigeria since Independence* (Bloomington: Indiana University Press, 1998), 41.

47. Willink et al., "Report of the Commission," 29.

48. Ibid., 95–96.

49. There appears to be some confusion as to the number of seats that the north was allocated after the census. According to Dieter Nohlen, Michael Krennerich, and Bernhard Thibaut, *Elections in Africa: A Data Handbook* (Oxford, UK: Oxford University Press, 1999), the number is 167. However, Eghosa Osaghae cites two different figures. On page 44 of Osaghae, *Crippled Giant*, he cites 174 as the number of seats in the north. However, on the very next page, his chart claims the number is 167. As the number of candidates elected in the north was 167, and none of the results were annulled, I use the number 167 and not Osaghae's erroneous 174.

50. Emmanuel Oladipo Ojo, "Minority Groups: Bridgeheads in Nigerian Politics, 1950s–1964," *Turkish Journal of Politics* 3, no. 2 (2012).

51. John P. Mackintosh, "The Struggle for Power in Nigeria," *Transition*, no. 22 (1965): 21.

52. Toyin Falola, *Development Planning and Decolonization in Nigeria* (Gainesville: University Press of Florida, 1996), 154.

53. Mackintosh, "The Struggle for Power in Nigeria," 22.

54. Allocation of mining royalties and rents: Nigerian Constitution Art. 134 Sec. 1. Distribution of funds in Distributable Pool Account: Nigerian Constitution Art. 135.

55. Ojo, "Minority Groups," 63.

56. Falola and Heaton, *A History of Nigeria*, 169.

57. Larry Jay Diamond, *Class, Ethnicity, and Democracy in Nigeria: The Failure of the First Republic* (Syracuse, NY: Syracuse University Press, 1988), 209.

58. Billy J. Dudley, *An Introduction to Nigerian Government and Politics* (Bloomington: Indiana University Press, 1982), 71.

59. Ibid.

60. Biodun Jeyifo, "Ogbeni's Victory; Omisore's Defeat: The 1965 Western Region Election Revisited," *The Nation*, August 17, 2014.

61. Osaghae, *Crippled Giant*, 46. *Wetie* is Nigerian pidgin that loosely translates *to wet (with gasoline) and burn*. Necklacing was a popular method that Apartheid resistance groups used to execute collaborators with South Africa's white minority government.

62. Ibid., 47.

2. COUP, COUNTERCOUP, AND SECESSION

1. Olusegun Obasanjo, *Nzeogwu: An Intimate Portrait of Major Chukwuma Kaduna Nzeogwu* (Ibadan, Nigeria: Spectrum, 1987), 78–79.

2. Ibid., 79.

3. Ibid., 82.

4. Ben Gbulie, *Nigeria's Five Majors: Coup D'état of 15th January 1966, First Inside Account* (Onitsha, Nigeria: Africana Educational Publishers [Nig], 1981), 11–12.

5. A. M. Mainasara, *The Five Majors: Why They Struck* (Zaria, Nigeria: Hudahuda, 1982), 25.

6. Ademoyega dates the meeting to November while Gbulie places it a month earlier, in October. As Gbulie did not attend the meeting and Ademoyega was a core participant, I use the latter's date for the meeting.

7. Adewale Ademoyega, *Why We Struck: The Story of the First Nigerian Coup* (Ibadan, Nigeria: Evans Bros., 1981), 55.

8. Gbulie, *Nigeria's Five Majors*, 59.

9. Ibid., 75.

10. Ibid., 82.

11. Ibid.

12. Ibid., 80.

13. Ibid., 81.

14. Ademoyega, *Why We Struck*, 85–86.

15. Siollun, *Oil, Politics and Violence*, 47.

16. The old NET building was replaced in 1979 with a newer modern building, today known as NECOM (previously NITEL) House, which has an iconic radio

tower that doubles as a lighthouse and dominates the Lagos skyline. The new tower suffered a catastrophic arson attack in 1983.

17. Frederick Forsyth, *The Biafra Story: The Making of an African Legend* (London: Leo Cooper, 2001), 30.

18. Siollun, *Oil, Politics and Violence*, 51.

19. Frederick Forsyth claims that the finance minister was killed in his home and his body transported, but his account was written in 1969, before the war ended and long before Ademoyega's firsthand account of his own actions.

20. Siollun, *Oil, Politics and Violence*, 62.

21. Ademoyega, *Why We Struck*, 89.

22. Ntieyong Udo Akpan, *The Struggle for Secession, 1966–1970: A Personal Account of the Nigerian Civil War* (London: F. Cass, 1972), 7.

23. Ken Saro-Wiwa, *On a Darkling Plain: An Account of the Nigerian Civil War* (Port Harcourt, Nigeria: Saros, 1989), 17.

24. Obasanjo, *Nzeogwu: An Intimate Portrait*, 135–36.

25. In 2014, a failed attempt to oust Gambian president Yahya Jammeh saw two Gambian expatriates arrested in the United States. The two men attempted to mobilize forces to remove Jammeh from power but failed largely because many of those who agreed to help did not know the lead conspirators and thus did not assist when the time came to execute the coup.

26. Akpan, *The Struggle for Secession*, 9.

27. Ademoyega, *Why We Struck*, 61.

28. One version of the story appears in Lekan Abayomi, "Post-Colonial Nigeria: Did Igbos Draw First Blood?," NewsRescue.com, last modified July 31, 2012, http://newsrescue.com/genesis-the-beginning-of-north-south-hausa-igbo-beef-in-nigeria. Archived at https://uchetreasure50.wordpress.com/2014/06/01/post-colonial-nigeria-did-igbos-draw-first-blood/.

29. A. H. M. Kirk-Greene, *Crisis and Conflict in Nigeria: A Documentary Sourcebook* (London: Oxford University Press, 1971), v. 1, 39.

30. Tyler Fleming and Toyin Falola, "Africa's Media Empire: 'Drum''s Expansion to Nigeria," *History in Africa* 32 (2005): 153.

31. Alexander A. Madiebo, *The Nigerian Revolution and the Biafran War* (Enugu, Nigeria: Fourth Dimension, 1980), 38.

32. Ibid., 41.

33. The issue of the number of dead in the 1966 riots, both in May and after the July countercoup, have long been a source of contention within Nigeria and are dealt with in the next chapter.

34. Charles Henry Robinson, "Jaraba," in *Dictionary of the Hausa Language* (London: Cambridge University Press, 1913), 148. The proliferation of the term to mean secession has been widely repeated and can be found in Patrick A. Anwunah, *The Nigeria-Biafra War (1967–1970): My Memoirs* (Ibadan, Nigeria: Spectrum, 2007), 118; and S. E. Orobator, "Nigeria: From Separatism to Secession 1950–1970,"

Africa: Rivista trimestrale di studi e documentazione dell'Istituto italiano per l'Africa e l'Oriente 42, no. 2 (1987): 309.

35. John de St. Jorre, *The Brothers' War; Biafra and Nigeria* (Boston: Houghton Mifflin, 1972), 61.

36. Akpan, *The Struggle for Secession*, 20.

37. Though most accounts agree that Ojukwu did indeed urge easterners to return to their homes in the north, John de St. Jorre, writing immediately after the war's end, disagreed, calling the account part of "the subsequent mythology of the crisis" and stating that Ojukwu and his aides created this appeal in October 1966 as a way of justifying the march toward secession. For more details, see De St. Jorre, *The Brothers' War*, 61–62.

38. Max Siollun, "The Danjuma Interview," last modified May 28, 2008, https://maxsiollun.wordpress.com/2008/05/28/the-danjuma-interview.

39. Madiebo, *The Nigerian Revolution*, 32.

40. Ibid., 35.

41. De St. Jorre, *The Brothers' War*, 78.

42. This account comes from *January 15, Before and After. Nigerian Crisis 1966. Vol. 7* (Enugu, Nigeria: Printed by the Government Printer, 1967), 46–47. Despite the authorship, the events of that night in the government lodge have been largely corroborated by the participants, including Danjuma.

43. BOAC would form British Airways in 1974.

44. "Pilot Flies for Rebels." *New York Times*, August 1, 1966.

45. *The Aburi Conference: Ghana, Jan. 4–5, 1967* (New York: Reprinted by the American Committee to Keep Biafra Alive, 1967), 12.

46. Madiebo, *The Nigerian Revolution*, 64.

47. Saro-Wiwa, *On a Darkling Plain*, 38.

48. De St. Jorre, *The Brothers' War*, 72.

49. Though Fajuyi was also killed in the coup, Yoruba leaders in the west agreed not to oppose Gowon.

50. Zdenek Cervenka, *A History of the Nigerian War, 1967–1970* (Ibadan, Nigeria: Onibonoje, 1972), 28.

51. Forsyth, *The Biafra Story*, 53.

52. Walter Schwarz, *Nigeria* (New York: Praeger, 1968), 211.

53. De St. Jorre, *The Brothers' War*, 74. Though he hints at some American and British involvement, he is clear that the foreign diplomats wanted Nigeria to remain unified, a thought echoed by most of the Nigerian leadership present at the meetings over the weekend. On July 30, 1975, Murtala Mohammed eventually took control of the country, ousting Gowon in a coup of his own. Mohammed's rule lasted barely seven months before he was gunned down on his way to Dodan Barracks. His bullet-riddled Mercedes is on display at the Nigerian National Museum in Lagos.

54. Forsyth, *The Biafra Story*, 54–56.

55. Philip Efiong, *Nigeria and Biafra: My Story* (Princeton, NJ: Sungai, 2003), 111.

56. *January 15, Before and After*, 73.
57. *New Nigerian*, October 19, 1966.
58. *The Aburi Conference: Ghana, Jan. 4–5, 1967.*
59. Colin Legum, "The Massacre of the Proud Ibos" *Observer*, October 16, 1966.
60. Information Ministry of Eastern Nigeria Division Publicity, *Nigerian Pogrom: The Organized Massacre of Eastern Nigerians* (Enugu, Nigeria: Publicity Division of the Ministry of Information, Eastern Nigeria, 1966).
61. "Massacre in Kano," *Time* 88, no. 16 (1966).
62. Information Ministry of Eastern Nigeria Division Publicity, *Nigerian Pogrom*, 18.
63. Siollun, *Oil, Politics and Violence*, 130.
64. Douglas A. Anthony, *Poison and Medicine: Ethnicity, Power, and Violence in a Nigerian City, 1966 to 1986* (Portsmouth, NH: Heinemann, 2002), 97.
65. Siollun, *Oil, Politics and Violence*, 135.
66. "Massacre in Kano."
67. Hunt FCO 51/169.
68. The ten thousand figure is quoted in *The Aburi Conference: Ghana, Jan. 4–5, 1967*, 30.
69. Cervenka, *A History of the Nigerian War*, 33.
70. The word comes from the Russian verb *gromit* (*громи́ть*), which means "to destroy with violence."
71. National Archives and Records Administration (NARA), Nixon Presidential Materials, NSC Files, Box 741, Country Files, Africa, Nigeria, Vol. I. Though the memo bears Kissinger's name, Roger Morris was the actual author of the piece and that particular phrase.
72. Olaudah Equiano, The Interesting Narrative of the Life of Olaudah Equiano (Project Gutenberg), https://www.gutenberg.org/files/15399/15399-h/15399-h.htm.
73. George Thomas Basden, *Among the Ibos of Nigeria: An Account of the Curious & Interesting Habits, Customs & Beliefs of a Little Known African People by One Who Has for Many Years Lived amongst Them on Close & Intimate Terms* (London: Cass, 1966). For details on the reception of Basden's work and its effect on the Igbo during colonial times, see Dmitri van den Bersselaar, "Missionary Knowledge and the State in Colonial Nigeria: On How G. T. Basden Became an Expert," *History in Africa* 33 (2006): 433–50.
74. A. E. Afigbo, "Traditions of Igbo Origins: A Comment," *History in Africa* 10 (1983): 10. Emphasis in original.
75. Ibid.
76. Saro-Wiwa, *On a Darkling Plain*, 40.
77. Roy Doron, "Forging a Nation While Losing a Country: Igbo Nationalism, Ethnicity and Propaganda in the Nigerian Civil War 1968–1970" (University of Texas at Austin, 2011).
78. Olukunle Ojeleye, *The Politics of Post-War Demobilisation and Reintegration in Nigeria* (London: Taylor & Francis, 2016), 62.

79. Peter Marson, "Prop Personailty–Hank Wharton," *Propliner Aviation Magazine*, December 1981.

80. Joel Calmettes, "The Secret History of Biafra" (Paris: Point du Jour International, 2001). US$140,000 in 1966 equals US$1,025,525 in 2015. (Source: "Cpi Inflation Calculator," Bureau of Labor Statistics, http://data.bls.gov/cgi-bin/cpicalc.pl.)

81. Frederick Forsyth, *Emeka* (Ibadan, Nigeria: Spectrum, 1982), 71.

82. Ibid.

83. Ibid., 69–72.

84. David Akpode Ejoor, *Reminiscences* (Lagos, Nigeria: Malthouse, 1989).

85. De St. Jorre, *The Brothers' War.*

86. *The Aburi Conference: Ghana, Jan. 4–5, 1967*, 6–7.

87. Ibid., 12.

88. Ibid., 15.

89. Ibid., 13.

90. Ibid., 20.

91. Ibid., 23–24.

92. Ejoor, *Reminiscences*, 89.

93. *The Aburi Conference: Ghana, Jan. 4–5, 1967*, 51.

94. Ibid., 57.

95. Ibid., 95–96.

96. Each region was given autonomy in appointing regional judges and civil servants, but any appointments above a certain rank in the civil service, police, or judiciary could be appointed only by the council.

97. Ejoor, *Reminiscences*, 63–64.

98. Ibid., 54.

99. Ibid., 92.

100. De St. Jorre, *The Brothers' War*, 103.

101. Press conference held on March 12, 1967, cited in Ibid.

102. Terhemba Wuam, "A Re-Examination of the Causes of the Nigerian Civil War," in *The Nigerian Civil War: Forty Years after, What Lessons?*, ed. Armstrong Matiu Adejo (Makurdi, Ibadan, Abuja: Aboki, 2008), 41.

103. Africa research bulletin 1967 v.4 n5.

104. Isaac Jasper Adaka Boro and Anthony Odogboro Tebekaemi, *The Twelve-Day Revolution* (Benin City, Nigeria: Idodo Umeh, 1982).

105. De St. Jorre, *The Brothers' War*, 98–100.

106. Cervenka, *A History of the Nigerian War*, 39.

107. Michael Gould, "The Struggle for Modern Nigeria the Biafran War, 1967–1970" (2012): 56.

108. Ibid., 57.

109. Madiebo, *The Nigerian Revolution*, 93.

110. Cervenka, *A History of the Nigerian War*, 40.

3. THE WAR BEGINS

1. For a full history of Dick Tiger's life and career, see Adeyinka Makinde, *Dick Tiger: The Life and Times of a Boxing Immortal* (Tarentum, PA: Word Association, 2004).

2. According to "2014 United Nations Demographic Yearbook," ed. Department of Economic and Social Affairs (New York: United Nations, 2015), Nigeria's total land area is 923,768 km^2. France's land area is 551,500 km^2 while Germany's is listed at 357,137 km^2. Nigeria's estimated population numbers are taken from "UN Population Division Data Portal," ed. United Nations Population Division (New York: United Nations).

3. Phia Steyn, "Oil Exploration in Colonial Nigeria, C. 1903–58," *Journal of Imperial & Commonwealth History* 37, no. 2 (2009): 250.

4. Ibid., 260.

5. Said Adejumobi and Adewale Aderemi, "Oil and the Political Economy of the Nigerian Civil War and Its Aftermath," in *The Nigerian Civil War and Its Aftermath*, ed. Eghosa E. Osaghae, Ebere Onwudiwe, and Rotimi T. Suberu (Ibadan, Nigeria: John Archers Limited, 2002), 195.

6. Peter Howe, *Shooting under Fire: The World of the War Photographer* (New York: Artisan, 2002). McCullin spent significant time in Biafra, and many of his photographs are among the most recognizable images of the war. He also covered the war in Vietnam and the Northern Ireland conflict. His work was so politically charged that in 1982 the Margaret Thatcher government refused to allow him access to cover the Falkland war.

7. Akpan, *The Struggle for Secession*, 156.

8. Saro-Wiwa, *Sozaboy*, 54.

9. Akpan, *The Struggle for Secession*, 156.

10. A. O. Y. Raji and T. S. Abejide, "Oil and Biafra: An Assessment of Shell-BP's Dilemma during the Nigerian Civil War, 1967–1970," *Kuwait Chapter of the Arabian Journal of Business and Management Review* 2, no. 11 (2013): 16. GB£300,000,000 is equivalent to GB£4,911717495.98 in 2015. Source: "Inflation Calculator Bank of England."

11. Ibid., 27.

12. Chibuike Uche, "Oil, British Interests and the Nigerian Civil War," *Journal of African History* 49, no. 1 (2008).

13. "Nigeria's Split Creates Oil Dilemma," *New York Times*, June 30, 1967.

14. *Financial Times*, July 6, 1967.

15. John Price, "Shell-BP Payment to Biafra," *The Times*, July 3, 1967

16. "Nigerians Hold Ship as Blockade Runner," *New York Times*, July 5, 1967.

17. Uche, "Oil, British Interests and the Nigerian Civil War," 113.

18. British High Commissioner Lagos to Secretary of State for Commonwealth Affairs, July 27, 1967 (PRO/FCO/38/112).

19. Roy Doron, "Ojukwu, Chukwuemeka Odumegwu," in *Dictionary of African Biography*, ed. Henry Louis Gates and Emmanuel K. Akyeampong (New York: Oxford University Press, 2012).

20. Though this was the start of the Nigerian invasion, the first report of hostilities along the Cameroonian border was reported on June 10. At the time, the Nigerians denied that any action took place, but the fighting was subsequently confirmed.

21. De St. Jorre, *The Brothers' War*, 149–50. Bukar would make a full recovery and after the war went on to become a colonel and commander of the Benin City brigade before he was executed in 1976 for his part in the coup attempt that killed Murtala Mohammed and installed Olusegun Obasanjo as military ruler.

22. Ibid., 149.

23. Ezenwa-Ohaeto, *Chinua Achebe: A Biography*, 127.

24. H. B. Momoh, *The Nigerian Civil War, 1967–1970: History and Reminiscences* (Ibadan, Nigeria: Sam Bookman, 2000), 68. Though the popular assumption is that Nzeogwu was killed at Obollo Afor, both Shelleng and Obasanjo in Olusegun Obasanjo, *My Command: An Account of the Nigerian Civil War, 1967–1970* (London: Heinemann, 1981), 17, assert that he was killed in Nsukka.

25. Michael I. Draper, *Shadows: Airlift and Airwar in Biafra and Nigeria, 1967–1970* (Aldershot, UK: Hikoki, 1999), 27. Later in the war, the Zambian government donated several C-47 Skytrains to the airlift effort, and in 1969, under the auspices of Carl Gustav von Rosen, several small Malmö MFI-9 planes were smuggled into Biafra to form the MiniCOIN.

26. Jan Zumbach, *On Wings of War: My Life as a Pilot Adventurer* (London: Deutsch, 1975). He is mistakenly credited as Jean in the book, which was originally written in French several years before.

27. S. E. Orobator, "The Nigerian Civil War and the Invasion of Czechoslovakia," *African Affairs* 82, no. 327 (1983).

28. Zumbach, *On Wings of War*.

29. Draper, *Shadows*, 34.

30. Nwabeze Reuben Ogbudinkpa, *The Economics of the Nigerian Civil War and Its Prospects for National Development* (Enugu, Nigeria: Fourth Dimension, 1985), 28.

31. Madiebo, *The Nigerian Revolution and the Biafran War*, 130.

32. Ibid., 138.

33. Ibid., 140.

34. De St. Jorre, *The Brothers' War*, 151. The Dornier Do 27 is a small single-engine trainer, and the 28 is a twin-engine light utility aircraft. Both are designated Short Take-Off and Landing (STOL) aircraft, meaning they would be indispensable in the environment of Eastern Nigeria.

35. Ibid.

36. Saro-Wiwa, *On a Darkling Plain*, 88.

37. Ken Saro-Wiwa, *Genocide in Nigeria: The Ogoni Tragedy* (London: Saros International, 1992), 27.

38. "Fight for Fatherland!," *Spectator*, August 1967, 2.

39. The NNS *Ibadan* was originally commissioned as the HMS *Montford*, a British Ford Class Seaward Defence Boat. On September 9, 1966, the ship was sold and transferred to the Nigerian navy and renamed the NNS *Ibadan*. Seaward Defence Boats were originally designed to protect ports against submarine incursions, but the *Ibadan* was redesignated as a frigate and used to patrol the approaches to the Niger Delta at Bonny to Port Harcourt and the Cross River to Calabar. For the differing versions on how the NNS *Ibadan* came to Biafra, see P. J. Odu, *The Future That Vanished: A Biafra Story* (United States: Xlibris, 2009), 101; Momoh, *The Nigerian Civil War*, 99.

40. Odu, *The Future That Vanished*, 101. Several years after the war, Fingesi was appointed to replace Anthony Enahoro as president of the organizing committee for the Second World Black and African Festival of Arts and Culture, known as FESTAC '77.

41. Momoh, *The Nigerian Civil War*.

42. Ibid., 640.

43. De St. Jorre, *The Brothers' War*, 152.

44. Momoh, *The Nigerian Civil War*, 624.

45. Ibid., 641.

46. All the Nigerian naval ships were repurposed from foreign militaries. Perhaps the ship with the most storied history was the NNS *Ogoja*. Commissioned in June 1942, the *Ogoja* began its life as a US Navy submarine chaser, the USS *PC-468*, before being transferred in August to the Dutch navy that was still fighting against Germany, especially from the Dutch islands in the Caribbean. Renamed the HNMS *Queen Wilhelmina*, the ship patrolled the Caribbean, where in 1944 it rescued survivors from an American tanker torpedoed off the coast of Colombia, near Aruba. In 1963, the Dutch navy loaned the ship to Nigeria, where it was renamed the *Ogoja*.

47. Momoh, *The Nigerian Civil War*, 642.

48. Ibid., 645.

49. Odu, who was captain of the *Ibadan* when she was sunk, wrote his memoir of the war but did not mention how the ship was sunk, claiming that he started writing his personal diary only on August 4 and started his recollection of the war then. He also did not explain why he did not include his account of the *Ibadan*'s sinking in his book.

50. Momoh, *The Nigerian Civil War*, 646.

4. THE MIDWEST OFFENSIVE AND THE TRANSFORMATION OF THE WAR

1. Not to be confused with the current Republic of Benin, which at the time was called the Republic of Dahomey. After a communist takeover of Dahomey in 1972, the coup's leader and the country's president, Mathieu Kérékou, changed the

name in 1975 to the People's Republic of Benin, in part because Dahomey became associated with the Fon ethnic group and the predatory slave-trading Kingdom of Dahomey from the nineteenth century. In 1991, with the establishment of a multiparty civilian republic, the country became the Republic of Benin.

2. Douglas Anthony, "'Resourceful and Progressive Blackmen': Modernity and Race in Biafra, 1967–70," *Journal of African History* 51, no. 1 (2010): 41–61.

3. Zumbach, *On Wings of War*, 29.

4. Ibid.

5. Whether his accusers knew that he played no part in the January coup has not been established. However, the word *falsely* implies that the accusers knew he was innocent yet was still imprisoned.

6. Madiebo, *The Nigerian Revolution and the Biafran War*, 156–57.

7. Ibid., 156.

8. Efiong, *Nigeria and Biafra: My Story*, 200.

9. Ibid.

10. Banjo's address on Benin radio. Cited in Ibid., 201–02.

11. Ademoyega, *Why We Struck*, 155–56.

12. Ibid., 159.

13. Madiebo, *The Nigerian Revolution and the Biafran War*, 157.

14. De St. Jorre, *The Brothers' War*, 160–61.

15. Madiebo, *The Nigerian Revolution and the Biafran War*, 158.

16. Ademoyega, *Why We Struck*, 155.

17. Or the Liberation Army, depending on whose definition was the correct one.

18. Godwin Alabi-Isama, *The Tragedy of Victory: On-the-Spot Account of the Nigeria-Biafra War in the Atlantic Theatre* (Ibadan, Nigeria: Spectrum, 2013), 46–47.

19. Ibid., 54.

20. Godwin Alaoma Onyegbula, *Memoirs of the Nigerian-Biafran Bureaucrat: An Account of Life in Biafra and within Nigeria* (Ibadan, Nigeria: Spectrum, 2005).

21. Anwunah, *The Nigeria-Biafra War*, 224–25. Emphasis mine.

22. Alfred Friendly Jr., "Nigerians Order a Step-up in War," *New York Times*, August 12, 1967.

23. Momoh, *The Nigerian Civil War*, 477.

24. Ibid., 86, 95.

25. De St. Jorre, *The Brothers' War*, 162.

26. Madiebo, *The Nigerian Revolution and the Biafran War*, 159.

27. Ibid., 145.

28. Anwunah, *The Nigeria-Biafra War*, 218–19.

29. Madiebo, *The Nigerian Revolution and the Biafran War*, 174.

30. Nelson Ottah, *Rebels against Rebels* (Ikeja, Nigeria: Manson, 1981). During the war, Ottah edited one of Biafra's publications, *Biafra Time*.

31. F. Adetowun Ogunsheye, *A Break in the Silence: A Historical Note on Lt. Colonel Victor Adebukunola Banjo* (Ibadan, Nigeria: Spectrum, 2001), 87.

32. For a recent account of the legal history of Biafra as it pertained to the trial and its aftermath, see Samuel Fury Childs Daly, "The Case against Victor Banjo: Legal Process and the Governance of Biafra," in *Postcolonial Conflict and the Question of Genocide: The Nigeria-Biafra War 1967–1970*, ed. Dirk Moses and Lasse Heerten, 95–112 (New York: Routledge, 2017).

33. Ogunsheye, *A Break in the Silence*, 86.

34. Madiebo, *The Nigerian Revolution and the Biafran War*, 167.

35. Alfred Friendly Jr., "Nigeria Detains Playwright after Cease-Fire Plea," *New York Times*, September 2, 1967.

36. Dan Sullivan, "The Theater: 2 Plays by Nigeria's Wole Soyinka," *New York Times*, November 10, 1967. His captivity renewed global interest in his poetry and plays. Several of his plays, including "The Trials of Brother Jero" and "The Strong Breed," featured as a double bill in New York City to rave reviews and starred renowned actor Harold Scott.

37. Emma Okocha, *Blood on the Niger: An Untold Story of the Asaba Massacre in the Nigerian Civil War* (Lagos, Nigeria: SUNRAY, 1994), 25.

38. Madiebo, *The Nigerian Revolution and the Biafran War*, 160.

39. Not much is known about Martins, but he has been referenced in several Nigerian newspaper editorials about the war, and according to these records, he returned to Nigeria in either 1921 or 1922. See Okocha, *Blood on the Niger*.

40. Ibid., 28.

41. Madiebo, *The Nigerian Revolution and the Biafran War*, 160.

42. Joe O. G. Achuzia, *Requiem Biafra* (Enugu, Nigeria: Fourth Dimension, 1986), 72–73.

43. Okocha, *Blood on the Niger*, 47.

44. Ibid., 63.

45. Ibid., 74.

46. Wole Soyinka, *The Man Died: Prison Notes* (Ibadan, Nigeria: Spectrum, 2002).

47. S. Elizabeth Bird and Fraser M. Ottanelli, *The Asaba Massacre: Trauma, Memory, and the Nigerian Civil War* (Cambridge, UK: Cambridge University Press, 2017).

48. Ogbudinkpa, *The Economics of the Nigerian Civil War*, 30.

49. Momoh, *The Nigerian Civil War*, 480.

50. Ibid., 73.

51. Madiebo, *The Nigerian Revolution and the Biafran War*, 173–74.

52. Momoh, *The Nigerian Civil War*, 846.

53. Madiebo, *The Nigerian Revolution and the Biafran War*, 176.

54. Momoh, *The Nigerian Civil War*, 848.

5. THE WORLD REACTS

1. I presented how the idea of genocide began in an earlier chapter, and I continue the discussion in the next one.

2. John J. Stremlau, *The International Politics of the Nigerian Civil War, 1967–1970* (Princeton, NJ: Princeton University Press, 1977).

3. For some examples of this type of work, see A. B. Akinyemi, "The British Press and the Nigerian Civil War," *African Affairs* 71, no. 285 (1972); George A. Obiozor, *The United States and the Nigerian Civil War: An American Dilemma in Africa, 1966–1970* (Lagos: Nigerian Institute of International Affairs, 1993); Roy Lewis, "Britain and Biafra," *Round Table* 60, no. 239 (1970): 241–48; E. Wayne Nafziger and William L. Richter, "Biafra and Bangladesh: The Political Economy of Secessionist Conflict," *Journal of Peace Research* 13, no. 2 (1976): 91–109.

4. Chinua Achebe, *There Was a Country: A Personal History of Biafra* (New York: Penguin, 2012).

5. See Marie-Luce Desgrandchamps, "Dealing with 'Genocide': The Icrc and the Un During the Nigeria–Biafra War, 1967–70," *Journal of Genocide Research* 16, no. 2–3 (2014): 281–97; Brian McNeil, "'And Starvation Is the Grim Reaper': The American Committee to Keep Biafra Alive and the Genocide Question During the Nigerian Civil War, 1968–70," *Journal of Genocide Research* 16, no. 2–3 (2014): 317–36; Kevin O'Sullivan, "Humanitarian Encounters: Biafra, Ngos and Imaginings of the Third World in Britain and Ireland, 1967–70," *Journal of Genocide Research* 16, no. 2–3 (2014): 299–315; Karen E. Smith, "The UK and 'Genocide' in Biafra," *Journal of Genocide Research* 16, no. 2–3 (2014): 247–62; Zach Levey, "Israel, Nigeria and the Biafra Civil War, 1967–70," *Journal of Genocide Research* 16, no. 2–3 (2014): 263–80.

6. PRO PREM 13–1661.

7. PRO PREM 13–1661. The author of the report, David Hunt, was a lifelong civil servant and high commissioner to Nigeria for most of the war. He retired from public life in 1973. In 1977, he was crowned champion of the popular television quiz show *Mastermind*.

8. Lyndon Baines Johnson Presidential Library (hereafter LBJ) CO 206 "Presentation on Nigeria," 105.

9. "Presentation on Nigeria," 105. B. 96, LBJ Archives.

10. "A Crisis Ahead in Nigeria?" 101. NARA, CIA Archives. (FOIA) /ESDN (CREST): CIA-RDP79R00967A001000020026-1.

11. "Comments on Nigeria Sitrep of 5/30/66," 99. B. 96, LBJ Archives.

12. Memorandum from Ed Hamilton to Walt Rostow, May 25, 1967. Emphasis in original. B. 96, LBJ Archives.

13. Memorandum from Ed Hamilton to Walt Rostow, July 3, 1967. B. 96 LBJ Archives.

14. Ibid.

15. Stremlau, *International Politics*.

16. Ibid., 80–81; Bruce D. Porter, *The USSR in Third World Conflicts: Soviet Arms and Diplomacy in Local Wars, 1945–1980* (Cambridge, UK: Cambridge University Press, 1984).

17. Stremlau, *International Politics*, 82.

18. In one embarrassing case, the Nigerian embassy in Moscow actually held a Biafran independence celebration in May 1967.

19. Stremlau, *International Politics*, 83. Tanzania at the time was not yet unified and was still the republics of Tanganyika and Zanzibar.

20. Ibid., 85.

21. Ibid., 85.

22. Of the five countries to recognize Biafra in 1968, Tanzania and Zambia were the only former British colonies to do so. The others were Gabon, Côte d'Ivoire, and Haiti.

23. For details see Ian Hancock, "The Buganda Crisis of 1964," *African Affairs* 69, no. 275 (1970): 109–23; Ali A. Mazrui, "Violent Contiguity and the Politics of Retribalization in Africa," *Journal of International Affairs* 23, no. 1 (1969): 89–105.

24. Stremlau, *International Politics*, 85. They did this without mentioning Biafra by name, an act that Ojukwu would have welcomed as de facto recognition of his regime.

25. Kirk-Greene, *Crisis and Conflict in Nigeria*, v. 2, 163–65.

26. Ibid., v. 2, 163.

27. James D. D. Smith, *Stopping Wars: Defining the Obstacles to Cease-Fire* (Boulder, CO: Westview Press Boulder, 1995). 150.

28. Stremlau believes that the Tanzanian or Zambian delegation distributed the memorandum for the Biafrans. Stremlau, *International Politics*, 90.

29. Kirk-Greene, *Crisis and Conflict in Nigeria*, v. 2, 168. Emphasis is mine.

30. Ibid., v. 2, 169.

31. Ibid., v. 2, 172.

32. "Convention on the Prevention and Punishment of the Crime of Genocide."

33. Ibid.

34. As of 2017, roughly two-thirds of African nations have acceded to the treaty. Nigeria joined the convention only in 2009, and other nations, such as Biafra's ally Zambia, Cameroon, and Botswana, have never acceded to the convention.

35. Stremlau, *International Politics*, 91.

36. Organization of African Unity, "OAU Charter" cited in https://au.int/sites/default/files/treaties/7759-file-oau_charter_1963.pdf.

37. Kirk-Greene, *Crisis and Conflict in Nigeria*, v.2, 175.

38. "T.K.O. to Gowon!," *Biafra Newsletter*, November 24, 1967, 5.

39. "Editorial," *Morning Post*, October 24, 1967.

40. Nigeria, *Report on the O.A.U. Consultative Mission to Nigeria* (Apapa, Nigeria: Printed by the Nigerian National Press, 1968).

41. Even Somalia, the most ethnically homogenous country in Africa, has suffered extreme violence due in some part to the differing colonial states that united to form modern Somalia.

42. Stremlau, *International Politics*, 100.

43. Kirk-Greene, *Crisis and Conflict in Nigeria*, v.2, 173.

6. GENOCIDE

1. The bunker and Ojukwu's adjacent residence in the city now constitute Nigeria's National War Museum.

2. See Stremlau, *International Politics,* 111; Efiong, *Nigeria and Biafra: My Story,* 213–14.

3. During the battle in Enugu, a Nigerian artillery battery had been able to locate and harass the station, temporarily silencing it. Whenever they heard it start broadcasting again, they renewed their barrage until the station moved.

4. Research Bureau Appraisal Committee, ed., *Guide Lines for Effective Propaganda* (Aba, Nigeria: Directorate for Propaganda, 1968).

5. The author uncovered this plan, as well as other publications, in the Nigerian National Archives in Enugu. However, at some point in the document's history, the plan's pages became separated and placed in two archival folders. I have since united the two halves of the report.

6. Research Bureau Appraisal Committee, *Guide Lines for Effective Propaganda.*"

7. Research Bureau Appraisal Committee, *Guide Lines for Effective Propaganda,* 39.

8. Ibid., 34.

9. Research & Publications Divisions Appraisal Committee, ed., *A Critique of Propaganda Radio Programmes* (Enugu, Nigeria: Ministry of Information, 1969), 18. The Agbekoya Parapo Revolt is discussed in a later chapter.

10. Research Bureau Appraisal Committee, *Guide Lines for Effective Propaganda,* 26.

11. Research Bureau Appraisal Committee, *Guide Lines for Effective Propaganda,* 35.

12. Research Bureau Appraisal Committee, *Guide Lines for Effective Propaganda,* 27.

13. "Why We Are Fighting," *Biafra Newsletter,* October 27, 1967.

14. "Biafran Rockets in Action: Enemy Reduced to Ashes," *Biafra Newsletter,* November 10, 1967.

15. "Fight for Fatherland!," Spectator, August 1967, 2.

16. "The Liberation of Mid-Western Nigeria," *The Spark,* September 1967, 7. This issue came out before Banjo's trial and execution.

17. Arthur Nwankwo, "Genocide not Internal Affair," *Biafra Newsletter,* November 24, 1967.

18. Ibid.

19. Nwankwo, "Genocide." Emphasis in original.

20. Ibid.

21. For an in-depth analysis of this thread in Biafra's public diplomacy offensive, see Anthony, "'Resourceful and Progressive Blackmen.'"

22. "Biafratoon," *Biafra Newsletter,* March 1, 1968.

23. "Anglo-Soviet Collusion: An Enigma," *Biafra Newsletter,* November 24, 1967.

24. "Newstalk: Russian Bridgehead in Nigeria," *Biafra Newsletter,* December 8, 1967. This article summarized a broadcast from the Voice of Biafra on November 16.

25. "Nigeria Becomes Soviet Satellite," *Biafra Newsletter*, December 8, 1967.

26. "Threat of Communist Takeover in Nigeria," *Biafra Newsletter*, March 1, 1968.

27. Madiebo, *The Nigerian Revolution and the Biafran War*, 381–82.

28. Doron, "Forging a Nation," 168.

29. "Convention on the Prevention and Punishment of the Crime of Genocide."

30. Among the many works that trace the events of 1968 around the world, perhaps the most accessible is Mark Kurlansky, *1968: The Year That Rocked the World* (New York: Random House, 2005).

31. All three wore pins in support of the Olympic Project for Human Rights, an organization that demanded the Olympic committee take a firmer stance against segregation in the United States and Apartheid in South Africa. Both Smith and Carlos went on to careers playing football in America. Norman was ostracized from the Australian athletics community, who refused to allow him to enter the 1972 Olympics despite the fact that he had qualified. He was also ignored during the celebrations for the Sydney Olympics in 2000. When he died in 2006, both Smith and Carlos were pallbearers at his funeral. The Australian government issued a formal apology to him and his family in 2012.

32. Though much of the literature on these events are in Polish, some English-language accounts exist. A brief English account exists in David Ost, *Solidarity and the Politics of Anti-Politics: Opposition and Reform in Poland since 1968* (Philadelphia: Temple University Press, 1991), 50–52.

33. Kieran Williams, *Prague Spring and Its Aftermath: Czechoslovak Politics, 1968–1970* (Cambridge,UK: Cambridge University Press, 2011), 42.

34. See Orobator, "The Nigerian Civil War."

35. "Nigeria's Civil War: Hate, Hunger and the Will to Survive," *Time*, August 23, 1968.

36. House of Commons, December 9, 1969. Cited in House of Commons Debates (HC Deb), 09 December 1969, v. 793, 328. After the war, it emerged that much of Cordle's advocacy for Nigeria had been enmeshed with corruption, as he became a major figure in the Poulson corruption scandal that forced his resignation. John Poulson, the architect at the center of the scandal, spent three years in prison for his role in bribing officials in the UK and abroad.

37. Open letter from H. Wm. Bernhardt to John Cordle, December 24, 1969.

38. Stremlau, *International Politics*, 116.

39. "Biafratoon," *Biafra Newsletter*, December 8, 1967.

40. Ibid.

41. Ibid.

42. "Genocide Is Their Aim," *Biafra Newsletter*, December 29, 1967.

43. "Genocide Is Their Aim."

44. "Genocide Is Their Aim."

45. "Address of His Excellency Lt. Col. Chukwuemeka Odumegwu Ojukwu, Head of State and Commander-in-Chief of the Armed Forces, Republic of Biafra,

to a Joint Meeting of the Consultative Assembly and Council of Chiefs held on Saturday, 27th of January, 1968," *Biafra* Newsletter, February 16, 1968, 9.

46. "Address of His Excellency," 14.

47. "Digging Up the Past? Yes!," *The Leopard,* May 31, 1968.

7. BIAFRA AND NIGERIA'S SECOND MILITARY COLLAPSE AND PEACE TALKS

1. Kogbara had a long history of involvement in Nigeria and Ogoni politics. He served as minister of industry in Ernest Shonekan's transitional government before Sani Abacha overthrew it in a coup. He narrowly escaped death in the murder the four Ogoni chiefs on May 21, 1994, the case that eventually led to Saro-Wiwa's judicial murder in 1995. He died in January 2002 in Port Harcourt after suffering a stroke.

2. Momoh, *The Nigerian Civil War,* 93.

3. Madiebo, *The Nigerian Revolution and the Biafran War,* 218.

4. Gould, "The Struggle for Modern Nigeria," 61–62. Gould's writing is based on interviews that he conducted with Achuzia and Maj. Gen. Julian Thompson, who stated that Achuzia's claims of a commission were not impossible but highly unlikely. Achuzia, oddly enough, did not touch on his early life in detail in his memoir, *Requiem Biafra.* Most of his boasts and claims came in the form of news interviews after the war. Achuzia's name is also sometimes alternatively spelled Achuzie. However, in virtually all interviews and in his memoirs, his name is spelled Achuzia, which is the spelling used in this volume.

5. Gould, "The Struggle for Modern Nigeria," 62.

6. Efiong, *Nigeria and Biafra: My Story,* 367.

7. Madiebo, *The Nigerian Revolution and the Biafran War,* 221.

8. Though some sources claim that Faulques fought in Biafra, there is no evidence to support that. His only role seemed to be to send men to Biafra to fight for the secessionists. There is no evidence that he was personally involved in the fighting in Biafra and no evidence that he even visited the country during the war.

9. Madiebo, *The Nigerian Revolution and the Biafran War,* 215–16.

10. Rolf Steiner and Yves-Guy Bergès, *The Last Adventurer,* 1st English language ed. (Boston: Little, Brown Boston, 1978).

11. Forsyth, *The Biafra Story,* 113.

12. Alternately spelled Goossens.

13. Claude Cookman, "Gilles Caron's Coverage of the Crisis in Biafra," *Visual Communication Quarterly* 15, no. 4 (2008): 239.

14. Achuzia, *Requiem Biafra,* 278; Forsyth's analysis of the mercenary impact on Biafra can be found in Forsyth, *The Biafra Story,* 112–14.

15. Madiebo, *The Nigerian Revolution and the Biafran War,* 223.

16. Ibid., 225.

17. Ibid., 228.

18. Achuzia, *Requiem Biafra*, 342.

19. Ibid., 343.

20. Ibid.

21. Madiebo, *The Nigerian Revolution and the Biafran War*, 229.

22. This operation is discussed in a later chapter.

23. Zdenek Červenka, *The Nigerian War, 1967–1970. History of the War; Selected Bibliography and Documents.* (Frankfurt am Main: Bernard & Graefe, 1971), 68.

24. Madiebo, *The Nigerian Revolution and the Biafran War*, 293.

25. Nicknamed Operation OAU, it is detailed in the next chapter.

26. The image can be accessed at https://www.worldpressphoto.org/collection/photo/1964/world-press-photo-year/don-mccullin.

27. Draper, *Shadows*.

28. PRO FCO 38/212.

29. "Arms for Nigeria; Approved: 1 June 1967—31 December 1967," "Arms for Nigeria; Approved: 1 January 1968—31 June 1968." PRO FCO 28/211.

30. "Arms," PRO FCO 28/211.

31. Memo from Johnson to Gowon. B. 96, LBJ Archives.

32. Proposed reply to Mayor Sam Yorty, March 28, 1968. B. 96, LBJ Archives.

33. Letter from Robert Schulman, May 3, 1968. B. 96, LBJ Archives.

34. Letter from Edward Riley, May 3, 1968. B. 96, LBJ Archives.

35. Letter from Bishop James Mathews (Boston Methodist Church), Rabbi Roland Gittelsohn, President Dana Greely of the Unitarian Universalist Organization, and Right Rev. Frederic T. Lawrence (Bishop of the Episcopal Church of Massachusetts), n.d. B. 96, LBJ Archives.

36. Letter from Conrad Brown, July 30, 1968. B. 96, LBJ Archives.

37. Letter from Simon Obi Anekwe to Ambassador Yitzhak Rabin, June 26, 1968.

38. Letter from the Biafran Students Association in the Americas to Consulate-General of Israel, New York, September 17, 1968.

39. Letter from Okey Anyadike to Yochanan Bein, Director Africa Dept., Israeli Foreign Ministry, April 14, 1968. 0009cin, Israel National Archives (INA).

40. Memo from Yochanan Bein, April 15, 1968. Translated by author. 000c9cs, INA.

41. Aside from sending search and rescue teams to earthquake sites, the Israeli government would not commit military personnel overseas again until 1994, when a similar medical team was dispatched to Rwanda.

42. Foreign Ministry Memo, n.d.001c9cs, INA.

43. Julius Nyerere speech, April 13, 1968. Cited in Godfrey Mwakikagile, *Nyerere and Africa, End of an Era* (Pretoria, South Africa: New Africa Press, 2007), 270.

44. Al J. Venter, *War Dog: Fighting Other Peoples' Wars* (Havertown, PA: Casemate, 2003), ix; Madiebo, *The Nigerian Revolution and the Biafran War*, 244–45.

45. As of 2021, Bonny still lacks a road link to the rest of Nigeria and is accessible only by river or small aircraft. Bonny has a small airstrip but neither it nor Opobo has reliable air travel. Italian company WeBuild, formerly called Salini Impregilo,

began constructing a road from Andoni to Opobo in 2005. They estimated completion in 2014, terrain issues and cost overruns meant the road is not completely open as of the writing of this book in 2023.

46. Madiebo, *The Nigerian Revolution and the Biafran War,* 248.

47. Achuzia, *Requiem Biafra,* 369.

48. Madiebo, *The Nigerian Revolution and the Biafran War,* 249.

49. Achuzia, *Requiem Biafra,* 448–49. SITREP is a British military term meaning situation report. It is generally a report on the current military situation in a given theater.

50. Ibid., 367–68.

51. Ibid., 368.

52. Ibid., 377–79.

53. Madiebo, *The Nigerian Revolution and the Biafran War,* 251.

54. They appear in Alabi-Isama, *The Tragedy of Victory,* 236–45. However, the plans and accompanying maps are unsourced. As the commander of the operation, Alabi-Isama had a major hand in planning the assault. Whether the maps and plans in his memoirs come from the Nigerian Military Archives, his own private collection, or memory is unclear.

55. The assault on Port Harcourt began on April 17, while Muhammed's division finally completed the conquest of Onitsha on March 21, having begun the assault the previous October with several catastrophic crossings of the Niger River.

56. Saro-Wiwa, *On a Darkling Plain.*

57. "Nightmare in Biafra," *Sunday Times.* London, April 26, 1968.

58. Alabi-Isama, *The Tragedy of Victory.*

59. Stremlau, *International Politics,* 165.

60. Ibid., 167.

61. Ibid.

62. Kirk-Greene, *Crisis and Conflict in Nigeria,* vol. 2, 217.

63. Stremlau, *International Politics,* 149.

64. Jimi Peters, *The Nigerian Military and the State,* Tauris Academic Studies, 1997, 118.

65. Ibid.

66. Kirk-Greene, *Crisis and Conflict in Nigeria,* vol. 2, 230.

67. Johnson Banjo was of no direct relation to Victor Banjo, who commanded Biafra's Liberation Army during the Midwest Offensive.

68. Stremlau, *International Politics,* 170–71.

69. Ibid., 173.

70. Ibid., 174.

71. Ibid.

72. Memo from Ed Hamilton, August 12, 1968; B. 96 D. 109, LBJ Archives.

73. He was US ambassador from 1960 to 1962, Soviet ambassador from 1966 to 1968, and scion to the famous chocolatier family.

74. Telegram from George Christian, August, 14, 1968; B. 96 D. 108a, LBJ Archives.

75. Doron, "Forging a Nation While Losing a Country," 191–92.

76. His father, Eric, founded the Swedish version of the Nazi Party, the Nationalsocialistiska Blocket, and his aunt Carin was wife to German Luftwaffe commander Hermann Göring. He had been accused of helping Göring loot Jewish assets and allegedly helped fly artwork and other Jewish valuables to Sweden. However, his wife fought in the Dutch resistance and was killed by the Nazis.

77. For a full account of Hammarskjold's death, see Williams, *Who Killed Hammarskjöld?*

78. Bush flying originated in the northern expanses of Canada and Alaska shortly after the First World War. It is still one of the most important ways of traversing remote, inhospitable expanses such as the Australian Outback with few amenities necessary for traditional flight operations.

79. Draper, *Shadows*, 125.

80. For a corrective on the logistics of the airlift, see Arua Oko Omaka, *Biafran Humanitarian Crisis, 1967–1970: International Human Rights and Joint Church Aid* (Vancouver, Canada: Fairleigh Dickinson University Press, 2018).

8. BIAFRA'S COLLAPSE AND REBIRTH

1. Madiebo gives his name as only Navy Captain Anuku. Others have called him Winifred or William Anuku. I go by the spelling of Wilfred, as that is the name in the most prominent naval memoir. See Odu, *The Future That Vanished*, 174; Madiebo, *The Nigerian Revolution and the Biafran War.*

2. Madiebo, *The Nigerian Revolution and the Biafran War*, 268.

3. Achuzia, *Requiem Biafra*, 453–54. Achuzia ends his narrative of the war after the fall of Port Harcourt with little explanation as to why he did not cover his subsequent escapades in Owerri and Oguta.

4. Alabi-Isama, *The Tragedy of Victory*, 338.

5. Ibid.

6. Madiebo, *The Nigerian Revolution and the Biafran War*, 259–60.

7. Ibid., 176.

8. Axel Harneit-Sievers, Jones O. Ahazuem, and Sydney Emezue, *A Social History of the Nigerian Civil War: Perspectives from Below* (Enugu, Nigeria: Jemezie, 1997), 97.

9. For most of 1967 and 1968, the Nigerian air force's MiG-17 fighter bombers were flown by Egyptian pilots, who were notoriously ill trained and limited to daylight bombing runs, making a return home at night a regular occurrence for those suffering the bombings.

10. One such example comes from Chief Z. C. Obi, a senator during the First Republic. After the war, his home at 24 Aggrey Road became the home of Ken Saro-Wiwa. In 1976, Obasanjo attempted some kind of restitution for properties

lost during the war, an act that incensed Saro-Wiwa. For a broader account of this incident, see Doron and Falola, *Ken Saro-Wiwa,* 63.

11. Dan Jacobs, *The Brutality of Nations* (New York: Paragon House, 1988), 238.

12. Harneit-Sievers, Ahazuem, and Emezue, *A Social History of the Nigerian Civil War,* 95.

13. Egodi Uchendu, *Women and Conflict in the Nigerian Civil War* (Trenton, NJ: Africa World Press, 2007), 141.

14. Odigwe A. Nwaokocha, "Remembering the Massacre of Civilians in Ani-omaland during the Nigerian Civil War," *Brazilian Journal of African Studies* 4, no. 7 (2019): 194; Uchendu, *Women and Conflict in the Nigerian Civil War,* 141.

15. For an in-depth discussion of the term and its meanings, see Harneit-Sievers, Ahazuem, and Emezue, *A Social History of the Nigerian Civil War,* 144–45.

16. Ibid., 139.

17. Uchendu, *Women and Conflict in the Nigerian Civil War*; Christie Achebe, "Igbo Women in the Nigerian-Biafran War 1967–1970: An Interplay of Control," *Journal of Black Studies* 40, no. 5 (2010): 785–811.

18. Harneit-Sievers, Ahazuem, and Emezue, *A Social History of the Nigerian Civil War,* 117.

19. Achebe, "Igbo Women in the Nigerian-Biafran War," 798–99.

20. Saro-Wiwa, *On a Darkling Plain,* 165.

21. Harneit-Sievers, Ahazuem, and Emezue, *A Social History of the Nigerian Civil War,* 151. Though the name Kpaberekpe has been cited in many publications from this source, I have not been able to determine its meaning.

22. Lloyd Garrison, "The 'Point of No Return' for the Biafrans," *New York Times,* June 8, 1968.

23. Alabi-Isama, *The Tragedy of Victory,* 340.

24. Sissons would report from Biafra until November 1968, when he was wounded covering the Nigerian offensive on Umuahia. He continued his reporting as ITN's news editor but did not return to the field.

25. Alabi-Isama, *The Tragedy of Victory,* 320.

26. "Nigerian Civil War: Battle for Biafra" (United Kingdom: ITN, 1968).

27. Madiebo, *The Nigerian Revolution and the Biafran War,* 263.

28. Both Alabi-Isama and Madiebo do not have any dates in their accounts of the battle. Sisson's reports are dated July 29, and the *New York Times* mentions the battle in two reports on July 29 and August 14.

29. Alabi-Isama, *The Tragedy of Victory,* 314.

30. "Some Progress in Biafran Peace Talks" (United Kingdom: ITN, 1968). All the videos have been accessed from Getty Images' website, and as such, the full citations may be incomplete, but they are viewable from the title alone on Getty's website.

31. "Nigerian Civil War: Battle for Biafra."

32. Alabi-Isama, *The Tragedy of Victory,* 314.

33. Madiebo, *The Nigerian Revolution and the Biafran War,* 265.

34. Alabi-Isama, *The Tragedy of Victory*, 315. He does not specify what piece it was, just that it was newly supplied and still being trained with. Most likely it was a 122mm 2A18 towed howitzer, which is still in use in Nigeria and was one of the main weapons used in the shelling of Kano during the Maitatsine revolt of 1980.

35. Momoh, *The Nigerian Civil War*, 173.

36. Alabi-Isama, *The Tragedy of Victory*, 323.

37. Madiebo, *The Nigerian Revolution and the Biafran War*, 268–69.

38. Ibid., 269–74. Details of Steiner's departure are outlined in the previous chapter.

39. Ibid., 299.

40. Efiong, *Nigeria and Biafra: My Story*, 334.

41. Madiebo, *The Nigerian Revolution and the Biafran War*, 272.

42. Ibid.; Alabi-Isama, *The Tragedy of Victory*.

43. See, among others, Efiong, *Nigeria and Biafra: My Story*, 213–14, 38; Anwunah, *The Nigeria-Biafra War (1967–1970): My Memoirs*, 188; Akpan, *The Struggle for Secession*, 98–100.

44. For a representation of this type of accusation, see Ihediwa Nkemjika Chimee, "The Nigerian-Biafran War, Armed Conflicts and the Rules of Engagement," in *Warfare, Ethnicity, and National Identity in Nigeria*, ed. Toyin Falola, Roy Doron, and Okpeh O. Okpeh (London: Africa World Press, 2013).

45. For the Soviets, forcing Czech pilots to fly for Nigeria was a way to assert control over the rogue Warsaw Pact member that attempted to relax the strict communist dictates from Moscow in what became known as the Prague Spring. For a detailed analysis, see Orobator, "The Nigerian Civil War."

46. Draper, *Shadows*, 86–89.

47. Madiebo, *The Nigerian Revolution and the Biafran War*, 275.

48. Alabi-Isama, *The Tragedy of Victory*, 348.

49. Ibid., 347.

50. Madiebo, *The Nigerian Revolution and the Biafran War*, 276.

51. Alabi-Isama, *The Tragedy of Victory*, 346–50.

52. Luke Nnaemeka Aneke, *The Untold Story of the Nigeria-Biafra War: A Chronological Reconstruction of the Events and Circumstances of the Nigerian Civil War* (New York: Triumph, 2007), 323. Nathan was a lifelong peace and humanitarian activist. In addition to his work in Biafra, he also flew mercy missions to Guatemala after a devastating 1976 earthquake that killed over twenty-three thousand people. He was repeatedly jailed in Israel and Egypt for his peace activism, which included attempted meetings with Egyptian officials in 1966 and a 1988 meeting with Palestinian leader Yasser Arafat. Nathan also invested much of his fortune in a radio station on board a ship that broadcast from international waters. Called the Voice of Peace, the station broadcast for twenty years, from 1973 until 1993, and was Israel's first unlicensed pirate radio station. Nathan died in 2008, after a series of strokes a decade earlier had left him paralyzed.

53. Smith, "The UK and 'Genocide' in Biafra"; Anthony Douglas, "'What Are They Observing?': The Accomplishments and Missed Opportunities of Observer Missions in the Nigerian Civil War," *Journal of African Military History* 2, no. 2 (2018).

54. For a representative example of this type of activist scholarship, see Chima J. Korieh, "History and the Politics of Memory: Introduction," in *The Nigeria-Biafra War: Genocide and the Politics of Memory*, ed. Chima J. Korieh (Amherst, NY: Cambria, 2012), 8–10.

55. See especially Douglas Anthony, "'Ours Is a War of Survival': Biafra, Nigeria and Arguments About Genocide, 1966–70," *Journal of Genocide Research* 16, no. 2/3 (2014): 219.

56. Alabi-Isama, *The Tragedy of Victory*; Momoh, *The Nigerian Civil War*.

57. Momoh, *The Nigerian Civil War*, 854–55.

58. For details about the process of Nigerianization, see Miners, *The Nigerian Army*; Siollun, *Oil, Politics and Violence*.

59. Momoh, *The Nigerian Civil War*, 702. After the war, Magoro would go on to be federal commissioner of transport under Obasanjo's military regime, and after the end of the Shagari government, Buhari appointed him as interior minister, where he orchestrated the deportation of nearly a million Ghanaians and other refugees in what became known as the "Ghana Must Go" operation. See "Nigeria: A Ragged Exodus of the Unwanted Once Again, Economic Woes Trigger the Mass Expulsion of Aliens," *TIME* 125, no. 20 (1985).

60. Madiebo, *The Nigerian Revolution and the Biafran War*, 286.

61. Ibid., 289–90.

62. Momoh, *The Nigerian Civil War*, 105.

63. Ibid.

64. Ibid., 79.

65. Madiebo, *The Nigerian Revolution and the Biafran War*, 293–94.

66. Ibid., 296.

67. Madiebo's account is the only one available for this operation, and his disdain for Achuzia has been well documented. As such, his evaluation of Achuzia's actions must be taken with caution, especially in cases when other versions of the operation do not exist.

68. Madiebo, *The Nigerian Revolution and the Biafran War*, 298–300.

69. Ibid., 304.

70. Alabi-Isama, *The Tragedy of Victory*, 356.

9. THE END (?) OF BIAFRA

1. Several works have examined the Land Army Scheme or Program. For fuller detail, see Achebe, "Igbo Women"; Chikwendu Christian Ukaegbu, "Lessons from Biafra: The Structuration of Socially Relevant Science in the Research and Production Directorate*," *Social Forces* 83, no. 4 (2005): 1395–423; Chima Korieh,

"The Nigeria-Biafra War, Oil and the Political Economy of State Induced Development Strategy in Eastern Nigeria 1967–1995," *Social Evolution and History* 17 (2018): 76–107.

2. Research Bureau Appraisal Committee, ed., *What Biafrans Know about the Nigeria/Biafra War* (Enugu (Aba), Nigeria: Appraisals Committee, Directorate for Propaganda, 1969), 35.

3. Ibid., 32.

4. Doron, "Forging a Nation While Losing a Country," 204–5.

5. Achebe, "Igbo Women"; Arua Oko Omaka, "The Forgotten Victims: Ethnic Minorities in the Nigeria-Biafra War, 1967–1970," *Journal of Retracing Africa* 1, no. 1 (2014), 5; Taiwo Bello, "'Your Offence Is That You By-Passed Us': Women, Violence and Agency in Biafra during the Nigeria-Biafra War, 1967–1970," *Gender & History* (2023), 9.

6. Eddie Iroh, *The Siren in the Night* (London: Heinemann, 2005); Nikolai Jeffs, "Ethnic 'Betrayal,' Mimicry, and Reinvention: The Representation of Ukpabi Asika in the Novel of the Nigerian-Biafran War," *LISA: Literature, History of Ideas, Images, and Societies of the English-SpeAking World* 10, no. 1 (2012): 280–306.

7. Efiong, *Nigeria and Biafra: My Story*, 272.

8. Chukwuemeka Odumegwu Ojukwu, *Ahiara Declaration: The Principles of Biafran Revolution* (Enugu, Nigeria: Biafra Information Service Corp., 1969).

9. Jago Morrison, "Imagined Biafras: Fabricating Nation in Nigerian Civil War Writing," *ARIEL* 36 (2005): 10.

10. Several Nigerian accounts, those of Mamman Jiya Vatsa and Mohammed Shuwa as well as a secondary account of the battle, appear in Momoh, *The Nigerian Civil War*. Madiebo dedicates several pages to the campaign in his memoir: Madiebo, *The Nigerian Revolution and the Biafran War*, 311–19.

11. Madiebo, *The Nigerian Revolution and the Biafran War*, 313.

12. The tactic is mentioned in several places, most notably in Momoh, *The Nigerian Civil War*, 903.

13. De St. Jorre, *The Brothers' War*, 211.

14. For a full treatment of France's support and abandonment of Biafra, see Christopher Griffin, "French Military Policy in the Nigerian Civil War, 1967–1970," *Small Wars & Insurgencies* 26, no. 1 (2015): 114–35.

15. De St. Jorre, *The Brother's War*, 211, 316.

16. Carl Gustav Von Rosen, "The Military Situation—an Overview," paper presented at the First International Conference on Biafra, Columbia University, December 7, 1968.

17. Equivalent to US$432,778 in 2020. Source: "CPI Inflation Calculator."

18. The pilots who joined von Rosen were the Swedes Martin Land and Gunnar Haglund and the Biafran air force pilots August Okpe and Willy Murray-Bruce, who had flown the Alouette helicopters earlier in the war.

19. Draper, *Shadows*, 225.

20. Though details are vague, Draper mentions that "Willy Bruce was still showing signs of 'battle stress'" in Ibid., 224.

21. Ibid., 227.

22. Ibid., 228–29.

23. Lloyd Garrison, "Swedish Count Describes Bombing Raids for Biafran Air Force," *New York Times*, 28 May 1969, 17.

24. "Reprieve for Eighteen," *Time*, June 13, 1969.

25. Roy Doron, "Biafra and the Agip Oil Workers: Ransoming and the Modern Nation State in Perspective," *African Economic History* 42 (2014): 149; Stremlau, *International Politics*, 333. Recent work by Arua Omaka challenges the existence of a ransom, citing denials by Biafran officials and the memoir by the head of Biafra's Civil Service, N. U. Akpan. Omaka emphasizes the recognition aspect and not the ransom as the main motive of Ojukwu's handling of the crisis. See Arua Oko Omaka, "The Nigerian Civil War and the 'Italian' Oil Workers," *War & Society* 38, no. 3 (2019): 208; Akpan, *The Struggle for Secession*, 22–23.

26. Achebe, *There Was a Country*, 220.

27. Stremlau, *International Politics*, 333–34; Draper, *Shadows*, 174–77.

28. Draper, *Shadows*, 177.

29. Equivalent to US$711 in 2020.

30. Forsyth, *The Biafra Story*, 222.

31. Obiozor, *The United States and the Nigerian Civil War*, 23–24. Alao would die several months later, as aforementioned.

32. R. W. Apple Jr., "Churchman Says Biafrans Face New Wave of Starvation Deaths," *New York Times*, June 29, 1969.

33. Marie-Luce Desgrandchamps, "'Organising the Unpredictable': The Nigeria-Biafra War and Its Impact on the Icrc," *International Review of the Red Cross* 94, no. 888 (2012): 1420.

34. Dan Dimancescu, "Red Cross Loses Its Grasp on Biafran Relief Efforts," *Boston Globe*, August 10, 1969.

35. For a complete treatment of the tensions the ICRC faced during the war, see Desgrandchamps, "Dealing with 'Genocide.'"

36. Paul Beran [pseud.], "Give Nigeria the Attention It Deserves," *Christian Science Monitor*, August 22, 1995. Abacha killed hundreds of his perceived enemies, both civilian and military, presiding over a summary execution of seventy military officers in March 1995 as well as dozens of petty criminals that same year. He ended 1995 with the execution of Ken Saro-Wiwa on November 10 after a widely condemned kangaroo court trial. Abacha's death from a heart attack has led to wild speculation that he was murdered, with some outlandish claims that Palestinian leader Yasser Arafat was working with Israeli security operatives to poison him or that he was poisoned by several prostitutes he was spending the night with. For

details, see Seun Opejobi, "Details of How Abacha Died in 1998—Al Mustapha," *Daily Post*, June 19, 2017; Tim Weiner, "U.S. Aides Say Nigeria Leader Might Have Been Poisoned," *New York Times*, July 11, 1998.

37. Alabi-Isama, *The Tragedy of Victory*, 409–10, 543–52.

38. Ibid., 567.

39. Obasanjo, *My Command*, 77.

40. Ibid., 79.

41. Madiebo, *The Nigerian Revolution and the Biafran War*, 342–48.

42. Ibid.

43. Siollun, *Oil, Politics and Violence*, 150.

44. Momoh, *The Nigerian Civil War*, 856. A kobo is the smallest denomination of Nigeria's currency, the naira. Though the naira and kobo were not in use until 1973, it has become a popular figure of speech in Nigeria today to denote the older subdivisions of the erstwhile Nigerian pound.

45. Doron, "Biafra and the Agip Oil Workers."

46. There is some confusion over the date that Bisalla and Jalo took over their respective commands. H. B. Momoh uses the same May 16, 1969 date that Obasanjo assumed command of the 3rd Marine Commando Division. This date conflicts with other literature on the war. According to Obasanjo, the appointments for the new divisional commands were all announced on May 12, 1969, and he took his command from Adekunle on May 16, the date that Momoh used to signify all transfer of power. However, Jalo did not take command of the 2nd division until June and by most accounts, including Shuwa, Siollun, and the Nigerian army's official chronology, Shuwa did not leave his command until September. I use the June and September dates as they seem much more likely given the war's general chronology.

47. Momoh, *The Nigerian Civil War*, 851.

48. Kirk-Greene, *Crisis and Conflict in Nigeria*, vol. 2, 415–16.

49. Ibid., 422.

50. Research & Publications Divisions Appraisal Committee, *A Critique of Propaganda Radio Programmes*, 27–28

51. Eric Pace, "Biafrans Shocked at Azikiwe's Views," *New York Times*, September 1, 1969.

52. Research & Publications Divisions Appraisal Committee, *A Critique of Propaganda Radio Programmes*, 27.

53. Stremlau, *International Politics*, 360.

54. Ben Gbulie, *The Fall of Biafra* (Enugu, Nigeria: Benlie, 1989), 109.

55. Madiebo, *The Nigerian Revolution and the Biafran War*, 357.

56. Gbulie, *The Fall of Biafra*, 146.

57. Madiebo, *The Nigerian Revolution and the Biafran War*, 358.

58. The British created marketing boards across their African colonies in an effort to stabilize prices and assist farmers and suppliers. However, many of these boards suppressed prices by preventing farmers from selling at market rates and,

instead of using the profits to aid local producers, used the revenue to loan money to colonial governments for infrastructure projects that the colony would then have to repay. For treatment of the cocoa boards in Nigeria and Ghana, see R. O. D. Alence, "Colonial Government, Social Conflict and State Involvement in Africa's Open Economies: The Origins of the Ghana Cocoa Marketing Board, 1939–46," *Journal of African History* 42, no. 3 (2001); Muojama Olisa Godson, "Cocoa Marketing Board and the Sustainable Cocoa Economy in Colonial Nigeria," *African Economic History* 47, no. 1 (2019): 1–31.

59. Toyin Falola and Akintunde Akinyemi, "Encyclopedia of the Yoruba," (Bloomington: Indiana University Press, 2016), 24–25; Tunde Adeniran, "The Dynamics of Peasant Revolt: A Conceptual Analysis of the Agbekoya Parapo Uprising in the Western State of Nigeria," *Journal of Black Studies* 4, no. 4 (1974): 363–75.

60. For a memoir on the author's participation in the revolt, see Toyin Falola, *Counting the Tiger's Teeth: An African Teenager's Story* (Ann Arbor: University of Michigan Press, 2016).

61. For the numbers, see Daniel Rothbart and Karina Korostelina, *Why They Die: Civilian Devastation in Violent Conflict* (Ann Arbor: University of Michigan Press, 2014), 18; Obasanjo's short account of the battle, including the ambush, can be found in Obasanjo, *My Command*, 71–72; for Alabi-Isama's commentary on Obasanjo's account, see Alabi-Isama, *The Tragedy of Victory*, 543–44.

62. Obasanjo, *My Command*.

63. Ibid., 82.

64. Randolph Baumann, "I Have to Kill the Ibos—Sorry!," *Stern*, August 18, 1968.

65. Obasanjo, *My Command*, 83.

66. Looting has been a constant concern in Nigerian military operations abroad. Nigerian peacekeepers in the Economic Community of West African States Monitoring Group (ECOMOG) mission to Liberia were so notorious for looting that a joke in country was that ECOMOG's true meaning was "Every Car or Moving Object Gone." For details, see Jennifer Ludden, "West African Peacekeepers Falter in Strife-Torn Liberia," *Christian Science Monitor*, May 22, 1996.

67. It is important to take many of Alabi-Isama's criticisms with skepticism, as he makes some disconcerting and inconceivable accusations against Obasanjo. In one instance, he accuses Obasanjo of purposely sending troops into harm's way, hoping for massive casualties so that he could pocket the dead soldiers' salaries. See Alabi-Isama, *The Tragedy of Victory*, 584–85.

68. Obasanjo, *My Command*, 89.

69. Madiebo, *The Nigerian Revolution and the Biafran War*; Obasanjo, *My Command*.

70. Alternately spelled Owasa in Obasanjo, *My Command*, 96, or Owazza in Madiebo, *The Nigerian Revolution and the Biafran War*, 332. The dates of this operation are somewhat unclear, though both Madiebo and Obasanjo discuss the same events in their respective sections; Obasanjo gives the date of July 15, or one day before he was to commence his operation in the area on July 16. Madiebo gives no

exact date for the operation but claims it took place in June 1969 as part of the rainy season offensives, mainly against the Nigerian 3rd Division. Regardless of the exact date, the battle took place during the crucial period when the Biafrans still had a sustainable offensive capacity and before Obasanjo was able to mount Operation Finishing Touch in October.

71. Madiebo, *The Nigerian Revolution and the Biafran War*, 330–41.

72. Ibid., 342.

73. Obasanjo, *My Command*, 97.

74. Department of State Telegram, "ICRC and Nigerian Relief," June 9, 1969; NARA RG 59, P 387, POL 27–9.

75. As with other operations, the dates are not accurately recorded in any of the sources, and the date I give is the most accurate based on the available news reports as well as cross-referencing dates at other battle zones to give a best estimate of the start of this operation.

76. Obasanjo, *My Command*, 100.

77. Momoh, *The Nigerian Civil War*, 108–9.

78. Obasanjo, *My Command*, 107.

79. Madiebo, *The Nigerian Revolution and the Biafran War*, 370.

80. Efiong, *Nigeria and Biafra: My Story*, 286.

81. Ibid., 290.

82. Kirk-Greene, *Crisis and Conflict in Nigeria*, vol. 2, 450.

83. Efiong, *Nigeria and Biafra: My Story*, 292.

84. Kirk-Greene, *Crisis and Conflict in Nigeria*, vol. 2, 451–51.

EPILOGUE

1. George Chimdi Mbara and Nirmala Gopal, "Peacebuilding Trajectories in Post-Conflict African States: A Re-Examination of The '3rs' In Post Nigeria-Biafra War," *African Journal of Peace and Conflict Studies* 10, no. 1 (2021): 16.

2. John Darnton, "Nigerians Fear New Revelations in Cement Scandal," *New York Times*, June 28, 1976.

3. The area on the western edge of Lagos, FESTAC Town, was originally the housing for the attendees and was later converted to housing for Lagos residents.

4. For accounts of the cement armada within the context of Nigerian politics, see Doron and Falola, *Ken Saro-Wiwa*; for an in-depth account of the business implications of the scandal, see Hanaan Marwah, "Untangling Government, Market, and Investment Failure during the Nigerian Oil Boom: The Cement Armada Scandal 1974–1980," *Business History* 62, no. 4 (2020): 566–87. For more on the culture of corruption in postwar Nigeria, see Childs Daly, *A History of the Republic of Biafra*.

5. Ebenezer Obadare. *Statism, Youth and Civic Imagination: A Critical Study of the National Youth Service Corps Programme in Nigeria*. (Dakar, Senegal, CODESRIA, 2010), 23.

6. Gowon did not return to Nigeria and instead moved to the United Kingdom, where he earned a doctorate in political science; he returned to Nigeria only in the 1980s, around the same time as his onetime adversary Ojukwu.

7. Momoh, *The Nigerian Civil War.*

8. "Boko Haram: Retired General, 40 Youths Killed in Renewed Violence," *The Nation* (Nigeria), last modified November 3, 2012, https://thenationonlineng.net/boko-haram-retired-general-40-youths-killed-in-renewed-violence.

9. Stephen Ellis, "West Africa's International Drug Trade," *African Affairs* 108, no. 431 (2009): 176.

10. Achebe, *There Was a Country,* 233.

11. Noo Saro-Wiwa, "There Was a Country: A Personal History of Biafra by Chinua Achebe—Review," *The Guardian,* October 5, 2012.

12. Moshood Kashimawo Olawale Abiola, nicknamed MKO, was the presumptive winner of the aborted June 12, 1993 elections in Nigeria. In the chaos that followed the election, Babangida stepped down from his role as head of state, and Sani Abacha took control of the government in a palace coup later that year. On June 11, 1994, Abiola declared himself the rightful winner of the election, and on June 23, Abacha's police arrested Abiola. He was never charged with a crime but was held in solitary confinement for over four years. He died on July 7, 1998, the morning of his release from prison, a fact that has spawned many conspiracy theories.

13. Sodiq Oyeleke, "Extradition: Nnamdi Kanu Files N25bn Suit against Fg," *Punch Nigeria,* March 25, 2022.

14. Ben Ezeamalu and Ruth Maclean, "More Than 1,800 Prisoners Are Broken Out of Jail in Nigeria," *New York Times,* April 6, 2021.

15. A prime example is the Abacha government's response to Ken Saro-Wiwa and the Ogoni movement. For a complete discussion of this, see Doron and Falola, *Ken Saro-Wiwa.*

16. Sarah Simpson, "General Strike over Rising Fuel Price Takes Hold in Nigerian Cities," *New York Times,* June 21, 2007.

17. Yemi Kale, *Nigerian Gross Domestic Product Report (Q2/2020)* (Abuja, Nigeria: National Bureau of Statistics, 2020); Kasirim Nwuke, *Nigeria's Petroleum Industry Act: Addressing Old Problems, Creating New Ones* (Washington, DC: Brookings Institution, 2021).

18. For a more complete discussion of the politics of oil and the government's crackdown on challenges, see Doron and Falola, *Ken Saro-Wiwa,* chapter 5; Ann Genova and Toyin Falola, "Oil in Nigeria: A Bibliographical Reconnaissance," *History in Africa* 30 (2003): 133–56.

19. Christopher Tuck, ""Every Car or Moving Object Gone": The Ecomog Intervention in Liberia," *African Studies Quarterly* 4, no. 1 (2000): 1–16; Herbert Howe, "Lessons of Liberia: Ecomog and Regional Peacekeeping," *International Security* 21, no. 3 (1996): 145–76.

20. Marie-Luce Desgrandchamps, "Revenir Sur Le Mythe Fondateur De Médecins Sans Frontières: Les Relations Entre Les Médecins Français Et Le Cicr Pendant La Guerre Du Biafra (1967–1970)," *Relations internationales* 146, no. 2 (2011): 95–108.

21. Desgrandchamps, "'Organising the Unpredictable'"; Marie-Luce Desgrandchamps et al., "Biafra, Humanitarian Intervention and History," *Journal of Humanitarian Affairs* 2, no. 2 (2020): 66–78; Desgrandchamps, "Dealing with 'Genocide.'"

22. Heerten, *The Biafran War and Postcolonial Humanitarianism*.

23. Karen Rothmyer, "What Really Happened in Biafra?," *Columbia Journalism Review* 9, no. 3 (1970): 43–47.

24. He naively first approached both Greenpeace and Amnesty International, and both told him his cause was not of interest to them. In fact Greenpeace, before 1990, did not work on the African continent at all, and Amnesty International was narrowly focused on "traditional" human rights violations and did not expand their mandate to include the kinds of problems that Saro-Wiwa embodied until after his imprisonment and execution. For more on how Saro-Wiwa penetrated the global consciousness, see Clifford Bob, *The Marketing of Rebellion: Insurgents, Media, and International Activism* (Cambridge, UK: Cambridge University Press, 2005), chapter 3; Clifford Bob, "Merchants of Morality," *Foreign Policy*, no. 129 (2002): 36–45; Doron and Falola, *Ken Saro-Wiwa*.

25. In the case of the Biafran war, many social, gendered, and recent legal histories minimize the ways the conflict has not only influenced but also driven the changes. See Harneit-Sievers, Ahazuem, and Emezue, *A Social History of the Nigerian Civil War*; Daly, *A History of the Republic of Biafra*.

26. Prunier, *Africa's World War*.

27. Draper, *Shadows*.

28. These tropes have long been part of the popular conception of Africa, and scholars have worked to dispel and correct them. Many classroom texts tackle these issues in creative ways. See Curtis A. Keim and Carolyn M. Somerville, *Mistaking Africa: Curiosities and Inventions of the American Mind* (New York: Routledge, 2019); Erik Reynolds Jonathan T. Gilbert, *Africa in World History: From Prehistory to the Present* (Boston: Pearson, 2012). But no attempts to deal with these issues has been more effective in its satire and humor than Binyavanga Wainaina, *How to Write about Africa* (Nairobi: Kwani Trust, 2006).

BIBLIOGRAPHY

ARCHIVAL SOURCES

British National Archives, Kew (PRO) Israel National Archives, Jerusalem (INA)
Lyndon Johnson Presidential Library Archives, Austin, TX (LBJ)
National Archives and Records Administration, College Park, MD (NARA)
Nigeria National Archives, Enugu (NNA-E)
Nigeria National Archives, Ibadan (NNA-I)
Nigerian Institute for International Affairs, Lagos (NIIA)

PUBLISHED SOURCES

Abayomi, Lekan. "Post-Colonial Nigeria: Did Igbos Draw First Blood?" NewsRescue.com. Last modified July 31, 2012. http://newsrescue.com/genesis-the-beginning-of-north-south-hausa-igbo-beef-in-nigeria.

Achebe, Chinua. *There Was a Country: A Personal History of Biafra*. New York: Penguin, 2012.

Achebe, Christie. "Igbo Women in the Nigerian-Biafran War 1967–1970: An Interplay of Control." *Journal of Black Studies* 40, no. 5 (2010): 785–811.

Achuzia, Joe O. G. *Requiem Biafra*. Enugu, Nigeria: Fourth Dimension, 1986.

———. *Requiem Biafra: The True Story of Nigeria's Civil War*. Asaba, Nigeria: Steel Equip Nigeria, 1993.

Ade Ajayi, J. F. "The Development of Secondary Grammar School Education in Nigeria," *Journal of the Historical Society of Nigeria* 2, no. 4 (1963): 517–35.

Adejo, Armstrong Matiu, ed. *The Nigerian Civil War: Forty Years After, What Lessons?* Makurdi, Nigeria: Aboki, 2008.

Adejumobi, Said, and Adewale Aderemi. "Oil and the Political Economy of the Nigerian Civil War and Its Aftermath." In *The Nigerian Civil War and Its Aftermath*, edited by Eghosa E. Osaghae, Ebere Onwudiwe, and Rotimi T. Suberu, 191–206. Ibadan, Nigeria: John Archers, 2002.

Adeleye, Rowland Aderemi. "The Dilemma of the Wazir: The Place of the Risat Al-Wazir 'Ila Ahl Al- Cilm Wa'l-Tadabbur in the History of the Conquest of the Sokoto Caliphate." *Journal of the Historical Society of Nigeria* 4, no. 2 (1968): 285–311.

Ademoyega, Adewale. *Why We Struck: The Story of the First Nigerian Coup*. Ibadan, Nigeria: Evans Bros., 1981.

Adeniran, Tunde. "The Dynamics of Peasant Revolt: A Conceptual Analysis of the Agbekoya Parapo Uprising in the Western State of Nigeria." *Journal of Black Studies* 4, no. 4 (1974): 363–75.

Afigbo, A. E. "The Aro Expedition of 1901–1902 (an Episode in the British Occupation of Iboland)." *Odù: Journal of Yoruba and Related Studies*, no. 7 (1972): 3–27.

———. "The Calabar Mission and the Aro Expedition of 1901–1902." *Journal of Religion in Africa* 5, no. 2 (January 1, 1973): 94–106.

———. "Traditions of Igbo Origins: A Comment." *History in Africa* 10 (1983): 1–11.

Akinjogbin, I. A. *War and Peace in Yorubaland, 1793–1893*. Ibadan, Nigeria: Heinemann Educational Books, 1998.

Akinyemi, A. B. "The British Press and the Nigerian Civil War." *African Affairs* 71, no. 285 (1972): 408–26.

Akpan, Ntieyong Udo. *The Struggle for Secession, 1966–1970: A Personal Account of the Nigerian Civil War.* London: F. Cass, 1972.

Alabi-Isama, Godwin. *The Tragedy of Victory: On-the-Spot Account of the Nigeria-Biafra War in the Atlantic Theatre*. Ibadan, Nigeria: Spectrum, 2013.

Alence, R. O. D. "Colonial Government, Social Conflict and State Involvement in Africa's Open Economies: The Origins of the Ghana Cocoa Marketing Board, 1939–46." *Journal of African History* 42, no. 3 (2001): 397–416.

Alexander, Boyd, Percy Amaury Talbot, and Arnold Edward. *From the Niger to the Nile*. London: Edward Arnold, 1907.

Aneke, Luke Nnaemeka. *The Untold Story of the Nigeria-Biafra War: A Chronological Reconstruction of the Events and Circumstances of the Nigerian Civil War.* New York: Triumph, 2007.

Anthony, Douglas. "'Ours Is a War of Survival': Biafra, Nigeria and Arguments about Genocide, 1966–70." *Journal of Genocide Research* 16, no. 2/3 (2014): 205–25.

———. "'Resourceful and Progressive Blackmen': Modernity and Race in Biafra, 1967–70." *Journal of African History* 51, no. 1 (2010): 41–61.

———. "'What Are They Observing?': The Accomplishments and Missed Opportunities of Observer Missions in the Nigerian Civil War." *Journal of African Military History* 2, no. 2 (October 24, 2018): 87–118.

Anthony, Douglas A. *Poison and Medicine: Ethnicity, Power, and Violence in a Nigerian City, 1966 to 1986*. Portsmouth, NH: Heinemann, 2002.

Anwunah, Patrick A. *The Nigeria-Biafra War (1967–1970): My Memoirs*. Ibadan, Nigeria: Spectrum, 2007.

Awa, E. O. "Federal Elections in Nigeria, 1959." *Indian Journal of Political Science* 21, no. 2 (1960): 101–13.

Awolowo, Obafemi. *Path to Nigerian Freedom*. London: Faber and Faber, 1947.

Ayoade, John A. A. "Party and Ideology in Nigeria: A Case Study of the Action Group." *Journal of Black Studies* 16, no. 2 (1985): 169–88.

Basden, George Thomas. *Among the Ibos of Nigeria: An Account of the Curious & Interesting Habits, Customs & Beliefs of a Little Known African People by One Who Has for Many Years Lived amongst Them on Close & Intimate Terms*. London: Cass, 1966.

Bello, Taiwo. "'Your Offence Is That You by-Passed Us': Women, Violence and Agency in Biafra during the Nigeria–Biafra War, 1967–1970." *Gender & History* (2023): 1–15

Bersselaar, Dmitri van den. "Missionary Knowledge and the State in Colonial Nigeria: On How G. T. Basden Became an Expert." *History in Africa* 33 (2006): 433–50.

Bird, S. Elizabeth, and Fraser Ottanelli. "The History and Legacy of the Asaba, Nigeria, Massacres." *African Studies Review* 54, no. 3 (2011): 1–26.

Bird, S. Elizabeth, and Fraser M. Ottanelli. *The Asaba Massacre: Trauma, Memory, and the Nigerian Civil War*. Cambridge, UK: Cambridge University Press, 2017.

Bob, Clifford. "Merchants of Morality." *Foreign Policy*, no. 129 (2002): 36–45.

———. *The Marketing of Rebellion: Insurgents, Media, and International Activism*. Cambridge, UK: Cambridge University Press, 2005.

Boro, Isaac Jasper Adaka, and Anthony Odogboro Tebekaemi. *The Twelve-Day Revolution*. Benin City, Nigeria: Idodo Umeh, 1982.

Bourne, Richard. *Nigeria: A New History of a Turbulent Century*. London: Zed, 2015.

Bovill, Mai, and George Rankin Askwith Askwith. *Roddy Owen; Brevet-Major Lancashire Fusiliers, D.S.O.: A Memoir*. London: J. Murray, 1897.

Calmettes, Joel. "The Secret History of Biafra." 54 minutes. Paris: Point du Jour International, 2001.

Carland, John M. *The Colonial Office and Nigeria, 1898–1914*. Stanford, CA: Hoover Institution Press, 1985.

Červenka, Zdenek. *A History of the Nigerian War, 1967–1970*. Ibadan, Nigeria: Onibonoje, 1972.

———. *The Nigerian War, 1967–1970. History of the War; Selected Bibliography and Documents*. Frankfurt am Main: Bernard & Graefe, 1971.

Childs Daly, Samuel Fury. "The Case against Victor Banjo: Legal Process and the Governance of Biafra." In *Postcolonial Conflict and the Question of Genocide: The Nigeria-Biafra War 1967–1970*, edited by Dirk Moses and Lasse Heerten, 95–112. New York: Routledge, 2017.

———. *A History of the Republic of Biafra: Law, Crime, and the Nigerian Civil War*. Cambridge, UK: Cambridge University Press, 2020.

Chimee, Ihediwa Nkemjika. "The Nigerian-Biafran War, Armed Conflicts and the Rules of Engagement." In *Warfare, Ethnicity, and National Identity in Nigeria*, edited by Toyin Falola, Roy Doron, and Okpeh O. Okpeh, 111–37. London: Africa World Press, 2013.

Coker, Increase Herbert Ebenezer. *Landmarks of the Nigerian Press: An Outline of the Origins and Development of the Newspaper Press in Nigeria, 1859 to 1965*. [Place of publication not identified]: [Publisher not identified], 1968.

Coleman, James Smoot. *Nigeria: Background to Nationalism*. Berkeley: University of California Press, 1958.

"Convention on the Prevention and Punishment of the Crime of Genocide." United Nations Treaty Collection. https://treaties.un.org/doc/Publication/UNTS/Volume%2078/volume-78-I-1021-English.pdf.

Cookey, S. J. S. *King Jaja of the Niger Delta: His Life and Times, 1821–1891*. New York, NY: NOK, 1974.

———. "Sir Hugh Clifford as Governor of Nigeria: An Evaluation." *African Affairs* 79, no. 317 (1980): 531–47.

Cookman, Claude. "Gilles Caron's Coverage of the Crisis in Biafra." *Visual Communication Quarterly* 15, no. 4 (2008): 226–42.

Crowder, Michael. *The Story of Nigeria*. London: Faber, 1978.

Daly, Samuel Fury Childs. *A History of the Republic of Biafra: Law, Crime, and the Nigerian Civil War*. Cambridge, UK: Cambridge University Press, 2020.

Daminabo, Amayanabo O. *Ken Saro-Wiwa, 1941–1995: His Life & Legacies*. Buguma, Nigeria: Hanging Gardens, 2005.

Darnton, John. "Nigerians Fear New Revelations in Cement Scandal." *New York Times*, June 28, 1976, 6.

Department of Economic and Social Affairs, ed. *2014 United Nations Demographic Yearbook*. New York: United Nations, 2015.

De St. Jorre, John. *The Brothers' War: Biafra and Nigeria*. Boston: Houghton Mifflin, 1972.

Desgrandchamps, Marie-Luce. "Dealing with 'Genocide': The ICRC and the Un during the Nigeria–Biafra War, 1967–70." *Journal of Genocide Research* 16, no. 2–3 (2014): 281–97.

———. "'Organising the Unpredictable': The Nigeria-Biafra War and Its Impact on the ICRC." *International Review of the Red Cross* 94, no. 888 (2012): 1409–32.

———. "Revenir Sur Le Mythe Fondateur De Médecins Sans Frontières: Les Relations Entre Les Médecins Français Et Le Cicr Pendant La Guerre Du Biafra (1967–1970)." *Relations internationales* 146, no. 2 (2011): 95–108.

Desgrandchamps, Marie-Luce, Lasse Heerten, Arua Oko Omaka, Kevin O'Sullivan, and Bertrand Taithe. "Biafra, Humanitarian Intervention and History." *Journal of Humanitarian Affairs* 2, no. 2 (May 1, 2020): 66–78.

Diamond, Larry Jay. *Class, Ethnicity, and Democracy in Nigeria: The Failure of the First Republic*. Syracuse, NY: Syracuse University Press, 1988.

Dictionary of the Hausa Language. London: Cambridge University Press, 1913.

Dike, K. Onwuka. *Trade and Politics in the Niger Delta, 1830–1885: An Introduction to the Economic and Political History of Nigeria*. Oxford, UK: Clarendon Press, 1956.

Dimancescu, Dan. "Red Cross Loses Its Grasp on Biafran Relief Efforts." *Boston Globe*, August 10, 1969.

Docherty, Paddy. *Blood and Bronze: The British Empire and the Sack of Benin*. Oxford, UK: C. Hurst, 2022.

Doron, Roy. "Biafra and the AGIP Oil Workers: Ransoming and the Modern Nation State in Perspective." *African Economic History* 42 (2014): 137–56.

———. "Forging a Nation While Losing a Country: Igbo Nationalism, Ethnicity and Propaganda in the Nigerian Civil War 1968–1970." PhD diss. University of Texas, 2011.

———. "Marketing Genocide: Biafran Propaganda Strategies During the Nigerian Civil War, 1967–70." *Journal of Genocide Research* 16, no. 2/3 (2014): 227–46.

———. "Ojukwu, Chukwuemeka Odumegwu." In *Dictionary of African Biography*, edited by Henry Louis Gates and Emmanuel K. Akyeampong. New York: Oxford University Press, 2012.

Doron, Roy, and Toyin Falola. *Ken Saro-Wiwa*. Athens: Ohio University Press, 2016.

Douglas, Anthony. "'What Are They Observing?': The Accomplishments and Missed Opportunities of Observer Missions in the Nigerian Civil War." *Journal of African Military History* 2, no. 2 (October 24, 2018): 87–118.

Draper, Michael I. *Shadows: Airlift and Airwar in Biafra and Nigeria, 1967–1970*. Aldershot, Hants, UK: Hikoki, 1999.

Dudley, Billy J. *An Introduction to Nigerian Government and Politics*. Bloomington: Indiana University Press, 1982.

Information Ministry of Eastern Nigeria and Division Publicity. *Nigerian Pogrom: The Organized Massacre of Eastern Nigerians*. Enugu, Nigeria: Publicity Division of the Ministry of Information, Eastern Nigeria, 1966.

Efiong, Philip. *Nigeria and Biafra: My Story*. Princeton, NJ: Sungai, 2003.

Ejoor, David Akpode. *Reminiscences*. Lagos, Nigeria: Malthouse, 1989.

Ellis, Stephen. "West Africa's International Drug Trade." *African Affairs* 108, no. 431 (2009): 171–96.

Equiano, Olaudah. *The Interesting Narrative of the Life of Olaudah Equiano*. Project Gutenberg), https://www.gutenberg.org/files/15399/15399-h/15399-.

European Court of Human Rights, ed. *European Convention on Human Rights*. Strasbourg, France: European Court of Human Rights, 1950.

Ezeamalu, Ben, and Ruth Maclean. "More Than 1,800 Prisoners Are Broken Out of Jail in Nigeria." *New York Times*, April 6, 2021.

Ezenwa-Ohaeto. *Chinua Achebe: A Biography*. Bloomington: Indiana University Press, 1997.

Falola, Toyin. *Colonialism and Violence in Nigeria*. Bloomington: Indiana University Press, 2009.

———. *Counting the Tiger's Teeth: An African Teenager's Story*. Ann Arbor: University of Michigan Press, 2016.

———. *Development Planning and Decolonization in Nigeria*. Gainesville: University Press of Florida, 1996.

Falola, Toyin, and Adam Paddock. *The Women's War of 1929: A History of Anti-Colonial Resistance in Eastern Nigeria.* Durham, NC: Carolina Academic Press, 2011.

Falola, Toyin, and Akintunde Akinyemi. "Encyclopedia of the Yoruba." Bloomington: Indiana University Press, 2016.

Falola, Toyin, and Matthew M. Heaton. *A History of Nigeria.* Cambridge, UK: Cambridge University Press, 2008.

"Fight for Fatherland!" *Spectator,* August 1967.

Fleming, Tyler, and Toyin Falola. "Africa's Media Empire: 'Drum''s Expansion to Nigeria." *History in Africa* 32 (2005): 133–64.

Forsyth, Frederick. *Emeka.* Ibadan, Nigeria: Spectrum, 1982.

———. *The Biafra Story: The Making of an African Legend.* London: Leo Cooper, 2001.

Friendly Jr., Alfred. "Nigeria Detains Playwright after Cease-Fire Plea." *New York Times,* September 2, 1967, 3.

———. "Nigerians Order a Step-up in War." *New York Times,* August 12, 1967, 7.

Gailey, Harry A. *Lugard and the Abeokuta Uprising: The Demise of Egba Independence.* London: F. Cass, 1982.

Garrison, Lloyd. "Swedish Count Describes Bombing Raids for Biafran Air Force." *New York Times,* May 28, 1969, 17.

Gbulie, Ben. *Nigeria's Five Majors: Coup D'état of 15th January 1966, First inside Account.* Onitsha, Nigeria: Africana Educational Publishers, 1981.

———. *The Fall of Biafra.* Enugu, Nigeria: Benlie, 1989.

Genova, Ann, and Toyin Falola. "Oil in Nigeria: A Bibliographical Reconnaissance." *History in Africa* 30 (2003): 133–56.

Gilbert, Erik Reynolds Jonathan T. *Africa in World History: From Prehistory to the Present.* Boston: Pearson, 2012.

Gould, Michael. *The Struggle for Modern Nigeria: The Biafran War, 1967–1970.* London and New York, NY: I. B. Tauris, 2012.

Griffin, Christopher. "French Military Policy in the Nigerian Civil War, 1967–1970." *Small Wars & Insurgencies* 26, no. 1 (January 2, 2015): 114–35.

Hancock, Ian. "The Buganda Crisis of 1964." *African Affairs* 69, no. 275 (1970): 109–23.

Harneit-Sievers, Axel. *Constructions of Belonging: Igbo Communities and the Nigerian State in the Twentieth Century.* Rochester, NY: University of Rochester Press, 2006.

Harneit-Sievers, Axel, Jones O. Ahazuem, and Sydney Emezue. *A Social History of the Nigerian Civil War: Perspectives from Below.* Enugu, Nigeria: Jemezie, 1997.

Haruna, Ibrahim. "The Nigerian Civil War—Causes and Courses." Paper presented at the Nigerian Warfare through the Ages, Umuahia, Nigeria, 1985.

Heerten, Lasse. *The Biafran War and Postcolonial Humanitarianism: Spectacles of Suffering.* Cambridge, UK: Cambridge University Press, 2018.

Howe, Herbert. "Lessons of Liberia: Ecomog and Regional Peacekeeping." *International Security* 21, no. 3 (1996): 145–76.

Howe, Peter. *Shooting under Fire: The World of the War Photographer.* New York: Artisan, 2002.

Iroh, Eddie. *The Siren in the Night*. London: Heinemann, 2005.

Jacobs, Dan. *The Brutality of Nations*. New York: Paragon House, 1988.

January 15, Before and After. Nigerian Crisis 1966. Vol. 7. Enugu, Nigeria: Printed by the Government Printer, 1967.

Jeffs, Nikolai. "Ethnic 'Betrayal,' Mimicry, and Reinvention: The Representation of Ukpabi Asika in the Novel of the Nigerian-Biafran War." *LISA: Literature, History of Ideas, Images, and Societies of the English-SpeAking World* 10, no. 1 (2012): 280–306.

Jeyifo, Biodun. "Ogbeni's Victory; Omisore's Defeat: The 1965 Western Region Election Revisited." *The Nation*, August 17, 2014.

Kale, Yemi. "Nigerian Gross Domestic Product Report (Q2/2020)." Abuja, Nigeria: National Bureau of Statistics, 2020.

Keim, Curtis A., and Carolyn M. Somerville. *Mistaking Africa: Curiosities and Inventions of the American Mind*. New York: Routledge, 2019.

Killingray, David, and Martin Plaut. *Fighting for Britain: African Soldiers in the Second World War*. Woodbridge, UK and Rochester, NY: Boydell & Brewer, 2010.

Kirk-Greene, A. H. M. *Crisis and Conflict in Nigeria: A Documentary Sourcebook*. London: Oxford University Press, 1971.

Korieh, Chima. "The Nigeria-Biafra War, Oil and the Political Economy of State Induced Development Strategy in Eastern Nigeria 1967–1995." *Social Evolution and History* 17 (2018): 76–107.

Korieh, Chima J. "History and the Politics of Memory: Introduction." In *The Nigeria-Biafra War: Genocide and the Politics of Memory*, edited by Chima J. Korieh, 1–39. Amherst, NY: Cambria, 2012.

Kurlansky, Mark. *1968: The Year That Rocked the World*. New York: Random House, 2005.

Levey, Zach. "Israel, Nigeria and the Biafra Civil War, 1967–70." *Journal of Genocide Research* 16, no. 2–3 (July 3, 2014): 263–80.

Lewis, Roy. "Britain and Biafra." *Round Table* 60, no. 239 (1970): 241–48.

Lovejoy, Paul E. "Nigeria: The Ibadan School and Its Critics." In *African Historiographies: What History for Which Africa?*, edited by Bogumil Jewsiewicki and Davis S. Newbury. New York: SAGE, 1985.

Ludden, Jennifer. "West African Peacekeepers Falter in Strife-Torn Liberia." *Christian Science Monitor*, May 22, 1996.

Lugard, Frederick D. *The Dual Mandate in British Tropical Africa*. Edinburgh, Scotland: W. Blackwood and Sons, 1922.

Mackintosh, John P. "Politics in Nigeria: The Action Group Crisis of 1962." *Political Studies* 11, no. 2 (1963): 126–55.

———. "The Struggle for Power in Nigeria." *Transition* no. 22 (1965): 21–25.

Macpherson, John. "Sovereign Nigeria." *Journal of the Royal Society of Arts* 109, no. 5059 (1961): 527–40.

Madiebo, Alexander A. *The Nigerian Revolution and the Biafran War*. Enugu, Nigeria: Fourth Dimension, 1980.

Mainasara, A. M. *The Five Majors: Why They Struck*. Zaria, Nigeria: Hudahuda, 1982.

Makinde, Adeyinka. *Dick Tiger: The Life and Times of a Boxing Immortal.* Tarentum, PA: Word Association, 2004.

Martinez, Jenny S. *The Slave Trade and the Origins of International Human Rights Law.* New York: Oxford University Press, 2012.

Marwah, Hanaan. "Untangling Government, Market, and Investment Failure during the Nigerian Oil Boom: The Cement Armada Scandal 1974–1980." *Business History* 62, no. 4 (2020): 566–87.

"Nigeria: Massacre in Kano." *Time*, October 14, 1966.

Mazrui, Ali A. "Violent Contiguity and the Politics of Retribalization in Africa." *Journal of International Affairs* 23, no. 1 (1969): 89–105.

Mbara, George Chimdi, and Nirmala Gopal. "Peacebuilding Trajectories in Post-Conflict African States: A Re-examination of the '3rs' In Post Nigeria-Biafra War." *African Journal of Peace and Conflict Studies* 10, no. 1 (April 2021): 9–32.

McNeil, Brian. "'And Starvation Is the Grim Reaper': The American Committee to Keep Biafra Alive and the Genocide Question During the Nigerian Civil War, 1968–70." *Journal of Genocide Research* 16, no. 2–3 (2014): 317–36.

Miners, Norman. *The Nigerian Army, 1956–66.* London: Methuen, 1971.

Momoh, H. B. *The Nigerian Civil War, 1967–1970: History and Reminiscences.* Ibadan, Nigeria: Sam Bookman, 2000.

Morrison, Jago. "Imagined Biafras: Fabricating Nation in Nigerian Civil War Writing." *ARIEL* 36 (January 2005–April 2005): 5+.

Moyd, Michelle. "African Military Historiography." *War & Society* (2022): 1–10.

———. *Violent Intermediaries: African Soldiers, Conquest, and Everyday Colonialism in German East Africa.* Athens: Ohio University Press, 2014.

Muffett, D. J. M. *Concerning Brave Captains: Being a History of the British Occupation of Kano and Sokoto and of the Last Stand of the Fulani Forces.* London: A. Deutsch, 1964.

Mwakikagile, Godfrey. *Nyerere and Africa, End of an Era.* Pretoria, South Africa: New Africa Press, 2007.

Nafziger, E. Wayne, and William L. Richter. "Biafra and Bangladesh: The Political Economy of Secessionist Conflict." *Journal of Peace Research* 13, no. 2 (1976): 91–109.

"Nigeria: A Ragged Exodus of the Unwanted Once Again, Economic Woes Trigger the Mass Expulsion of Aliens." *Time*, May 20, 1985.

"Nigerian Civil War: Battle for Biafra." 00:04:05. United Kingdom: ITN, 1968.

"Nigerians Hold Ship as Blockade Runner." *New York Times*, July 5, 1967.

Nigeria. *Report on the O.A.U. Consultative Mission to Nigeria.* Apapa, Nigeria: Nigerian National Press, 1968.

"Nigeria's Split Creates Oil Dilemma." *New York Times*, June 30, 1967.

Nohlen, Dieter, Michael Krennerich, and Bernhard Thibaut. *Elections in Africa: A Data Handbook.* Oxford, UK: Oxford University Press, 1999.

Nwaokocha, Odigwe A. "Remembering the Massacre of Civilians in Aniomaland during the Nigerian Civil War." *Brazilian Journal of African Studies* 4, no. 7 (2019): 189–208.

Nwuke, Kasirim. "Nigeria's Petroleum Industry Act: Addressing Old Problems, Creating New Ones." Washington, DC: Brookings Institution, 2021.

Obadare, Ebenezer. *Statism, Youth and Civic Imagination: A Critical Study of the National Youth Service Corps Programme in Nigeria*. Dakar, Senegal: CODESRIA, 2010.

Obasanjo, Olusegun. *My Command: An Account of the Nigerian Civil War, 1967–1970*. London: Heinemann, 1981.

———. *Nzeogwu: An Intimate Portrait of Major Chukwuma Kaduna Nzeogwu*. Ibadan, Nigeria: Spectrum, 1987.

Obiozor, George A. *The United States and the Nigerian Civil War: An American Dilemma in Africa, 1966–1970*. Lagos: Nigerian Institute of International Affairs, 1993.

Odu, P. J. *The Future That Vanished: A Biafra Story*. United States: Xlibris, 2009.

Ogbudinkpa, Nwabeze Reuben. *The Economics of the Nigerian Civil War and Its Prospects for National Development*. Enugu, Nigeria: Fourth Dimension, 1985.

Ogunsheye, F. Adetowun. *A Break in the Silence: A Historical Note on Lt. Colonel Victor Adebukunola Banjo*. Ibadan, Nigeria: Spectrum, 2001.

Ojeleye, Olukunle. *The Politics of Post-War Demobilisation and Reintegration in Nigeria*. London: Taylor & Francis, 2016.

Ojo, Emmanuel Oladipo. "Minority Groups: Bridgeheads in Nigerian Politics, 1950s - 1964." *Turkish Journal of Politics* 3, no. 2 (2012): 53–66.

Ojukwu, Chukwuemeka Odumegwu. *Ahiara Declaration: The Principles of Biafran Revolution*. Enugu, Nigeria: Biafra Information Service Corp., 1969.

Okocha, Emma. *Blood on the Niger: An Untold Story of the Asaba Massacre in the Nigerian Civil War*. Lagos, Nigeria: SUNRAY, 1994.

Olisa Godson, Muojama. "Cocoa Marketing Board and the Sustainable Cocoa Economy in Colonial Nigeria." *African Economic History* 47, no. 1 (2019): 1–31.

Olorunfemi, A. "Effects of War-Time Trade Controls on Nigerian Cocoa Traders and Producers, 1939–45: A Case-Study of the Hazards of a Dependent Economy." *International Journal of African Historical Studies* 13, no. 4 (1980): 672–87.

Omaka, Arua Oko. *Biafran Humanitarian Crisis, 1967–1970: International Human Rights and Joint Church Aid*. Vancouver, Canada: Fairleigh Dickinson University Press, 2018.

———. "The Forgotten Victims: Ethnic Minorities in the Nigeria-Biafra War, 1967–1970." *Journal of Retracing Africa* 1, no. 1 (2014): 25–40.

———. "The Nigerian Civil War and the 'Italian' Oil Workers." *War & Society* 38, no. 3 (July 3, 2019): 203–24.

Onyegbula, Godwin Alaoma. *Memoirs of the Nigerian-Biafran Bureaucrat: An Account of Life in Biafra and within Nigeria*. Ibadan, Nigeria: Spectrum, 2005.

Opejobi, Seun. "Details of How Abacha Died in 1998—Al Mustapha." *Daily Post*, June 19, 2017.

Orobator, S. E. "Nigeria: From Separatism to Secession 1950–1970." *Africa: Rivista trimestrale di studi e documentazione dell'Istituto italiano per l'Africa e l'Oriente* 42, no. 2 (1987): 301–14.

———. "The Nigerian Civil War and the Invasion of Czechoslovakia." *African Affairs* 82, no. 327 (1983): 201–14.

Osaghae, Eghosa E. *Crippled Giant: Nigeria since Independence*. Bloomington: Indiana University Press, 1998.

Ost, David. *Solidarity and the Politics of Anti-Politics: Opposition and Reform in Poland since 1968*. Philadelphia: Temple University Press, 1991.

O'Sullivan, Kevin. "Humanitarian Encounters: Biafra, Ngos and Imaginings of the Third World in Britain and Ireland, 1967–70." *Journal of Genocide Research* 16, no. 2–3 (2014): 299–315.

Ottah, Nelson. *Rebels against Rebels*. Ikeja, Nigeria: Manson, 1981.

Oyeleke, Sodiq. "Extradition: Nnamdi Kanu Files N25bn Suit against Fg." *Punch Nigeria*, March 25, 2022.

Peters, Jimi. *The Nigerian Military and the State*. London: Tauris Academic Studies, 1997.

Porter, Bruce D. *The USSR in Third World Conflicts: Soviet Arms and Diplomacy in Local Wars, 1945–1980*. Cambridge, UK: Cambridge University Press, 1984.

Prunier, Gérard. *Africa's World War: Congo, the Rwandan Genocide, and the Making of a Continental Catastrophe*. New York: Oxford University Press, 2012.

Raji, A. O. Y., and T. S. Abejide. "Oil and Biafra: An Assessment of Shell-BP's Dilemma during the Nigerian Civil War, 1967–1970." *Kuwait Chapter of the Arabian Journal of Business and Management Review* 2, no. 11 (July 2013): 15–32.

Rake, Alan. "Nigeria after Elections: What Happened?" *Africa Today* 12, no. 1 (1965): 5–12.

"Reprieve for Eighteen." *Time*, June 13, 1969, 46.

Research & Publications Divisions Appraisal Committee, ed. *A Critique of Propaganda Radio Programmes*. Enugu (Aba), Nigeria: Ministry of Information, 1969.

Research Bureau Appraisal Committee, ed. *Guide Lines for Effective Propaganda*. Aba, Nigeria: Directorate for Propaganda, 1968.

Research Bureau Appraisal Committee, ed. "What Biafrans Know about the Nigeria/Biafra War." Enugu (Aba), Nigeria: Appraisals Committee, Directorate for Propaganda, 1969.

Robins, Jonathan E. *Oil Palm: A Global History*. Chapel Hill: University of North Carolina Press, 2021. https://doi.org/10.5149/northcarolina/9781469662893.001.0001.

Rothbart, Daniel, and Karina Korostelina. *Why They Die: Civilian Devastation in Violent Conflict*. Ann Arbor: University of Michigan Press, 2014.

Rothmyer, Karen. "What Really Happened in Biafra?" *Columbia Journalism Review* 9, no. 3 (Fall 1970): 43–47.

Saro-Wiwa, Ken. *Genocide in Nigeria: The Ogoni Tragedy*. London: Saros International, 1992.

———. *On a Darkling Plain: An Account of the Nigerian Civil War*. Port Harcourt, Nigeria: Saros, 1989.

Saro-Wiwa, Noo. "There Was a Country: A Personal History of Biafra by Chinua Achebe—Review." *The Guardian*, October 5, 2012.

Schwarz, Walter. *Nigeria*. New York: Praeger, 1968.

Simpson, E. S. "Electricity Production in Nigeria." *Economic Geography* 45, no. 3 (1969): 239–57.

Simpson, Sarah. "General Strike over Rising Fuel Price Takes Hold in Nigerian Cities." *New York Times*, 2007, A5.

Siollun, Max. *Oil, Politics and Violence Nigeria's Military Coup Culture (1966–1976)*. New York: Algora, 2009.

———. "The Danjuma Interview." Last modified May 28, 2008. https://maxsiollun.wordpress.com/2008/05/28/the-danjuma-interview.

Smith, James D. D. *Stopping Wars: Defining the Obstacles to Cease-Fire*. Boulder, CO: Westview Press Boulder, 1995.

Smith, Karen E. "The UK and 'Genocide' in Biafra." *Journal of Genocide Research* 16, no. 2–3 (2014): 247–62.

"Some Progress in Biafran Peace Talks." 00:04:04. United Kingdom: ITN, 1968.

Soyinka, Wole. *The Man Died: Prison Notes*. Ibadan, Nigeria: Spectrum, 2002.

Stapleton, Timothy J. *A Military History of Africa*. Santa Barbara, CA: Praeger, 2013.

———. *No Insignificant Part: The Rhodesia Native Regiment and the East Africa Campaign of the First World War*. Waterloo, ON: Wilfrid Laurier University Press, 2006.

Steiner, Rolf, and Yves-Guy Bergès. *The Last Adventurer*. 1st English language ed. Boston, MA: Little, Brown Boston, 1978.

Steyn, Phia. "Oil Exploration in Colonial Nigeria, C. 1903–58." *Journal of Imperial & Commonwealth History* 37, no. 2 (2009): 249–74.

Stremlau, John J. *The International Politics of the Nigerian Civil War, 1967–1970*. Princeton, NJ: Princeton University Press, 1977.

Sullivan, Dan. "The Theater: 2 Plays by Nigeria's Wole Soyinka." *New York Times*, November 10, 1967, 60.

Sunday, Simon Echewofun. "Kainji Turbine Get First Turnaround Maintenance in 40 Years." *Daily Trust*, October 29, 2013.

Tamuno, Tekena N., ed. *Proceedings of the National Conference on Nigeria since Independence. Zaria, March, 1983*. 3 vols. Vol. 3, National Conference on Nigeria since Independence. Zaria: The Panel on Nigeria Since Independence History Project, 1983.

The Aburi Conference: Ghana, Jan. 4–5, 1967. New York: Reprinted by the American Committee to Keep Biafra Alive, 1967.

Thomas, Charles G., and Roy Doron. "Out of Africa: The Challenges, Evolution, and Opportunities of African Military History." *Journal of African Military History* 1, no. 1–2 (2017): 3–23.

Thomson, Graeme. "Some Problems of Administration and Development in Nigeria." *Journal of the Royal African Society* 26, no. 104 (1927): 305–14.

Thornton, John K. "The Art of War in Angola, 1575–1680." *Comparative Studies in Society and History* 30, no. 2 (1988): 360–78.

———. *Warfare in Atlantic Africa, 1500–1800*. London: Routledge, 1999.

Tuck, Christopher. "'Every Car or Moving Object Gone': The ECOMOG Intervention in Liberia." *African Studies Quarterly* 4, no. 1 (2000): 1–16.

Uche, Chibuike. "Oil, British Interests and the Nigerian Civil War." *Journal of African History* 49, no. 1 (2008): 111–35.

Uchendu, Egodi. *Women and Conflict in the Nigerian Civil War.* Trenton, NJ: Africa World Press, 2007.

Ukaegbu, Chikwendu Christian. "Lessons from Biafra: The Structuration of Socially Relevant Science in the Research and Production Directorate." *Social Forces* 83, no. 4 (2005): 1395–423.

United Nations Population Division, ed. "UN Population Division Data Portal." New York: United Nations.

Uzoigwe, G. N. *Britain and the Conquest of Africa: The Age of Salisbury.* New York: NOK, 1978.

———. "European Partition and Conquest of Africa: An Overview." In *General History of Africa, VII, Africa under Colonial Domination, 1880–1935,* edited by Albert Adu Boahen. Ibadan, Nigeria: Heinemann, 1985.

———. "The Warrior and the State in Precolonial Africa: Comparative Perspectives." *Journal of Asian and African Studies* 12, no. 1–4 (1977).

Vandervort, Bruce. *Wars of Imperial Conquest in Africa, 1830–1914.* London: UCL Press, 1998.

Venter, Al J. *War Dog: Fighting Other Peoples' Wars.* Havertown, PA: Casemate, 2003.

Vickers, Michael. *A Nation Betrayed: Nigeria and the Minorities Commission of 1957.* Trenton, NJ: Africa World, 2010.

Von Rosen, Carl Gustav, "The Military Situation—an Overview," paper presented at the First International Conference on Biafra, Columbia University, December 7, 1968.

Wainaina, Binyavanga. *How to Write about Africa.* Nairobi, Kenya: Kwani Trust, 2006.

Weiner, Tim. "U.S. Aides Say Nigeria Leader Might Have Been Poisoned." *New York Times,* July 11, 1998, 4.

Williams, Kieran. *Prague Spring and Its Aftermath: Czechoslovak Politics, 1968–1970.* Cambridge, UK: Cambridge University Press, 2011.

Williams, Susan. *Who Killed Hammarskjöld?: The UN, the Cold War, and White Supremacy in Africa.* Oxford, UK: Oxford University Press, 2017.

Willink, Henry, Grodon Hadow, Philip Mason, and J. B. Shearer. "Report of the Commission Appointed to Enquire into the Fears of Minorities and the Means of Allaying Them." edited by Colonial Office. London: Her Majesty's Stationary Office, 1958.

Wuam, Terhemba. "A Re-examination of the Causes of the Nigerian Civil War." In *The Nigerian Civil War: Forty Years after, What Lessons?,* edited by Armstrong Matiu Adejo, 28–27. Makurdi, Nigeria: Aboki, 2008.

Zumbach, Jan. *On Wings of War: My Life as a Pilot Adventurer.* London: Deutsch, 1975.

INDEX

ROY DORON IS CD Spangler Distinguished Professor of African and African American History at Winston-Salem State University. He is author, with Toyin Falola, of *Ken Saro-Wiwa* and editor, with Falola and Okpeh Ochayi Okpeh, of *Warfare, Ethnicity and National Identity in Nigeria*.

For Indiana University Press

Sabrina Black, Editorial Assistant
Tony Brewer, Artist and Book Designer
Anna Francis, Assistant Acquisitions Editor
Anna Garnai, Production Coordinator
Katie Huggins, Production Manager
Alyssa Nicole Lucas, Marketing and Publicity Manager
Darja Malcolm-Clarke, Project Manager/Editor
Bethany Mowry, Acquisitions Editor
Dan Pyle, Online Publishing Manager
Jennifer Witzke, Senior Artist and Book Designer